# HISTORIC PHOTOS OF LEXINGTON

Text and Captions by W. Gay Reading

TURNER
PUBLISHING COMPANY

College of the Bible (built 1895) at Transylvania University (then Kentucky University), 1898.

# HISTORIC PHOTOS OF LEXINGTON

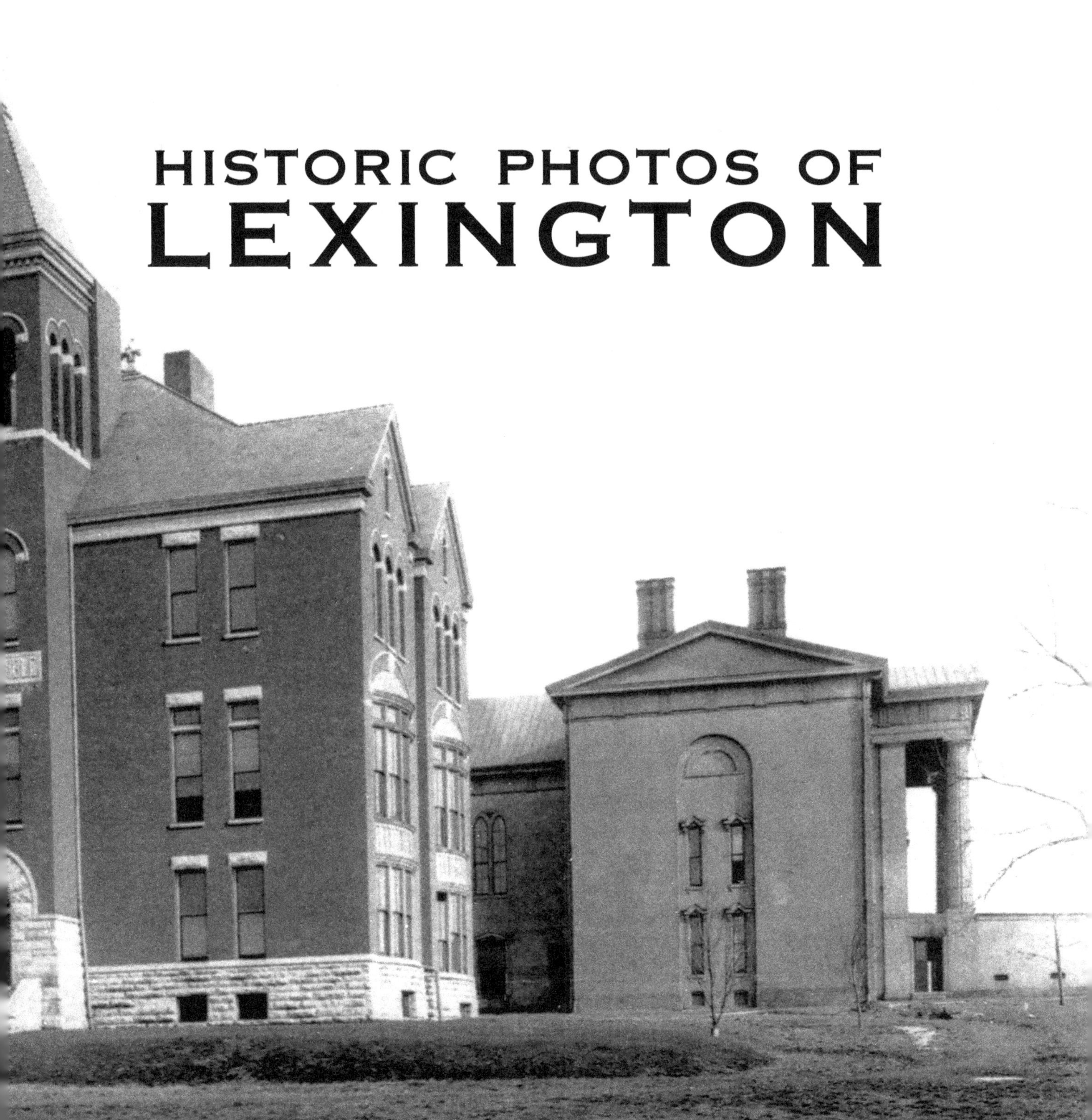

Turner Publishing Company
www.turnerpublishing.com



Library of Congress Control Number: 2006902321

ISBN-13: 978-1-59652-262-6

Printed in the United States of America.

ISBN 978-1-68336-914-1 (hc)

# Contents

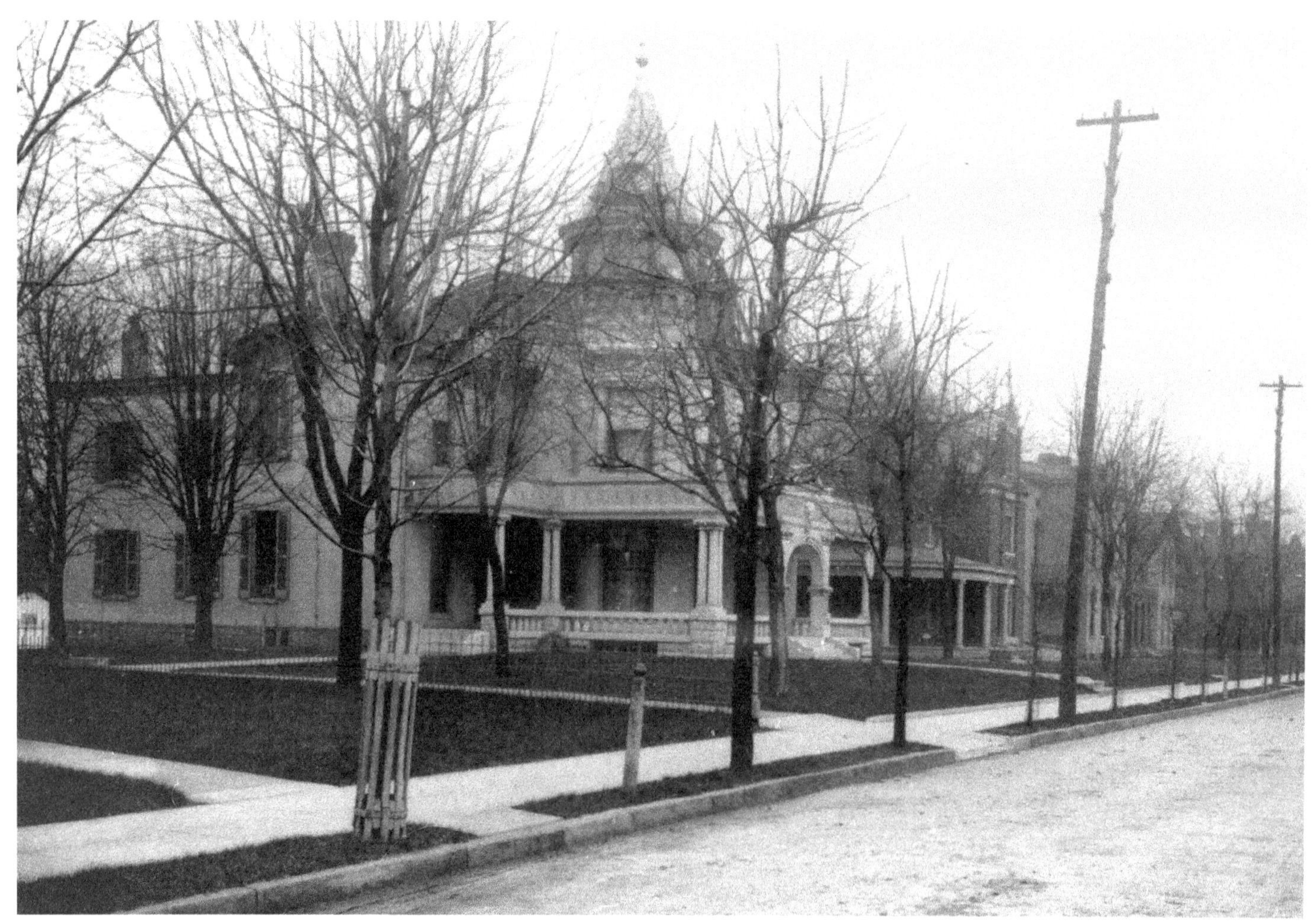

View of Third Street, late 19th century.

# Acknowledgments

This volume, *Historic Photos of Lexington,* is the result of the cooperation and efforts of many individuals, organizations, institutions, and corporations. It is with great thanks that we acknowledge the valuable contribution of the following for their generous support.

Equus Standardbred Station
Georgetown College
University of Kentucky Libraries
Transylvania University Special Collections Library
Lexington Opera House/Lexington Center Corporation
Keeneland
Kentucky American Water Company

Our appreciation goes to Tamara Farnsworth for her professional guidance and assistance in research and verification.

We would also like to thank the following individuals for their valuable contribution and assistance in making this work possible

Jason Flahardy, Audio Visual Archivist, University of Kentucky Libraries
Luanne Franklin, Program Director, Lexington Opera House
BJ Gooch, Special Collections Librarian and University Archivist, Transylvania University Library
Susan Lancho, Communications Manager, Kentucky American Water
Cathy Schenck, Librarian, Keeneland Library
Glen Edward Taul, Ph.D., Director, Archives, Georgetown College

# PREFACE

Lexington has thousands of historic photographs that reside in private and public archives. These photographs give us an important link to the city's past. During a time when Lexington is looking ahead and evaluating its future course, many people are wondering how to treat the city's past. These decisions affect every aspect of the city – architecture, public spaces, commerce, and infrastructure – and these, in turn, affect the way that people live their lives. This book seeks to provide easy access to a valuable, objective look into Lexington's history.

The power of photographs is that they are less subjective in their treatment of history. While the photographer can make decisions regarding what subject matter to capture and some limited variation in its presentation, photographs do not provide the breadth of interpretation that text does. For this reason, they provide an original, untainted perspective that allows the viewer to interpret and observe.

The project represents countless hours of review and research. The researchers and author have reviewed thousands of photographs in numerous archives. We greatly appreciate the generous assistance of the archivists listed in the acknowledgements of this work, without whom, this project could not have been completed.

The goal in publishing this work is to provide broader access to a set of extraordinary photographs. We hope to inspire, provide insight and perspective using the past as a lesson for the future. Equally as important, this book seeks to preserve the past with respect and reverence.

The photographs we have selected for this book represent the technology of that era. With the exception of touching up imperfections caused by time, no other changes have been made. The focus and clarity of many images is limited to the technology and ability of the photographer at the time they were taken.

The work is divided into eras. Beginning with some of the earliest known photographs of Lexington, the first section records events from the Civil War era through the end of the nineteenth century. The second section spans the first two decades of the twentieth century. The third section moves through the depression. The final section takes us through World War II up to the 1970's.

In each of these sections we have made an effort to capture various aspects of life through our selection of photographs. People, commerce, transportation, infrastructure, religious institutions, and educational institutions are included to provide a broad perspective.

We encourage readers to reflect as they walk down Main Street, through Gratz Park, or visit Transylvania. Streetcar tracks once ran down Broadway, houses and shopping centers now sit on land where horses once grazed, and the site of the city's first marketplace is once again bustling with downtown businesses. It is the publisher's hope that in utilizing this work, long time residents will learn something new, and new residents will gain insight on where Lexington has been, so that each can contribute to its future.

*Todd Bottorff, Publisher*

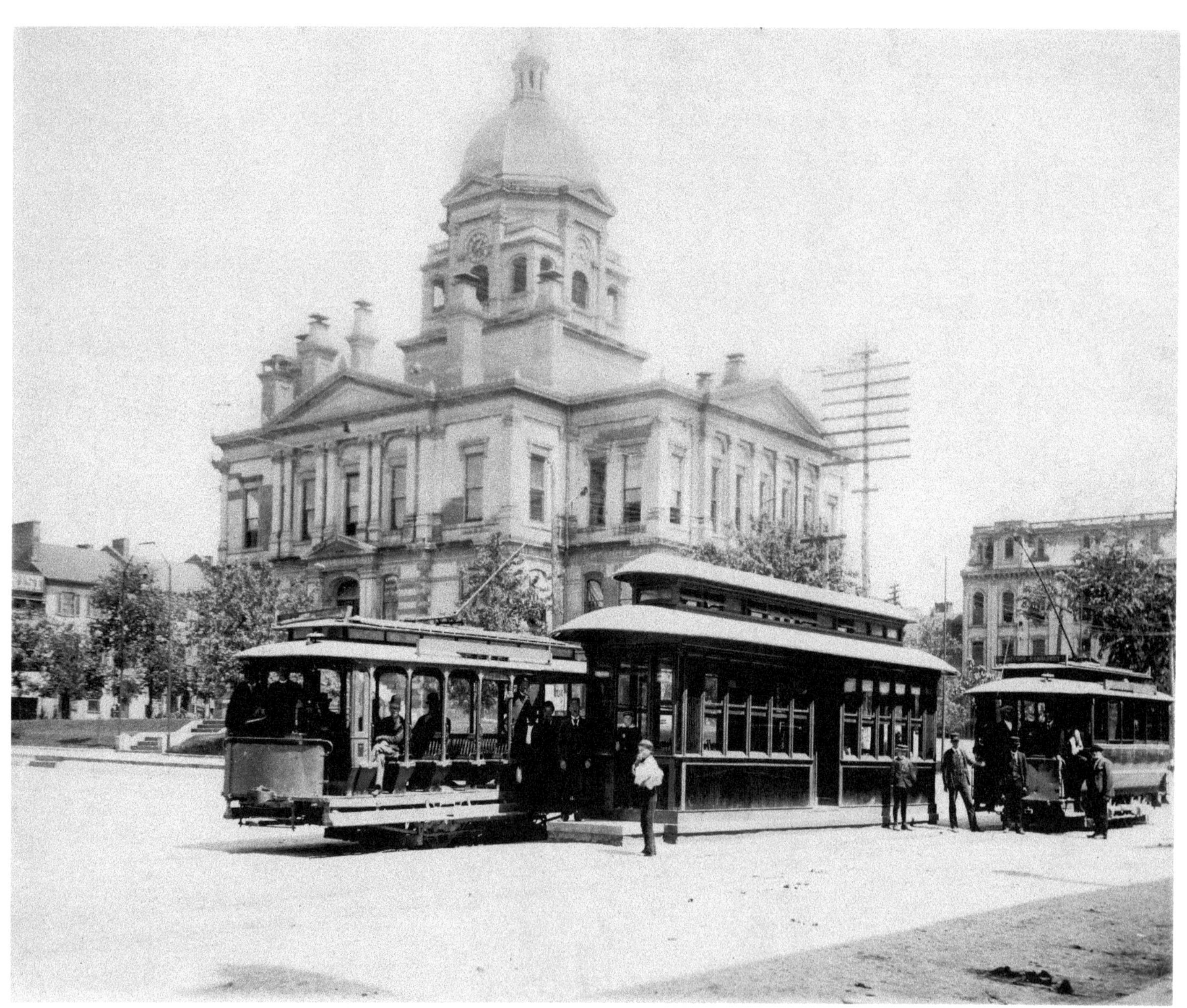

Street car center at Lexington's fourth courthouse (built 1883-84), burned 1897.

# Birth of a City and Post Civil War Changes

## 1775-1899

The earth rich region known today as Lexington, Kentucky was named by a group of land seekers camped by a spring in the area upon hearing of the first bloodshed of the American Revolution. Lexington became the seat of Fayette County and the town was officially created in 1782. It is better known as the heart of the Bluegrass country (named for the color effect of the seed plume of a grass native to this savannah plateau seen in certain lighting conditions).

It would be hard to overestimate the role Transylvania University played in the cultural and social development of Lexington. This oldest institution of higher learning west of the Alleghenies can be seen as a main reason Lexington was called "The Athens of the West".

Henry Clay, one of the most popular political figures in the country of his day and an icon of the flourishing "West", stands as the best known of a number of gentlemen of means and endeavor who built the institutions and fabric of the city. Men such as Clay championed compromises that postponed the Civil War for better or worse. Lexington was both for the Union and for slavery.

It is never to be forgotten that the slave trade flourished in this community although the institution of slavery was not of great economic viability in the agricultural structure of the region. Neutrality was the most commonly sought position. Lexington seemed to prosper during the Civil War. Local building continued while the South burned. Slavery was not abolished here until after the war. A community that had remained with the Union began to have increasingly "Southern" sympathies. It is often said that Kentucky, and especially Lexington, waited until after the Civil War to secede. But this is a simplified truth.

The prosperity the city enjoyed during the Civil War brought with it challenges. Lexington did not have an adequate waterworks system until 1885. The city had avoided this necessary improvement for years. A drought in 1883 forced action and Lexington could proceed with other enterprises. Increased rail transport connected the city with the natural raw material riches of the state. Public transportation within the city grew. By the end of the century, public roads maintained at public expense had replaced an outdated system of toll turnpikes. Electric lights flickered here in 1882. The telephone first appeared about two years earlier.

The funeral procession of Senator Henry Clay on Main Street, Lexington, 10 July 1852.

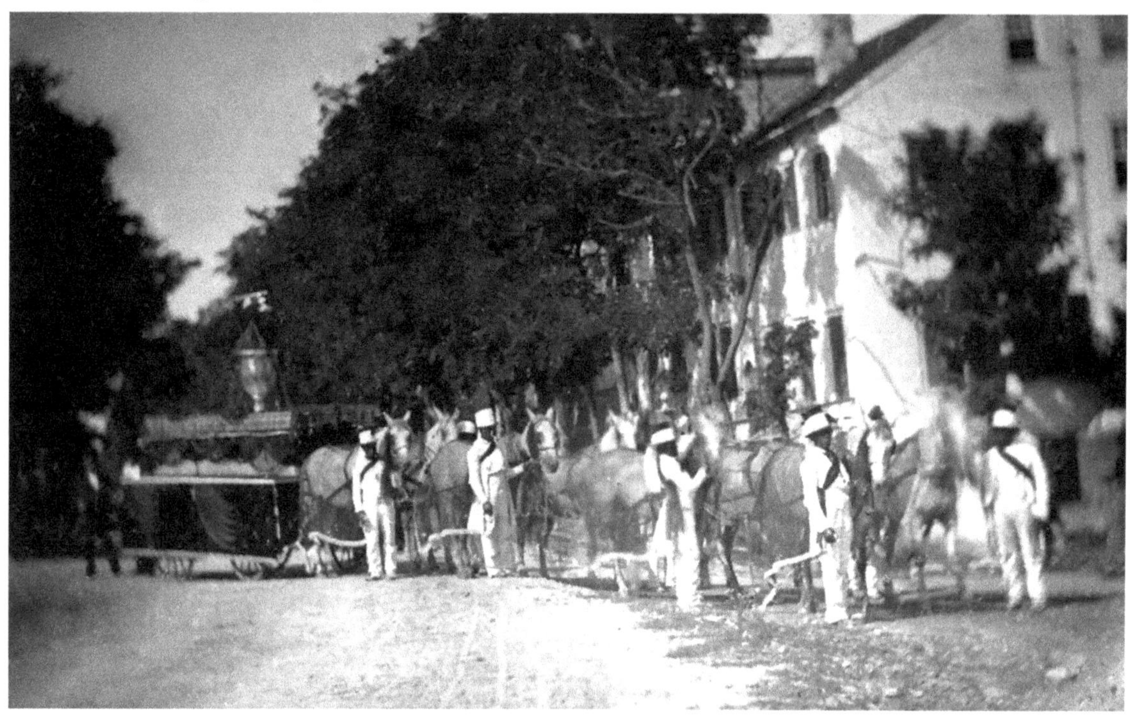

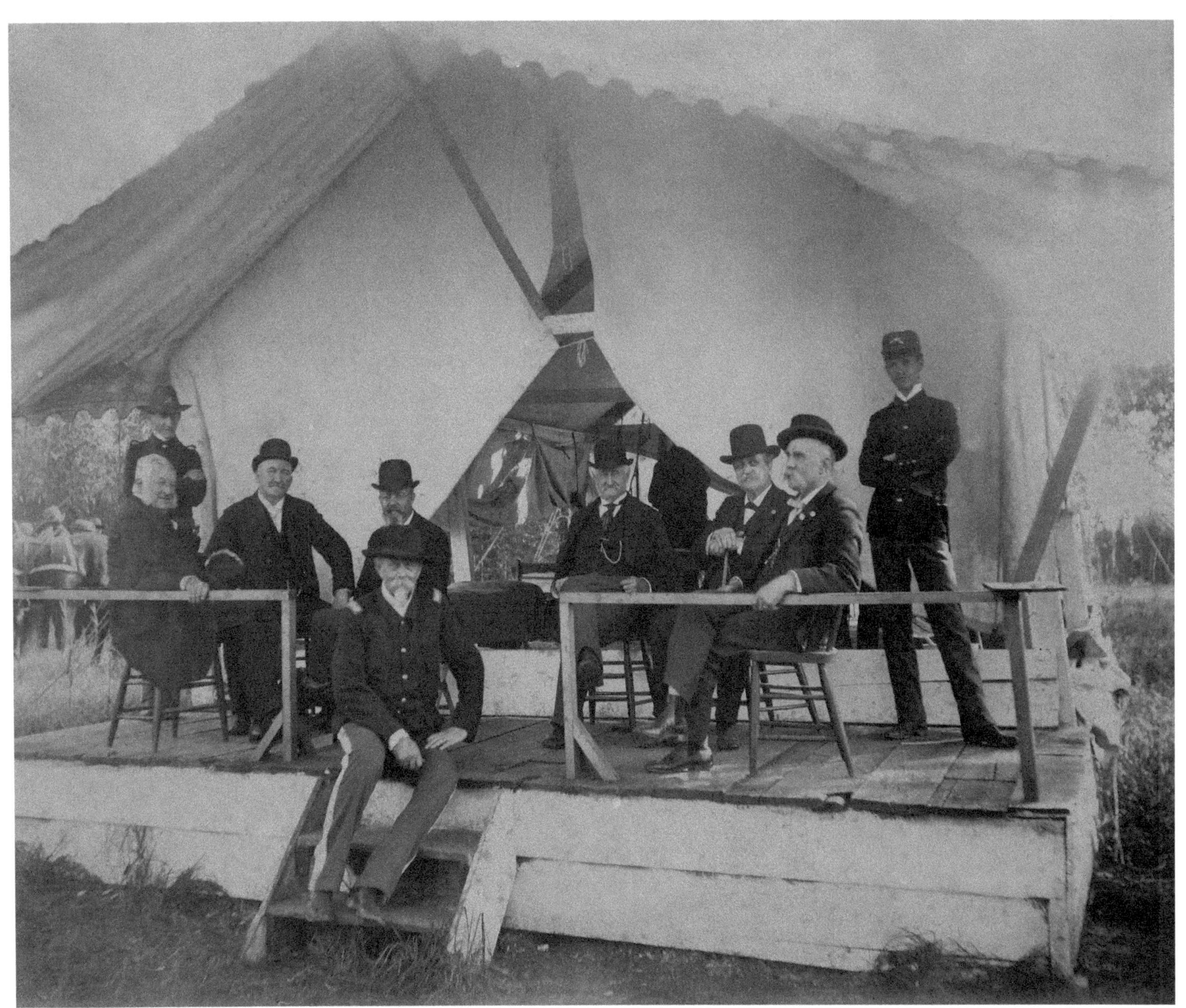

Old soldiers' reunion (some in Union uniforms), late 19th century.

Lexington's third courthouse (built in 1806), late 19th century.

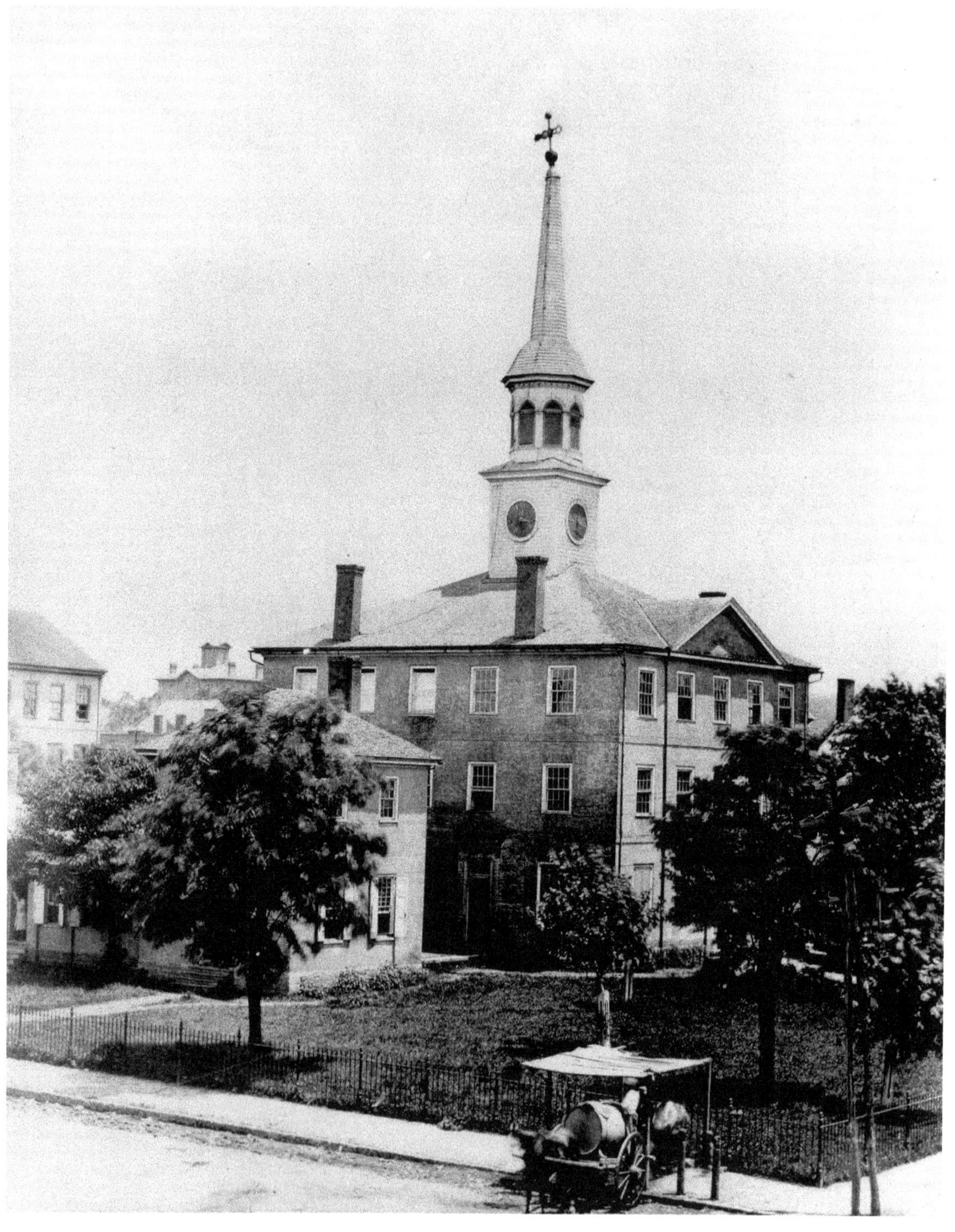

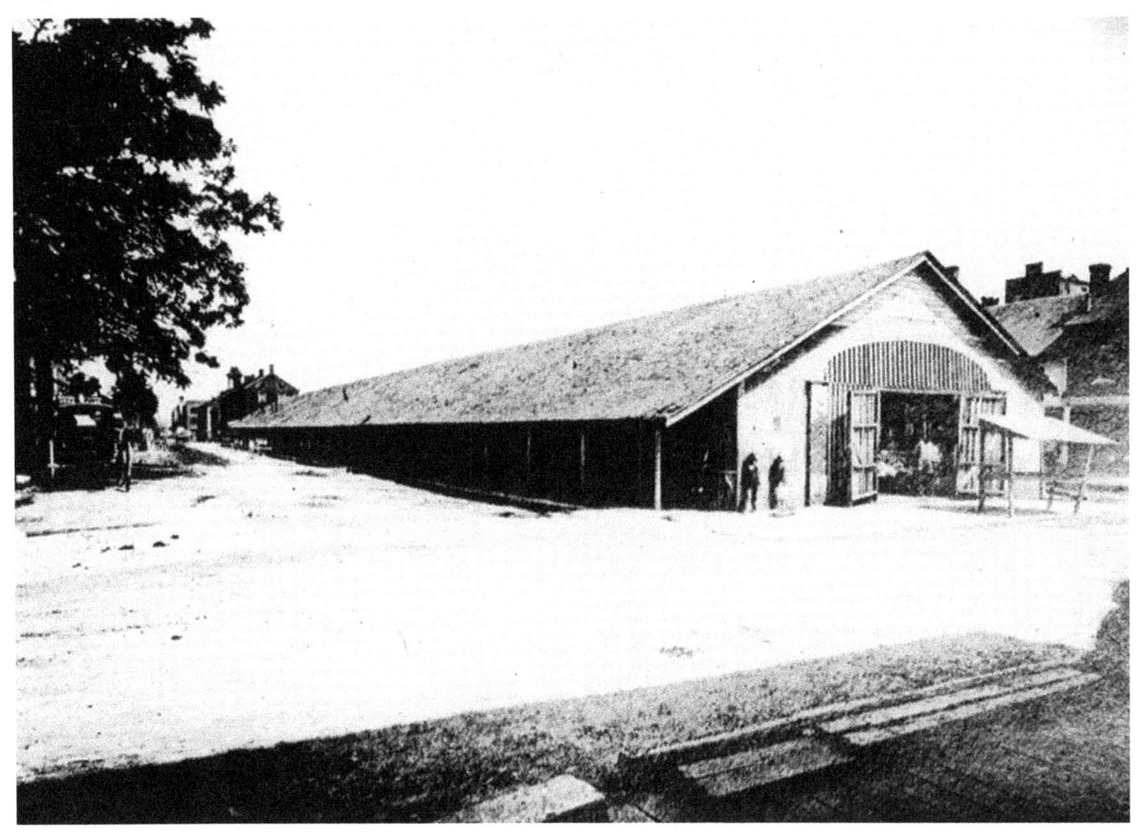

Upper Market House (built 1844), Vine Street,
demolished 1879.

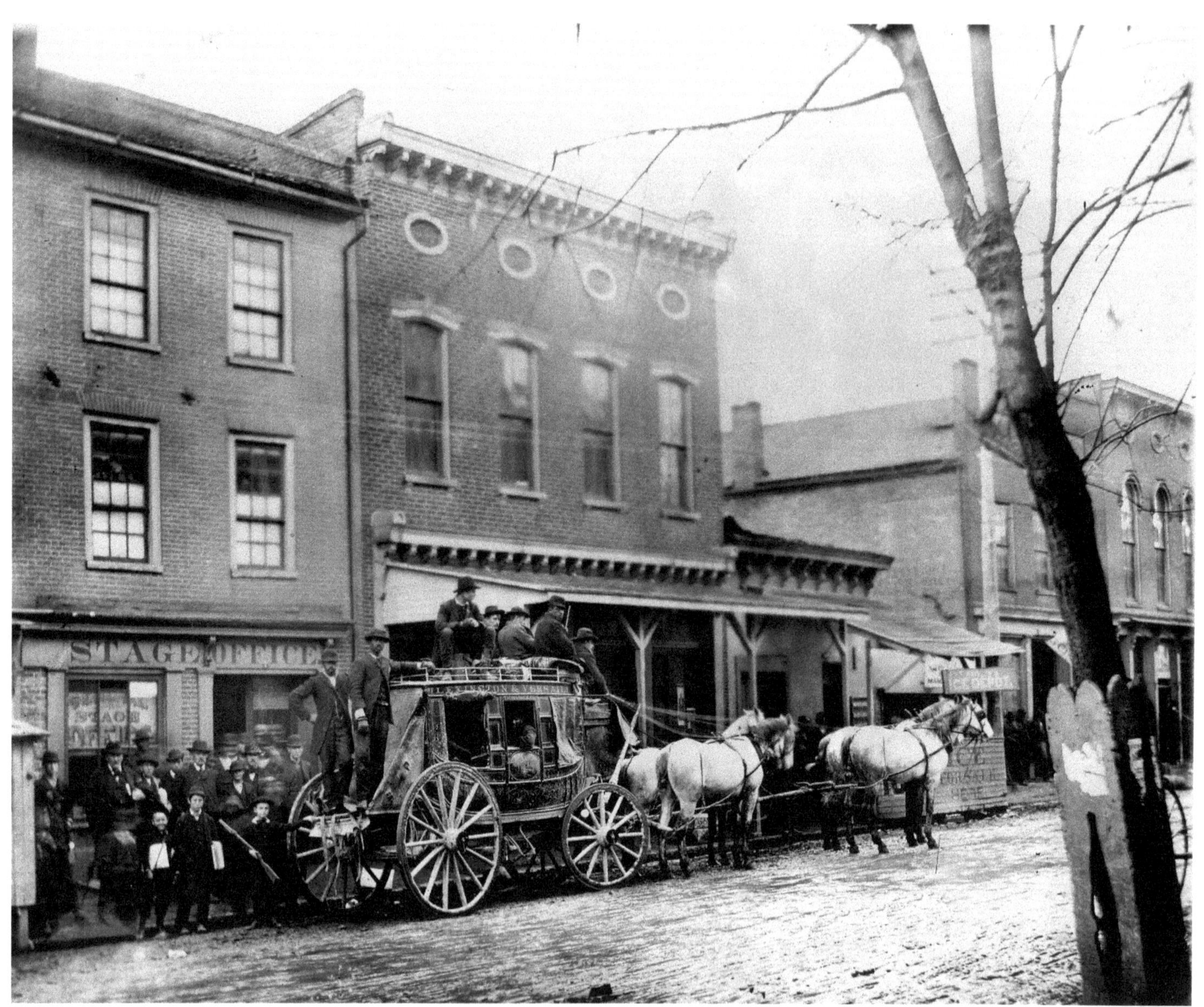

Stage coach stop on Short Street, ca. 1885.

Lexington Fire Department on Short Street, ca. 1875.

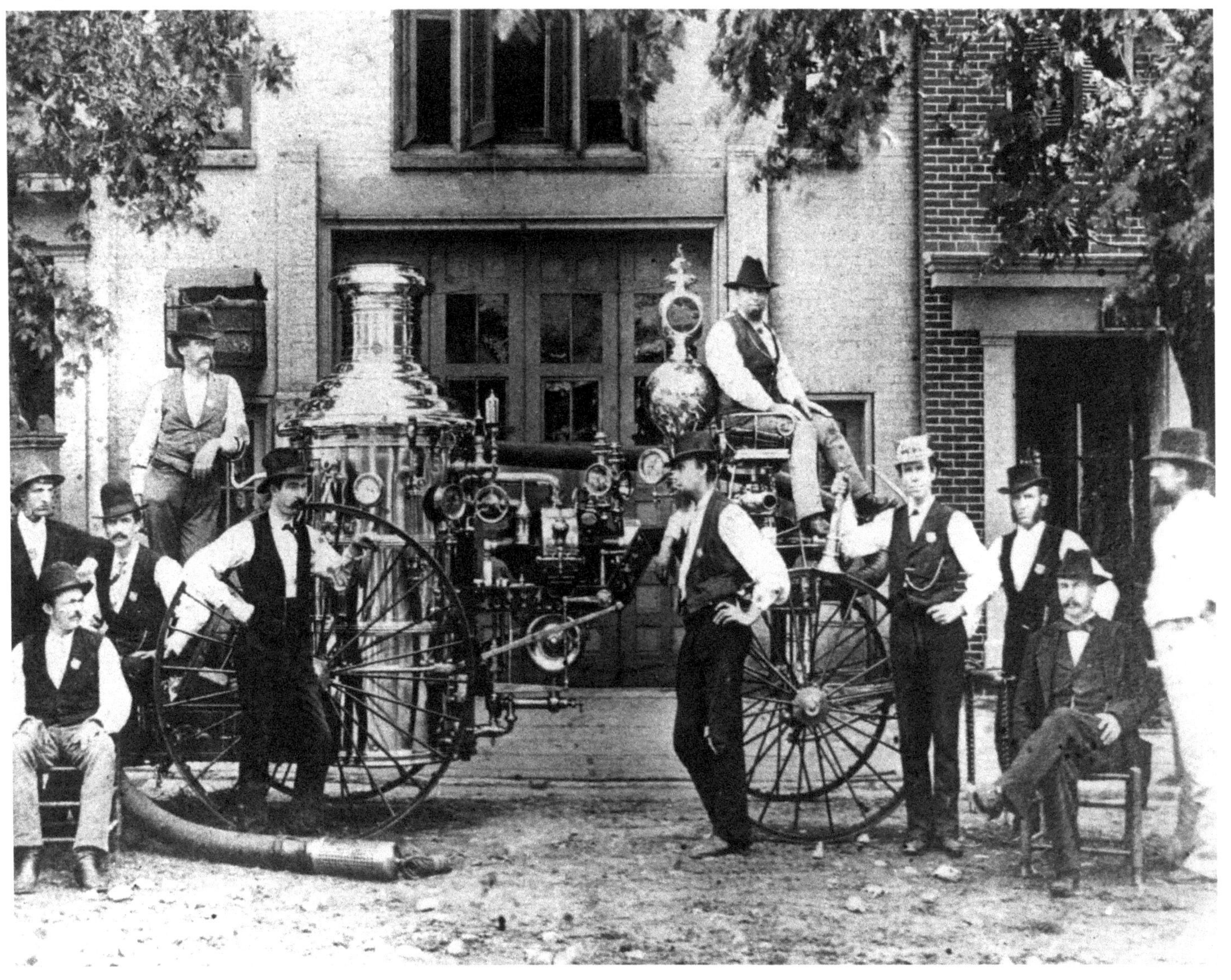

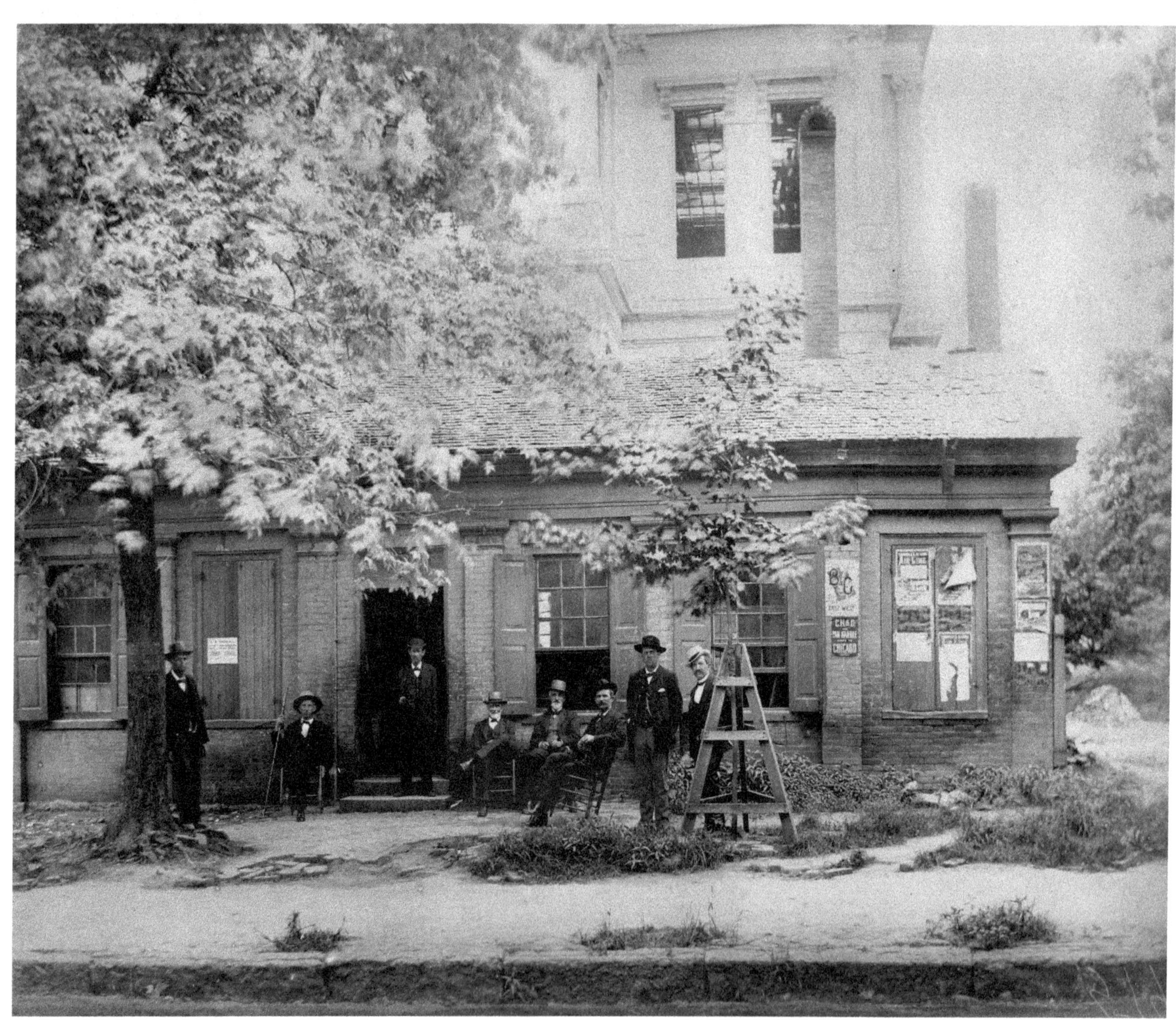

Sheriff's office on Upper Street, 1815 (burned 1897).

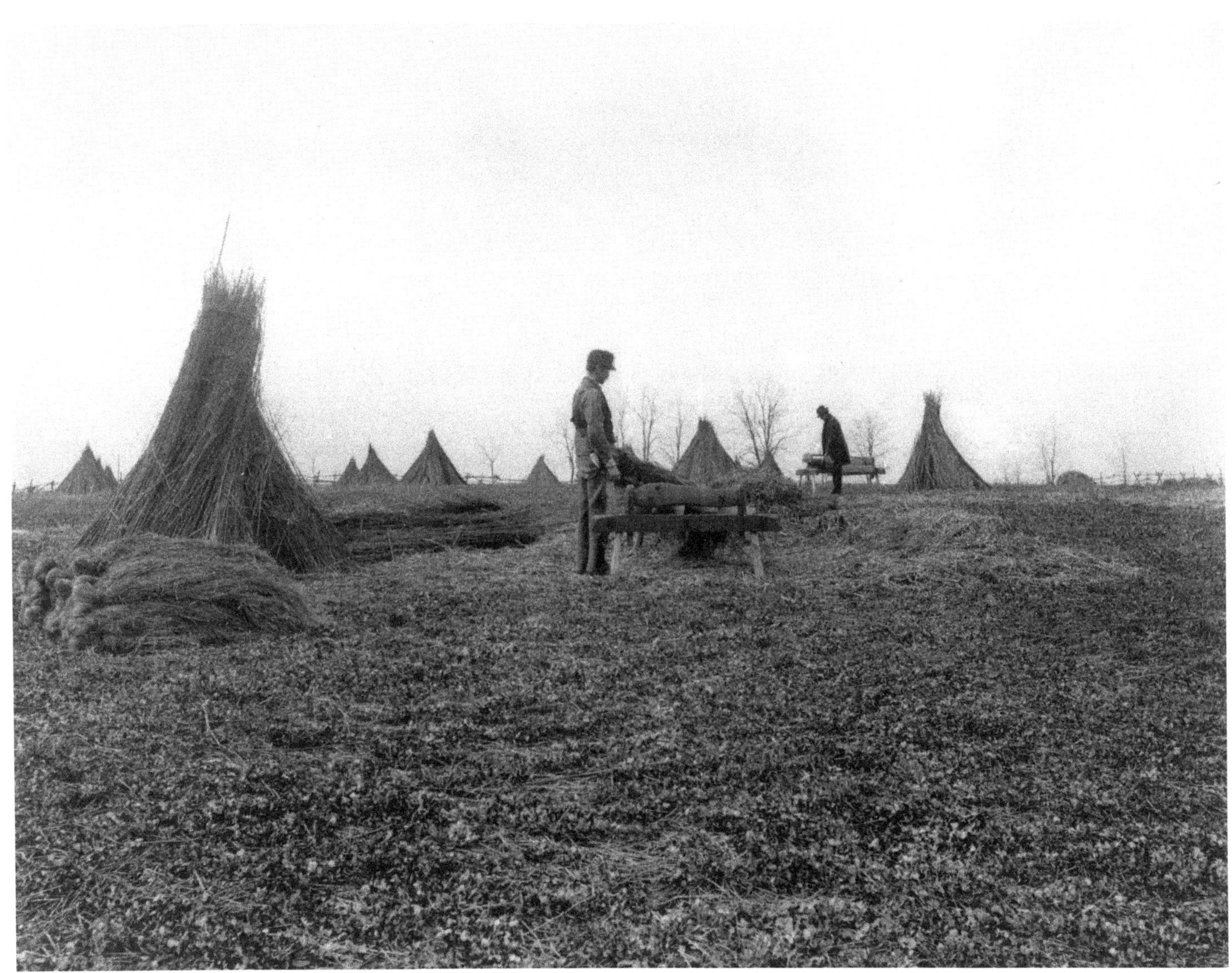

Breaking hemp in the field, late 19th century.

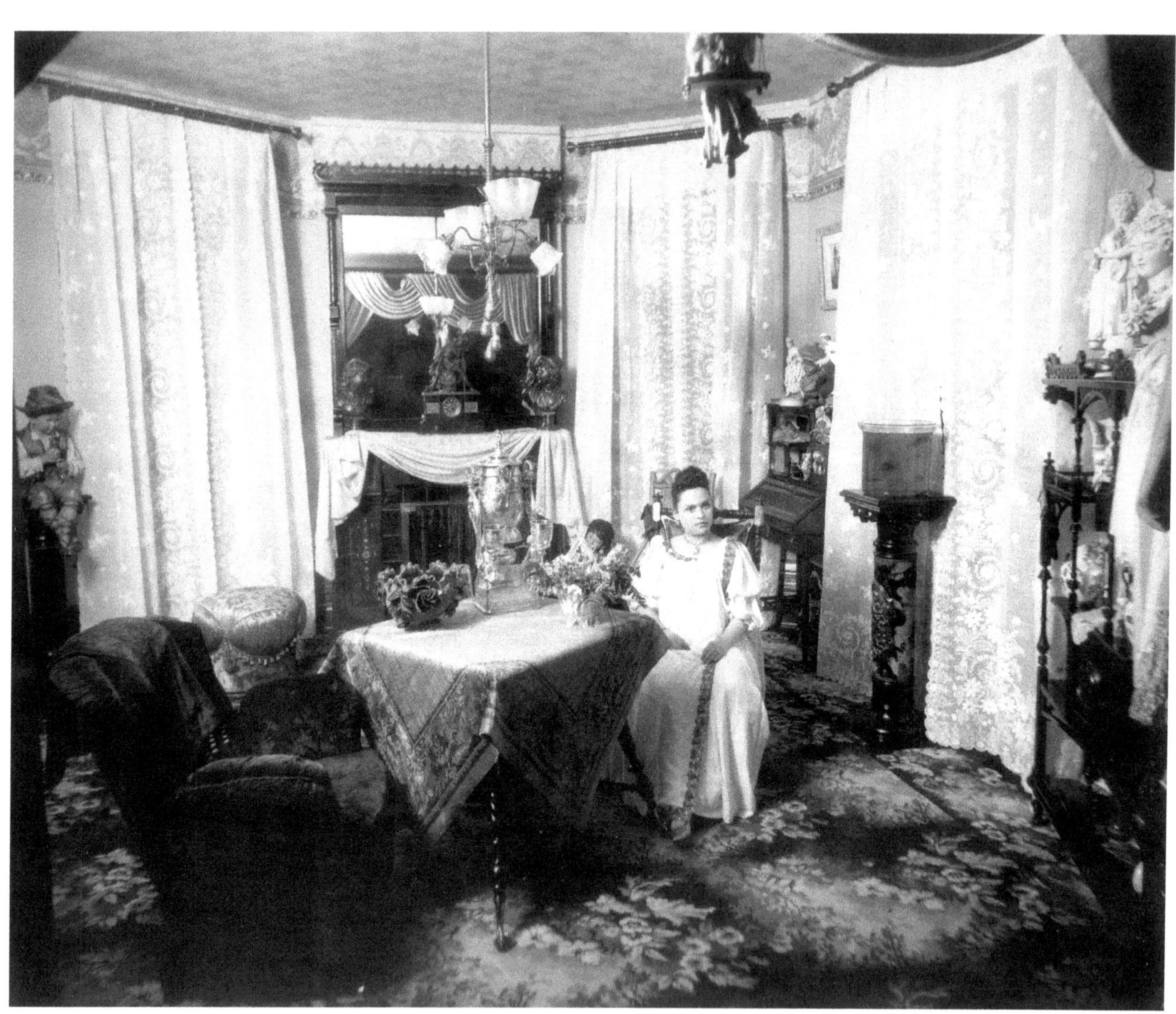

"Madam" Belle Brezing in her private parlor in her bordello at 59 Megowan Street, 1890.

Kentucky State Guard encamped in Woodland Park, 1899.

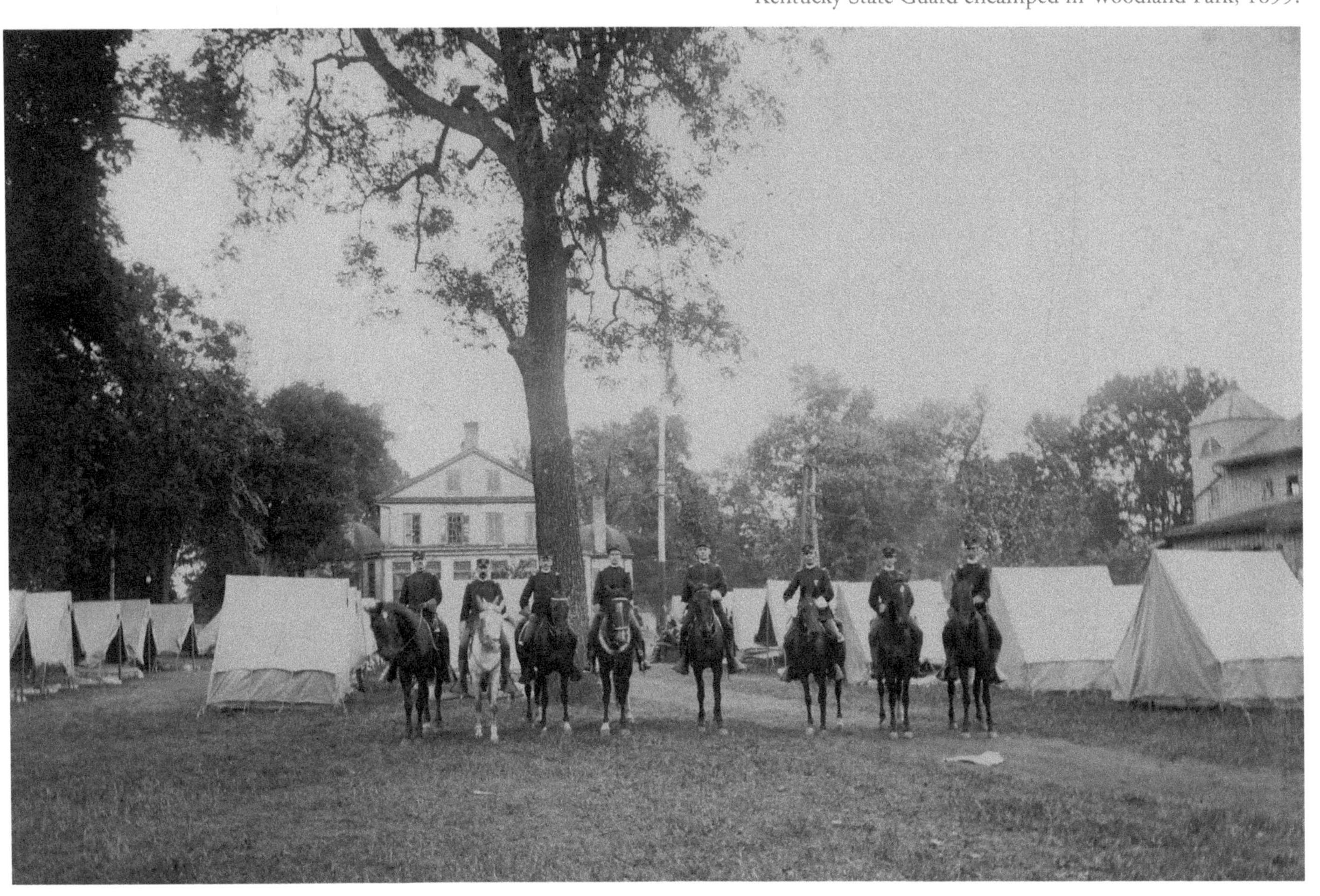

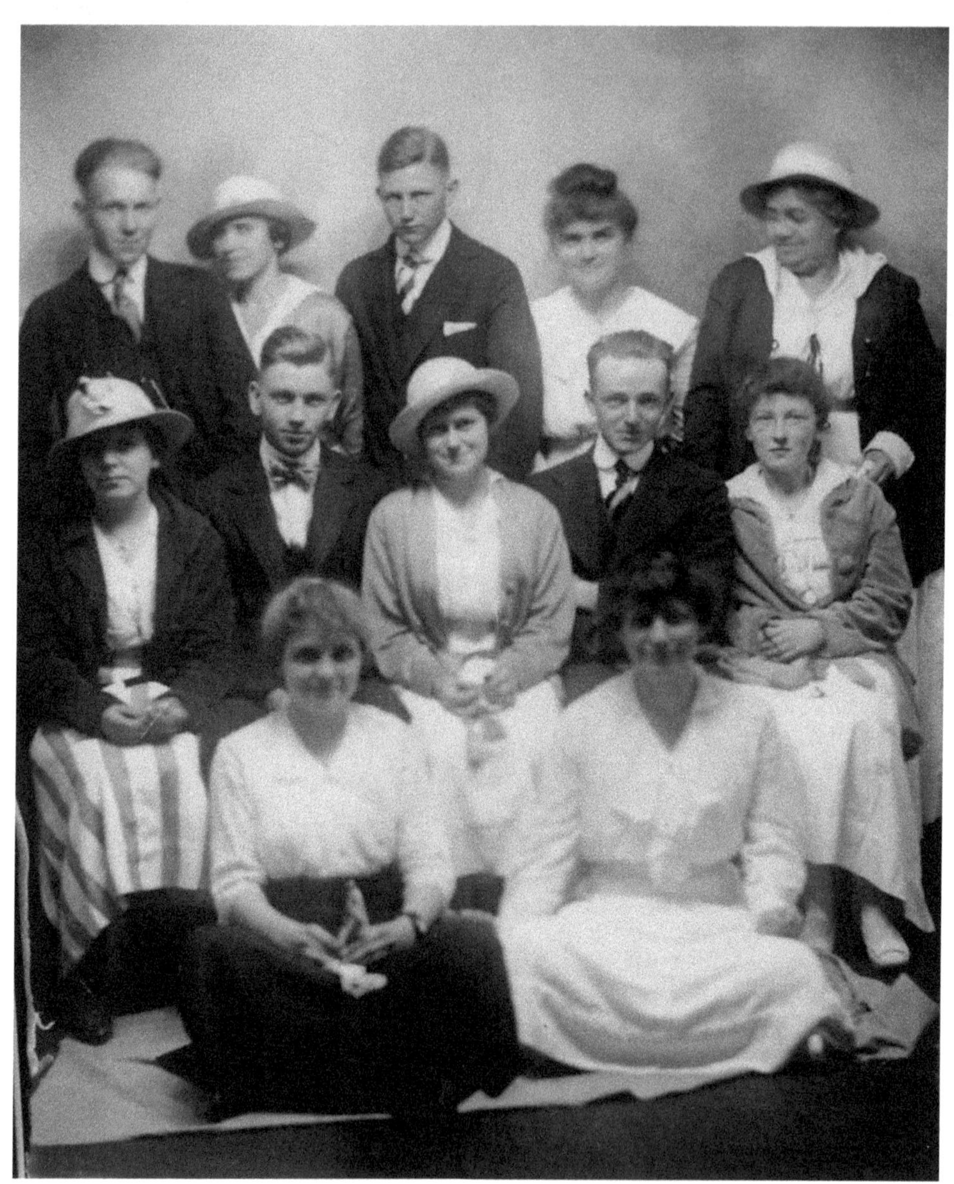

Morton School seniors on a picnic in Bluegrass Park, 1891.

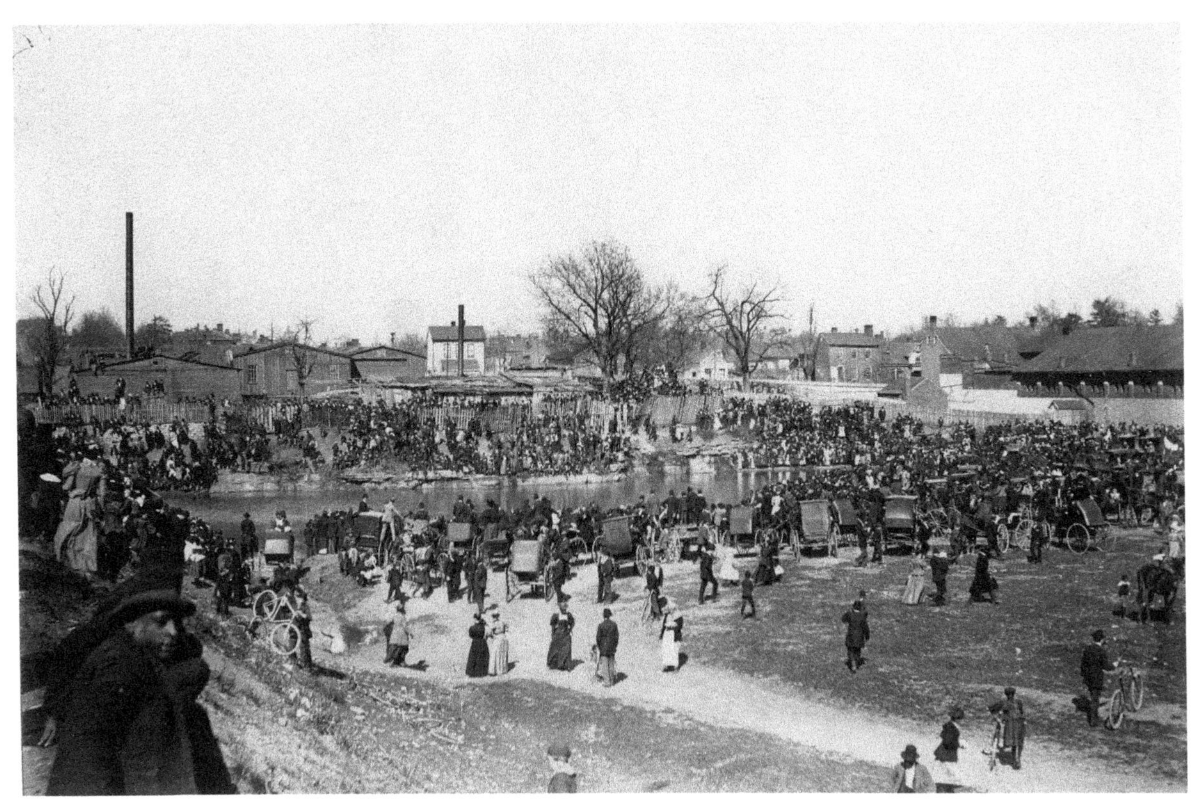

African-American Baptism at Work House pond, late 19$^{th}$ century.

Lexington's fifth courthouse, built in 1989. It still stands and is the current home of the Lexington History Museum.

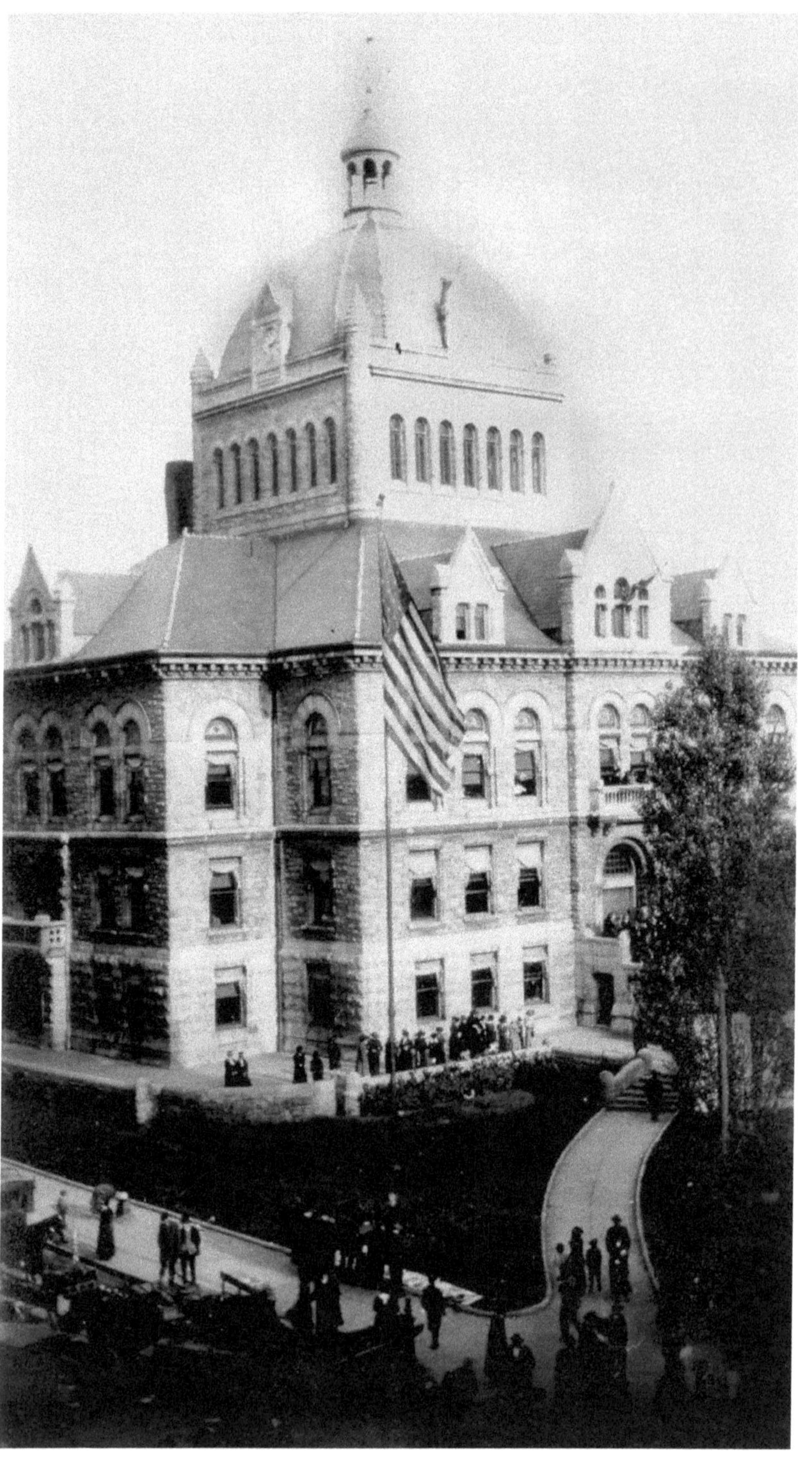

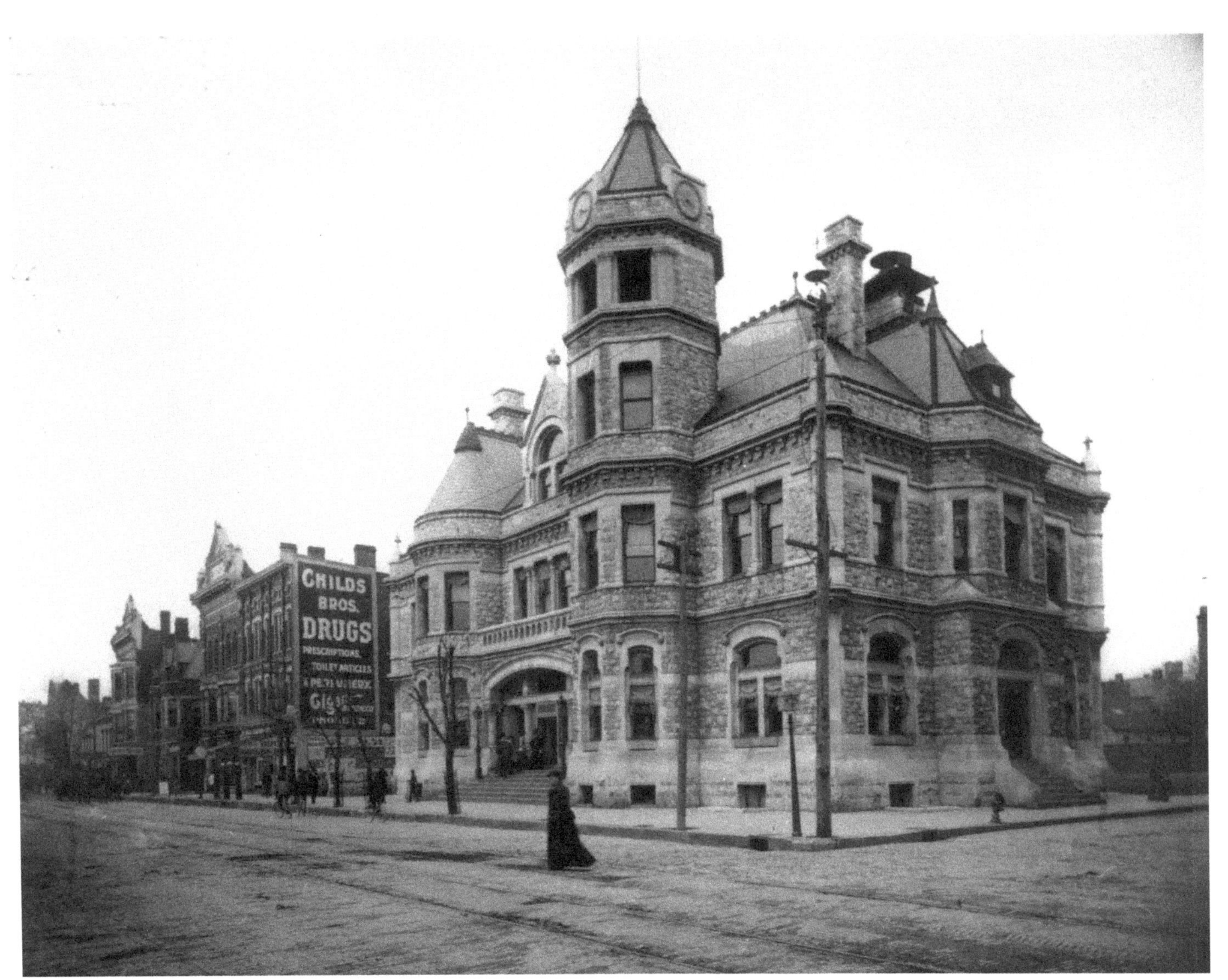


Lexington Post Office, 1898.

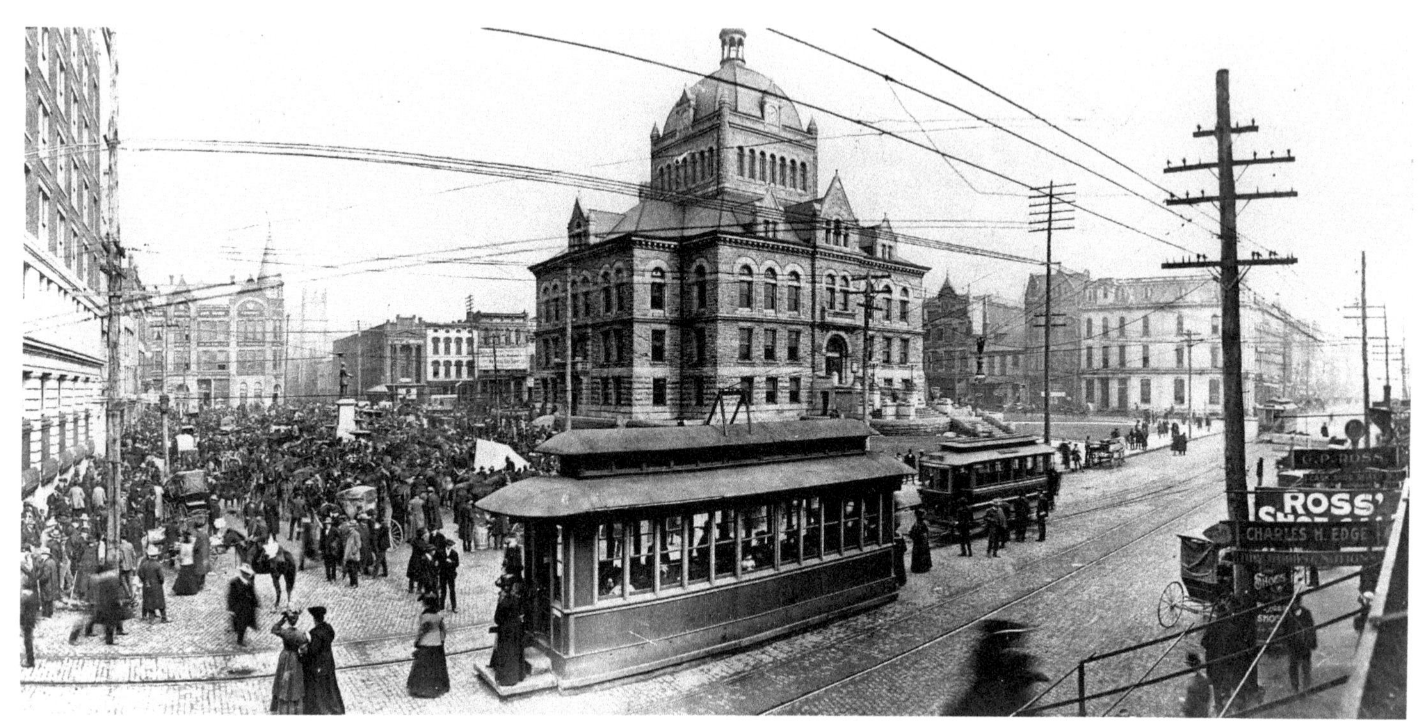


Courthouse looking north on Cheapside, 1890's.

Court day on Cheapside looking south, 1897.

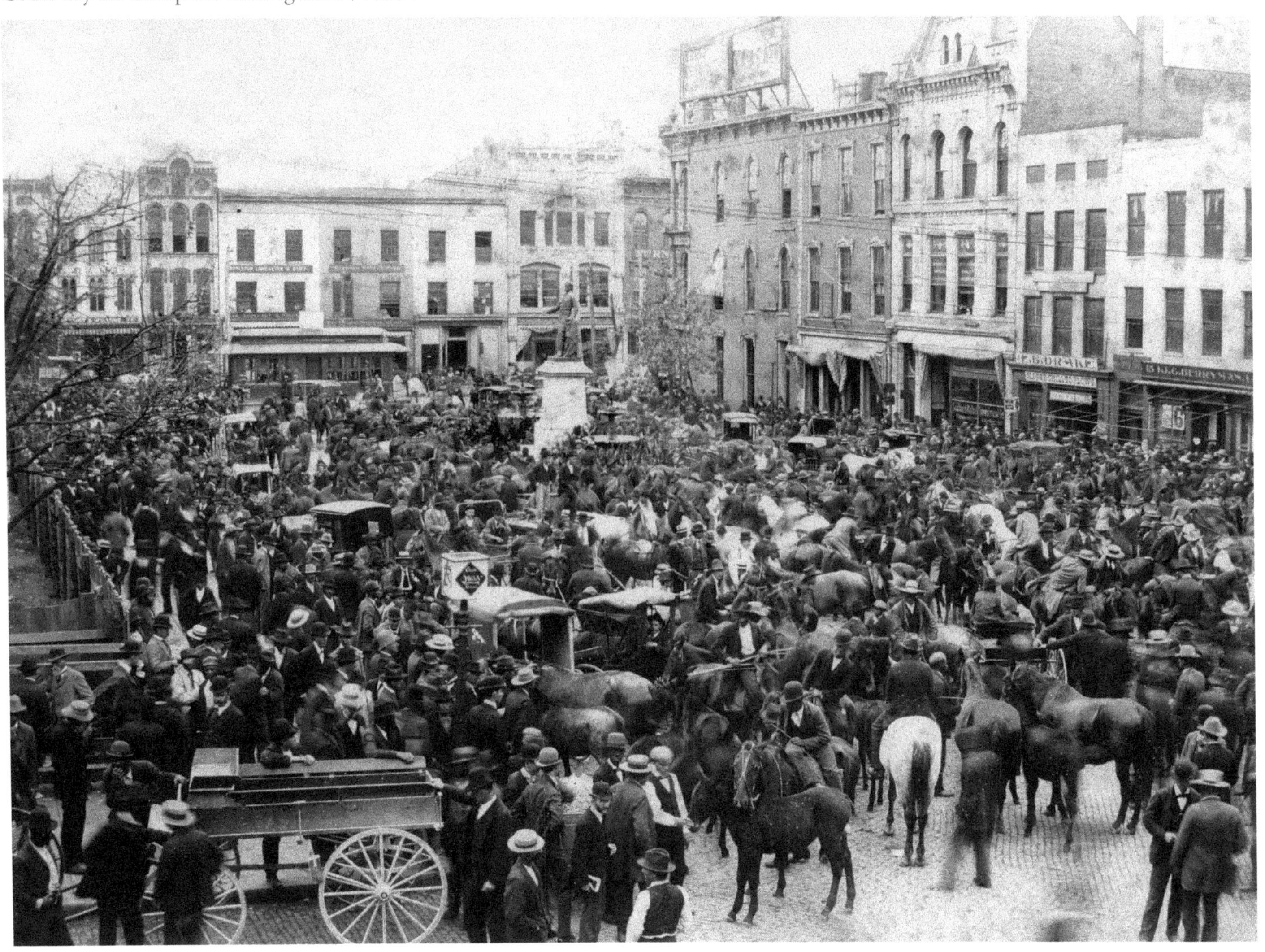

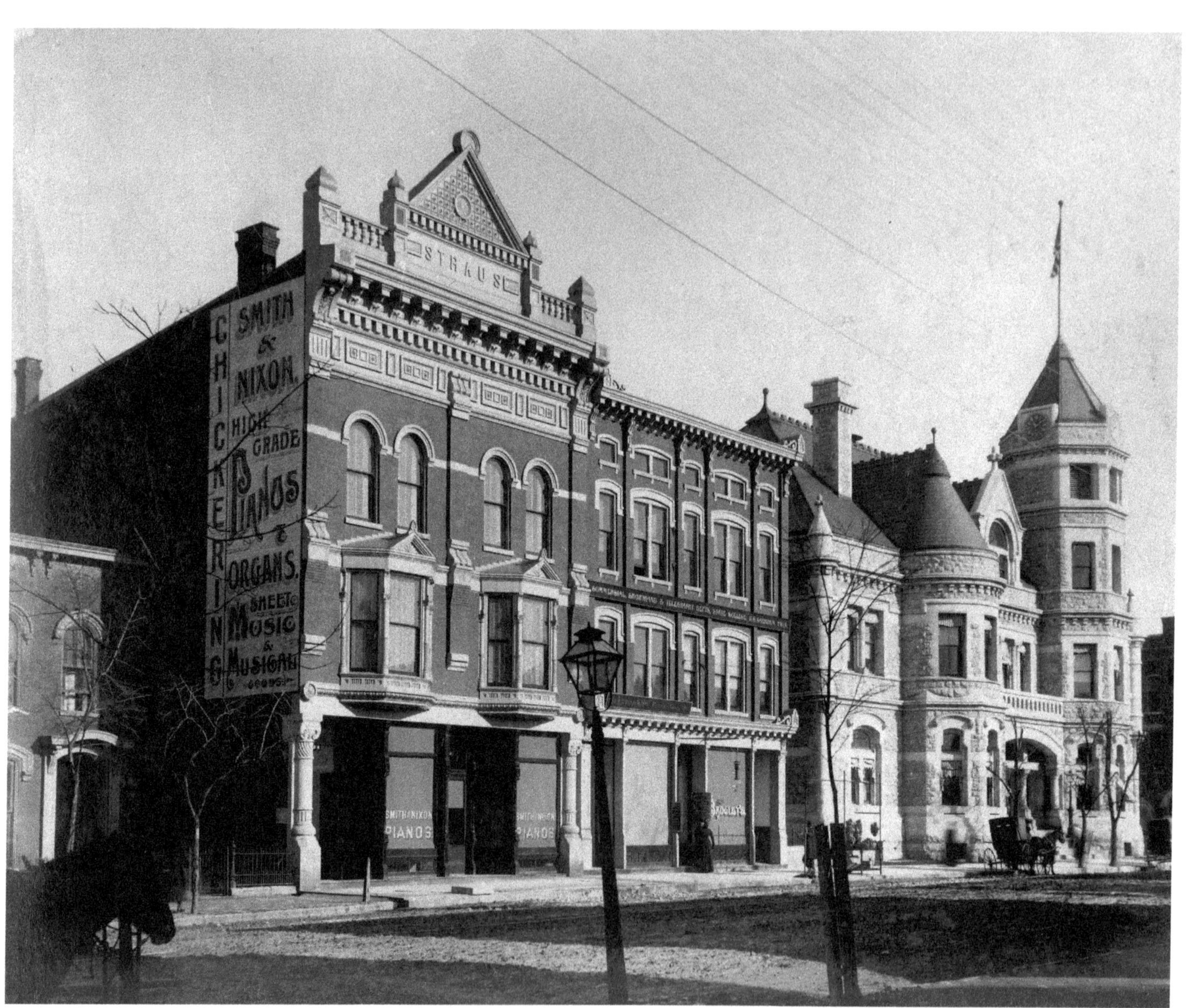


The Straus Building, located next to the post office, 1889.

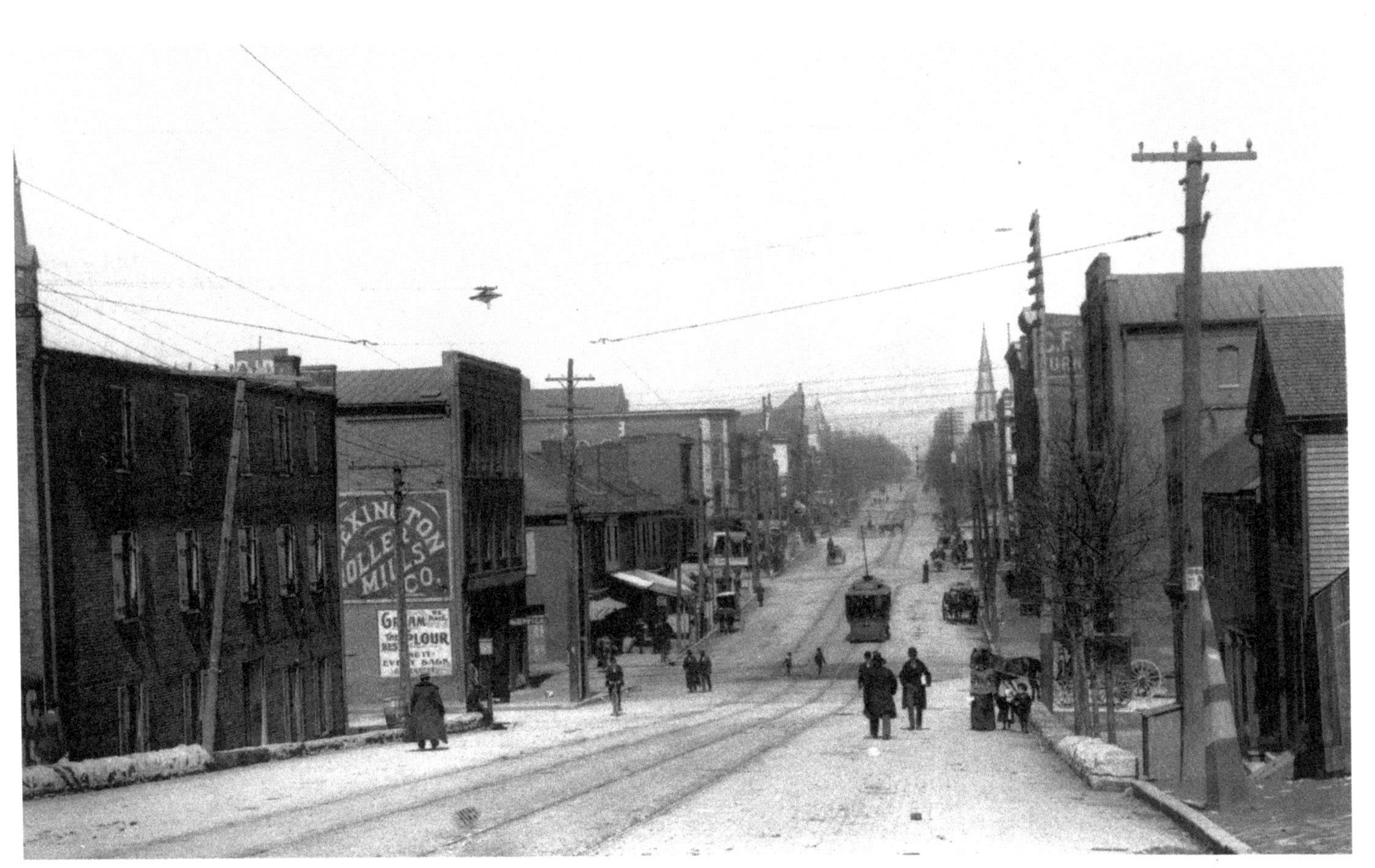

View showing street car tracks on Broadway, ca. 1898.

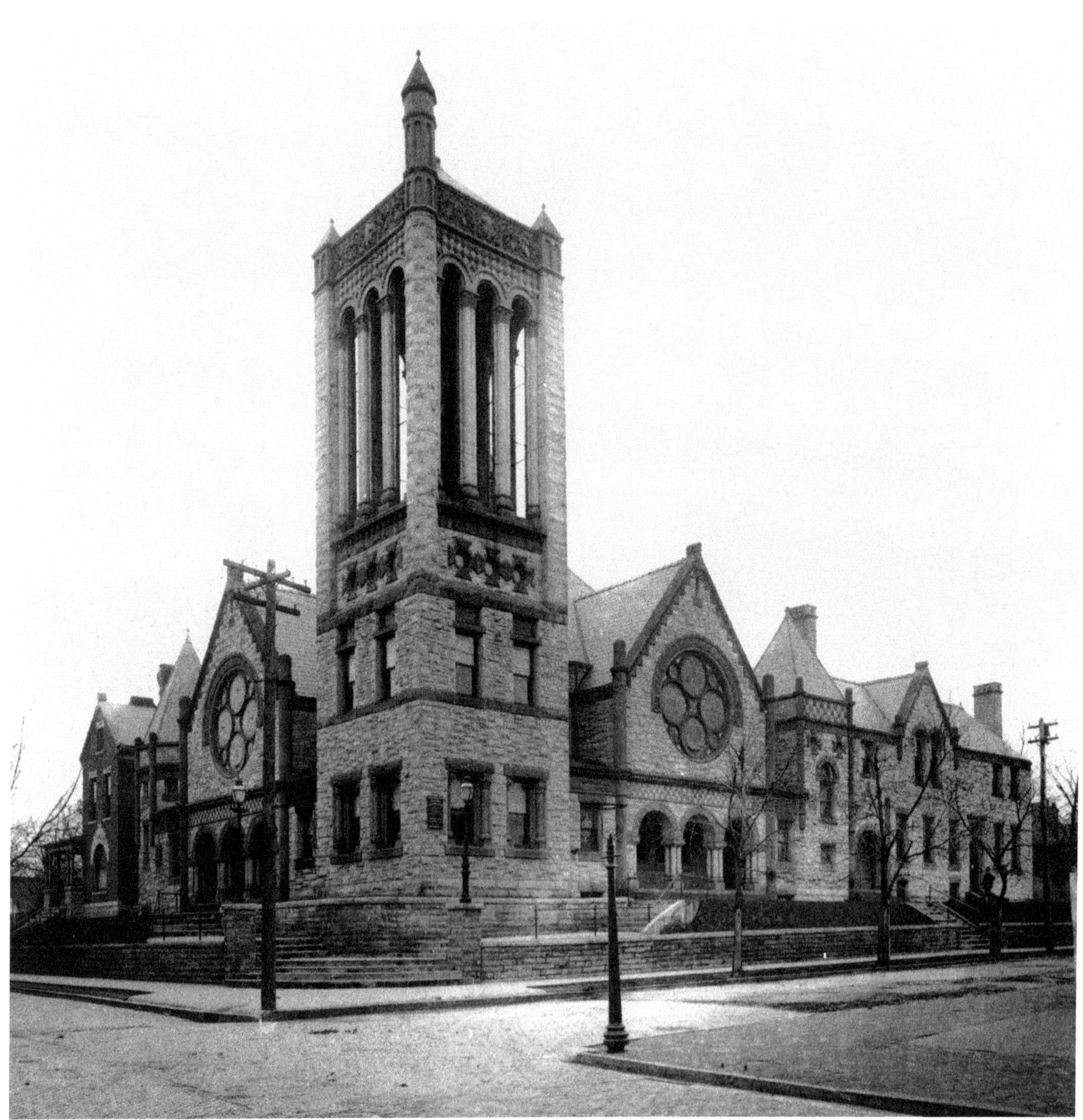

Central Christian Church (built 1893-94 by local architect), late 19th century.

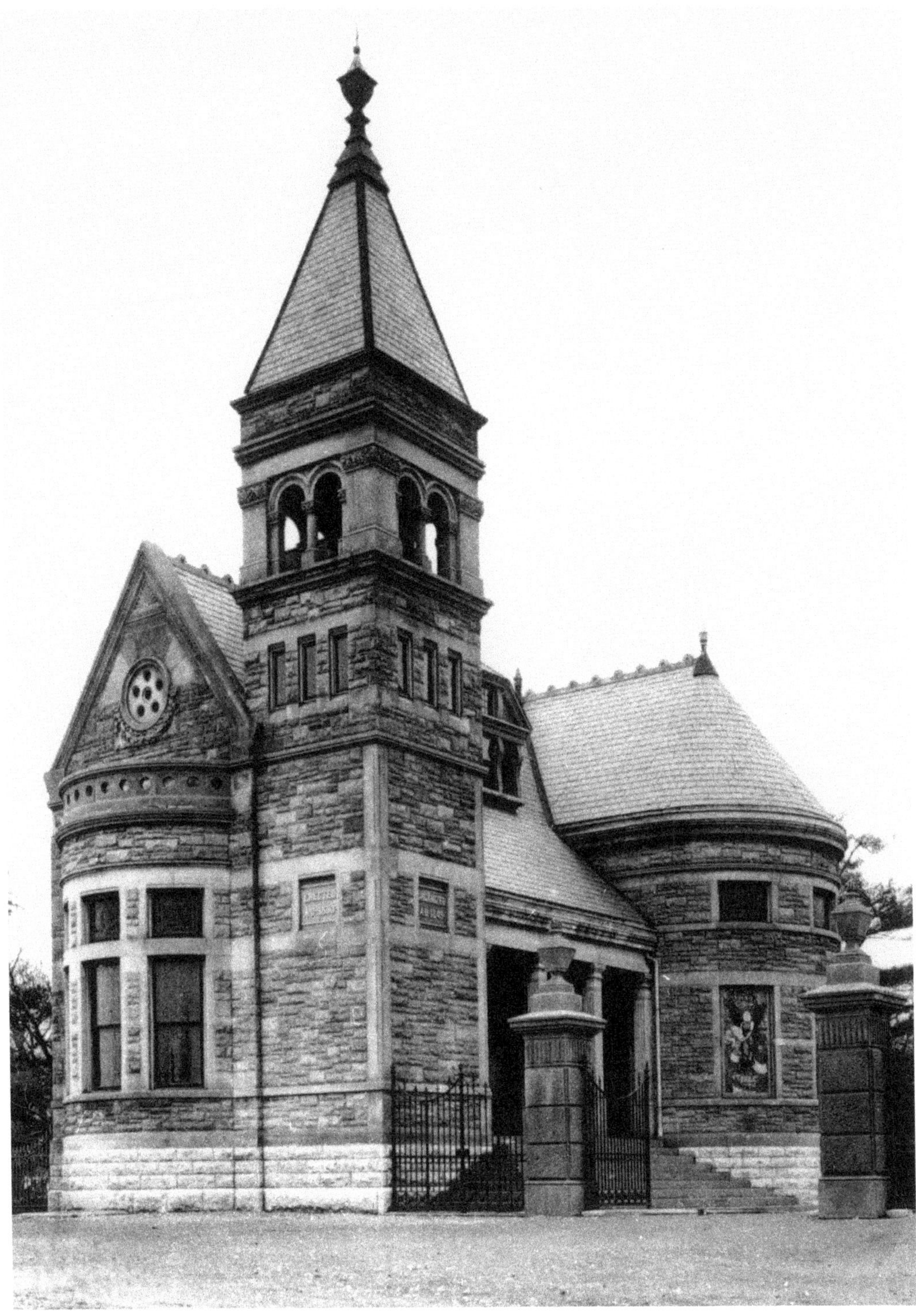

Lexington Cemetery entrance, 1898.

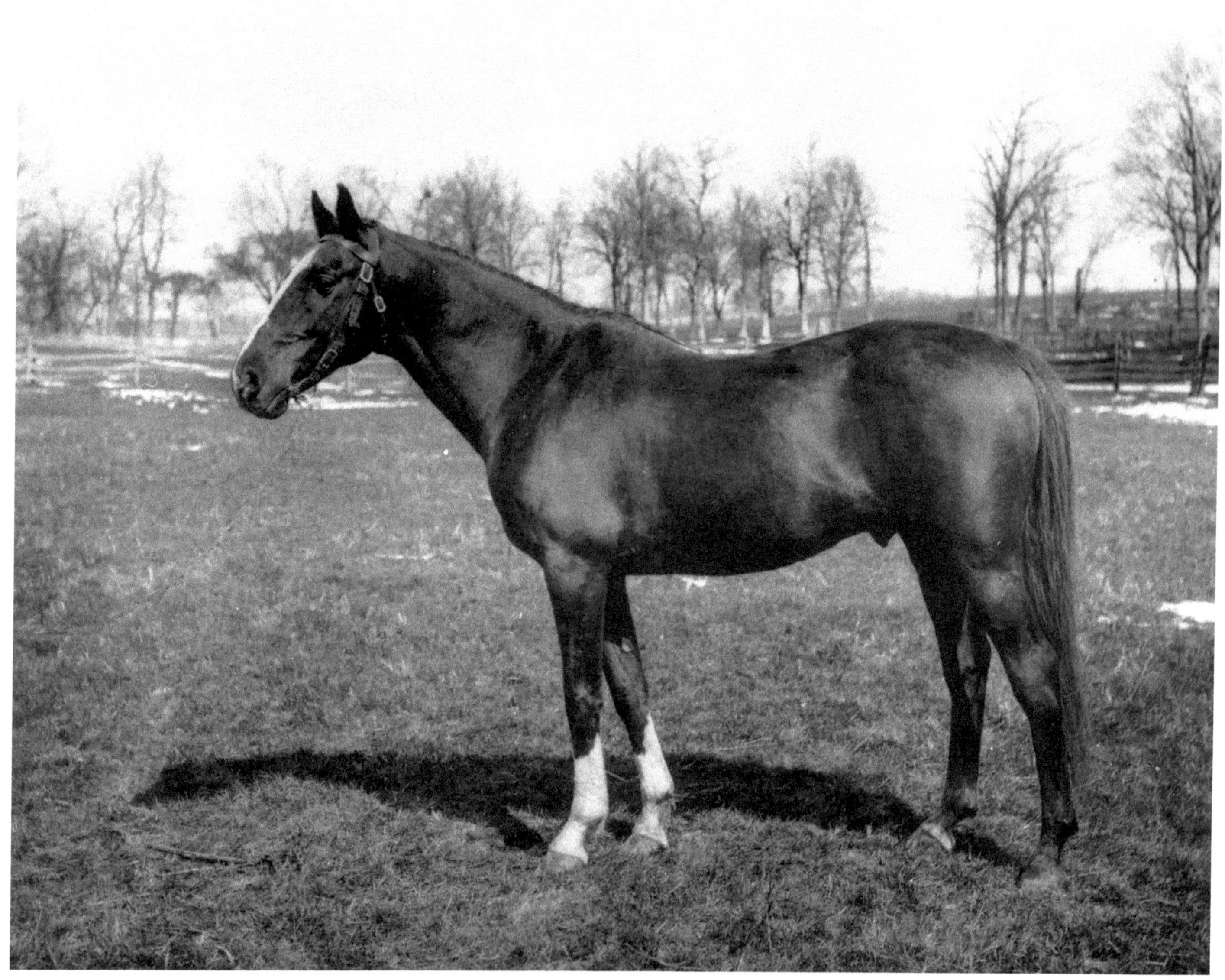

"Hanover" (1884-1899) won 32 of his 50 starts. In 1889, he was purchased by Colonel Milton Young who sent him to his McGrathiana Farm near Lexington. Hanover led U.S. sire lists in four successive years.

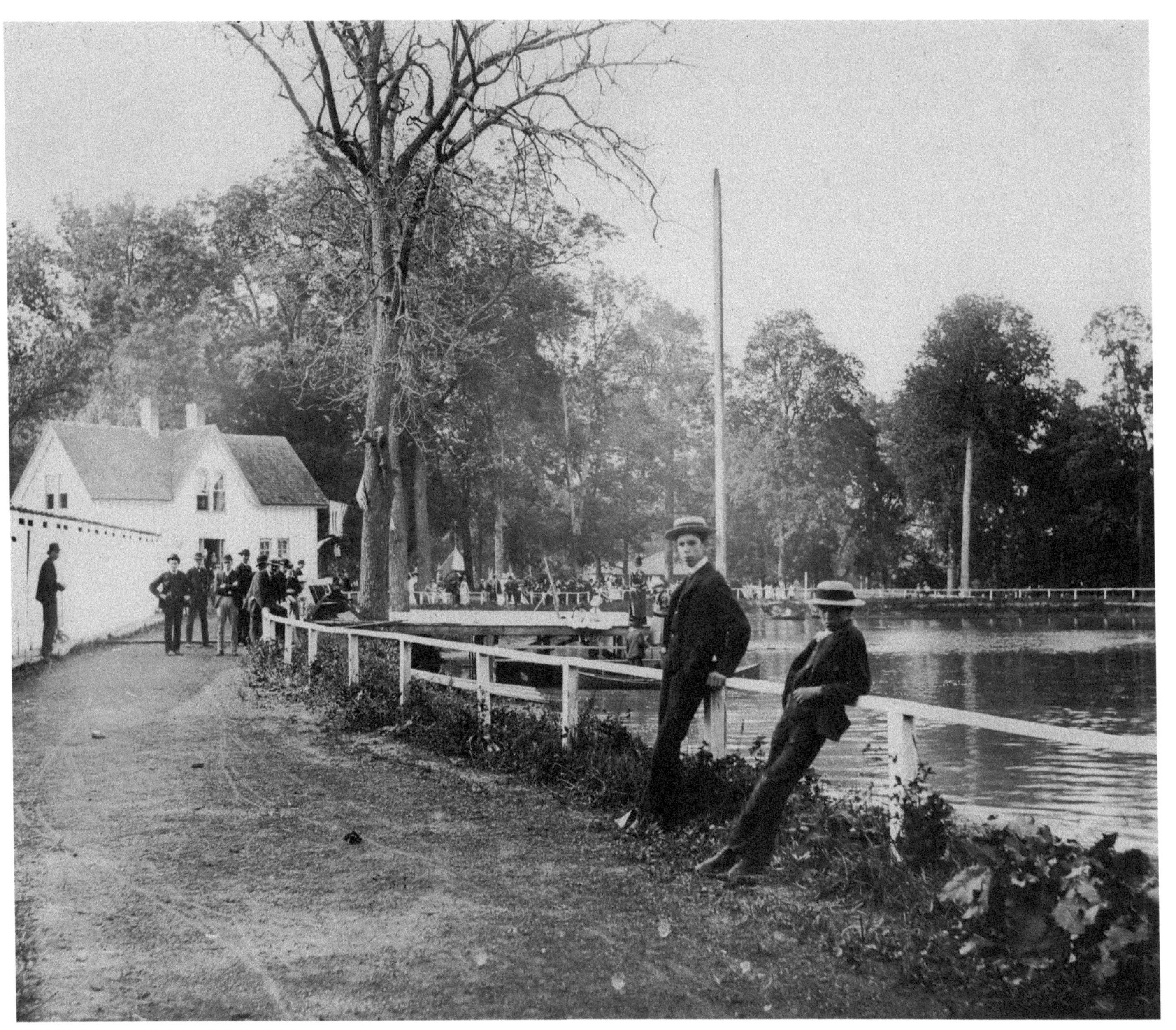

Chenosa Lake in Woodland Park (filled in about 1895), 1890.

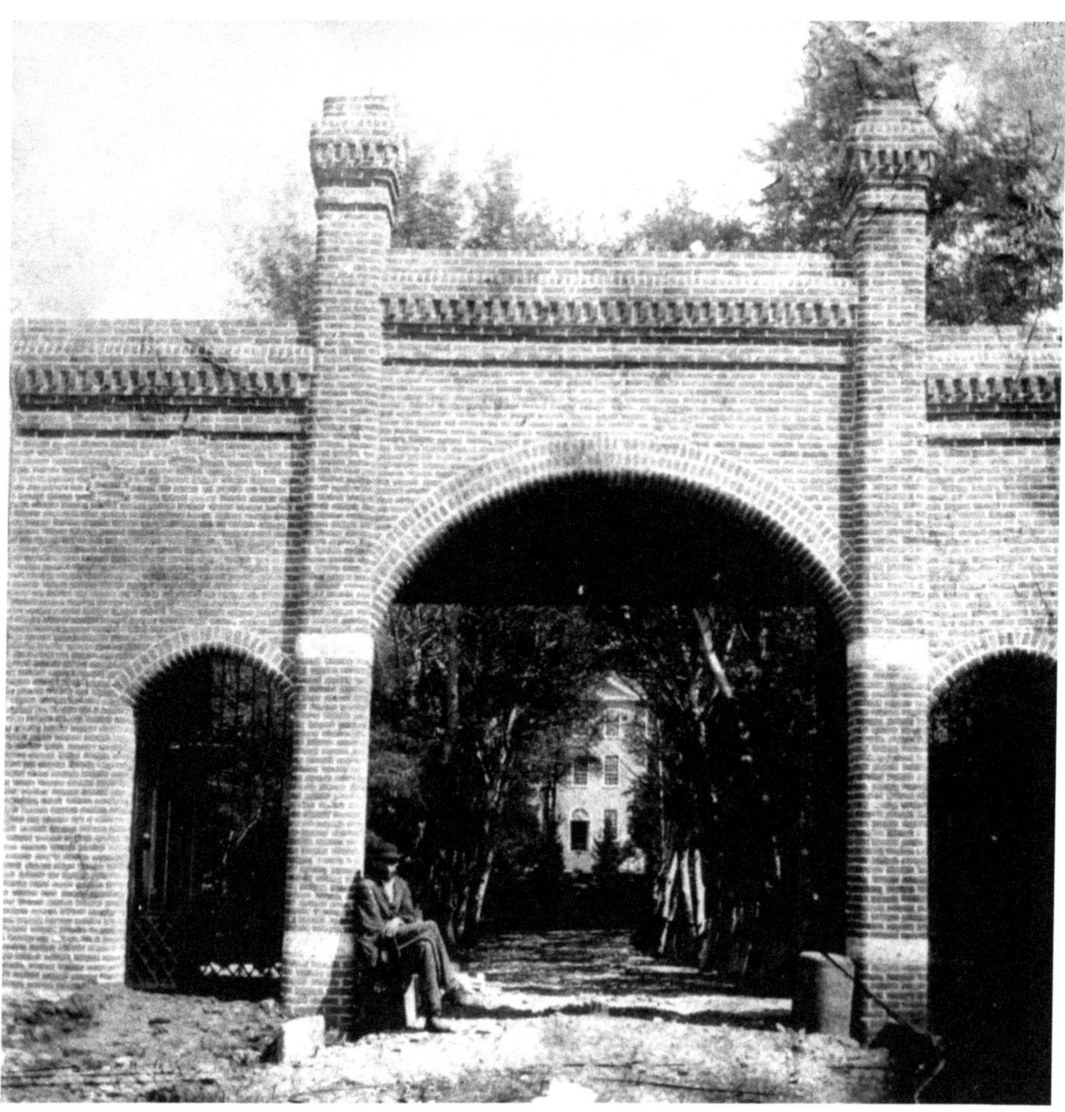

Asylum gatehouse on 4$^{th}$ Street (built by 1869), important 1820's original building viewed through arch, end of 19$^{th}$ century.

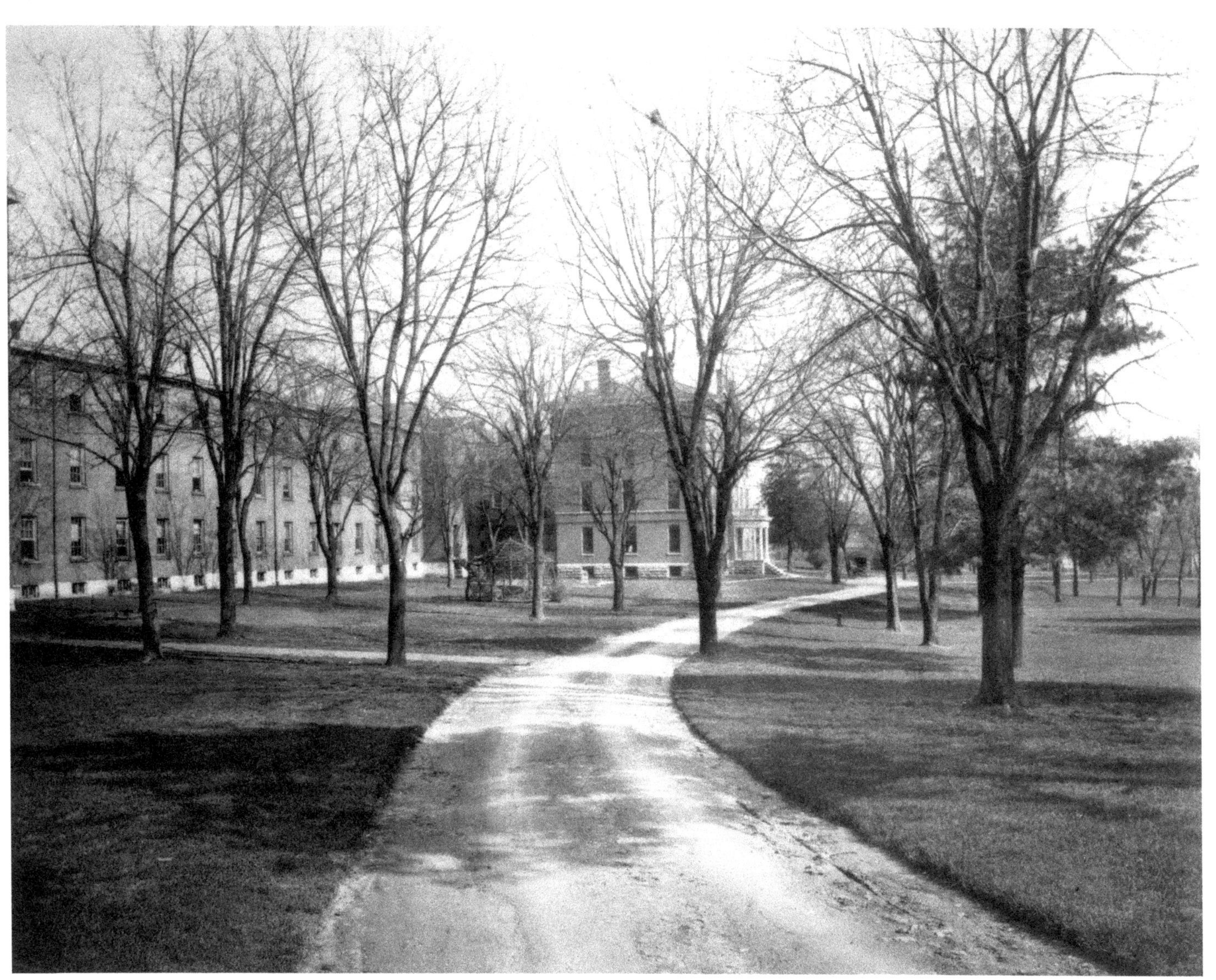

Eastern Kentucky Asylum for the Insane (established 1816), second oldest in the Nation, 1898.

"Hopemont", the Hunt-Morgan House (built by 1814), ca. 1890.

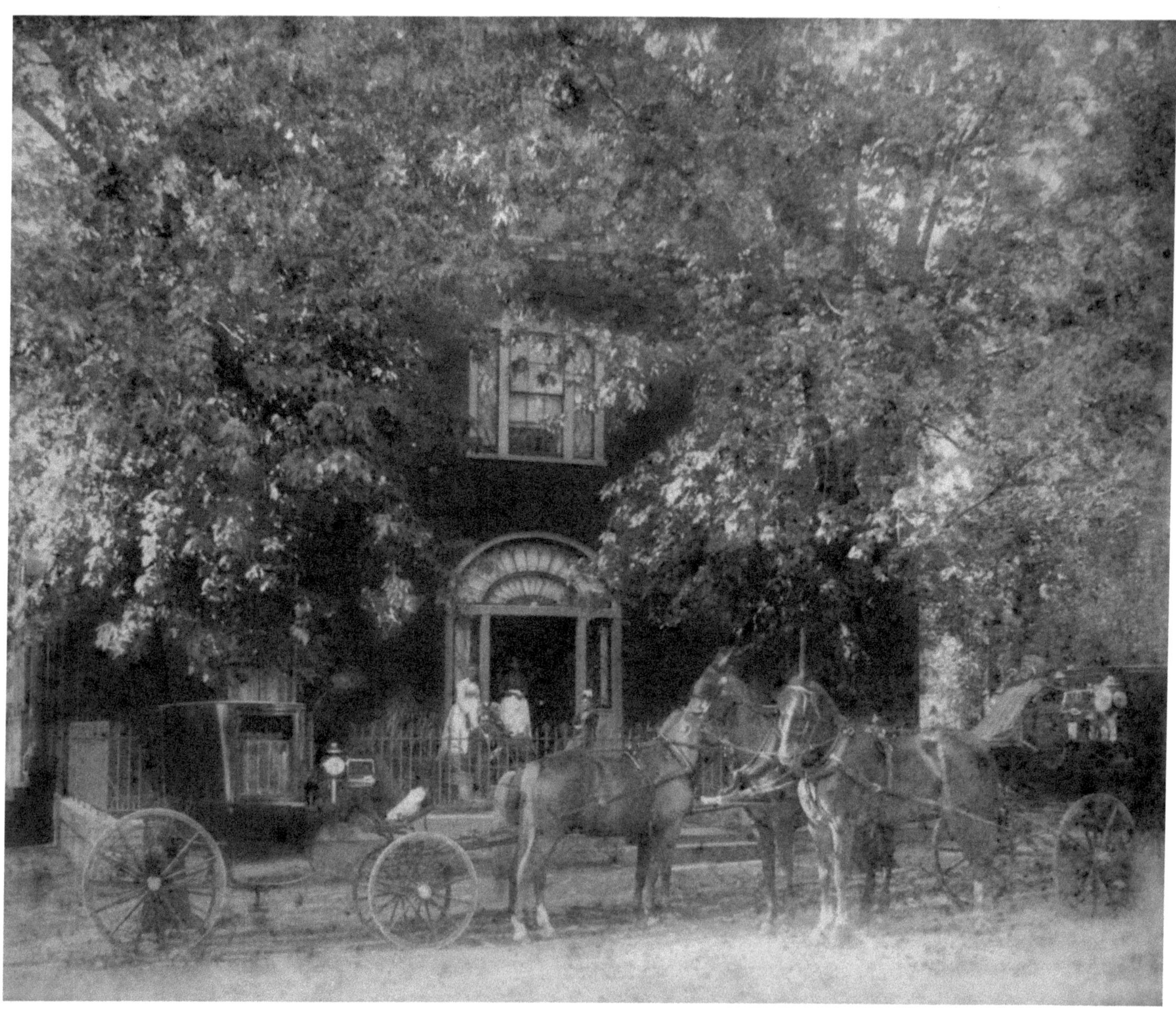

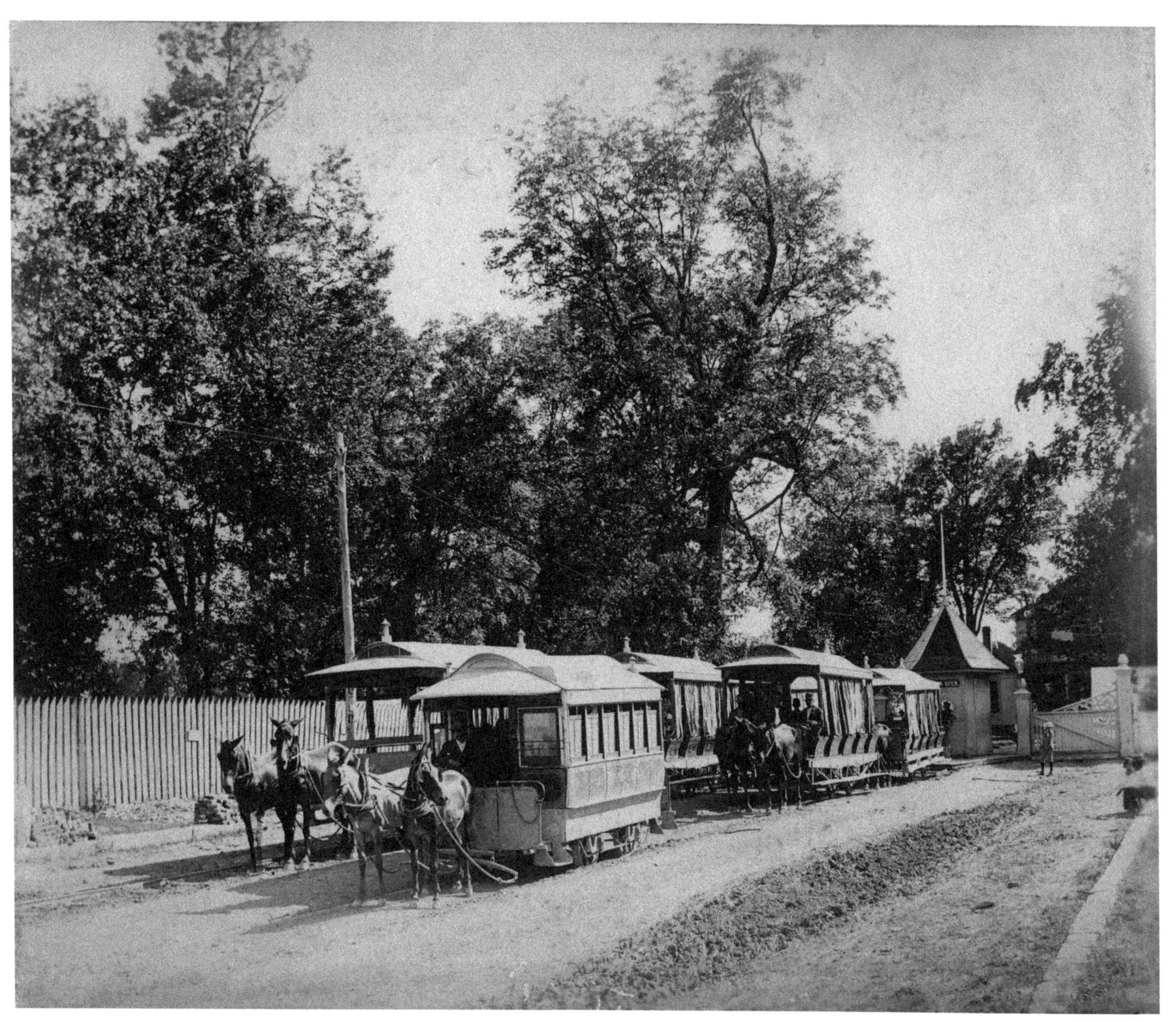

Mule drawn trolleys at Woodland Park, late 1890's.

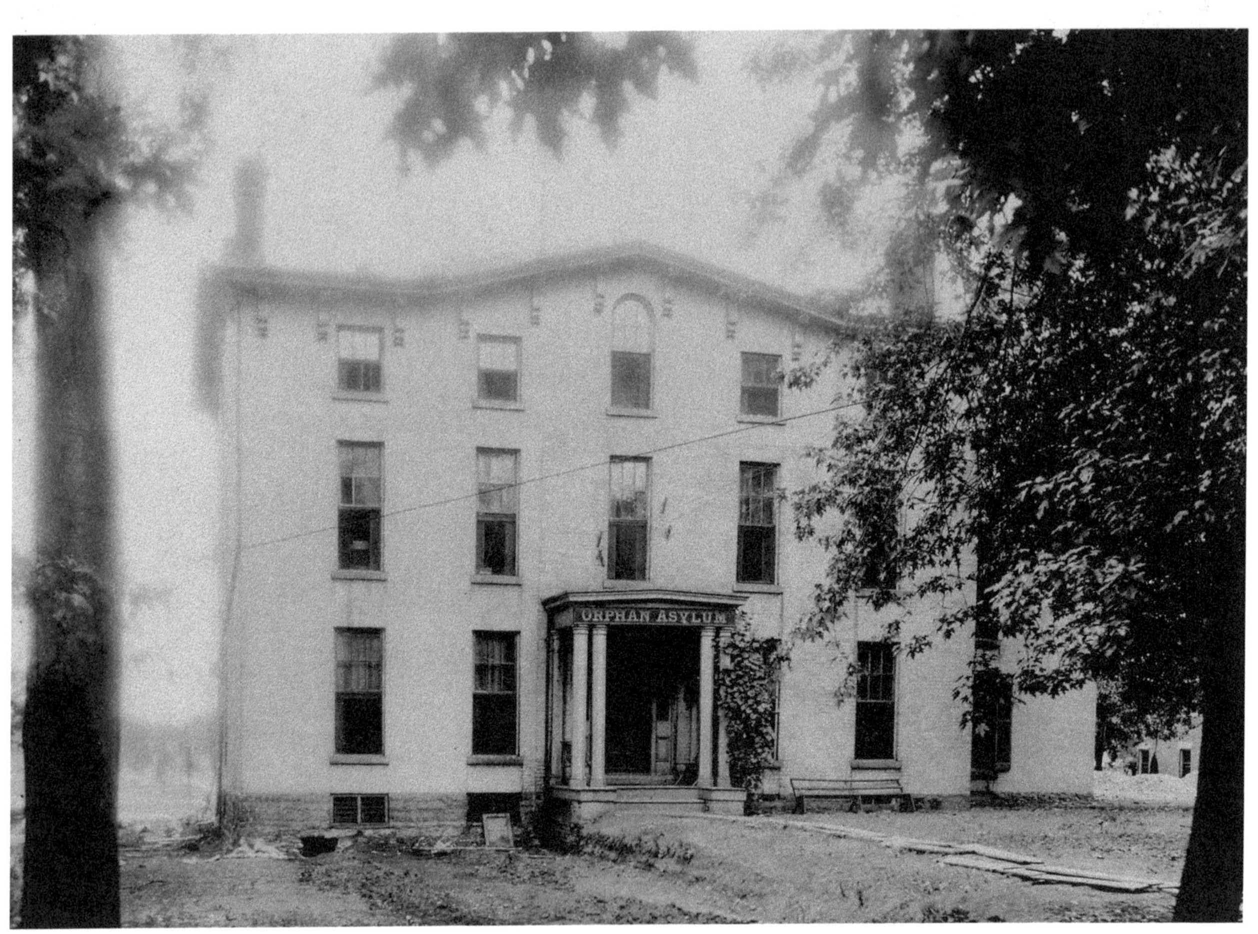

Orphan Asylum on Third Street, near the turn of the century.

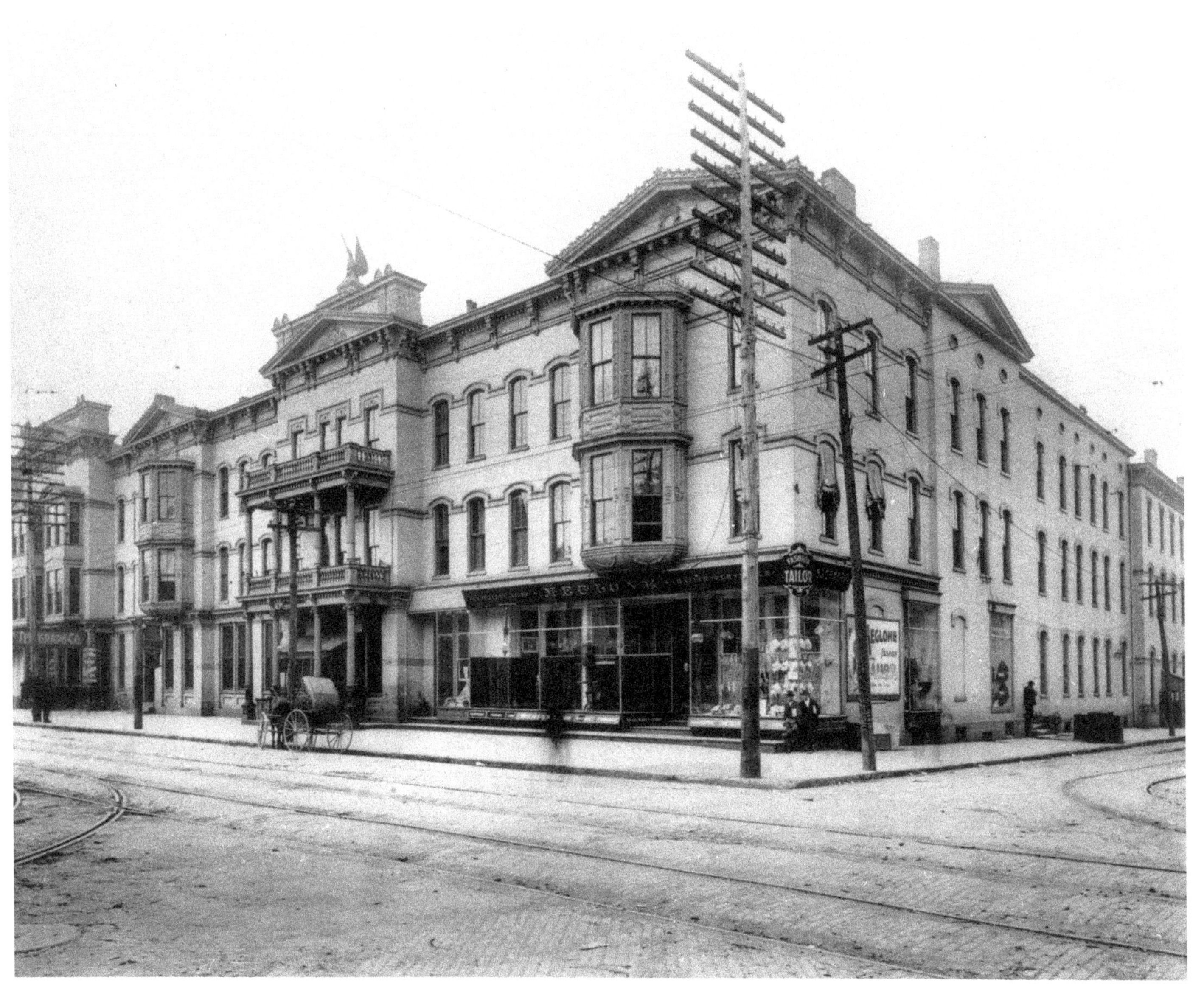


Phoenix Hotel on Main, built in 1870's.

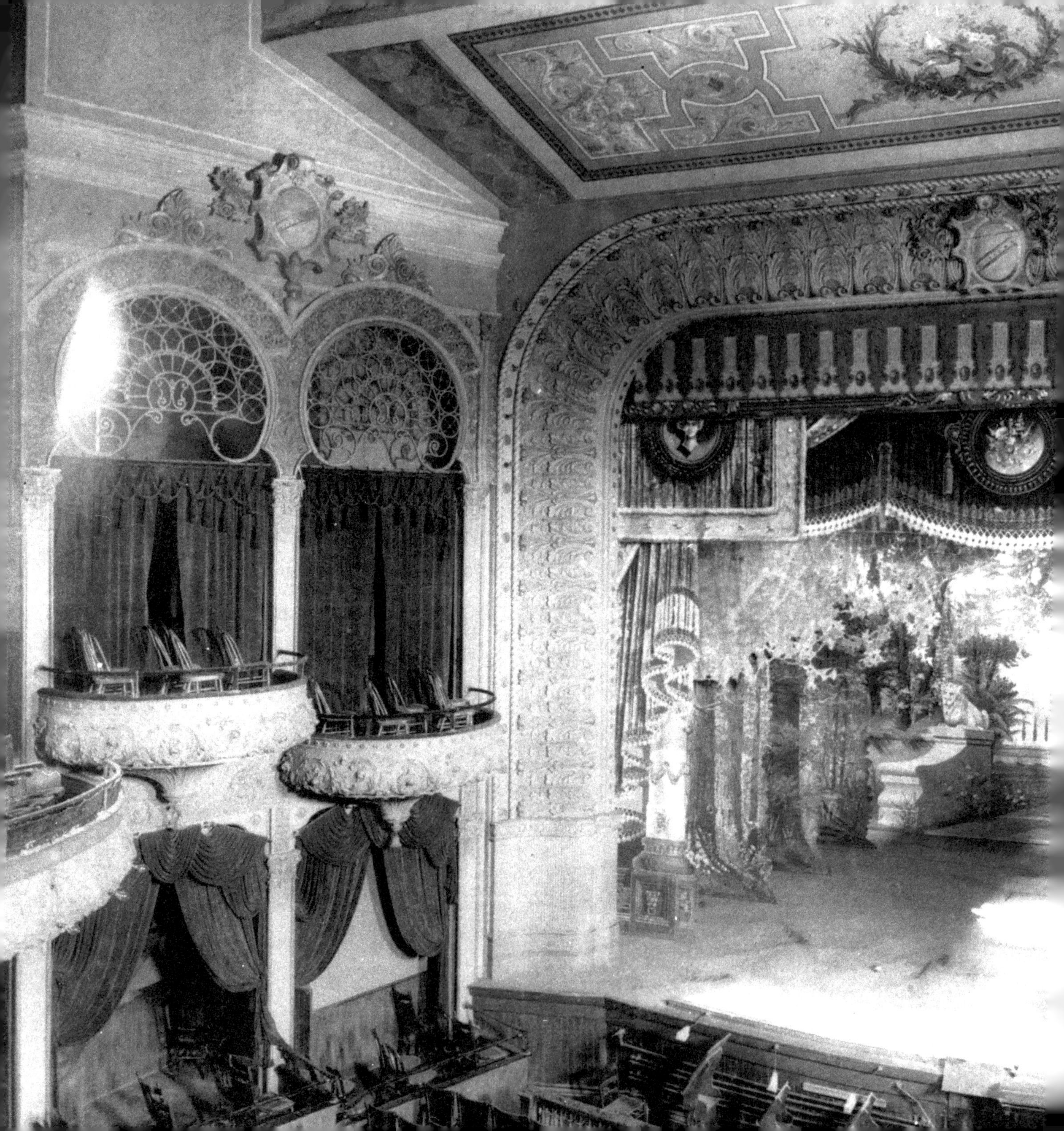

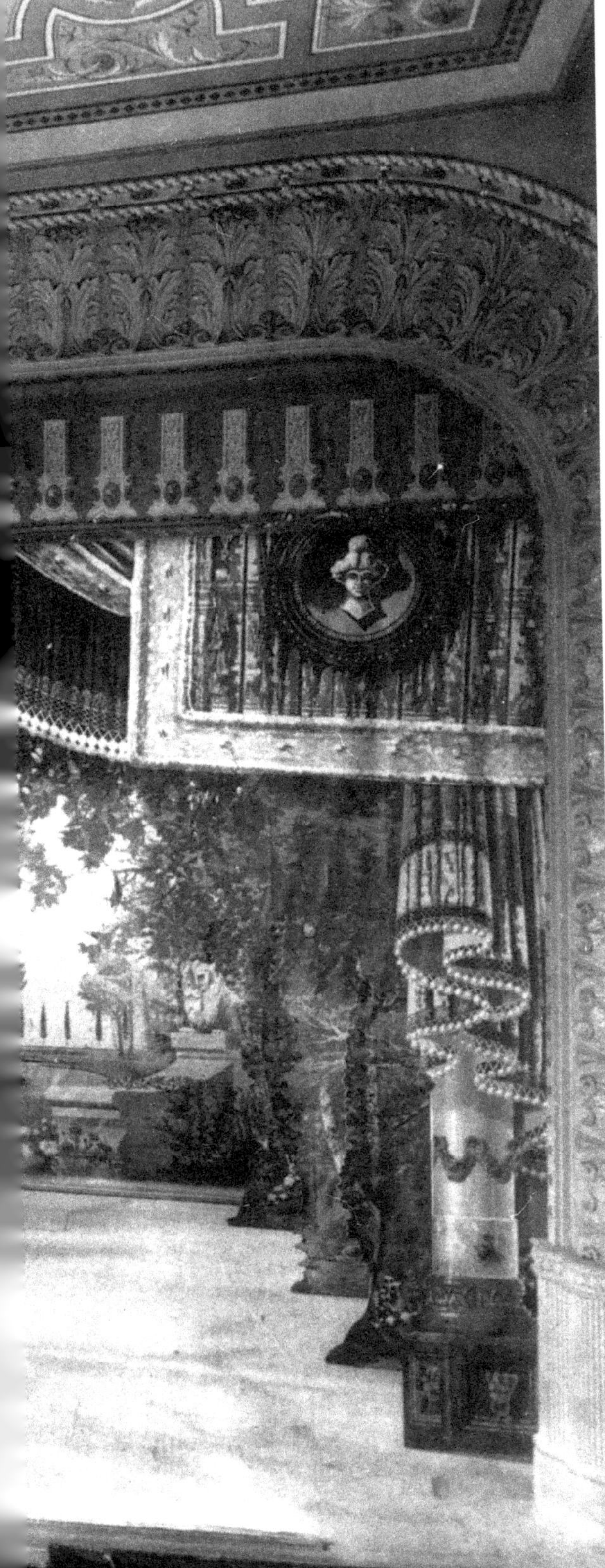

Lexington Opera House interior view, late 1890's.

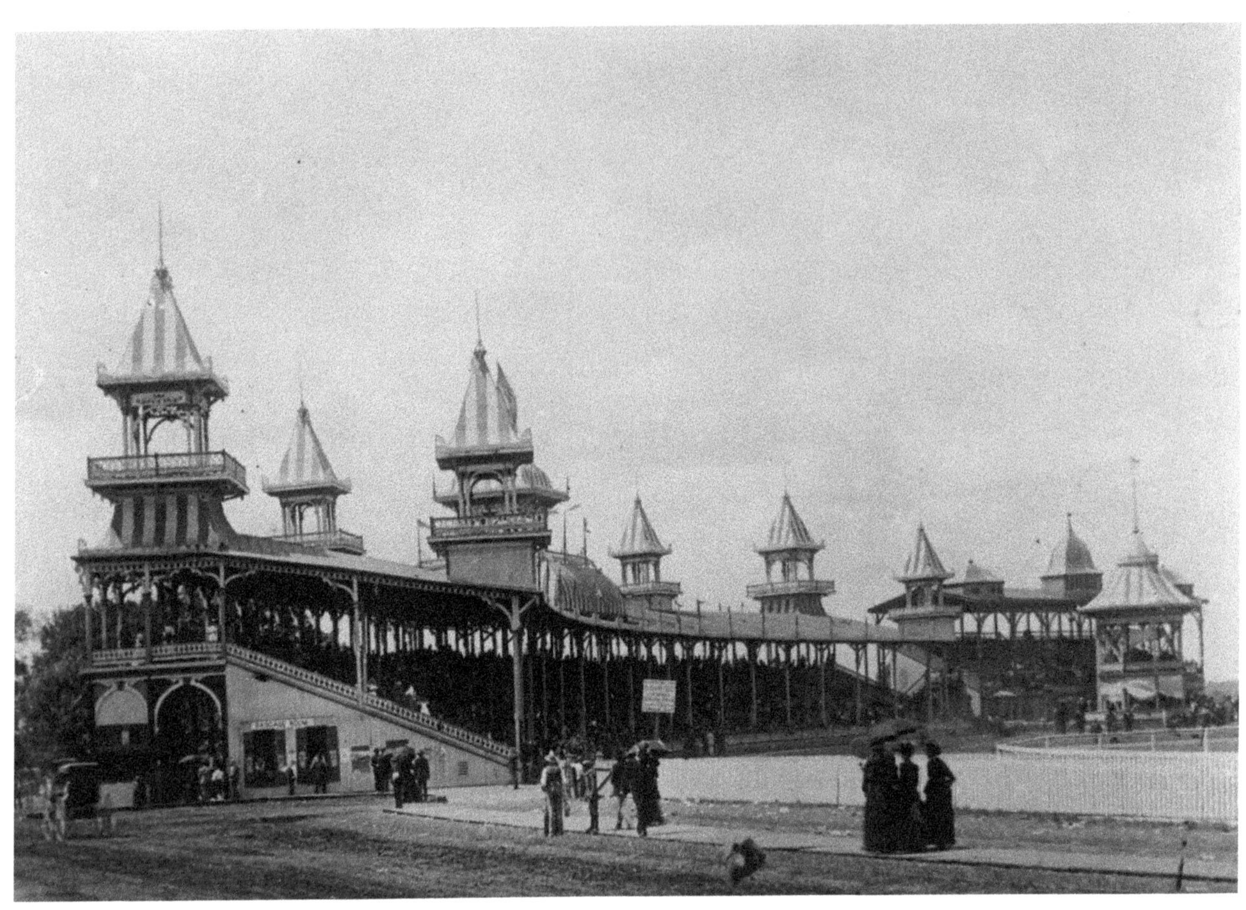

Grandstand and trotting track at the fairgrounds ("The Red Mile"), ca. 1882.

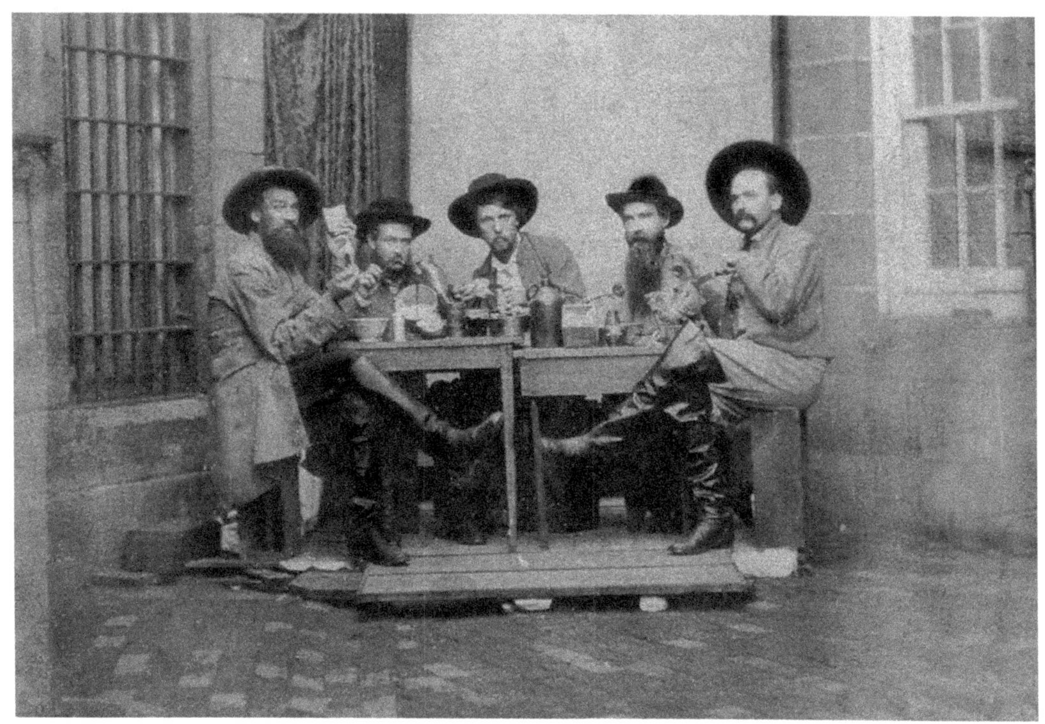

"Morgan's Men" imprisoned during the Civil War.

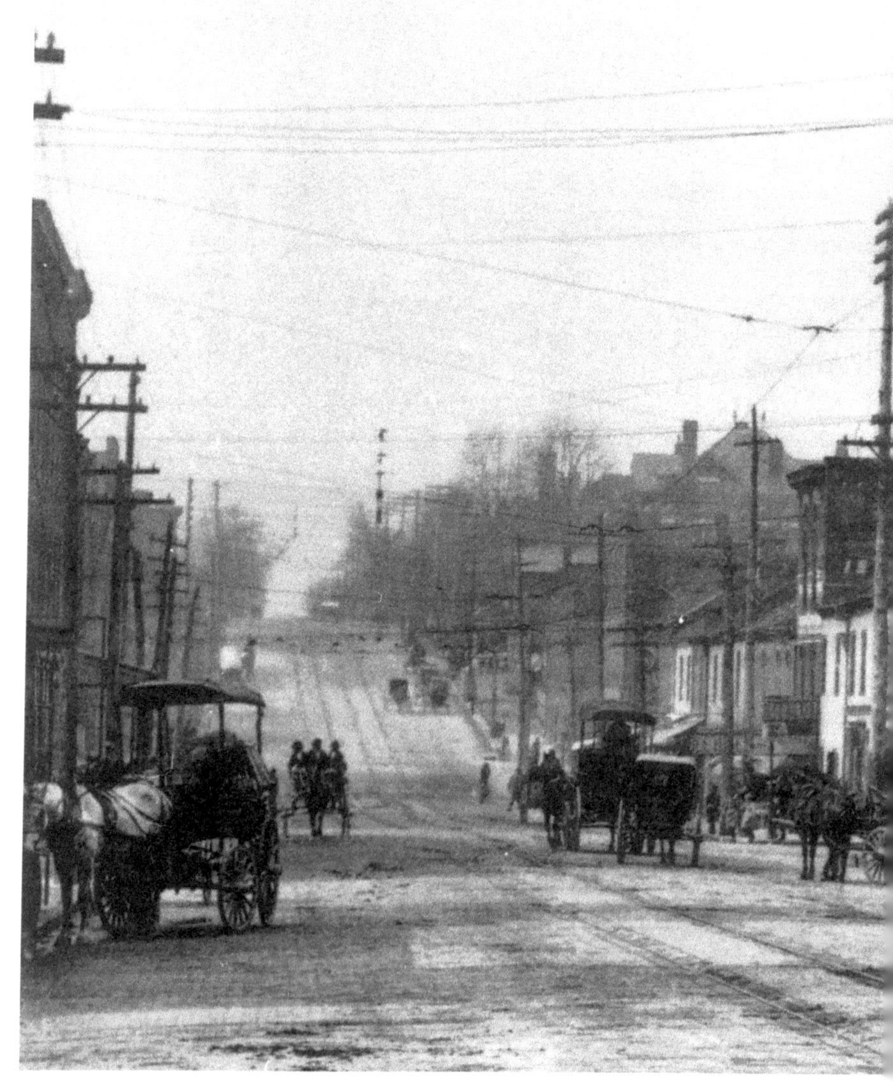

View on Broadway, 1898.

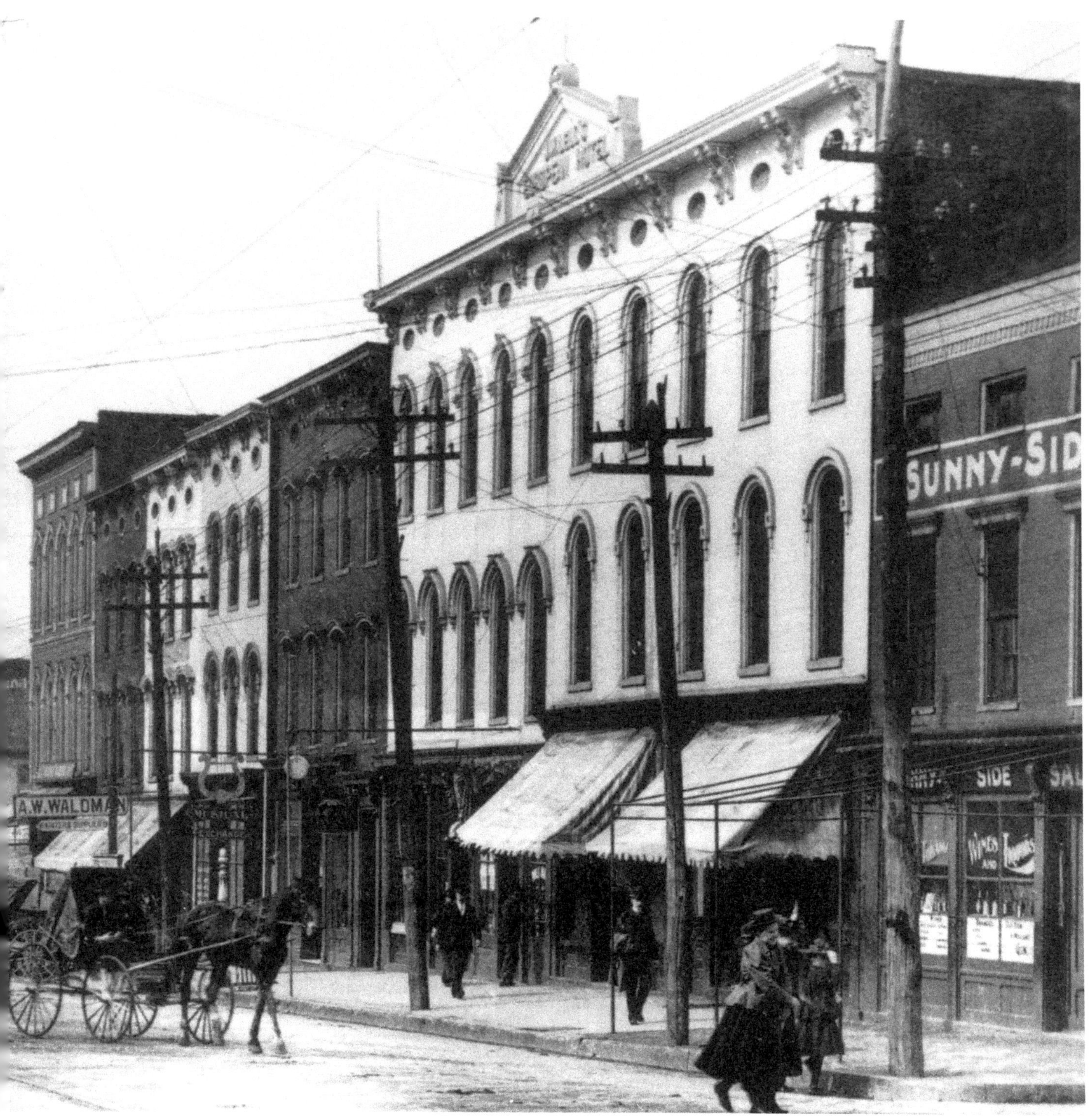
A.W. WALDMAN
SUNNY-SID
SIDE

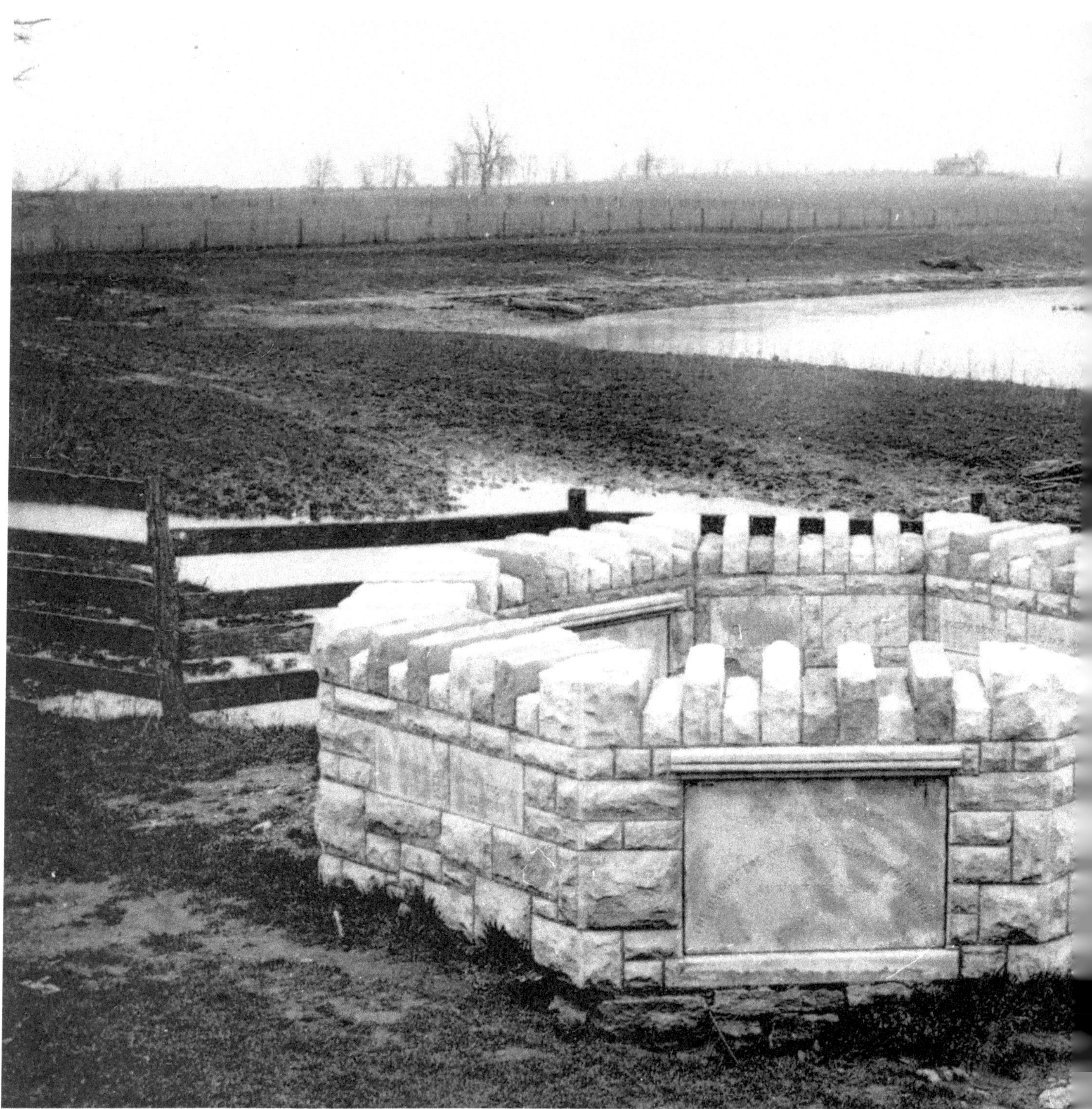

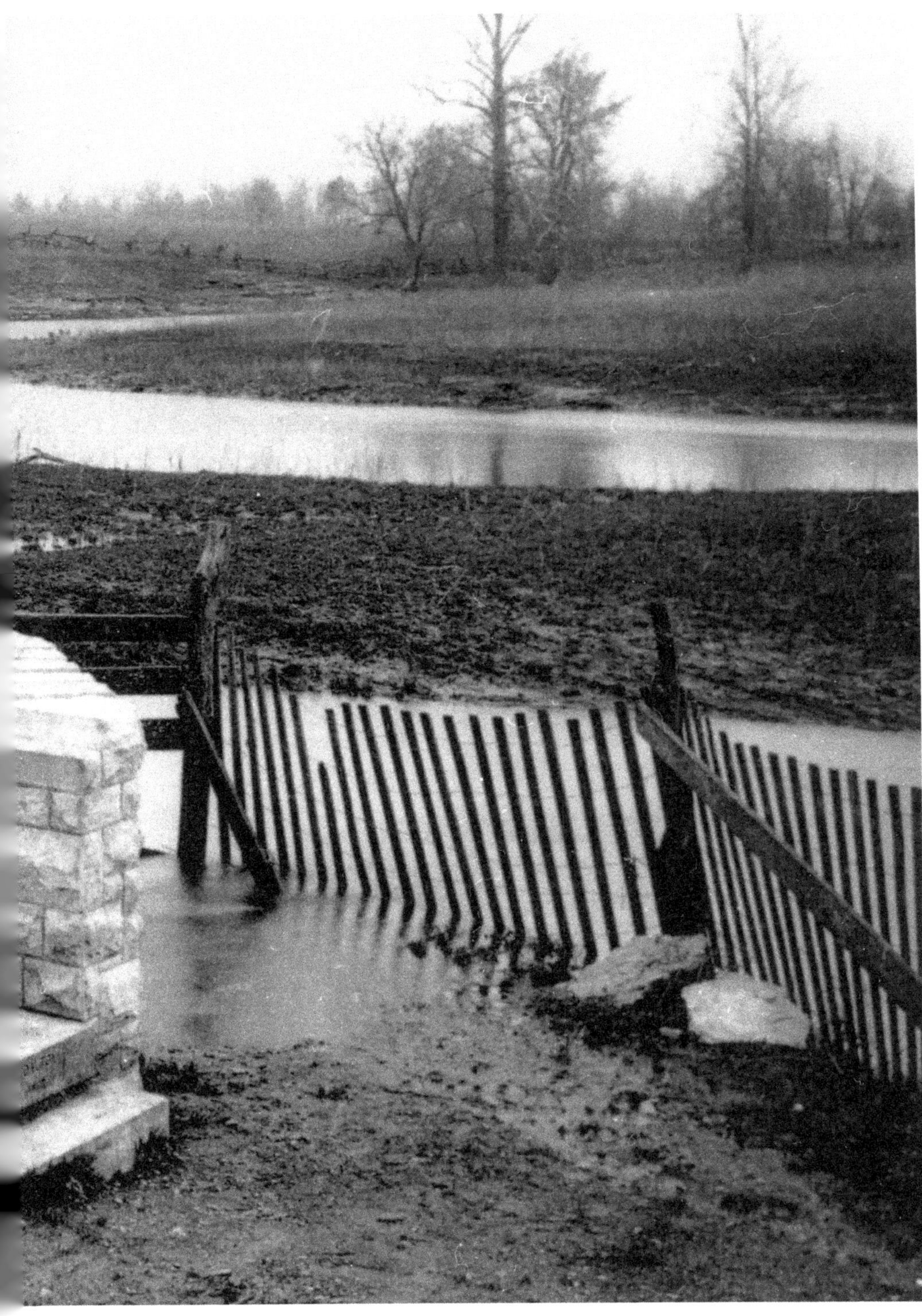

Memorial at Bryan Station spring, site of historic fort, ca. 1898.

Race track of the Kentucky Association for the Improvement of the Breeds of Stock, (this grandstand replaced in 1889), 1888.

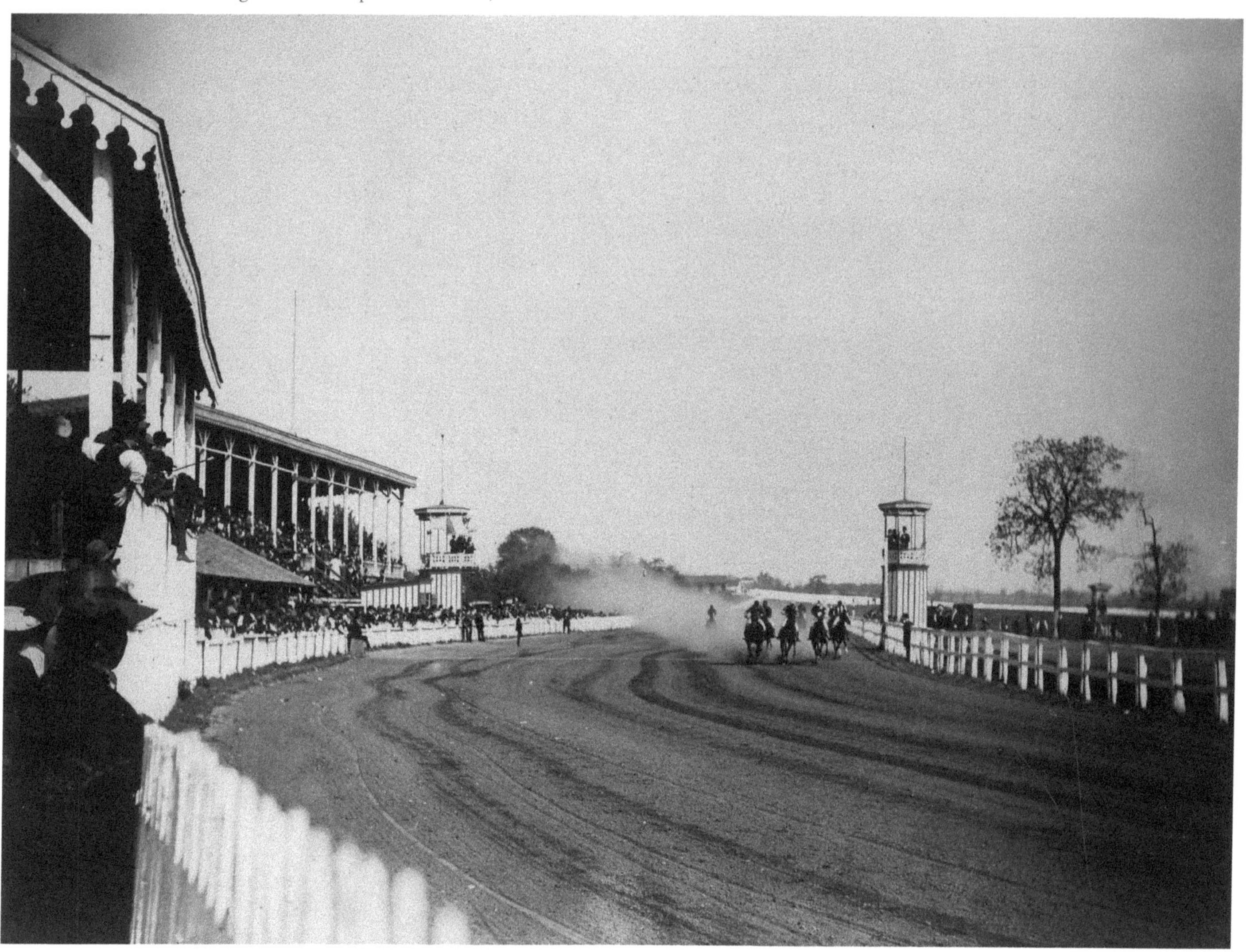

"Old Morrison" of Transylvania University seen from Gratz Park, late 1900's.

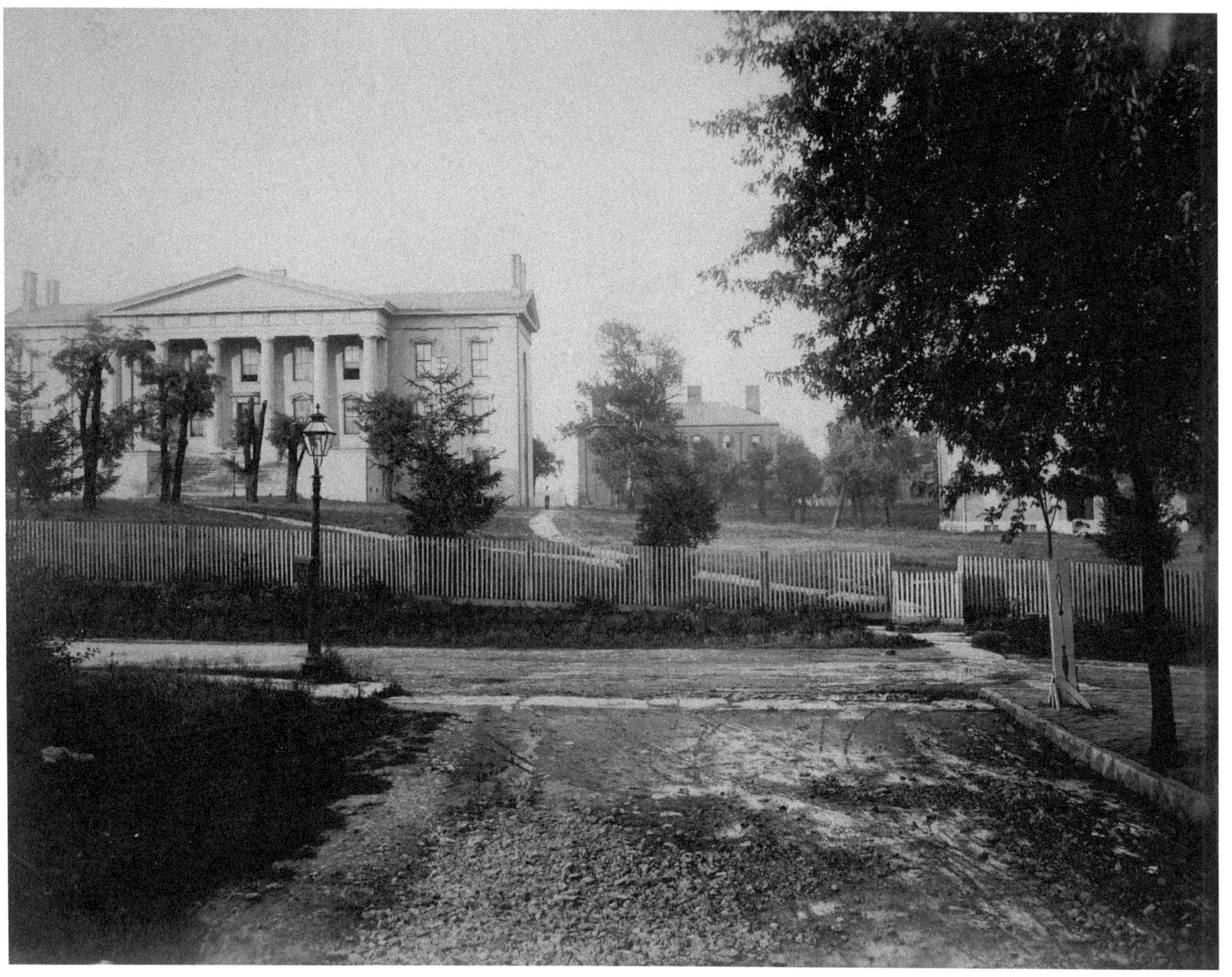

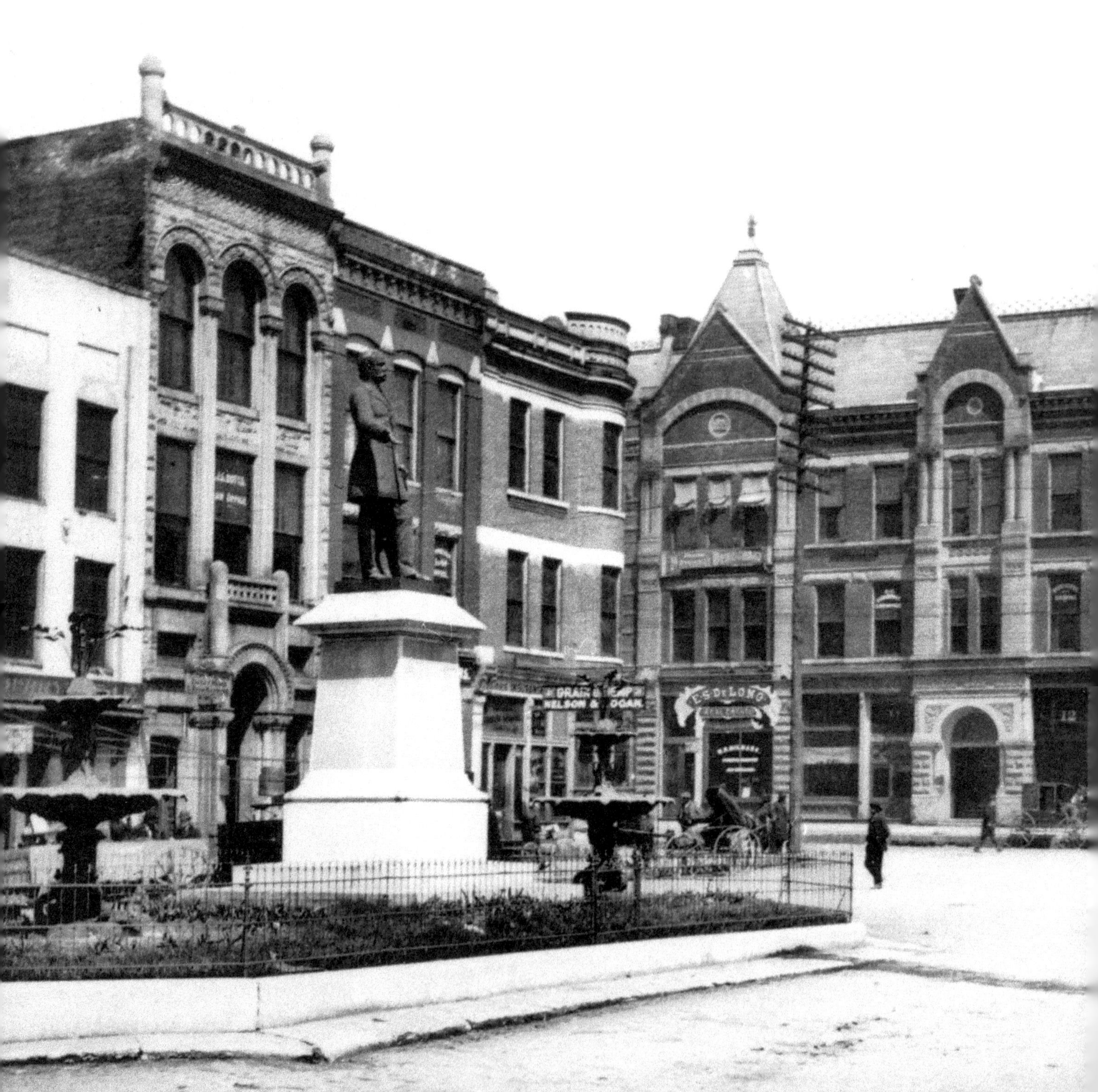
E.S. DeLONG

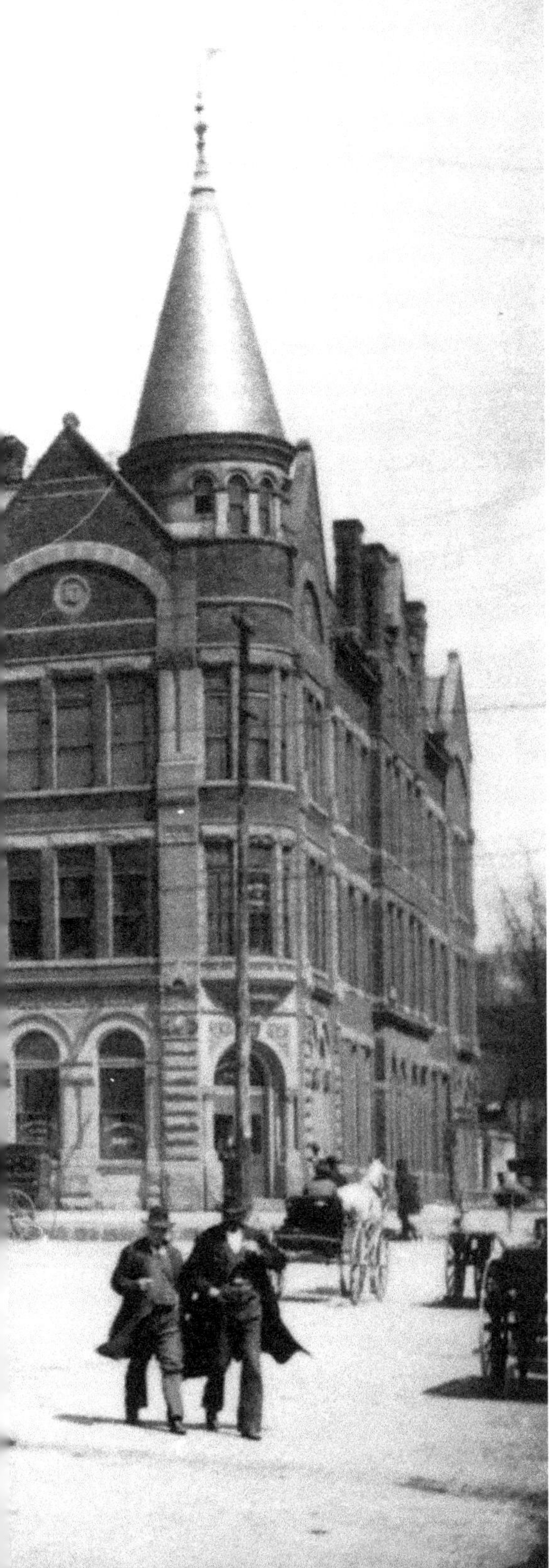

Monument to John C. Breckinridge on Cheapside, 1898.

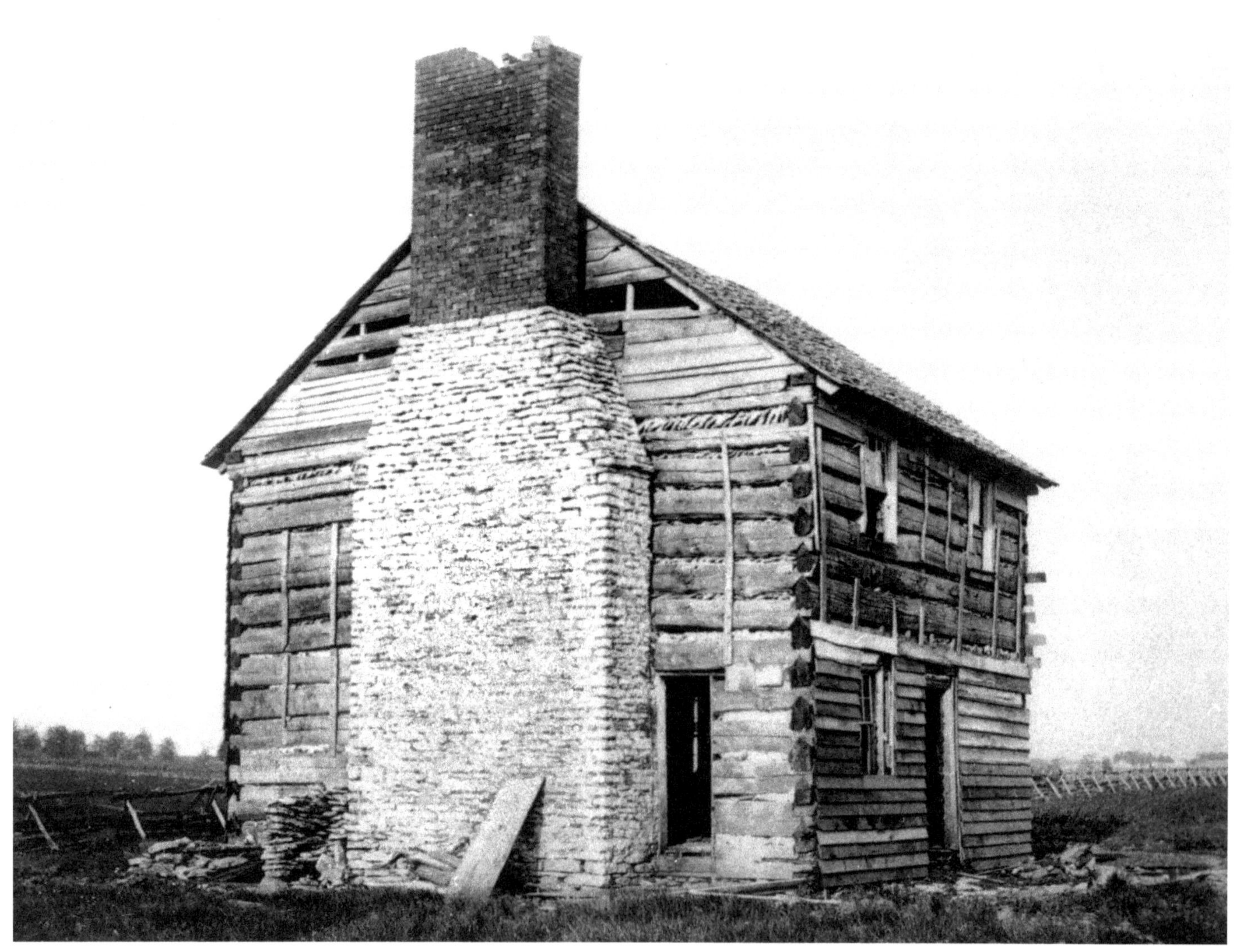

Masterson's Station (site of first Methodist Church conference in Kentucky in 1790), 1898.

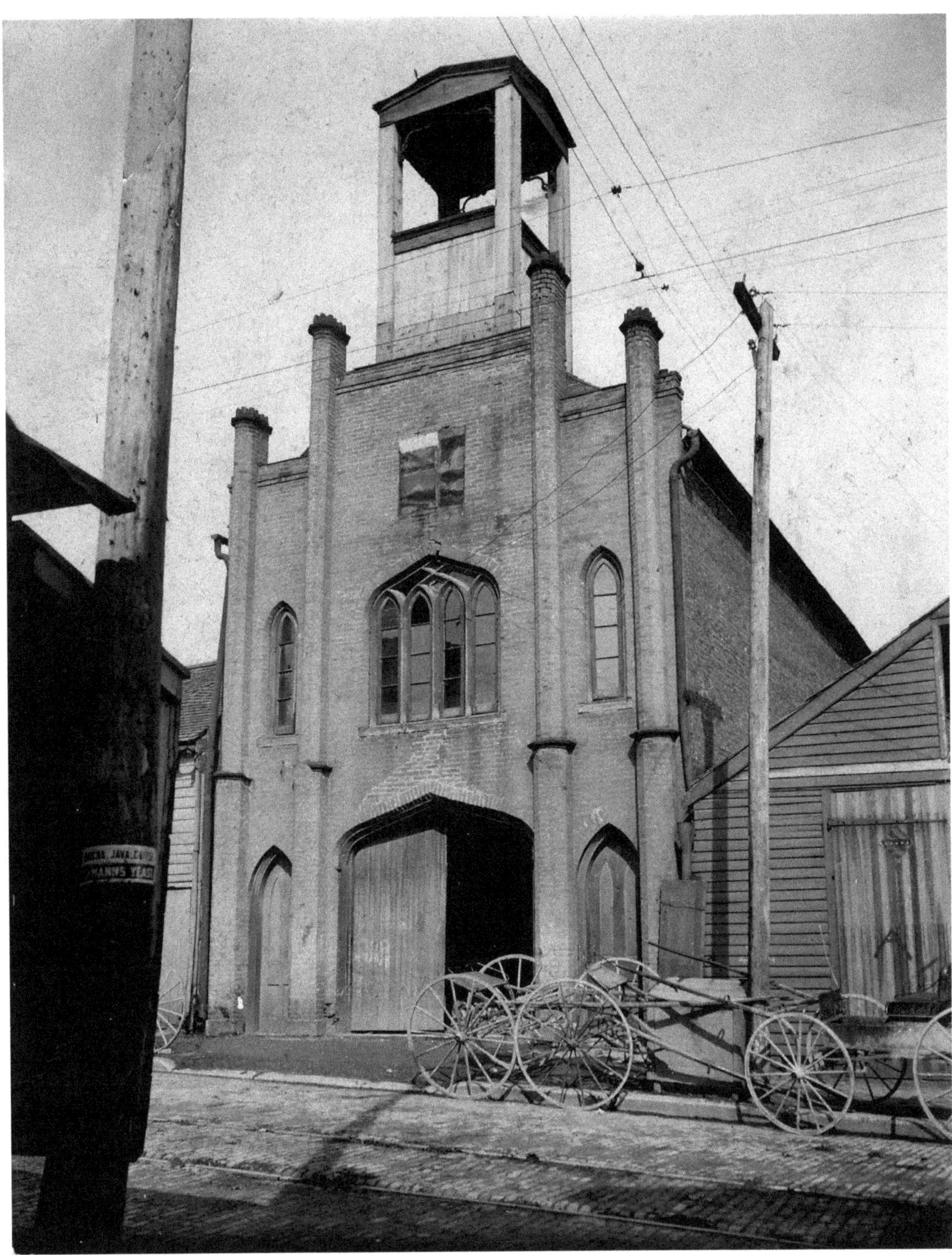

Lyon Firehouse on Limestone, late 19th century

Photo on next page: Revival in Woodland Park, late 1800's.

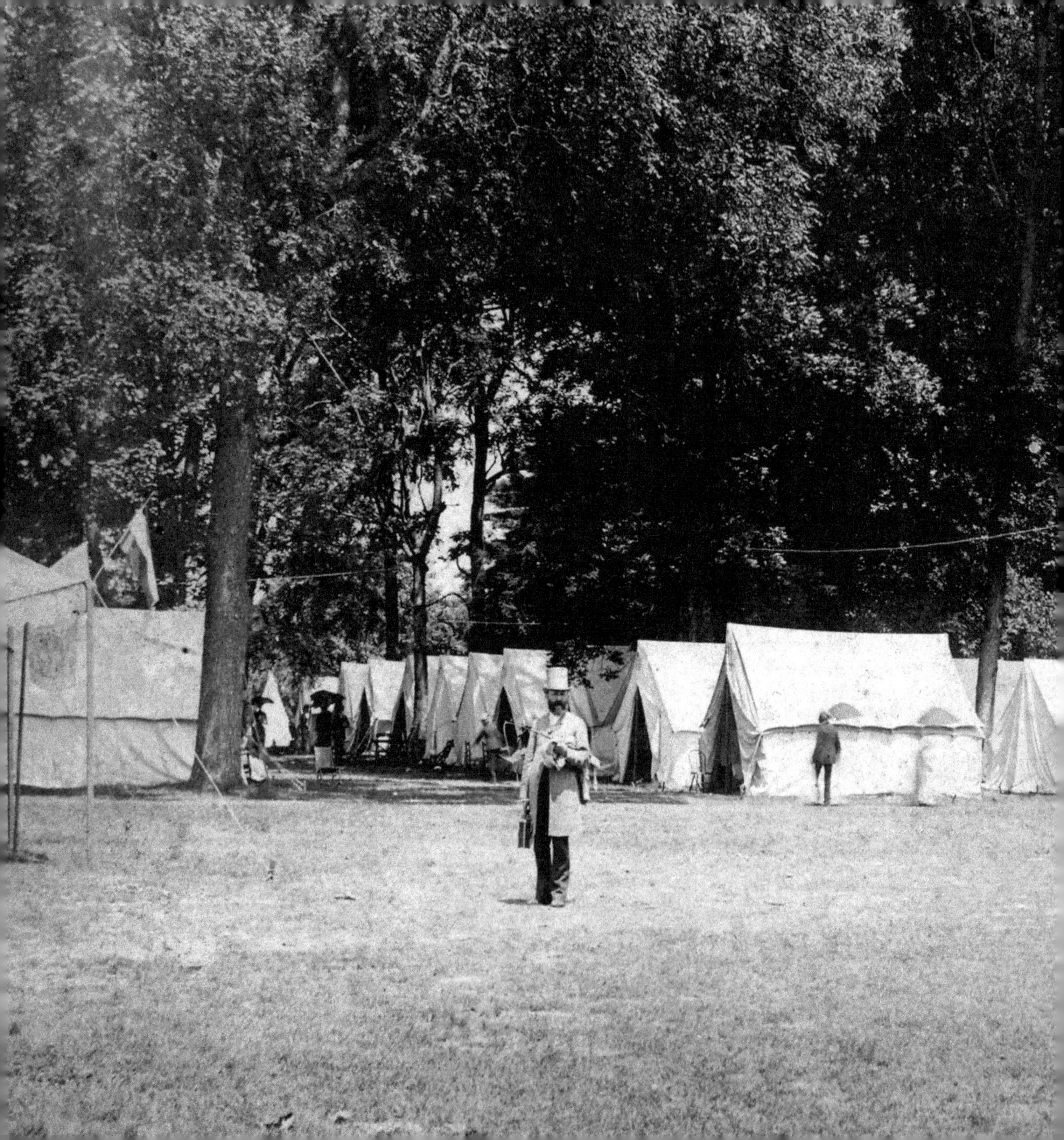

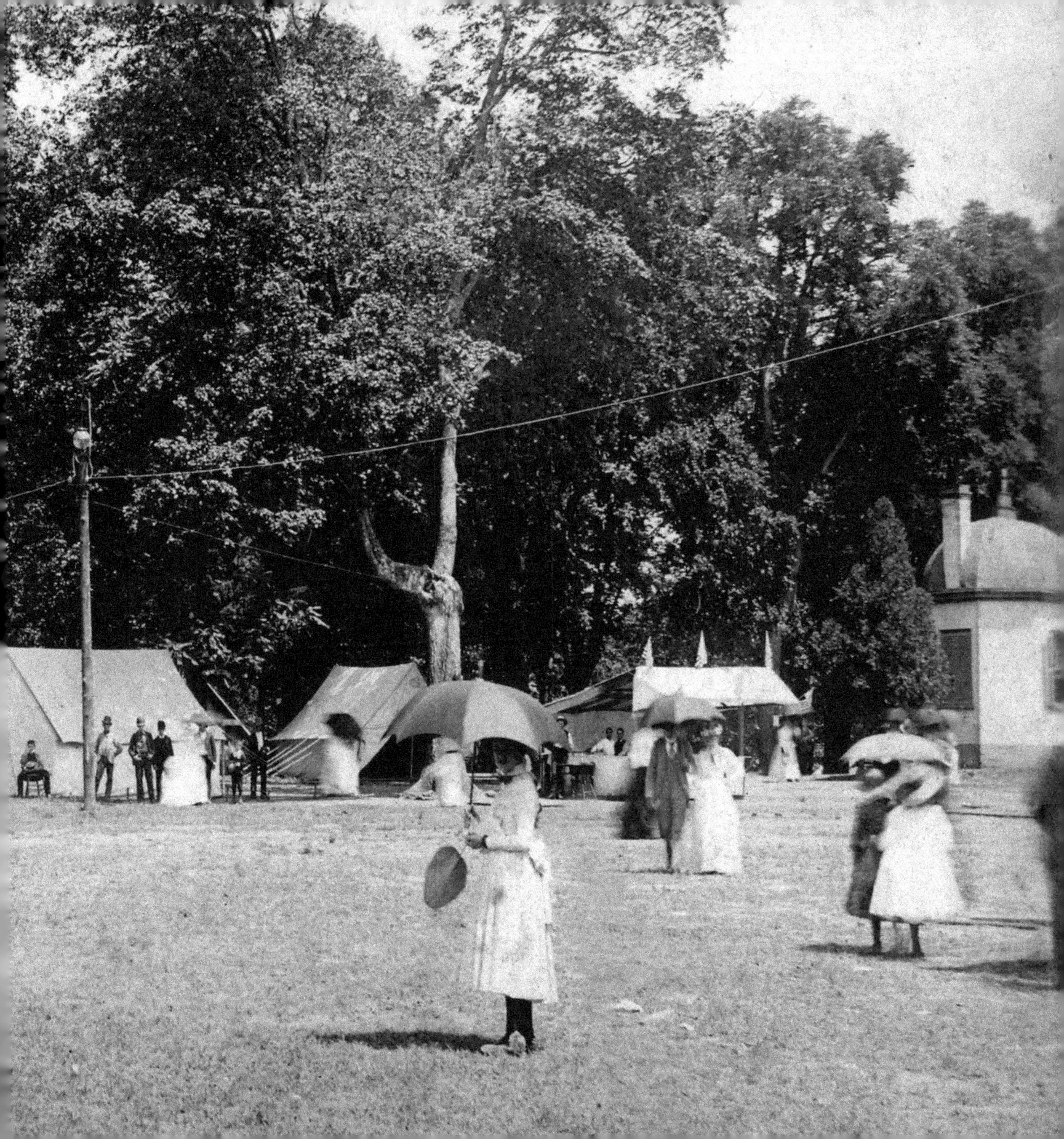

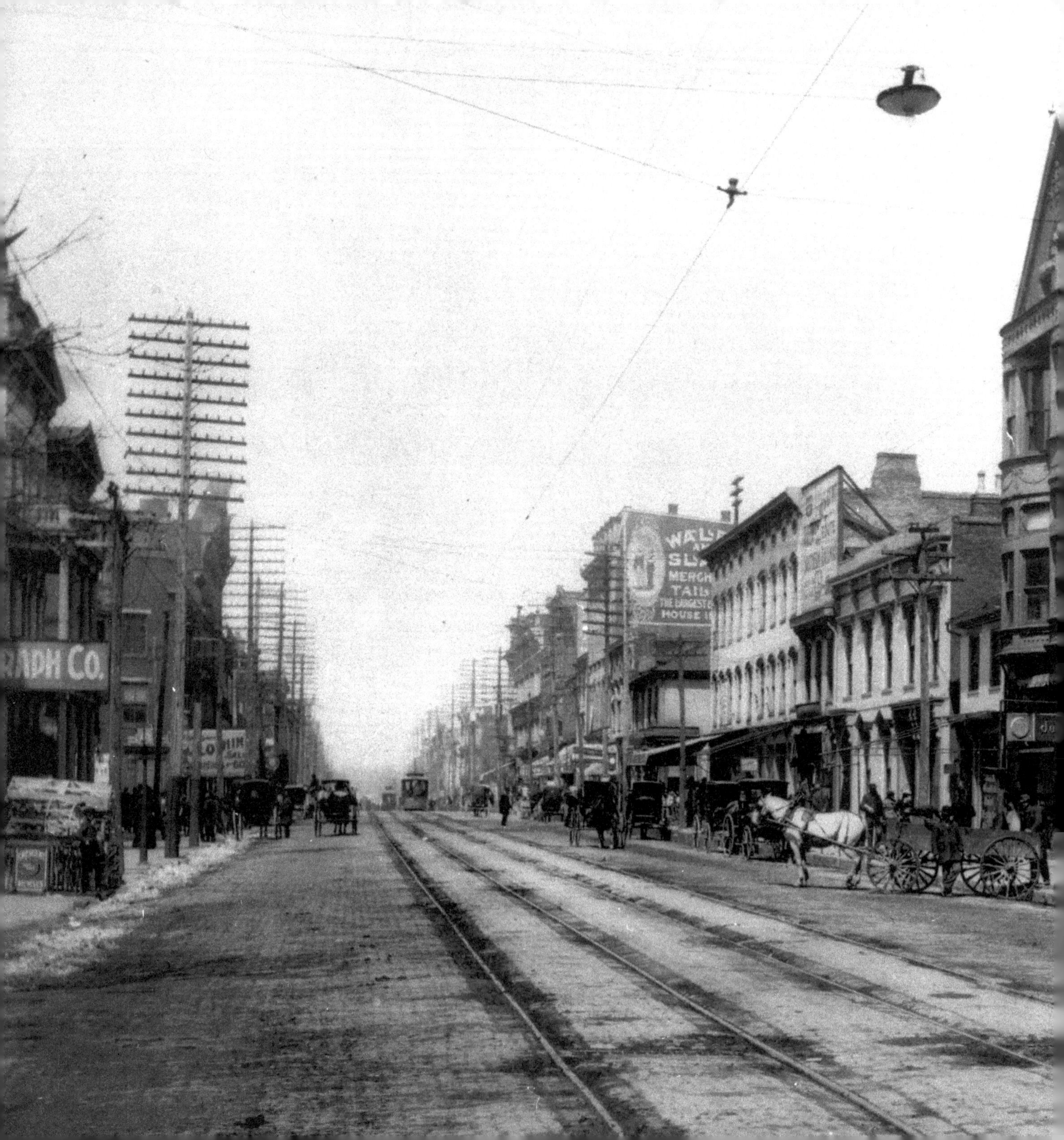

RAPH CO.
MERCH
HOUSE

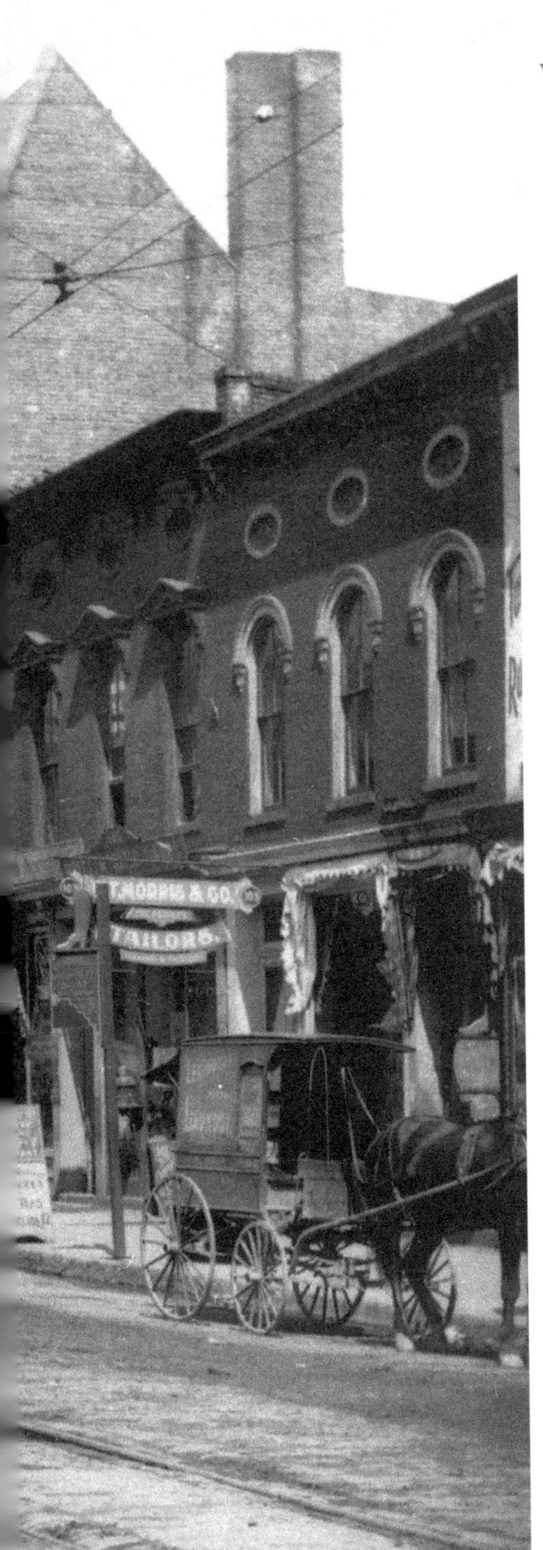


View of Main Street, 1898.

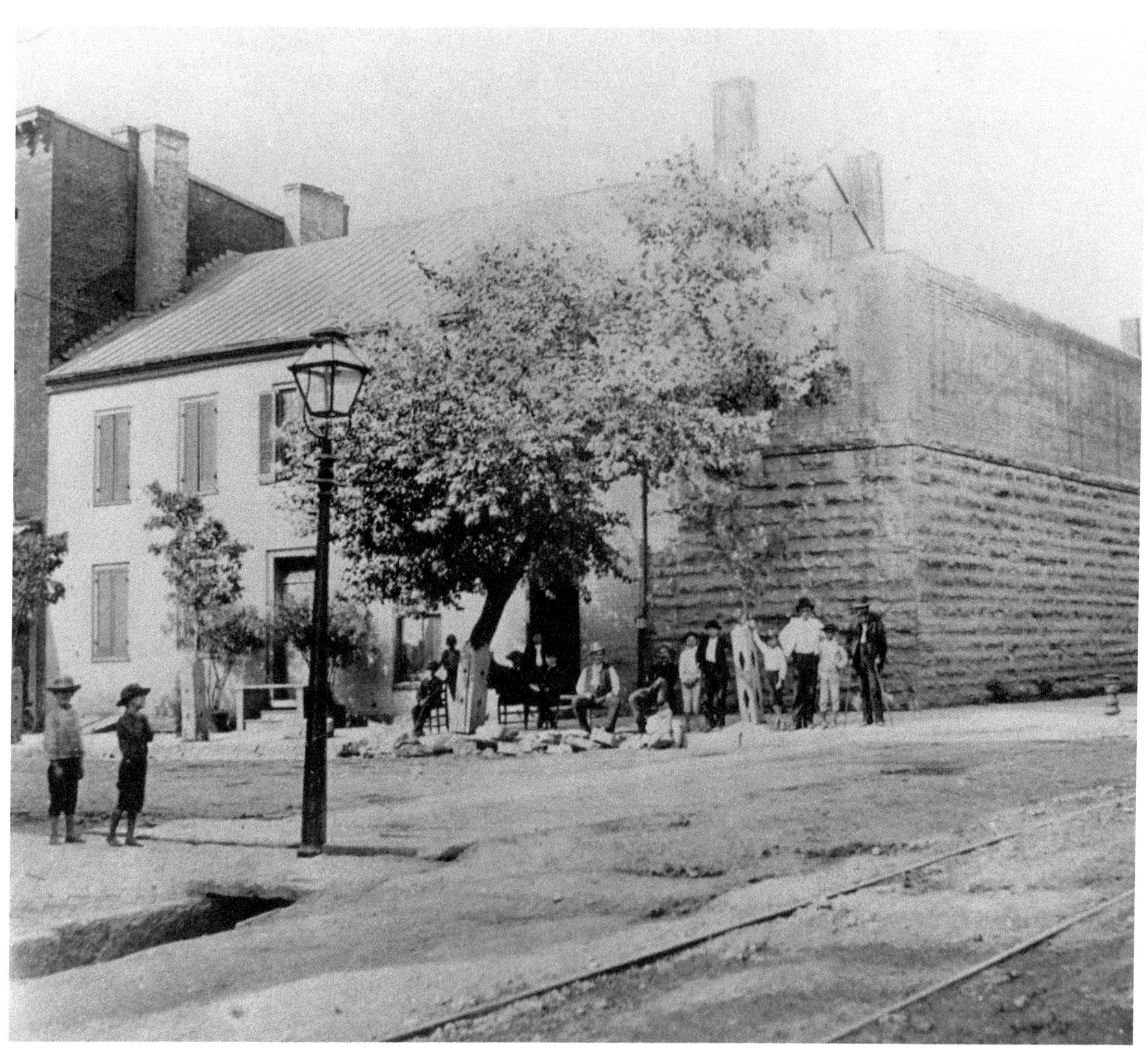

Fayette County jail, Short and Limestone Streets, ca. 1890.

Kitchen in Graz Park (only remaining part of original Transylvania University campus) as it was when occupied by Howard Graz, ca. 1880.

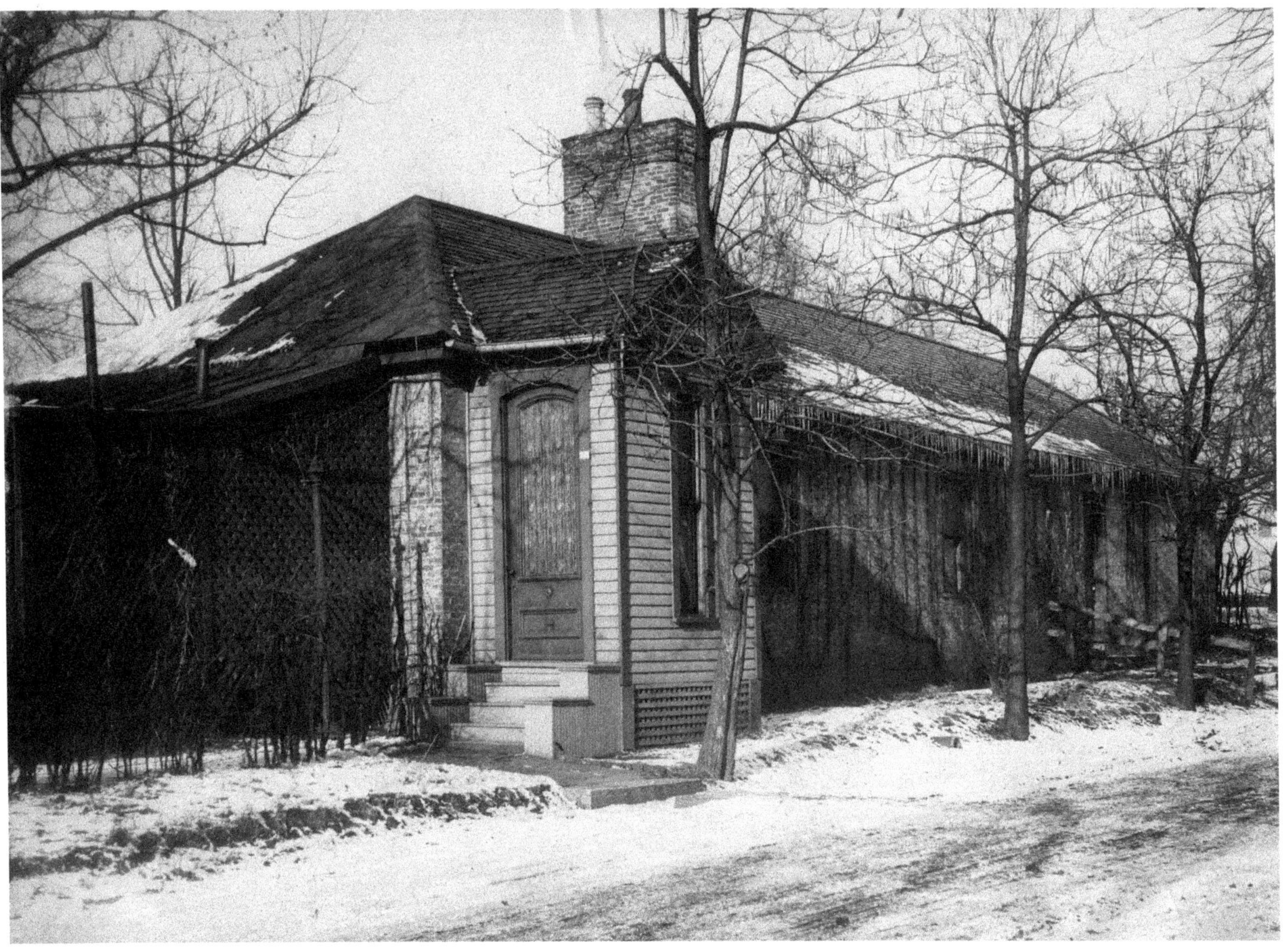

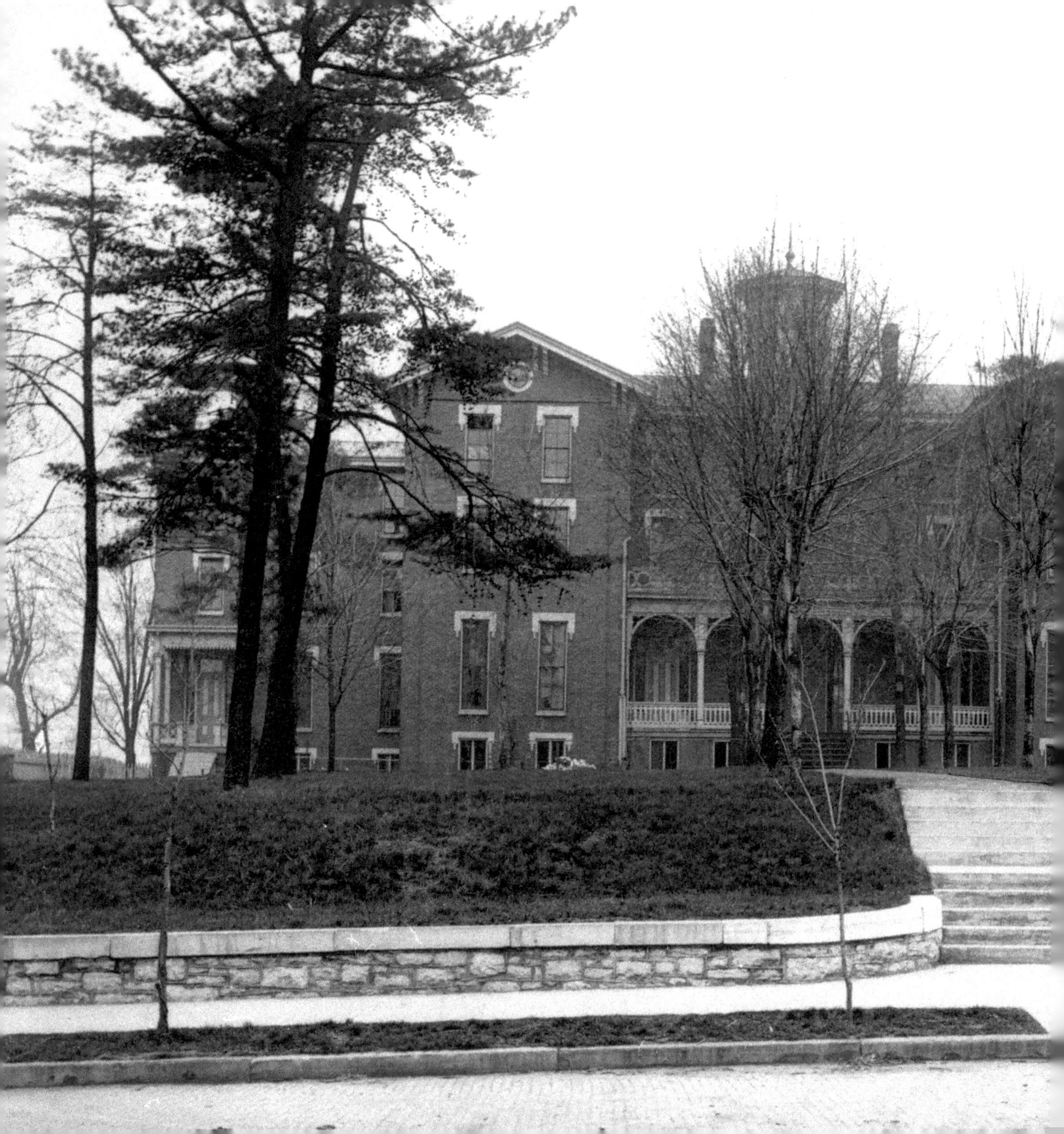

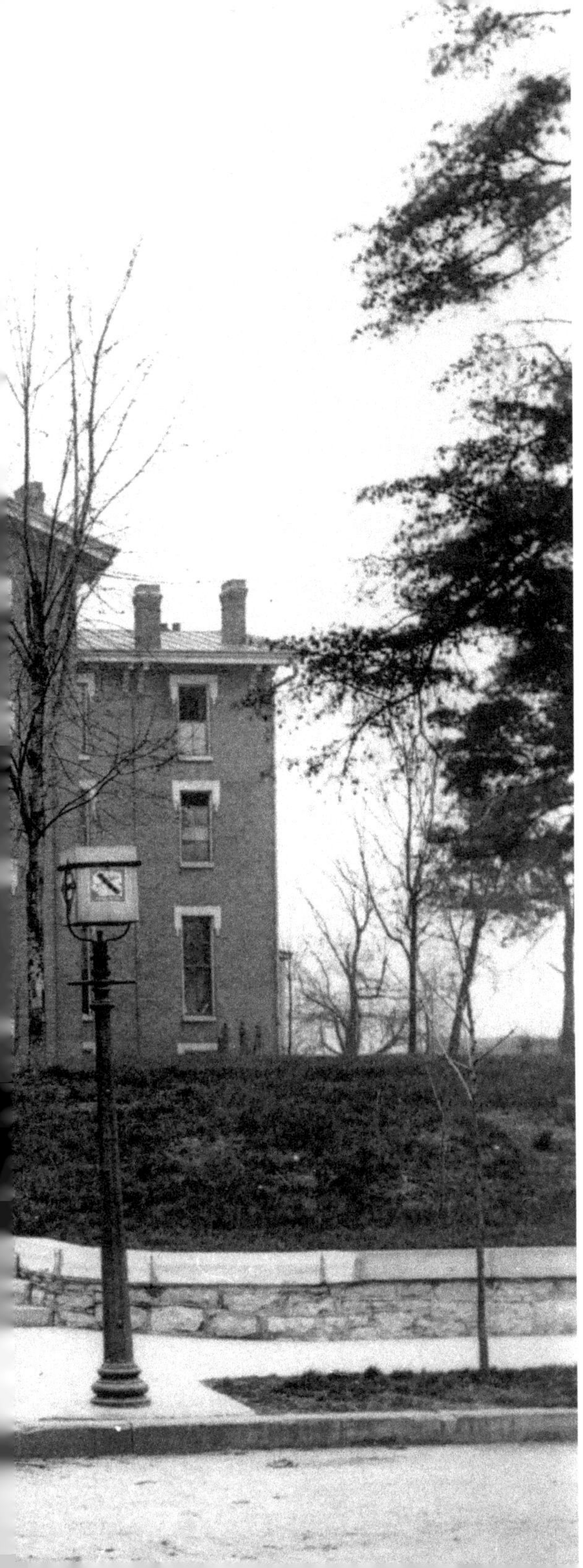

Hamilton Female College, ca. 1898. Founded in 1869 as Hocker Female College, it became part of Transylvania University in 1903.

View of Short Street, ca. 1898.

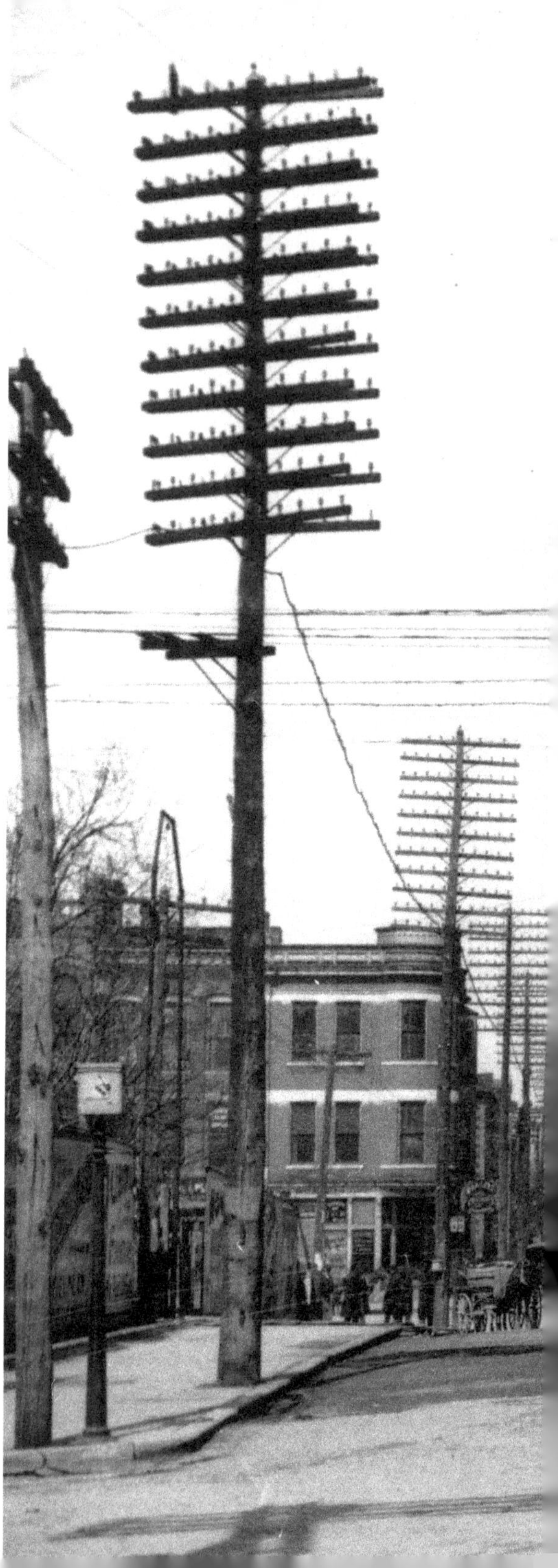

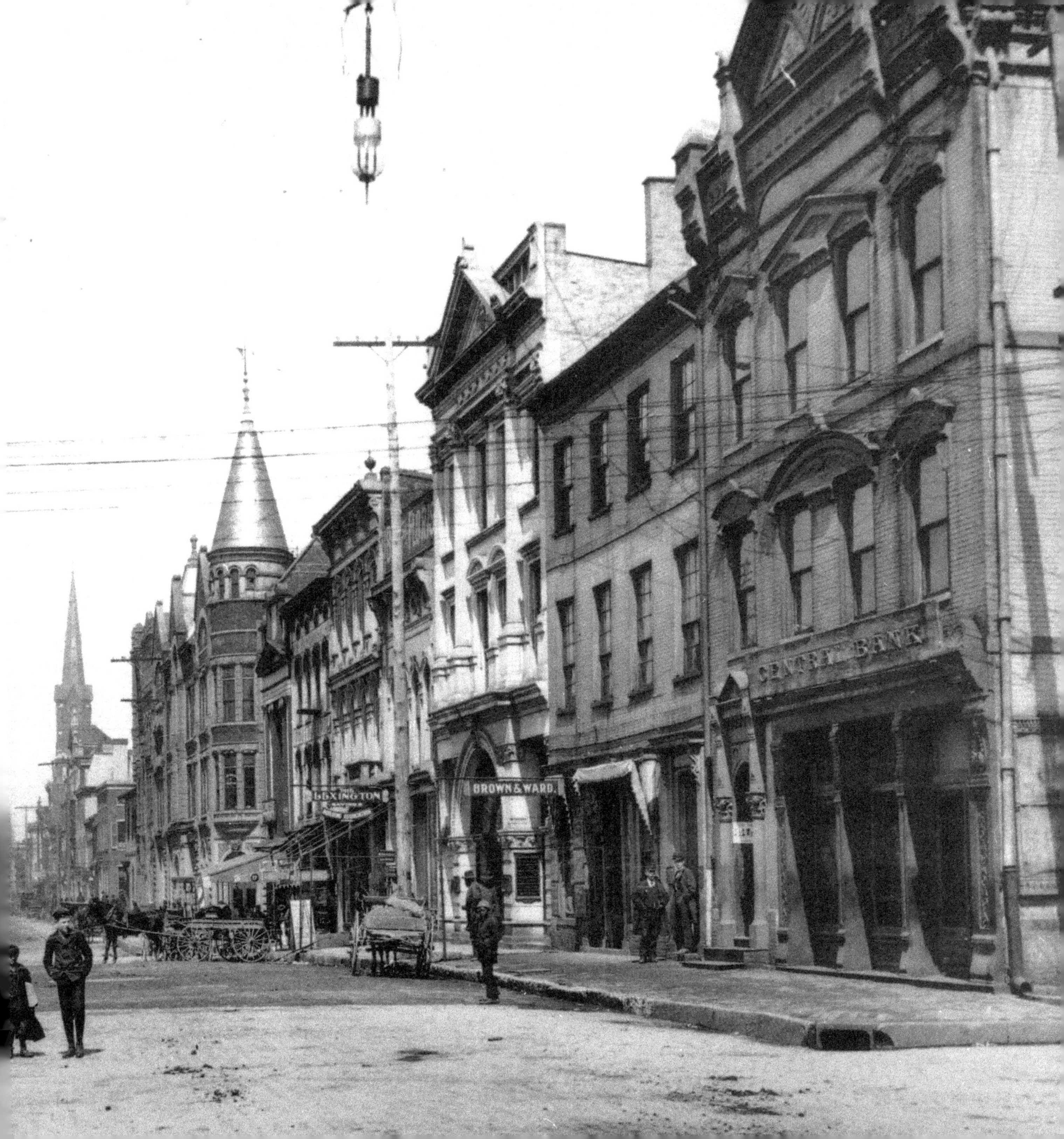
LEXINGTON
BROWN & WARD.
BANK

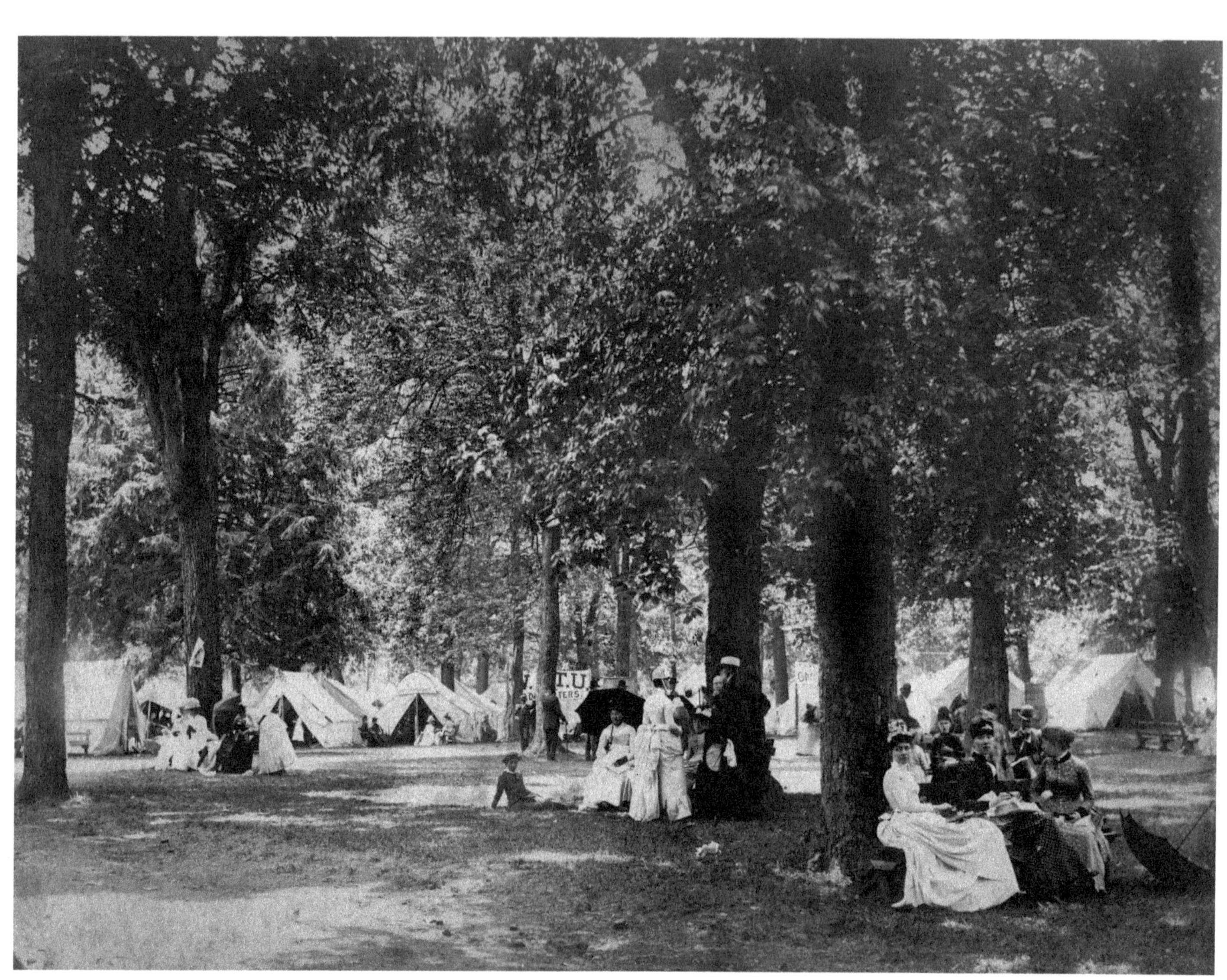

Women and Christian Temperance Union convocation in Woodland Park, late 19th century.

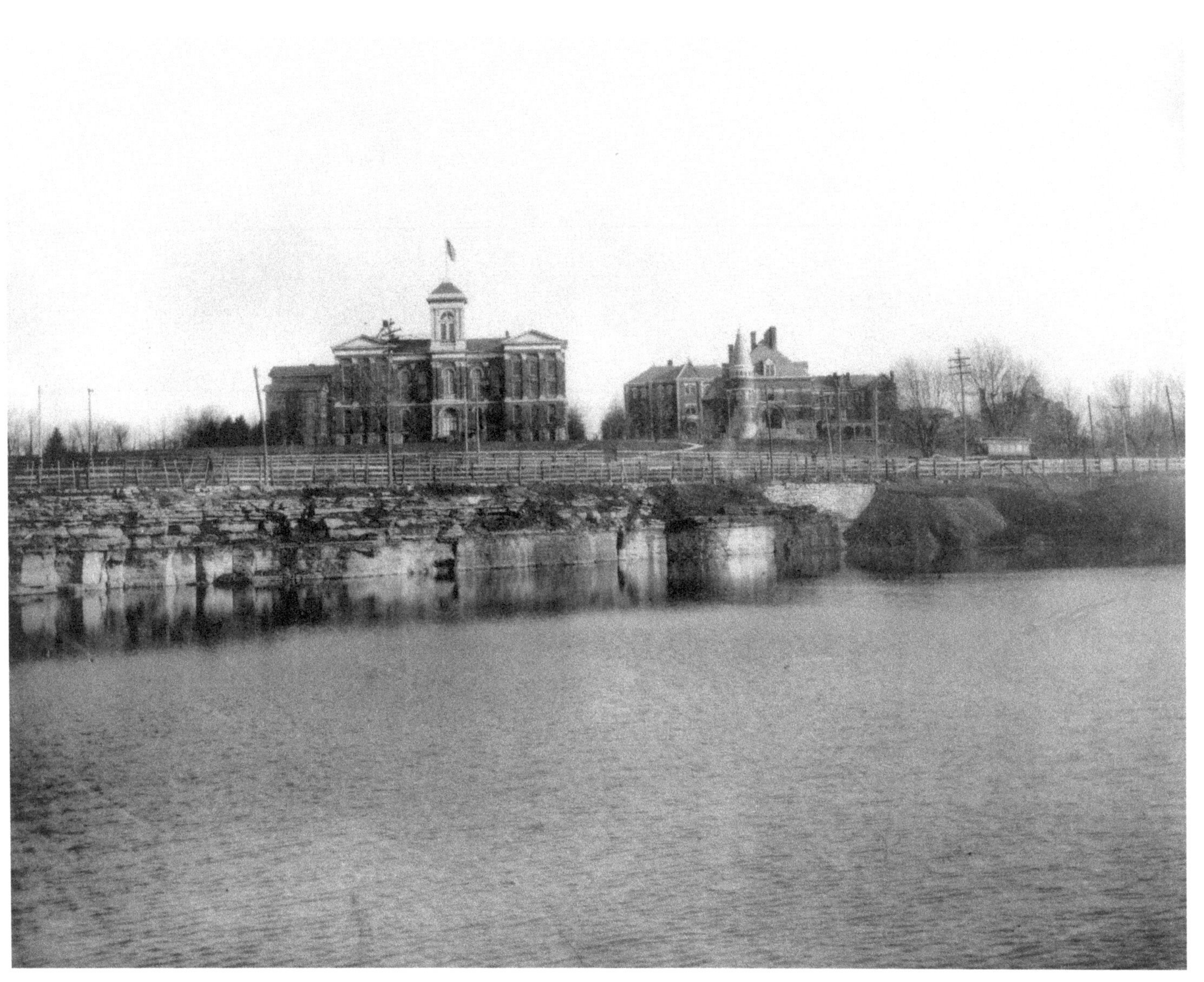

Agricultural and Mechanical College of Kentucky (now the University of Kentucky), late 19th century.

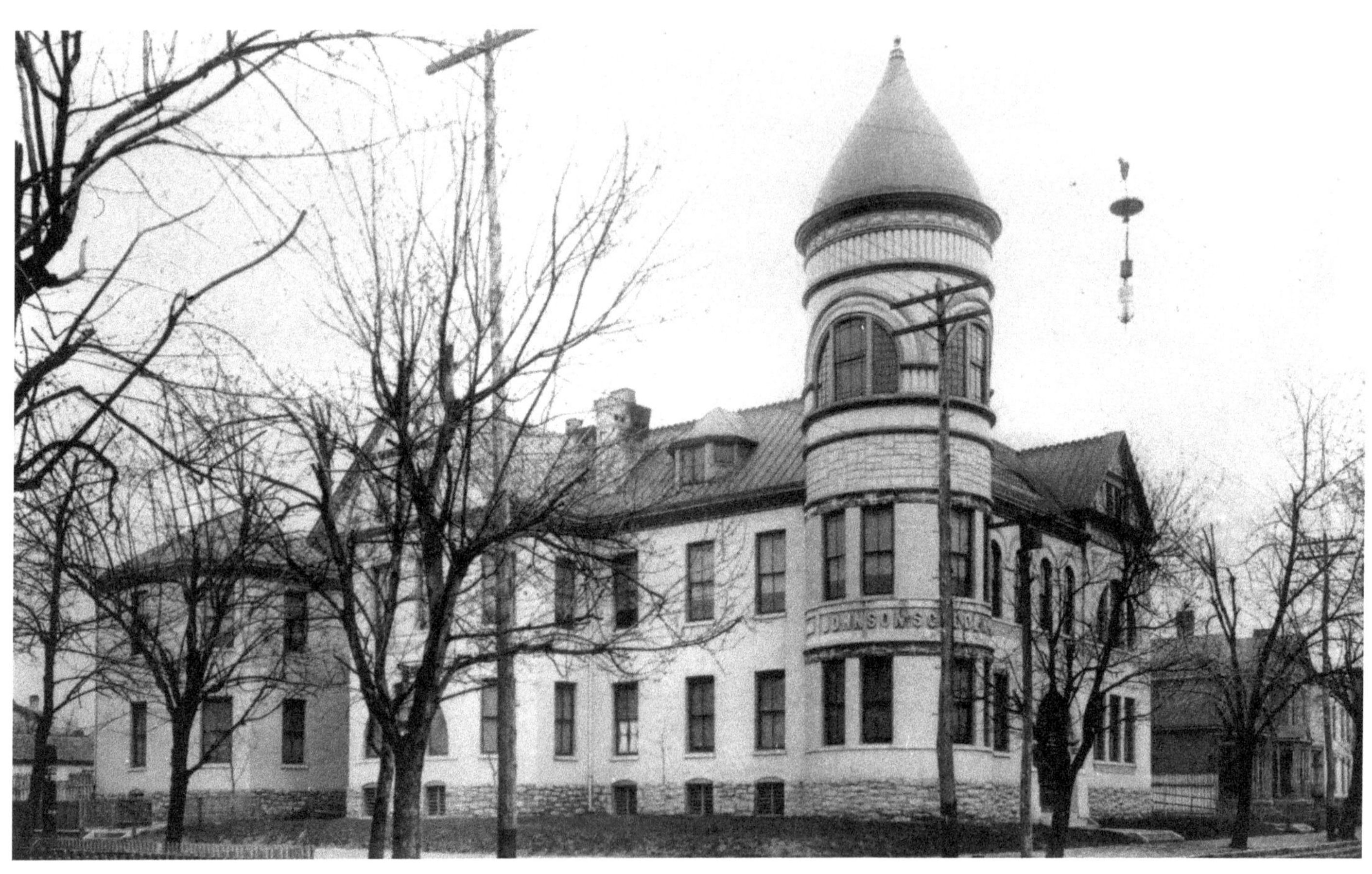


Johnson School, late 19th century.

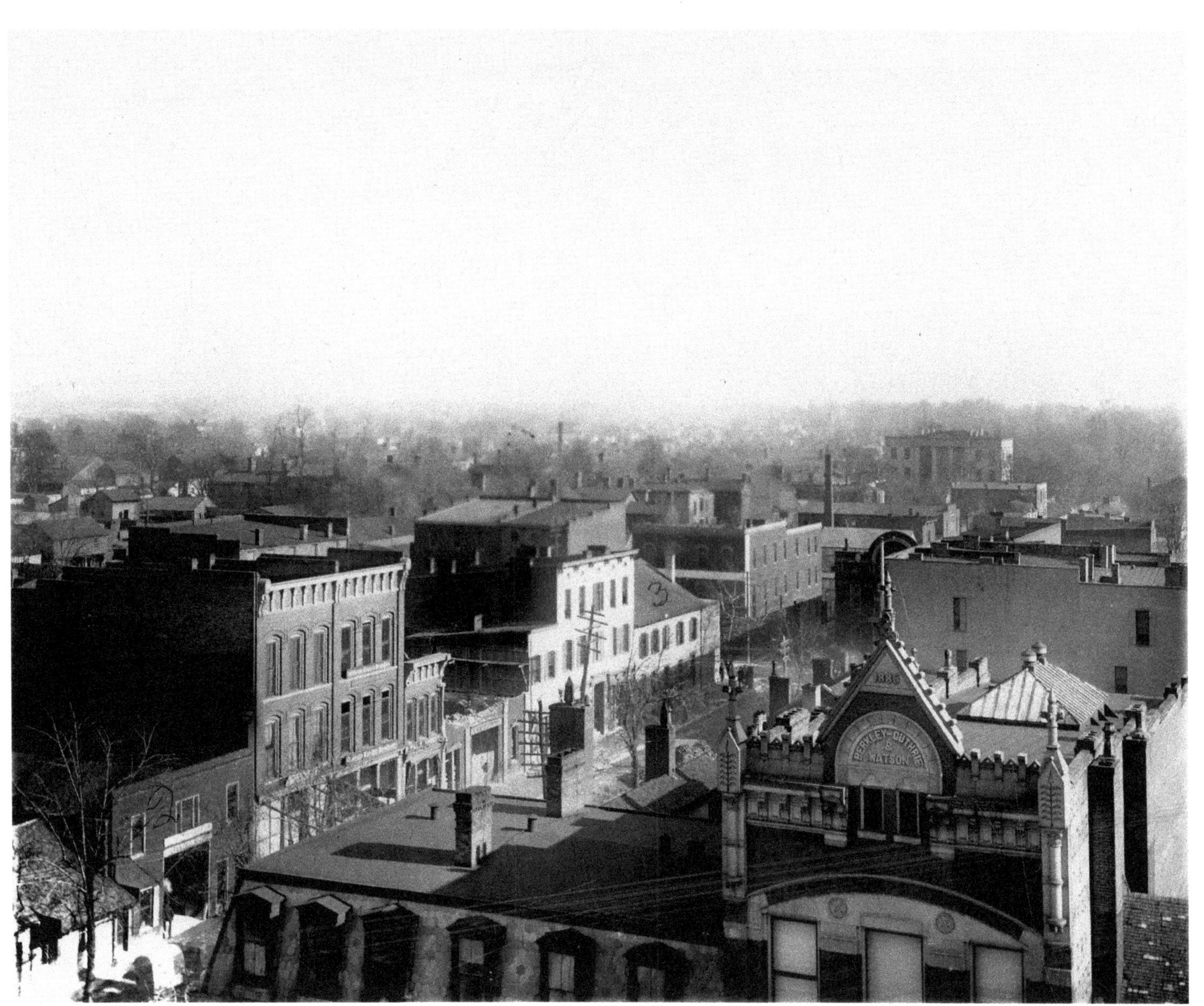


View toward Short Street from the Court House, 1885.

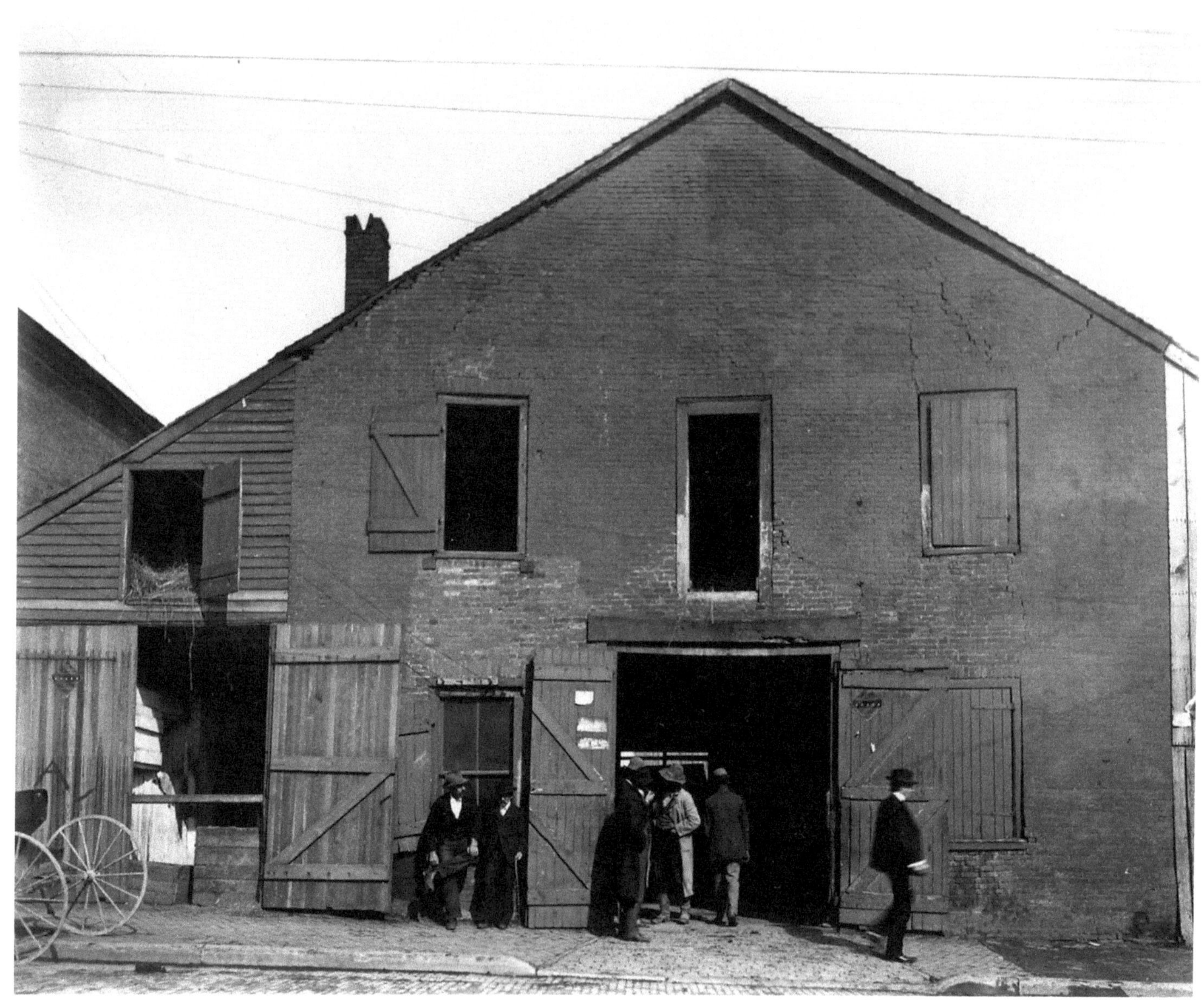

Stable on South Limestone, 1898.

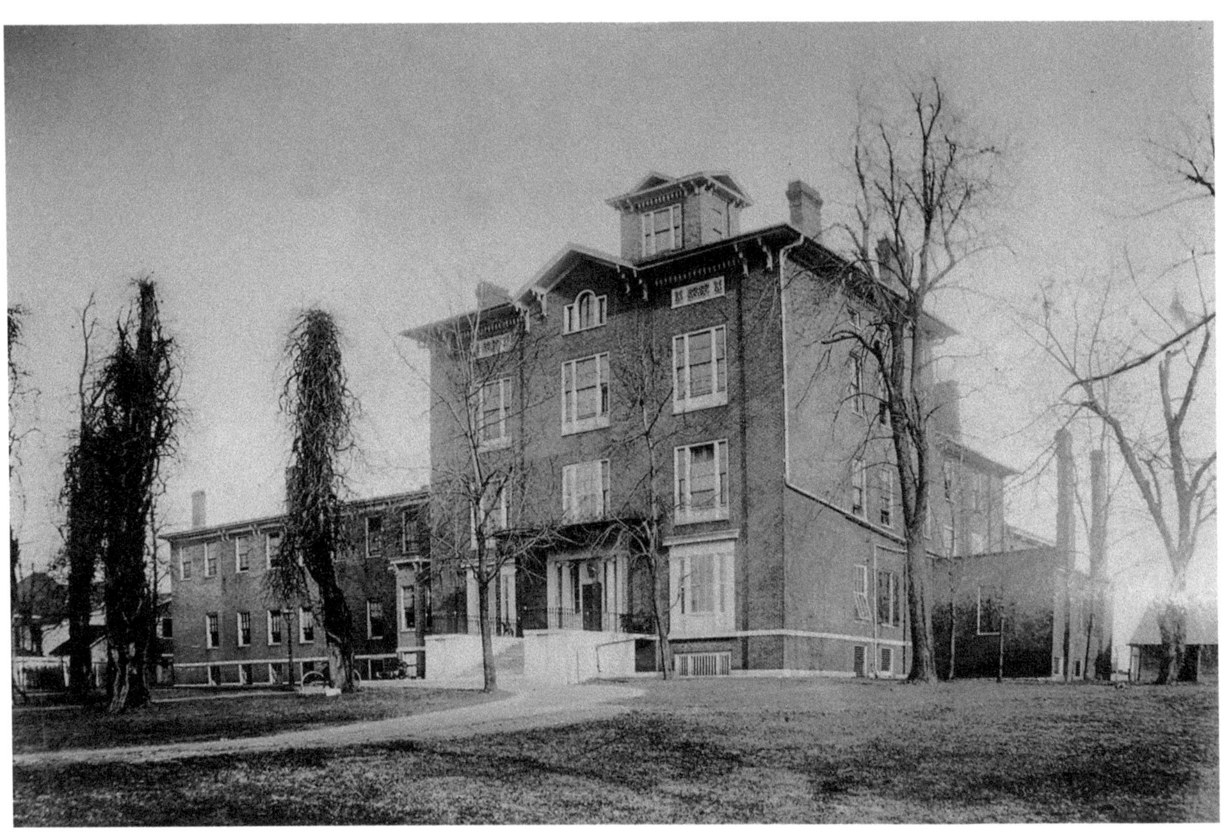

Sayre Female Institute, late $19^{th}$ c. Founded in 1854 as the Transylvania Female Seminary it was renamed the Sayre Female Institute in 1954 and moved to a five acre tract that included two small houses and a brick mansion on North Limestone.

Students on the lawn of Sayre Academy, late 19th century.

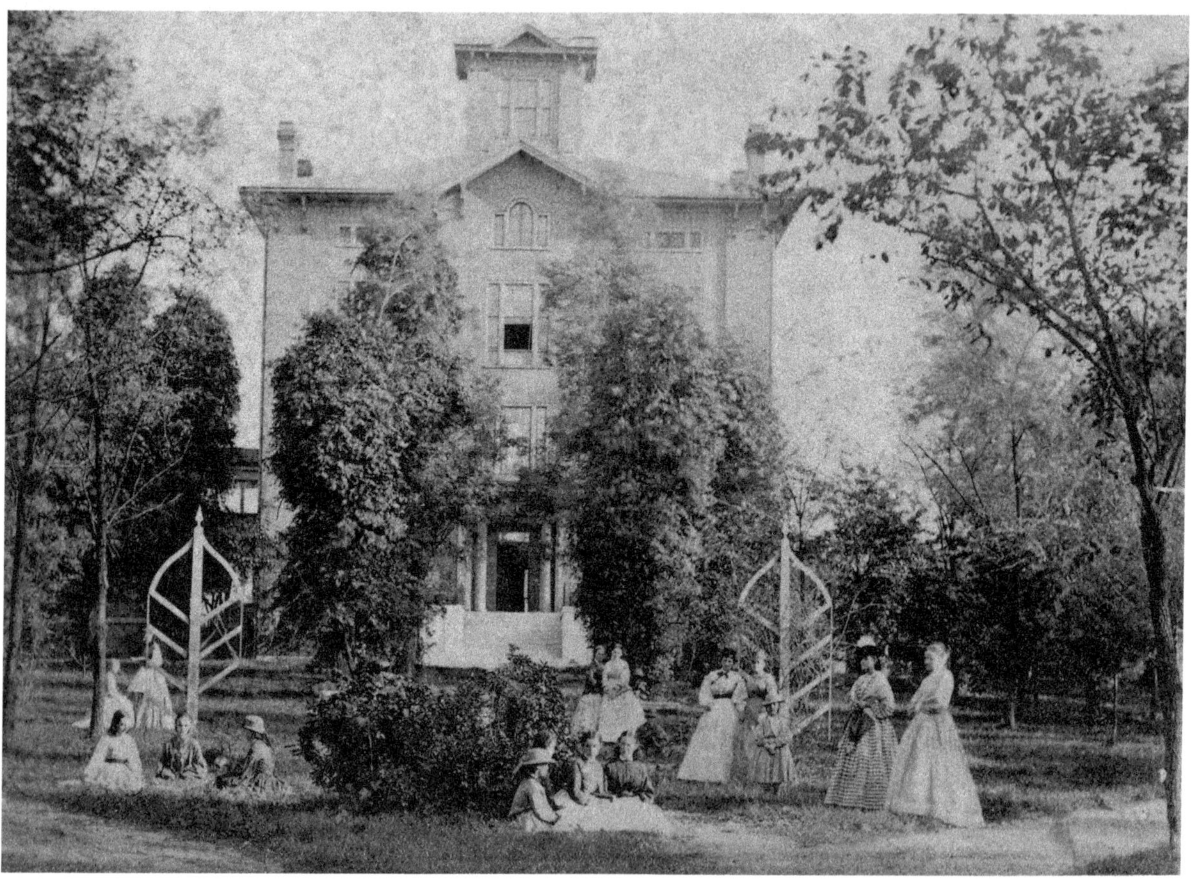

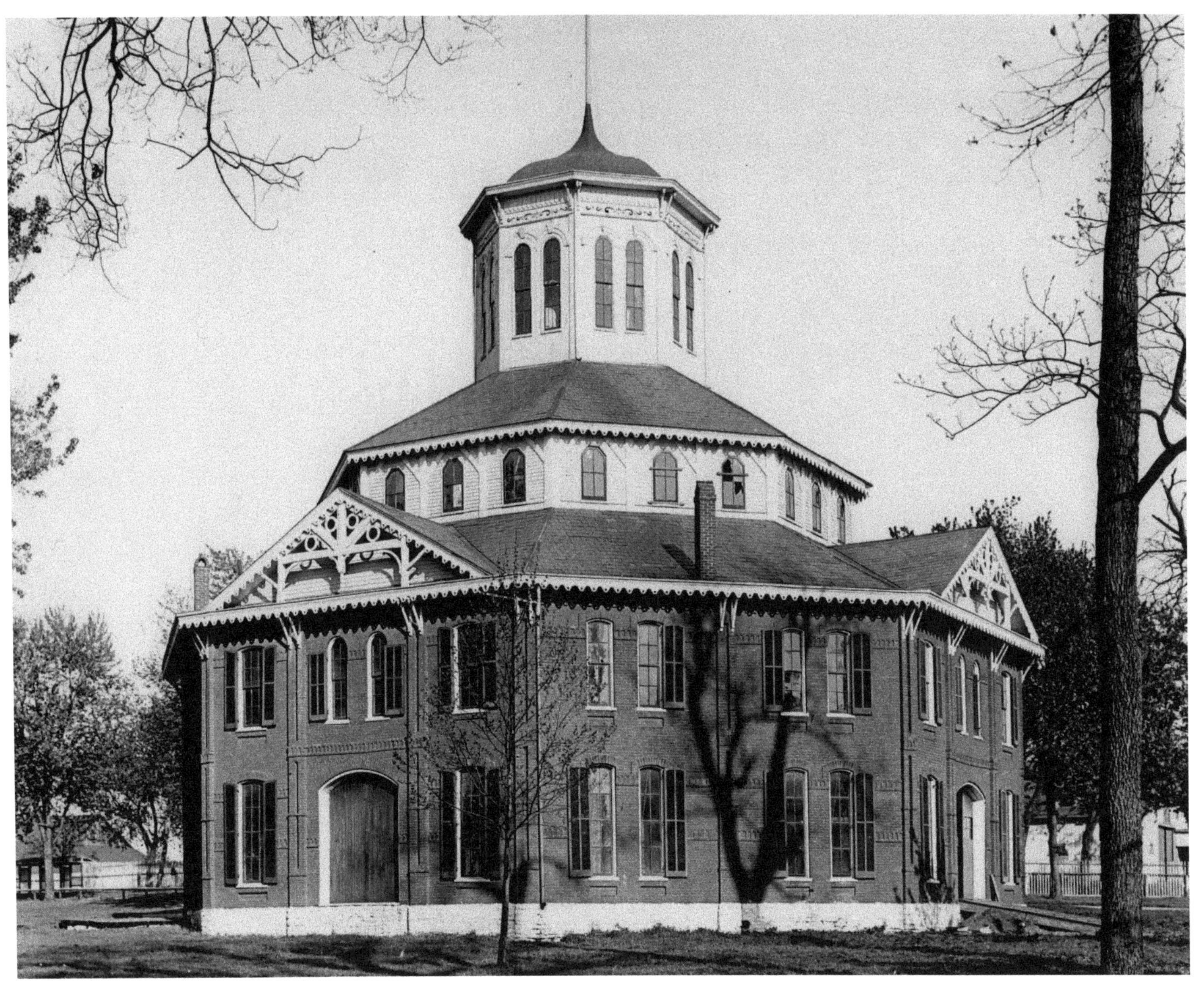

Floral Hall at the Red Mile, built 1882.

Officers and gentlemen before police station on Water Street, early 1900's.

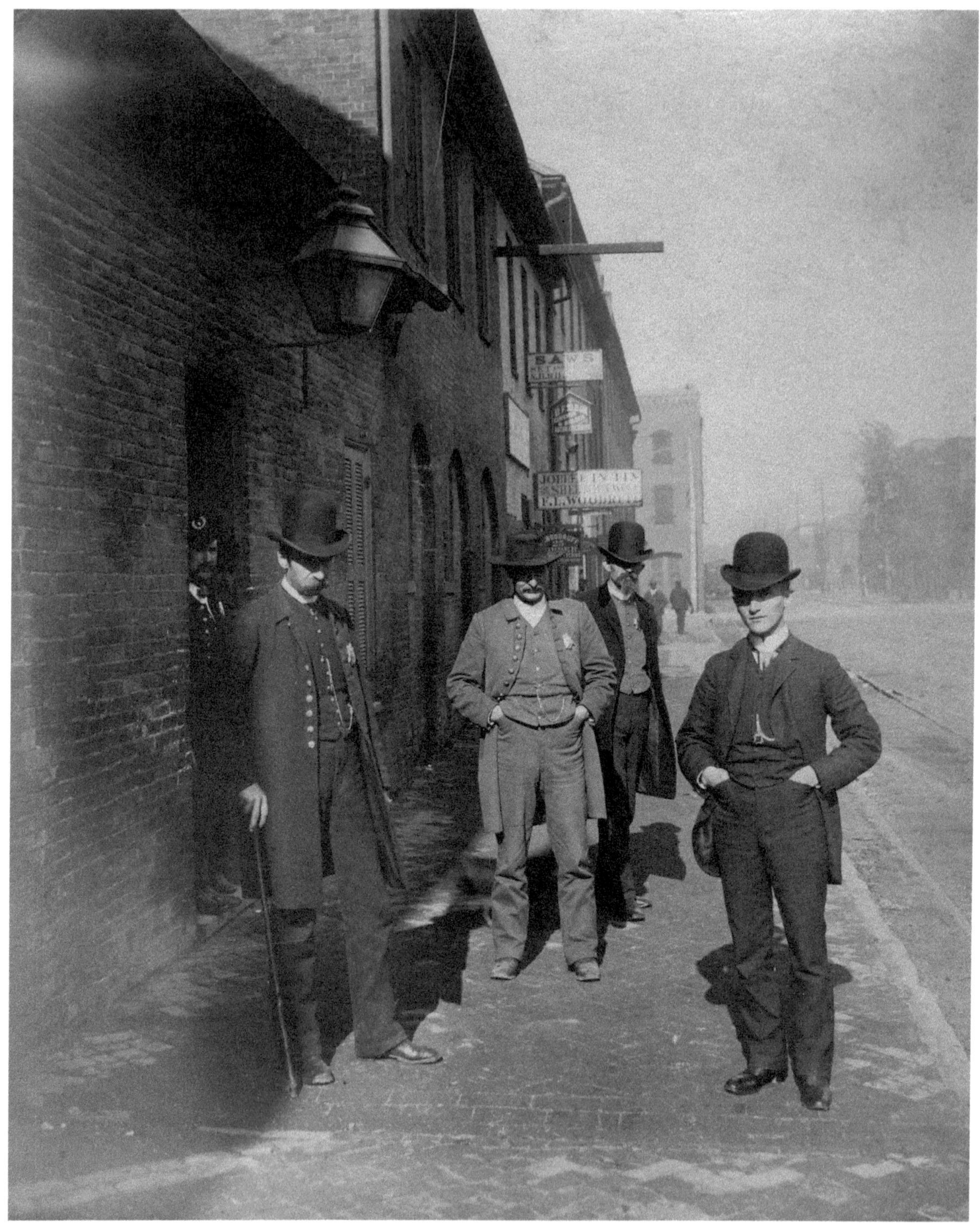

# Growth from Slumber

## 1900-1917

As the 19th Century drew to its end, necessary social and political changes began to take place in Lexington. Cultural and religious factions had to deal with economic realities and modern vitality. It was a time to expand the agrarian base and to develop an industrial one. There was a need to increase transportation ties both internal and external. The city was slow in acting. A major change to the whole region came when the production of burley tobacco outstripped that of hemp, the premier cash crop in earlier days.

The influx of former rural slaves to the town after the Civil War forever changed patterns of urban development. A type of inexpensive housing came to dominate areas of infill that would remain well into the century. But soon there was expansion and development away from the center of the city into areas that had heretofore known only suburban villas. New parks could be reached by new means of transport and enjoyed by most of the citizens. Thus was opened the path to housing development well outside the original town plan.

Public schools were well established and accepted, although segregated. Transylvania University was, in the early twentieth century, a liberal arts college rather than the great institution of Lexington's "golden age", but the State University had grown across town and was to become the University of Kentucky. Lexington's Opera House was called "the best one night stand in the country."

The land itself had always been the chief attraction of Lexington and this land was glorified by the development of the great horse farms and the various racing attractions. Horses thrived in the bluegrass fields around the city. The landed families had developed the horse industry as an adjunct to their other agrarian interests. Both sides in the Civil War had prized the horses as tools of conflict. From the later nineteenth century onwards however, numerous new people, often of great wealth, came to also be stewards of the horse lands. The great breeds of sport and pleasure gave fame to the place and viability to the preservation of beautiful country estates.

Assembly on steps of the fourth courthouse, late 19th century.

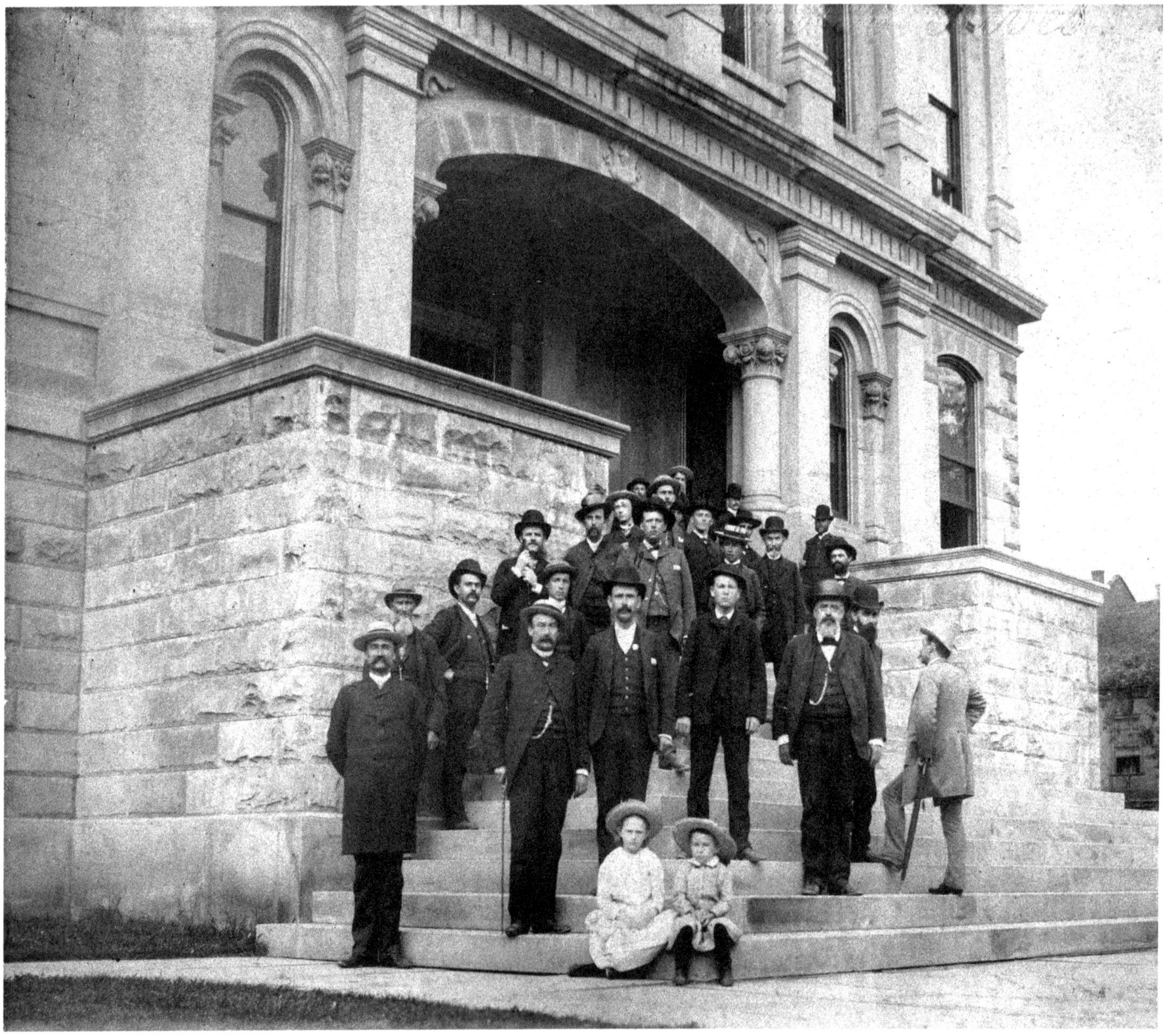

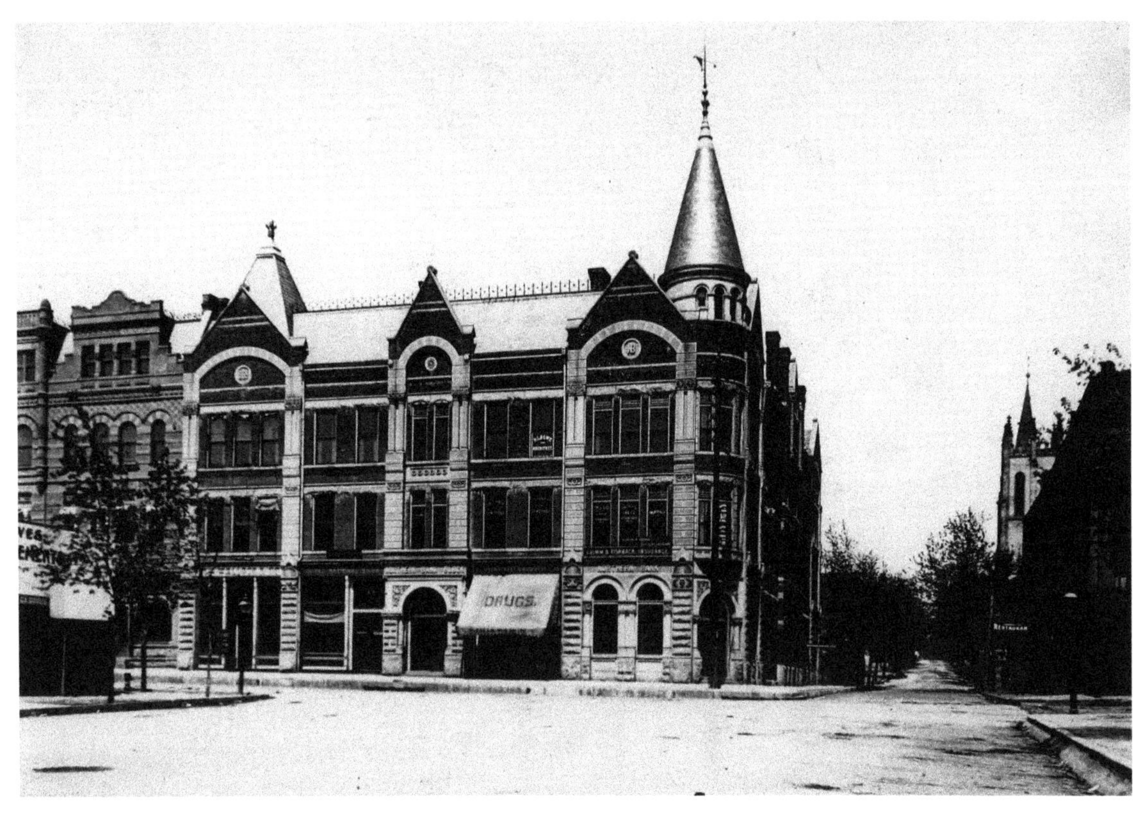


Northern Bank Building (built 1889), Short and Market Streets, as it appeared in the early 1900's.

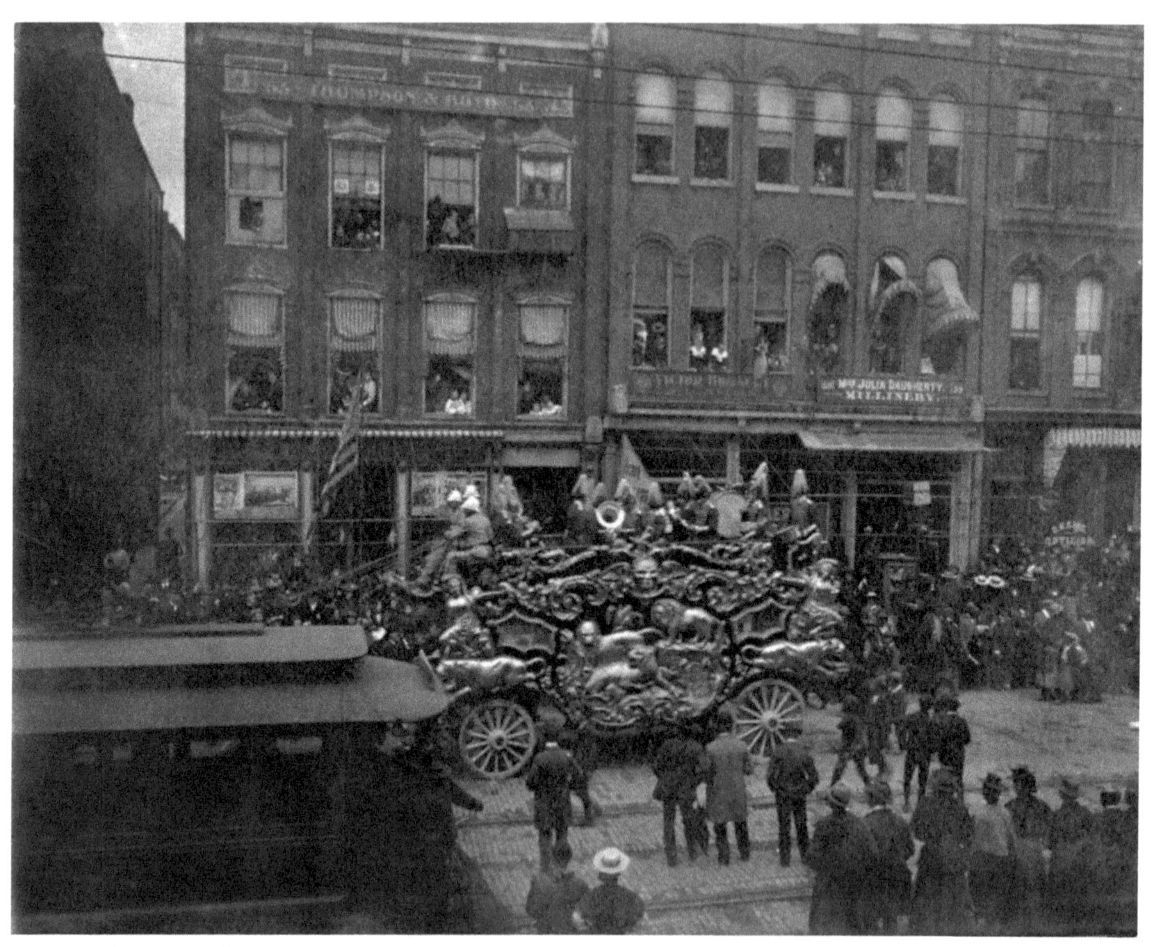

Ringling Circus Parade on Main Street, ca. 1900.

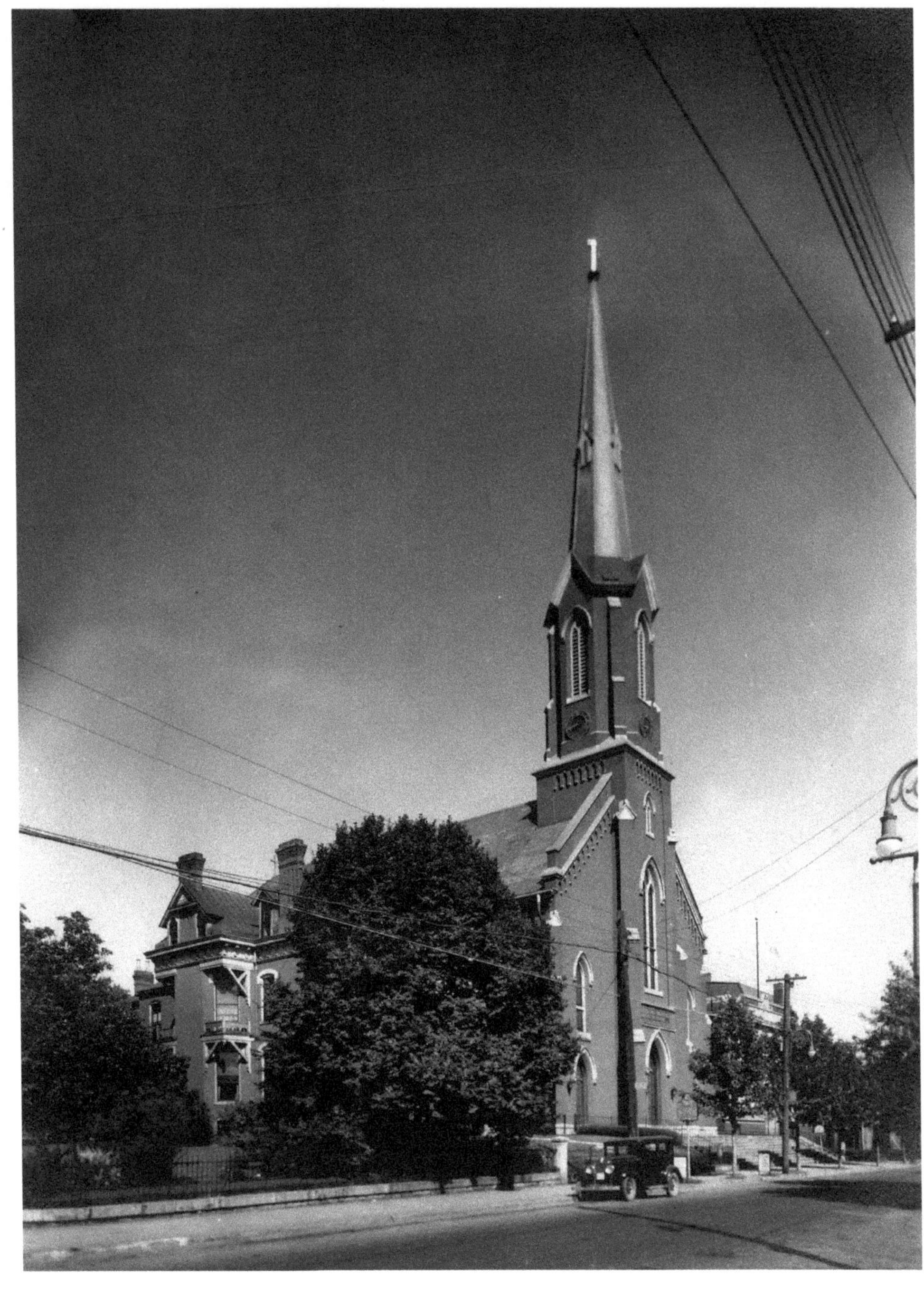

St. Paul's Catholic Church with later parsonage and school, early 20th century.

Soldiers arriving at Union Station on Main Street in July, 1918 for military technical training at the University of Kentucky.

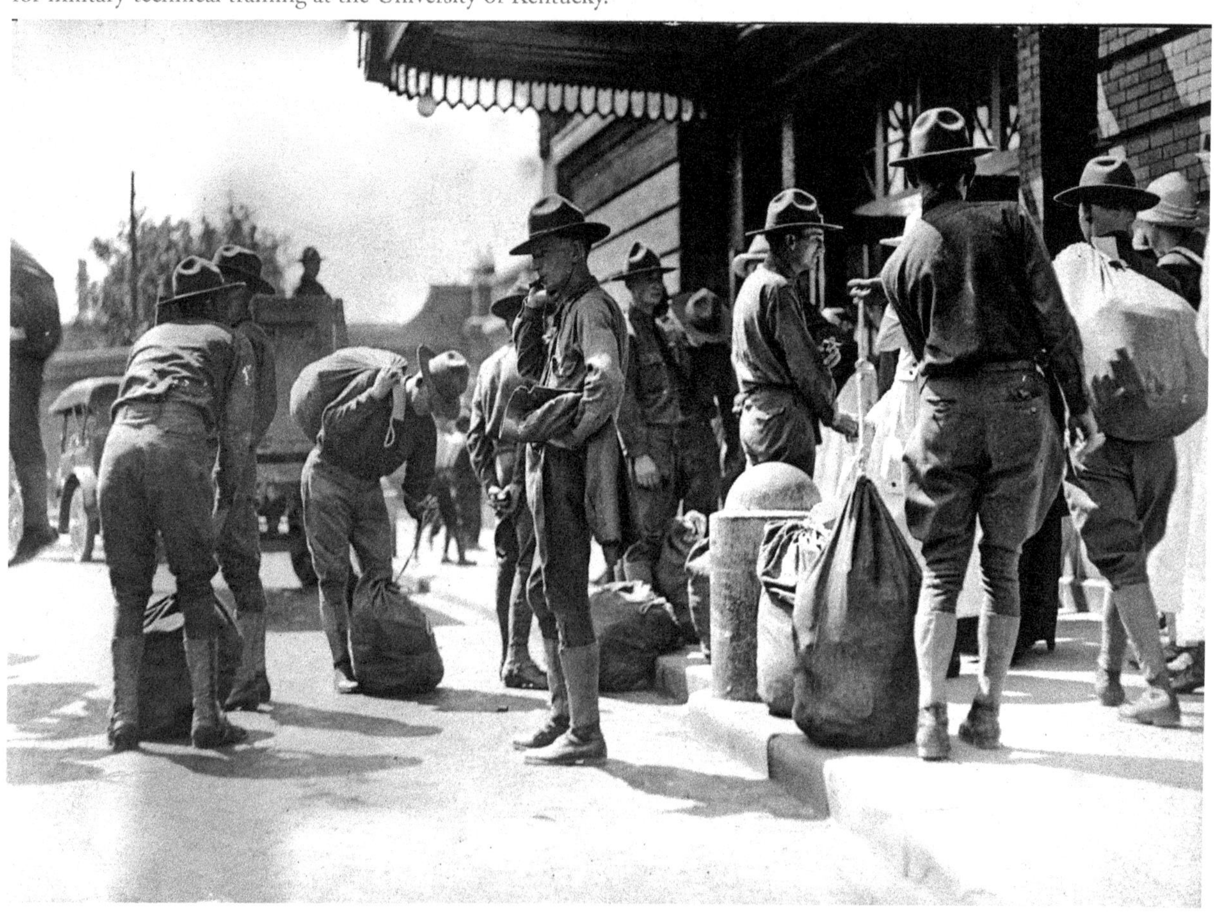

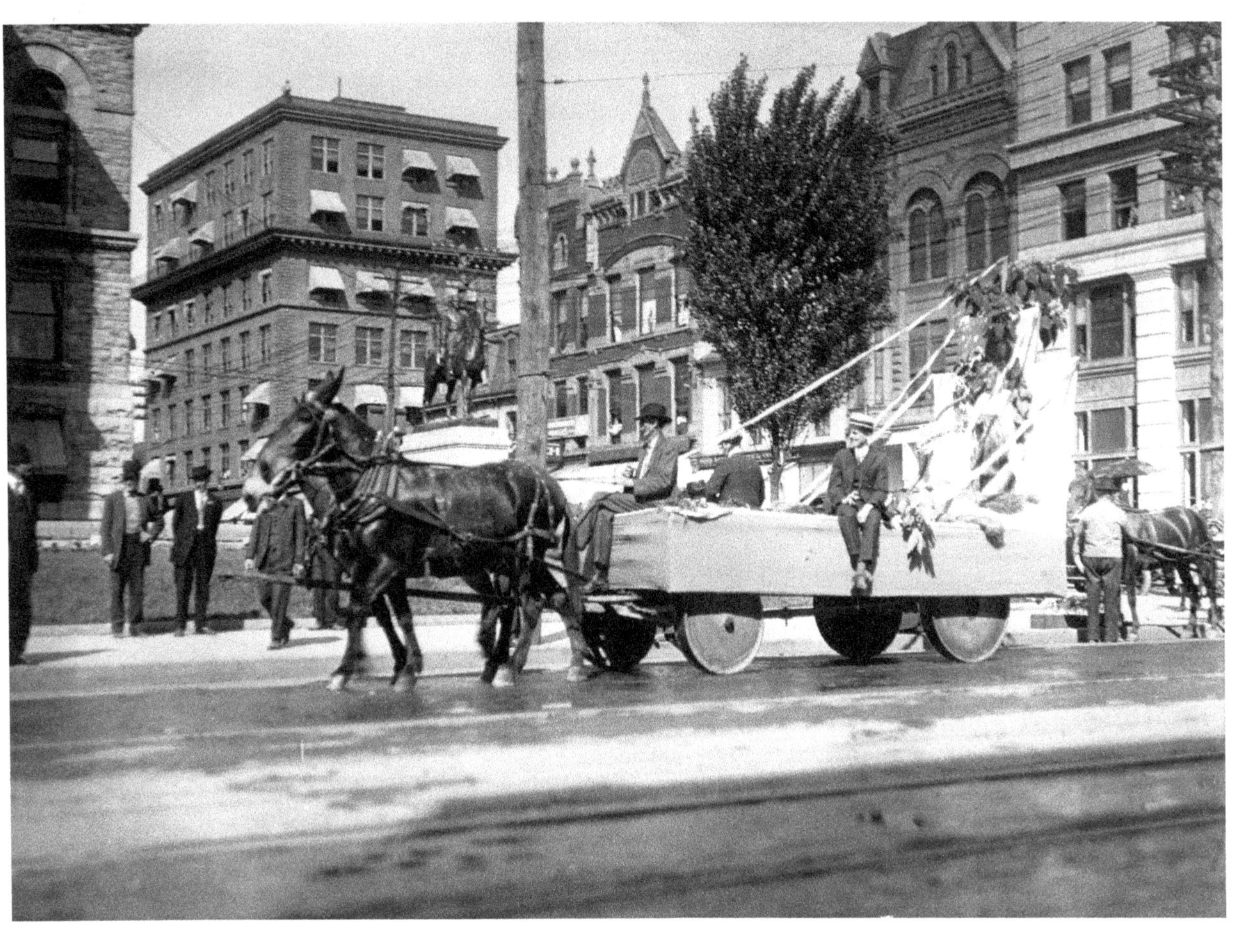

Golden Jubilee Parade at Main and Upper, 1916.

Choir of the Second Presbyterian Church, early 20th century.

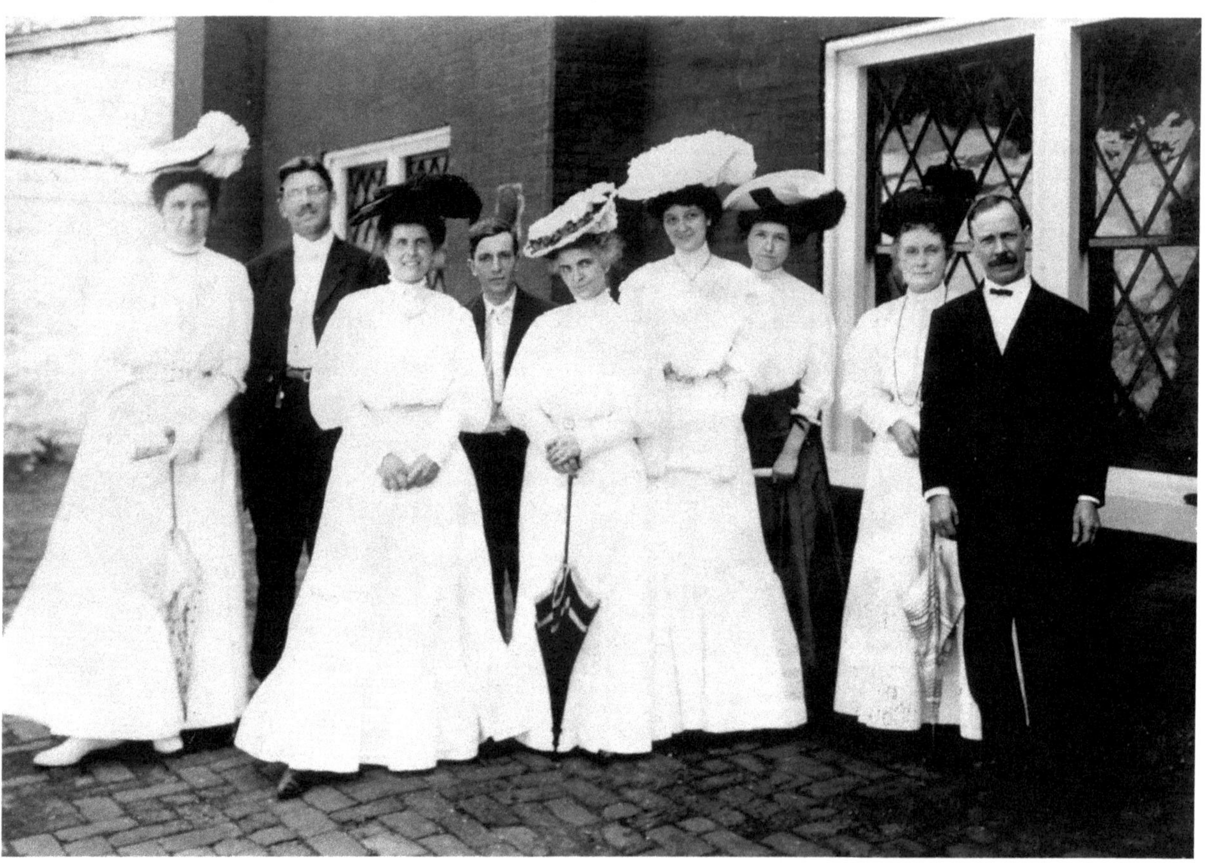

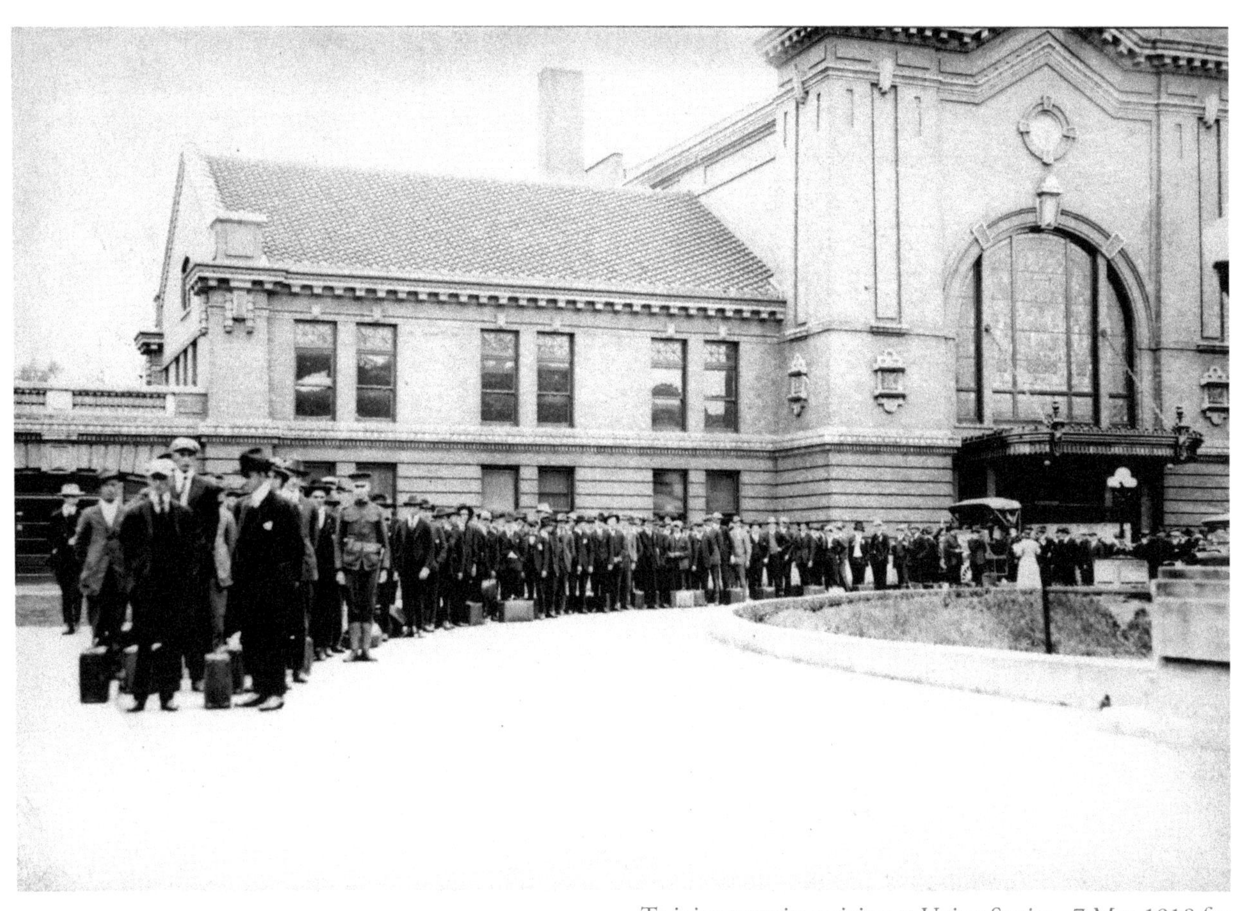

Training recruits arriving at Union Station, 7 May 1918 for military technical training at the University of Kentucky.

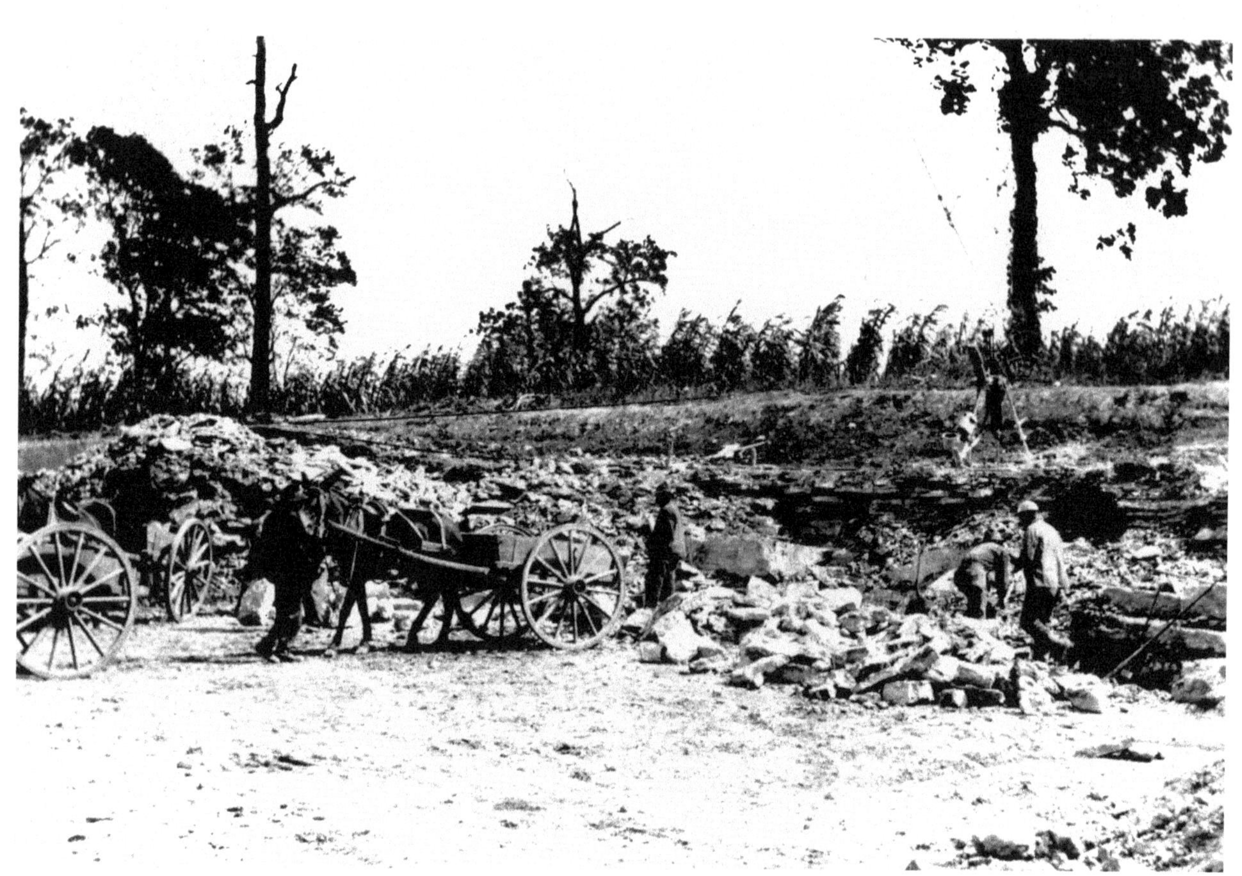

Mule carts were used to excavate for spillway water reservoirs , early 1900's.

State College Band, ca. 1908.

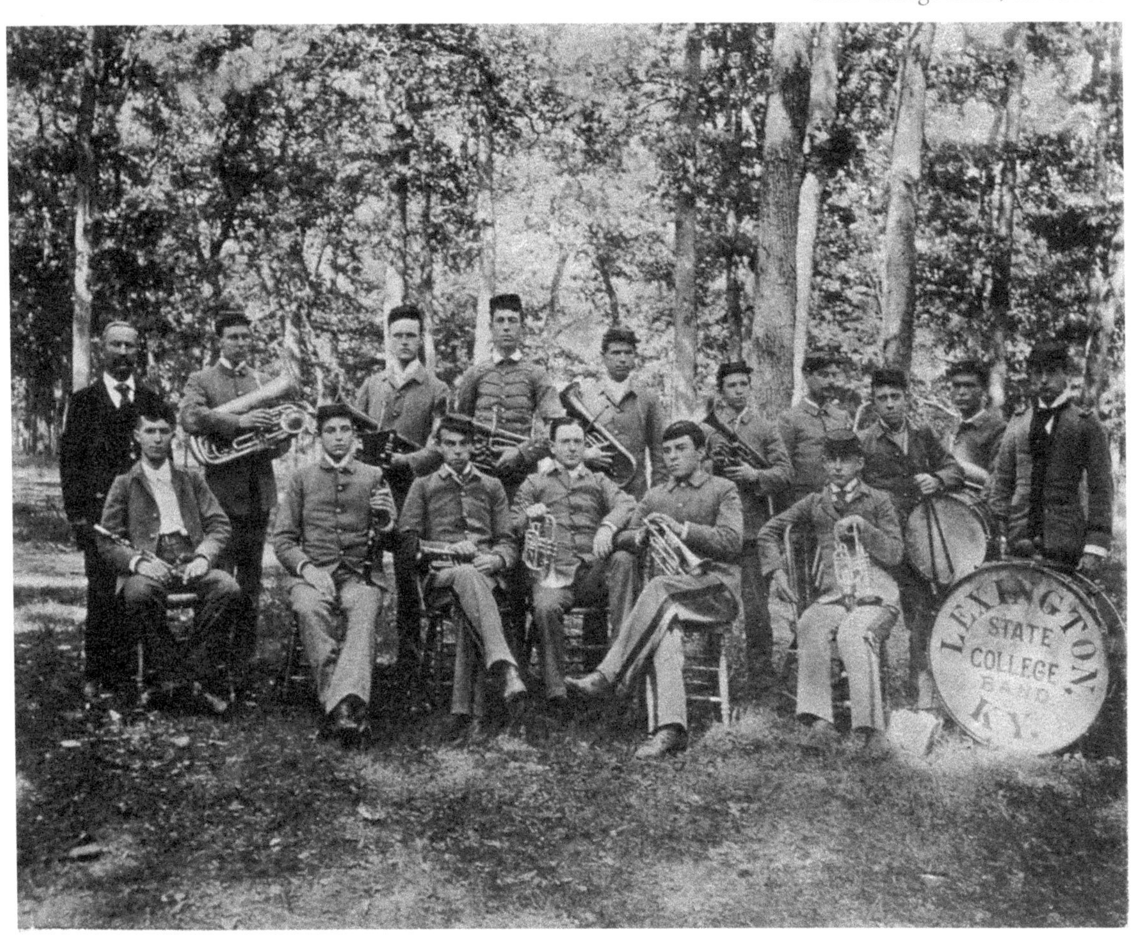

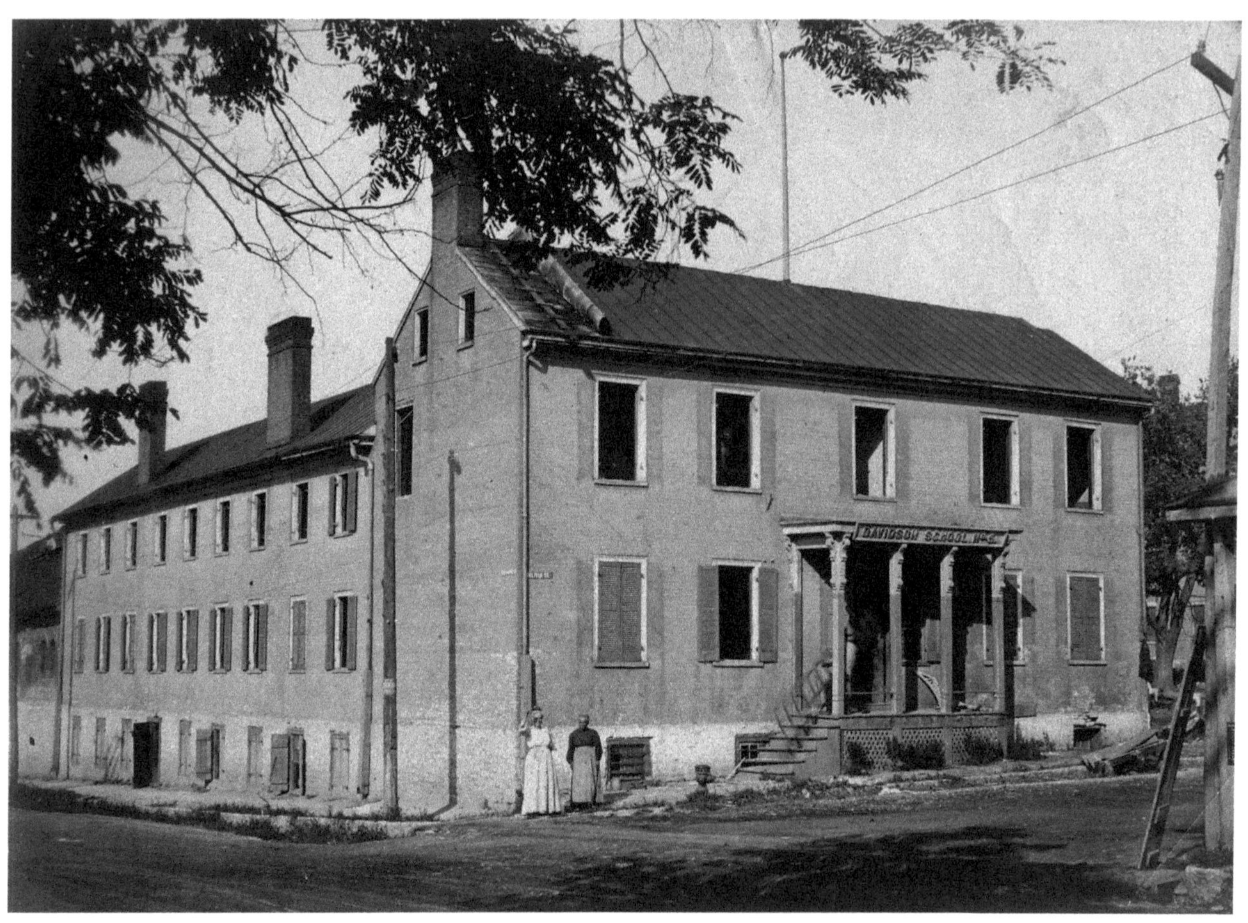

Davidson School (built on the foundation of the old Work House), demolished 1903-05.

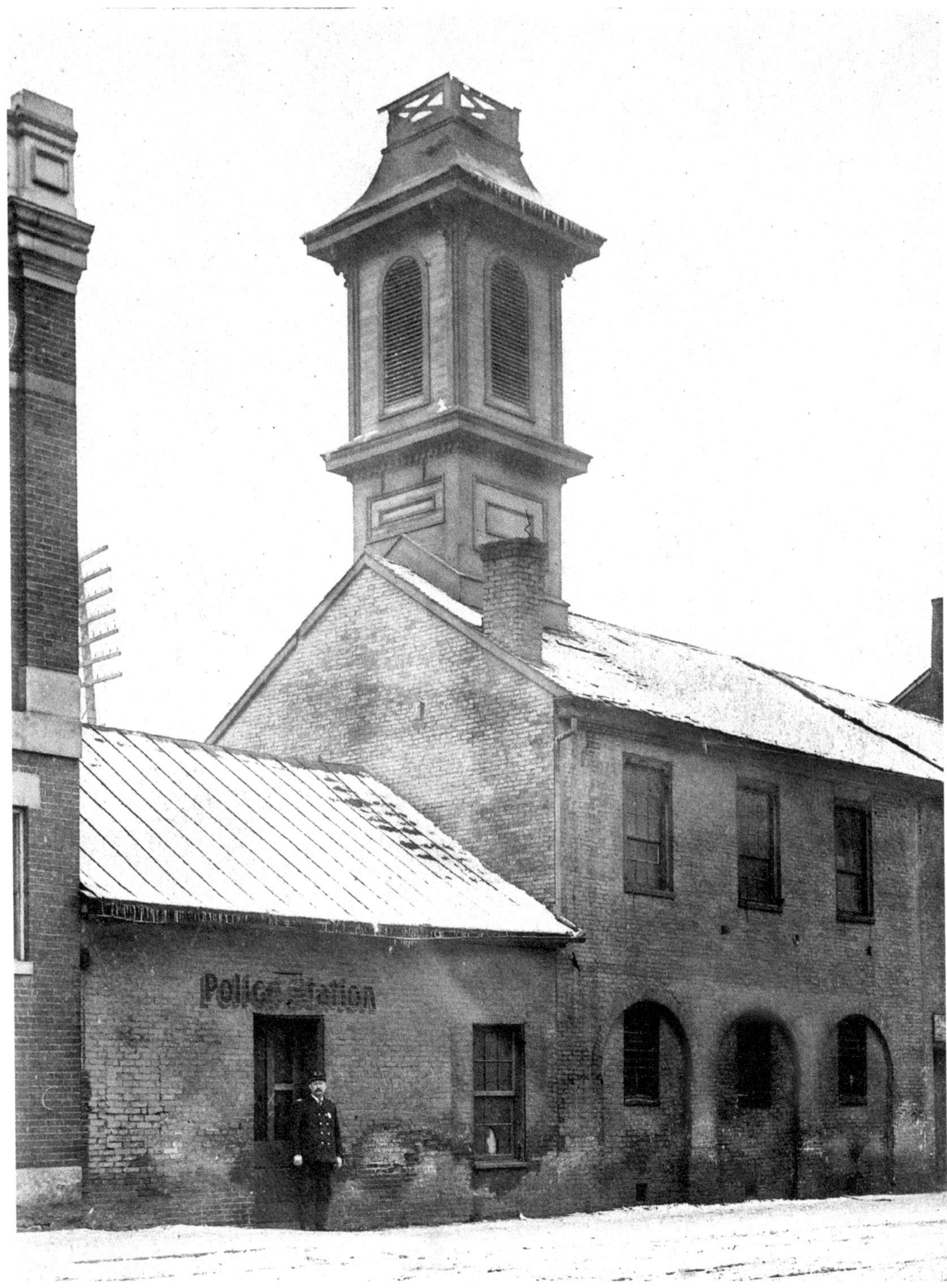


Police station or watch house (formerly a mustard factory), standing in 1910.

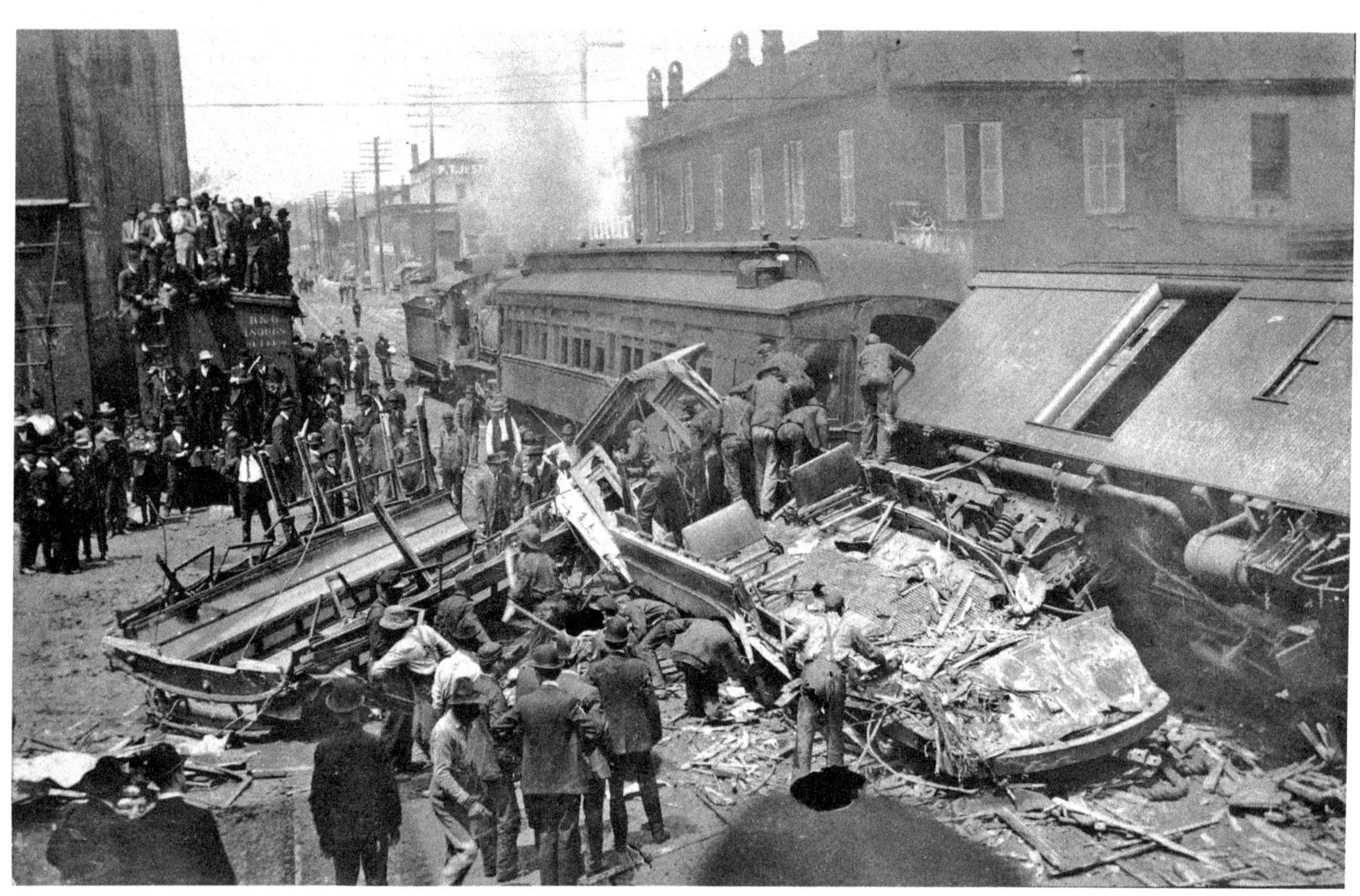

Streetcar and C&O train accident, 1907.

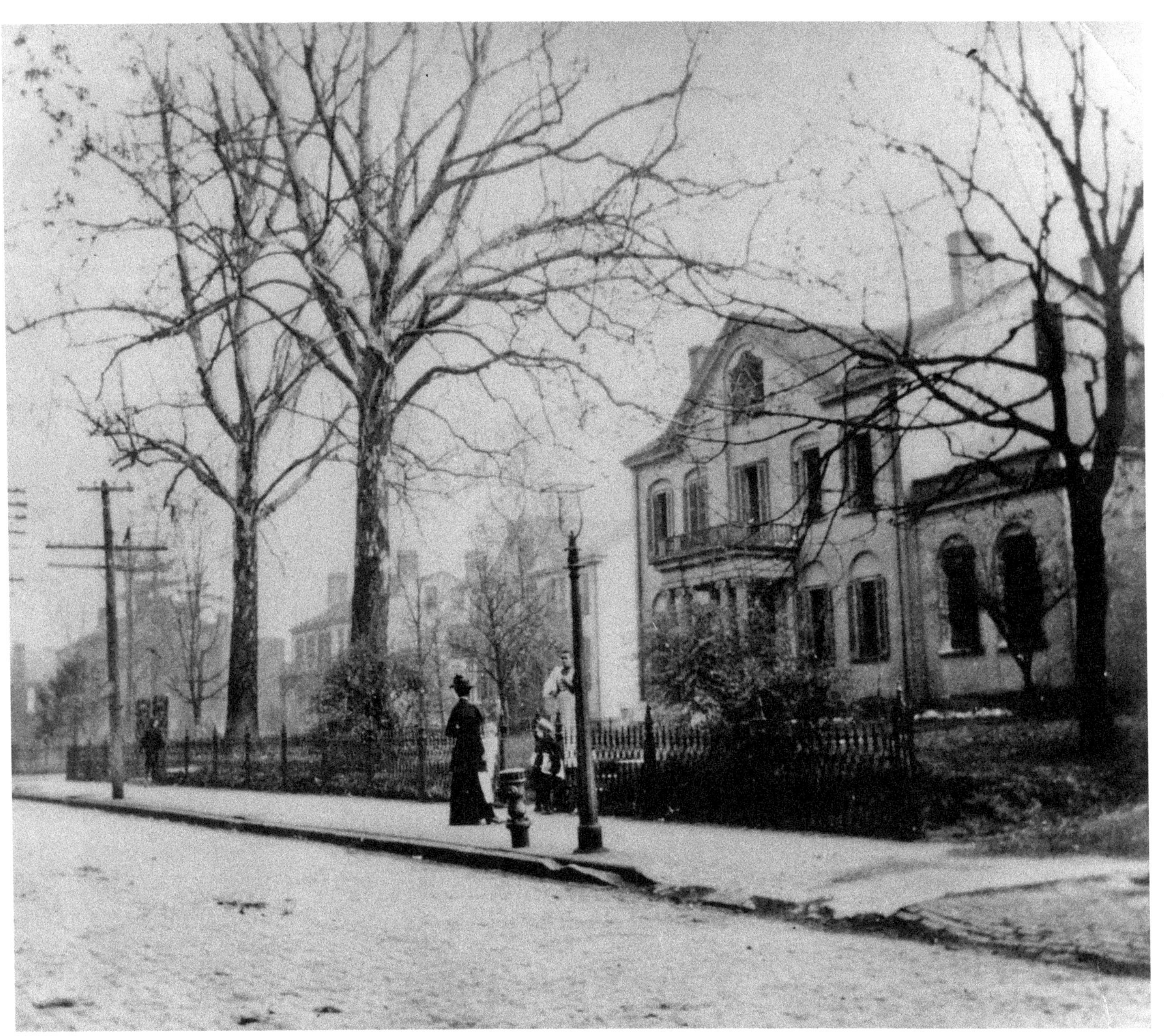

Swift House on East High Street in the early 1900's. This was the home of Dr. Lyman Beecher Todd, Lexington Civil War postmaster and is now the site of Calvary Baptist Church.

Old Mount Horeb Church, burned 1925.

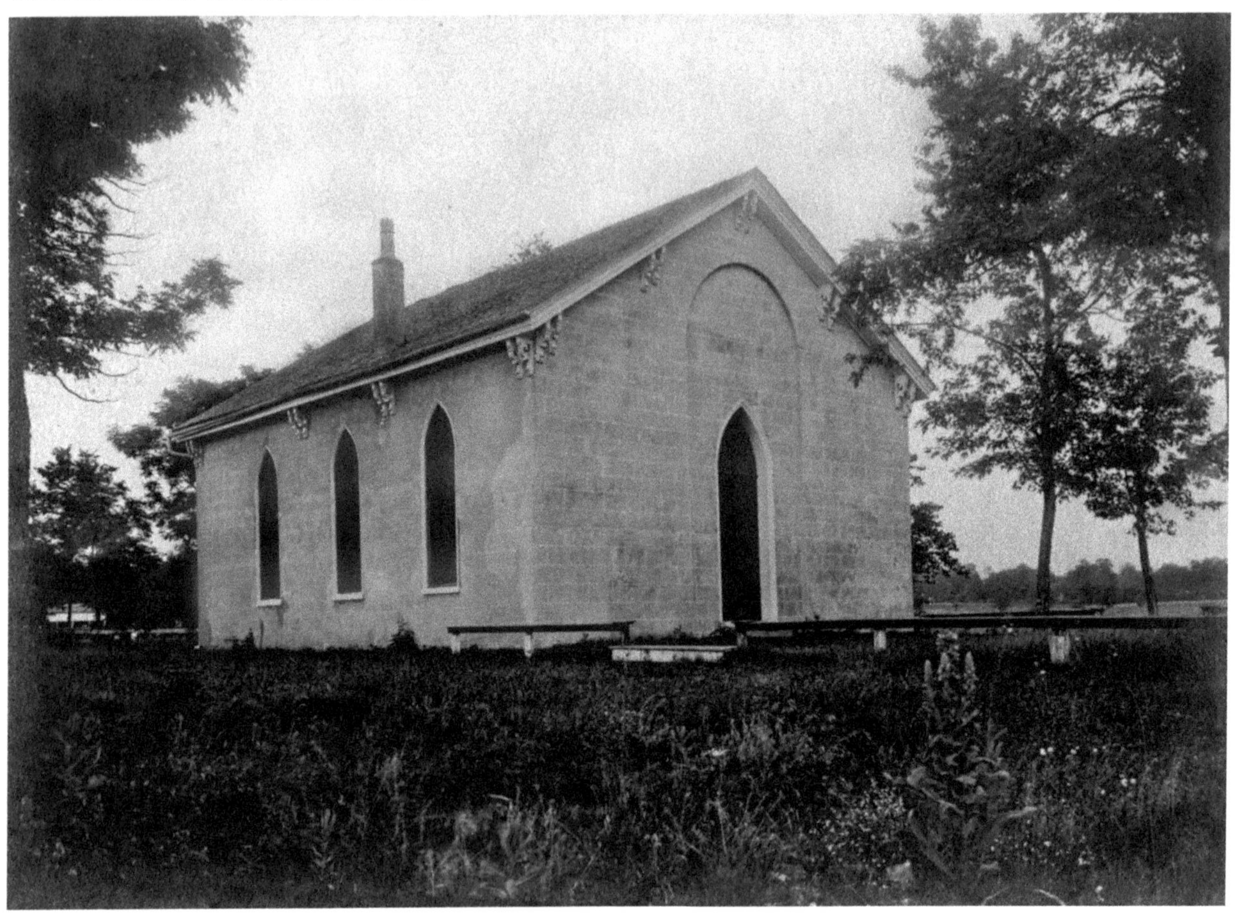

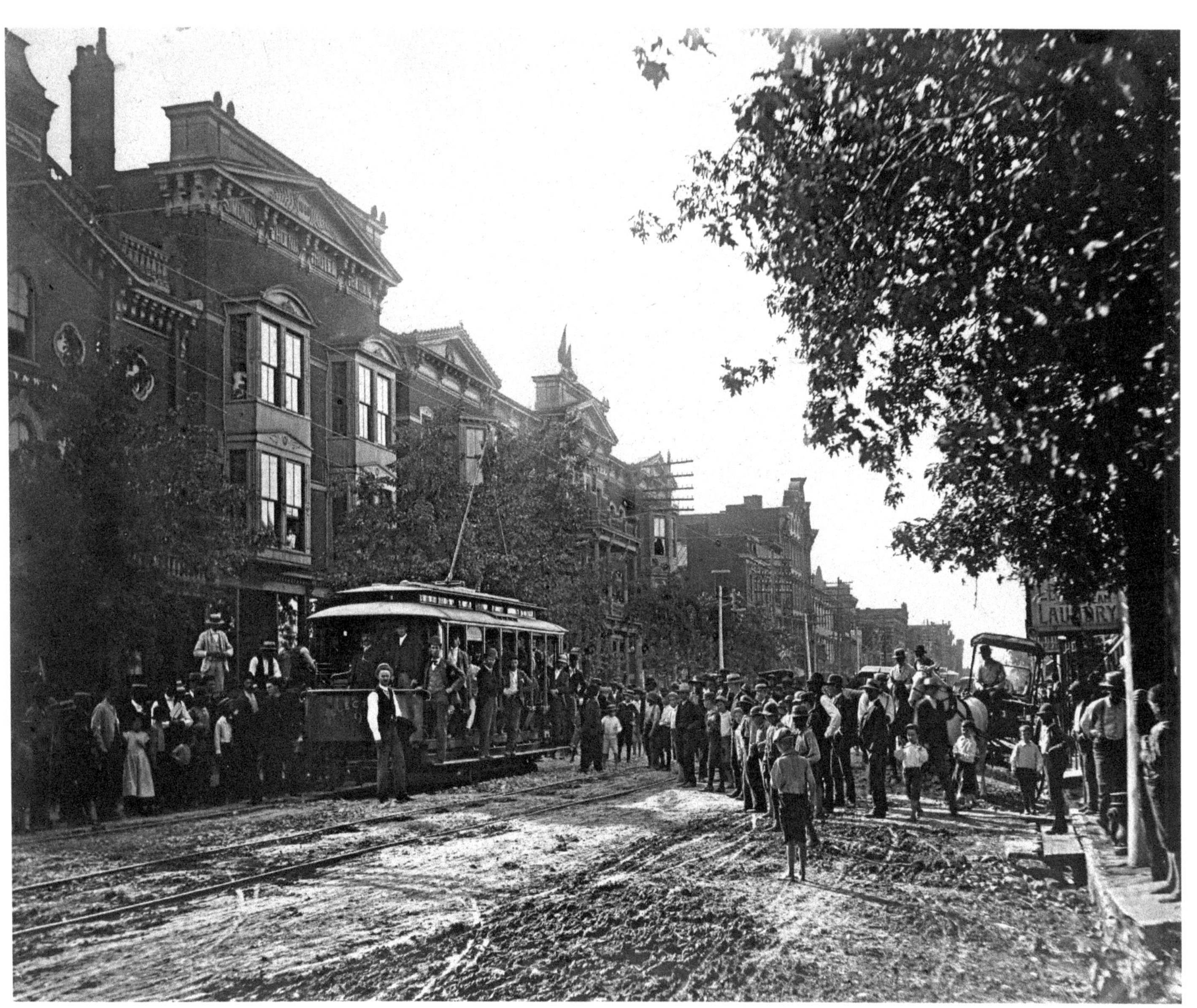

An electric streetcar passing in front of the Phoenix Hotel, Main Street, in the early 1900's.

Main and Broadway looking east.

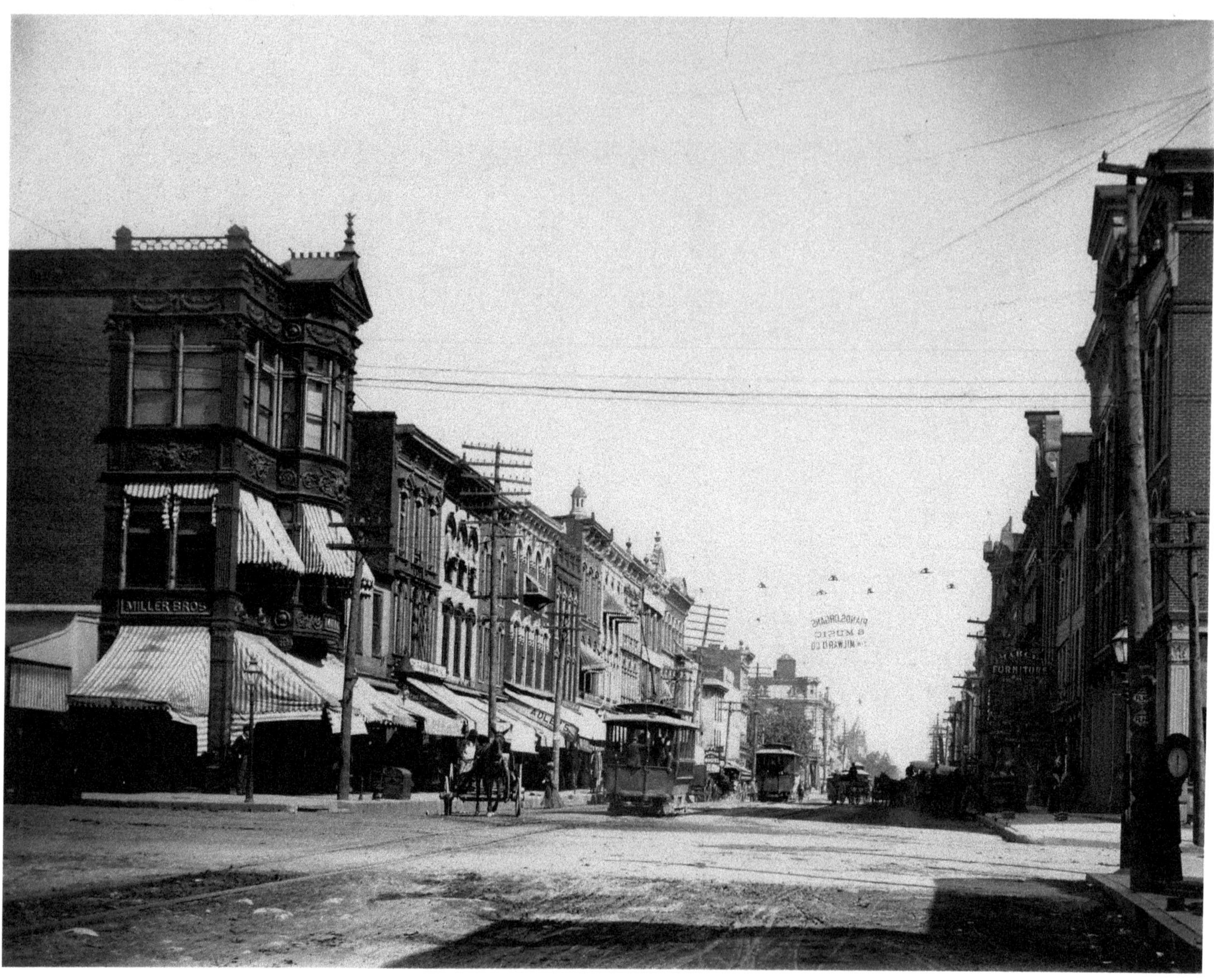

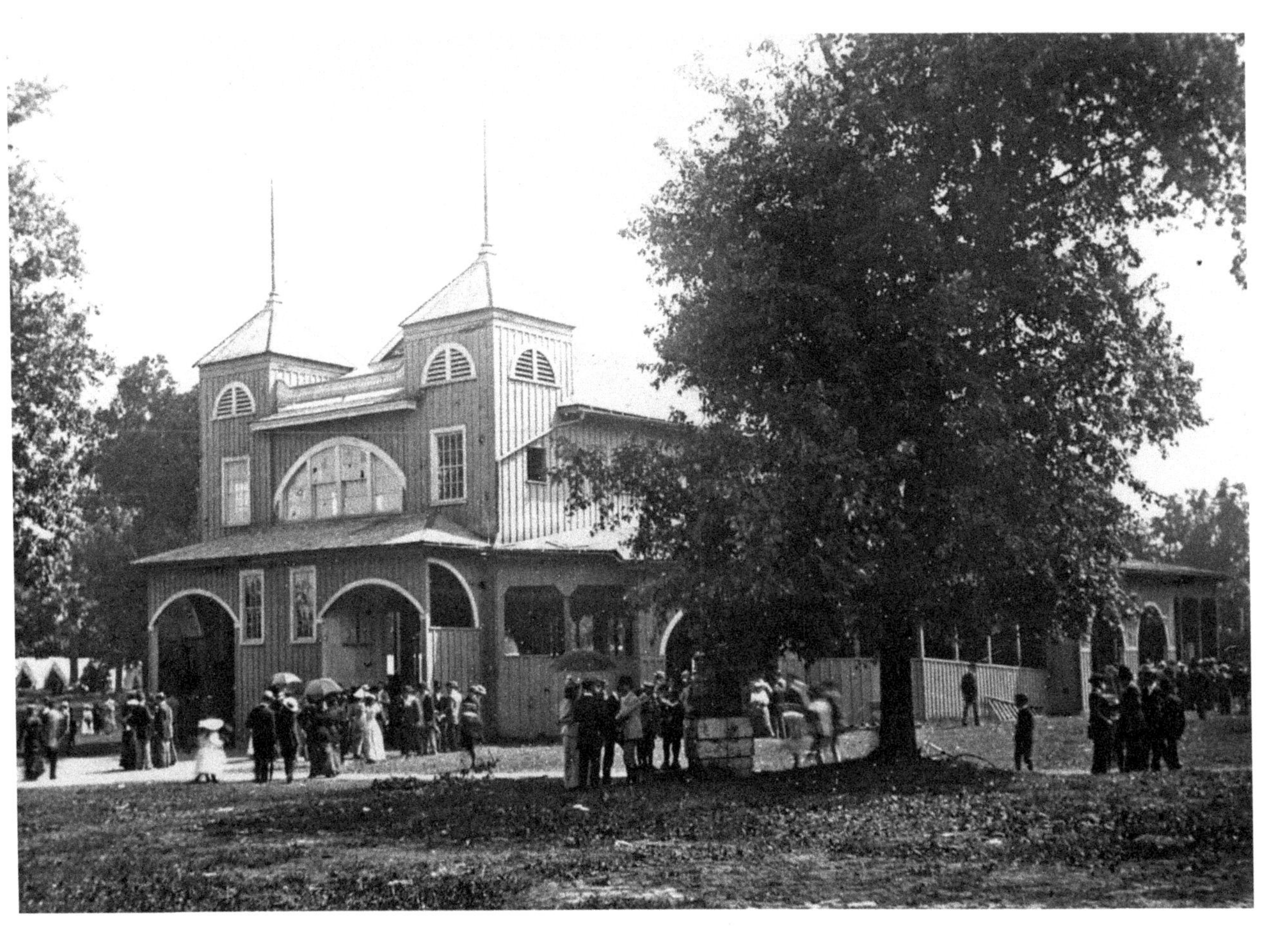

Woodland Park Auditorium, frame construction, moved to Greentree Farm, early 20$^{th}$ century.

Interior of Main Street Christian Church (built 1841), replaced by Union Station, demolished in 1904.

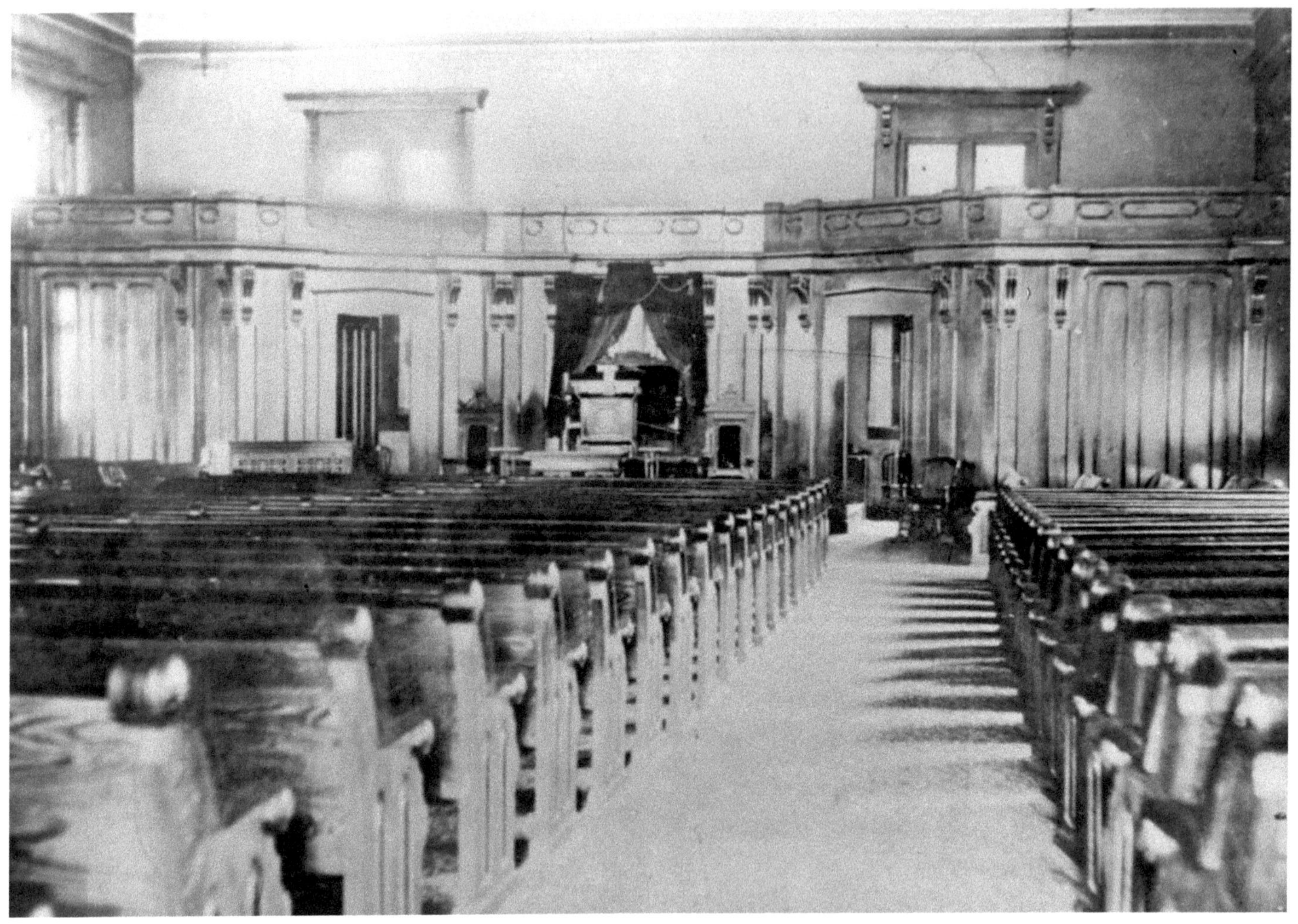

Construction of First National Bank at Main and Upper in 1912. When it was completed two yearrs later, the 15-story building was the tallest building between Cincinnati and Atlanta.

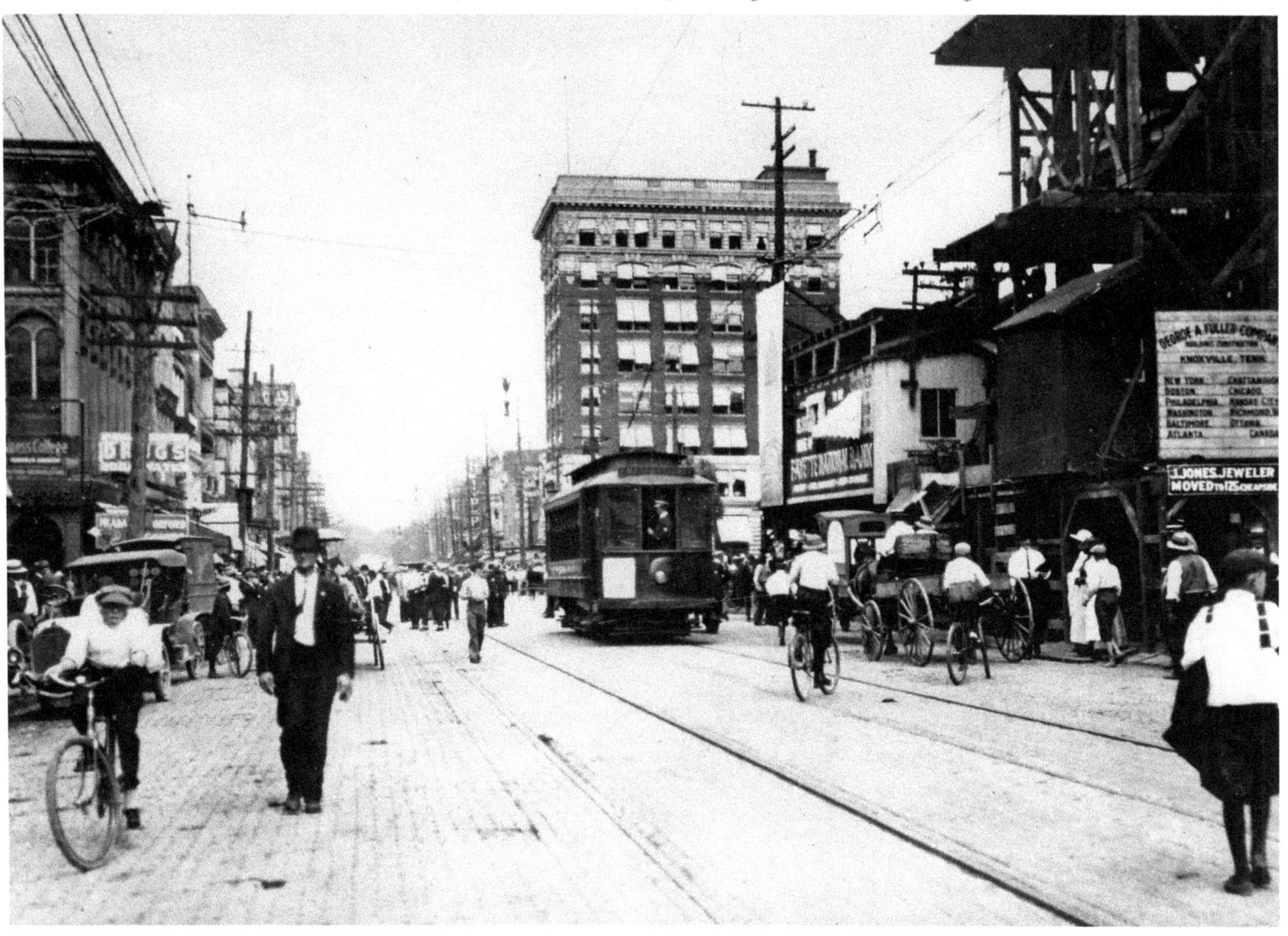

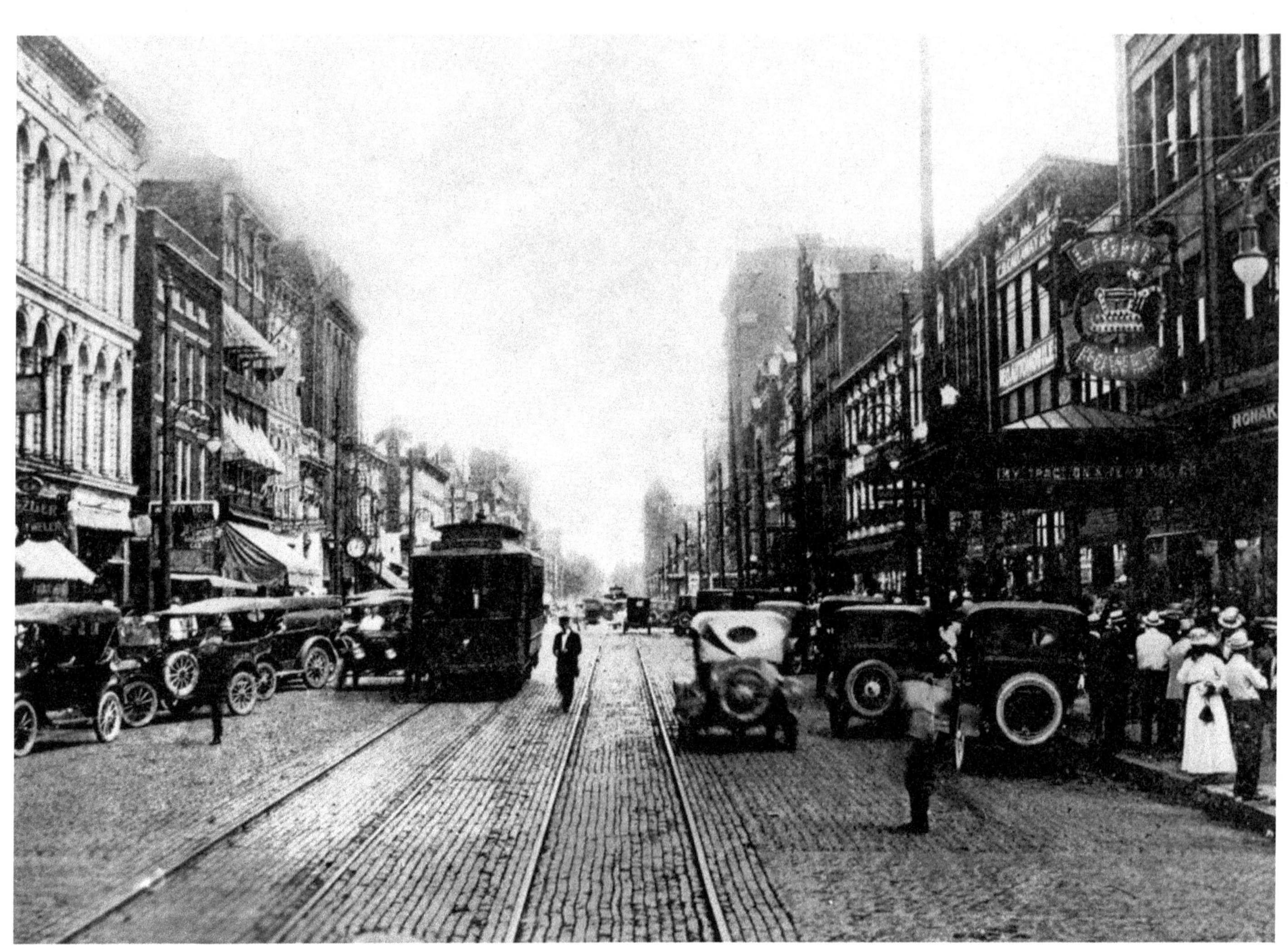

View of Main Street looking east from Upper Street, ca. 1919.

Old Central Fire Department on Short Street, c. 1919.

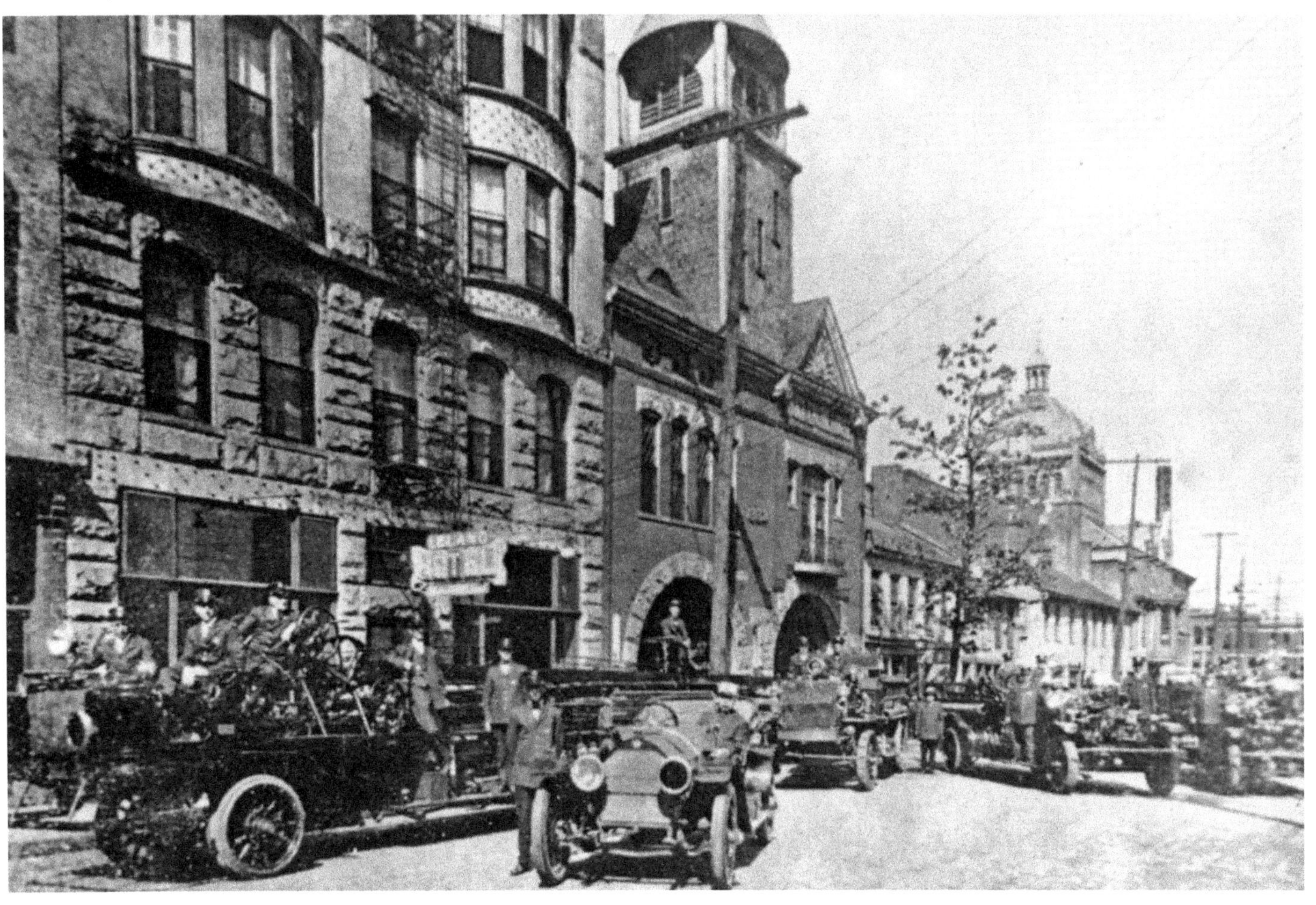

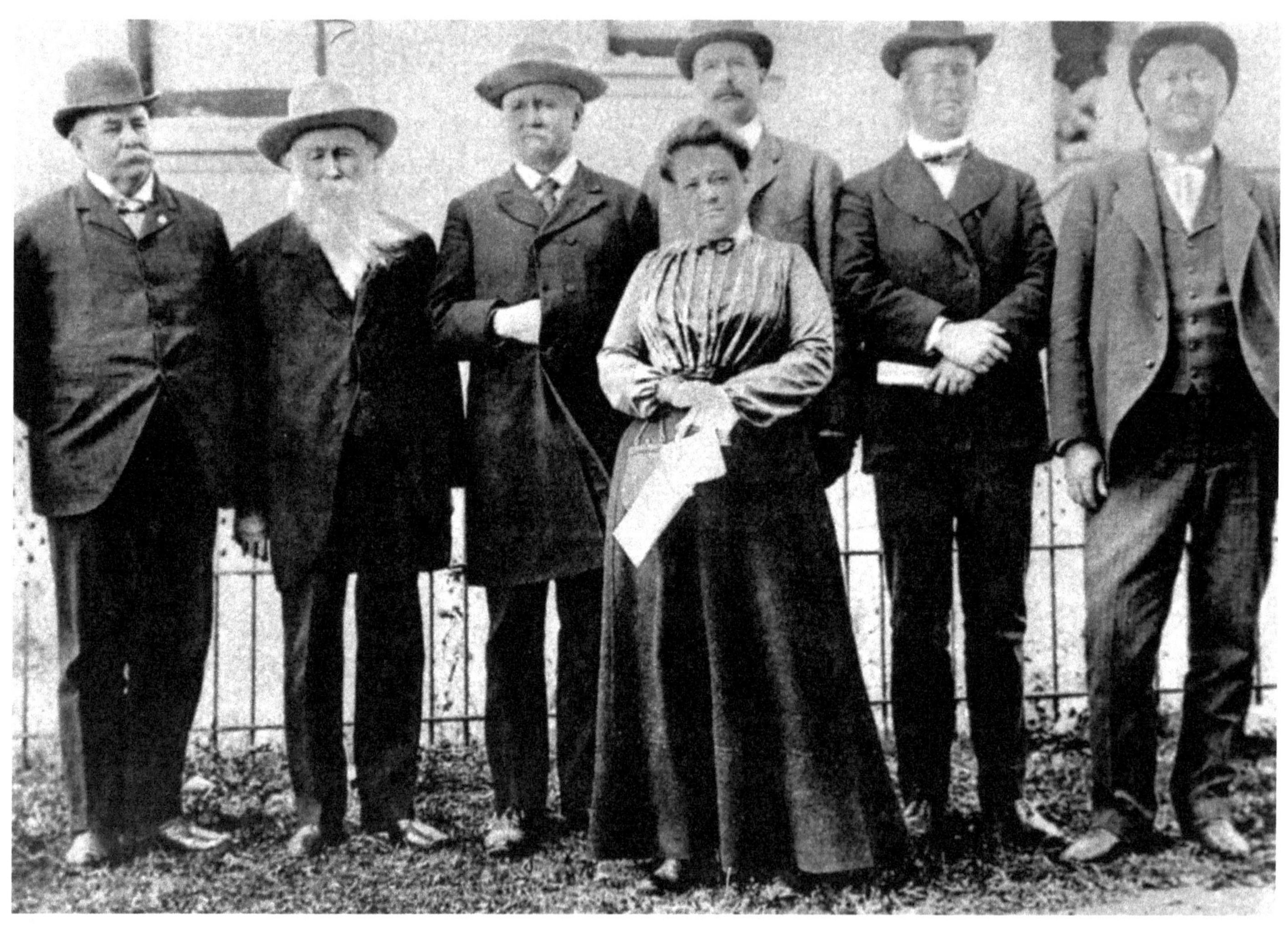

Prominent horsemen and the secretary of the Kentucky Association, ca. 1908.

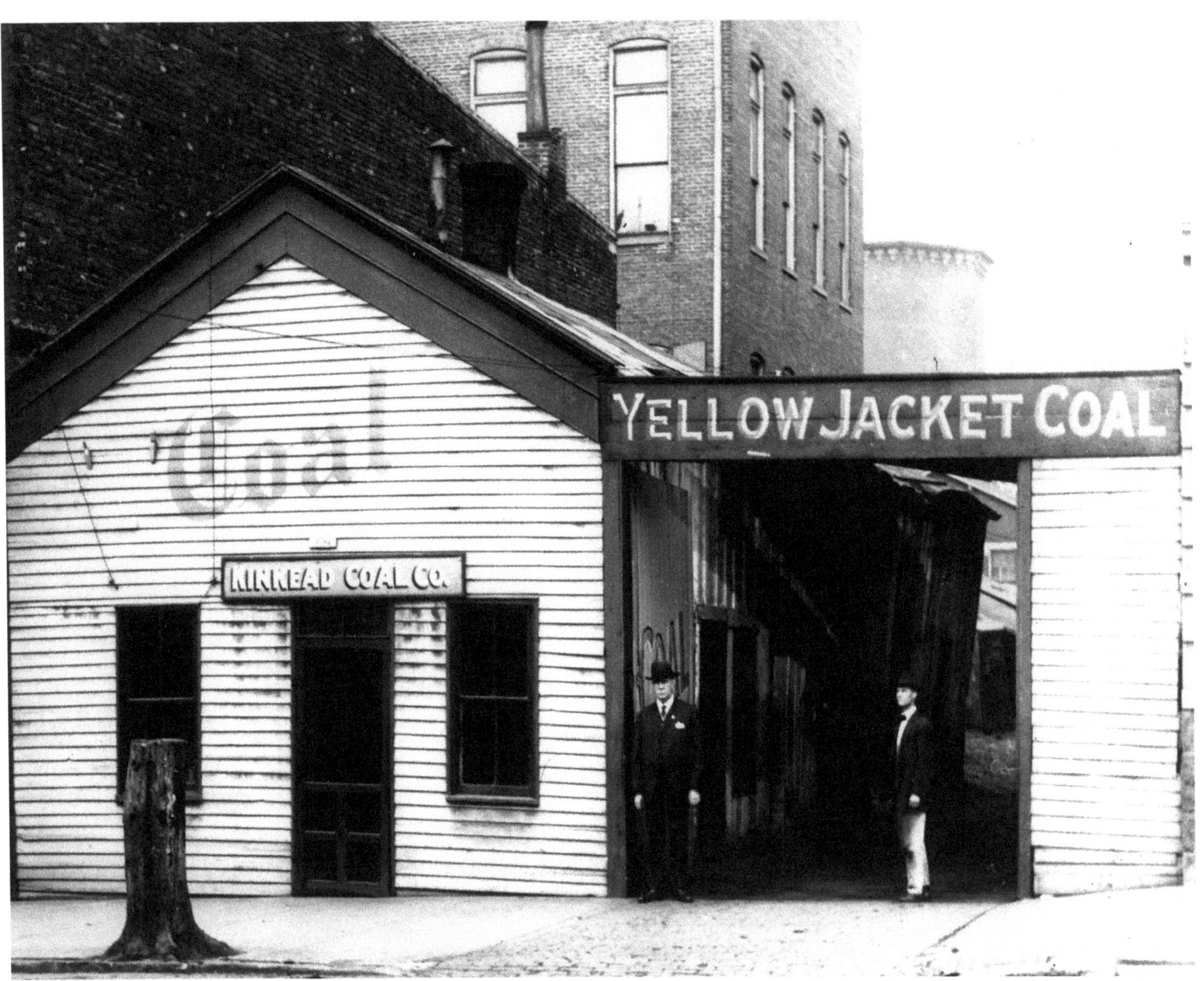


Coal companies on Broadway, early 20th century.

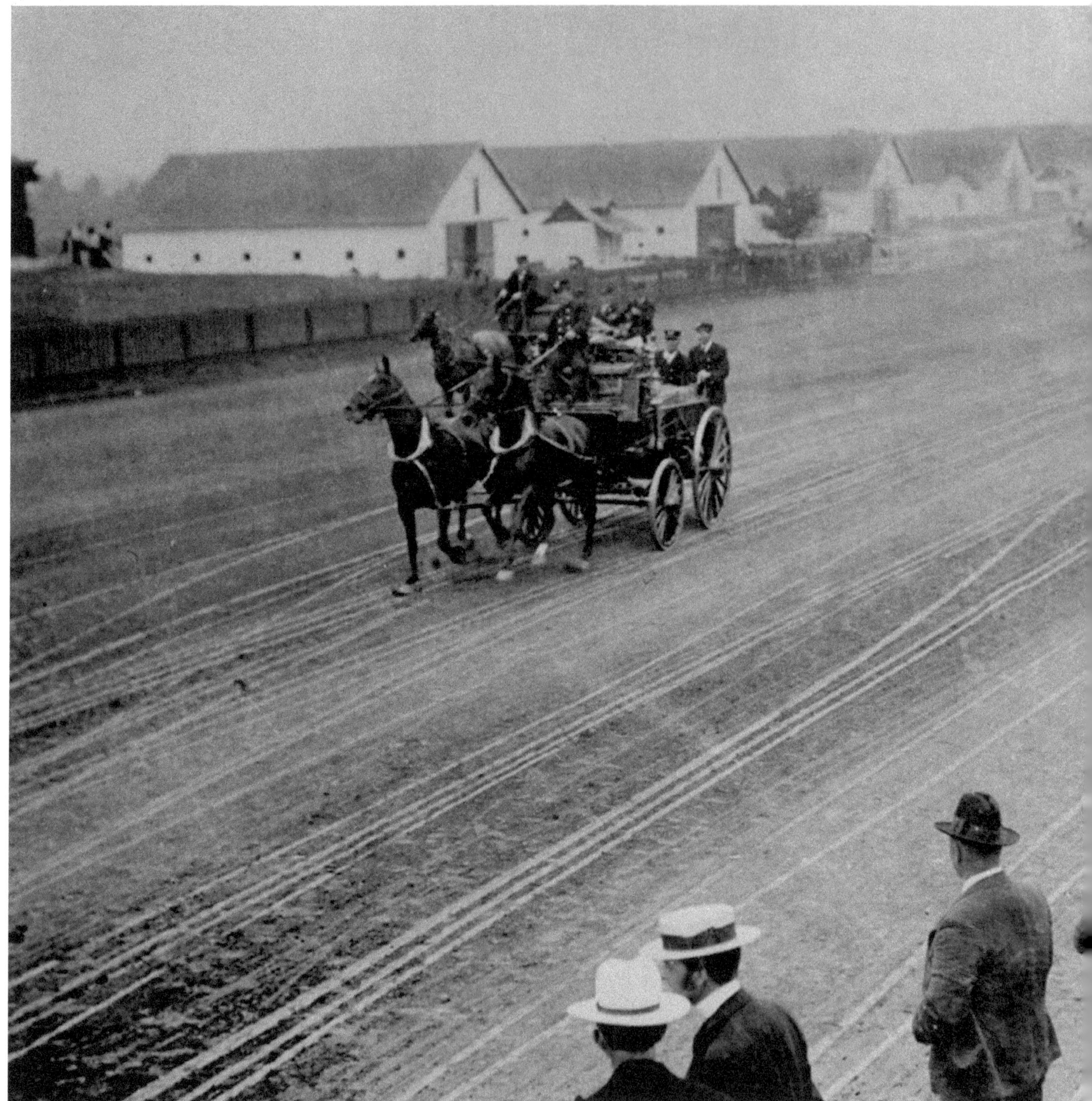

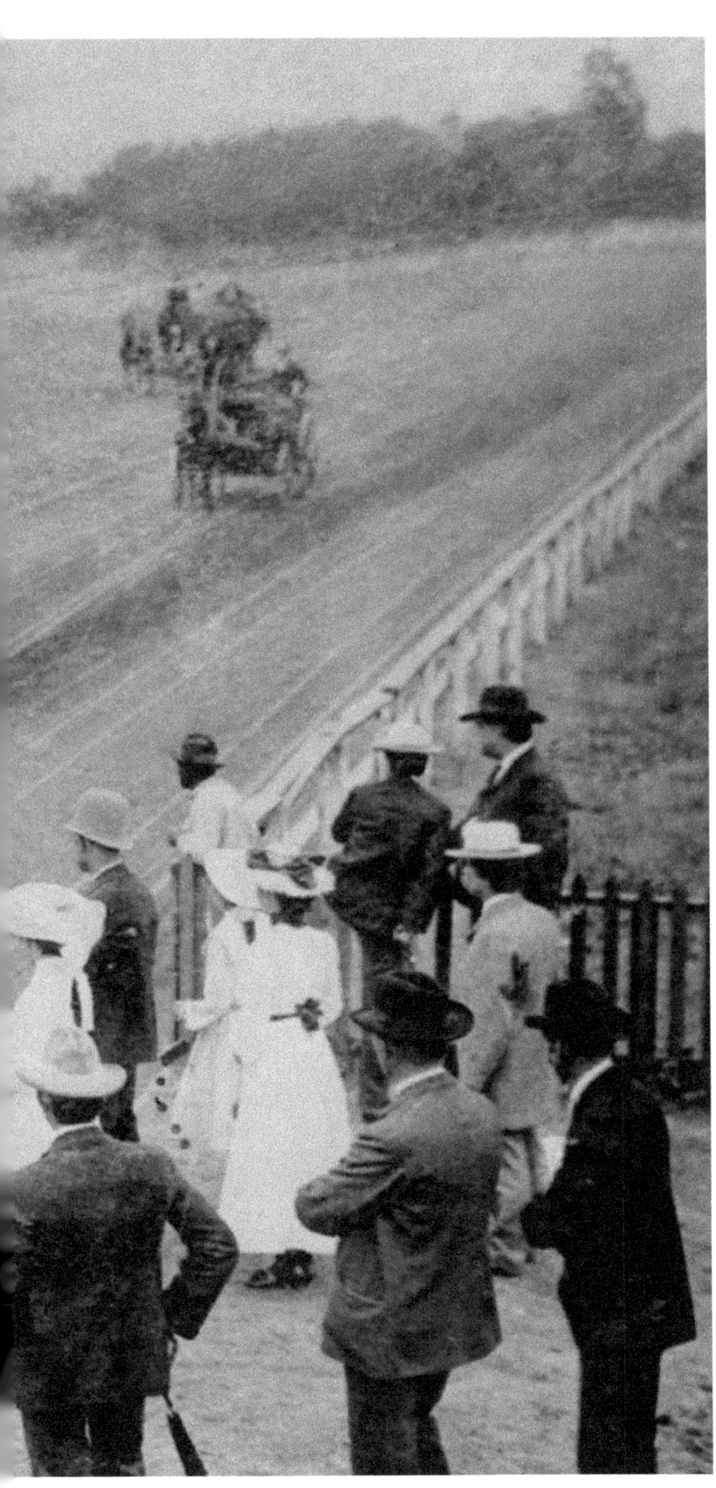

Fire companies race at the trotting track, ca. 1900.

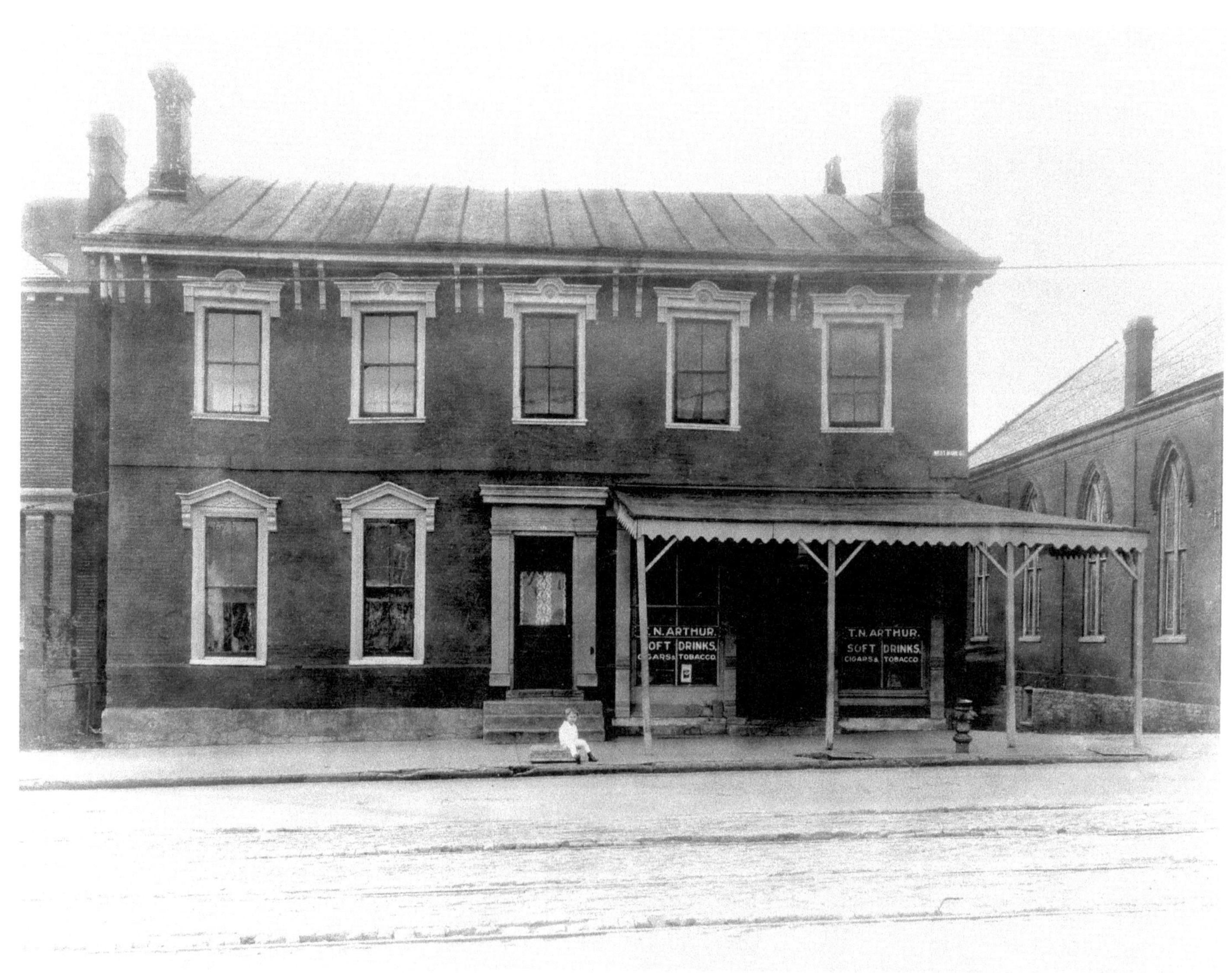


Mary Todd Lincoln's girlhood home on West Main was built in 1803-1806 as an inn.

Jail on Short Street (built 1871, razed 1978), 20th century.

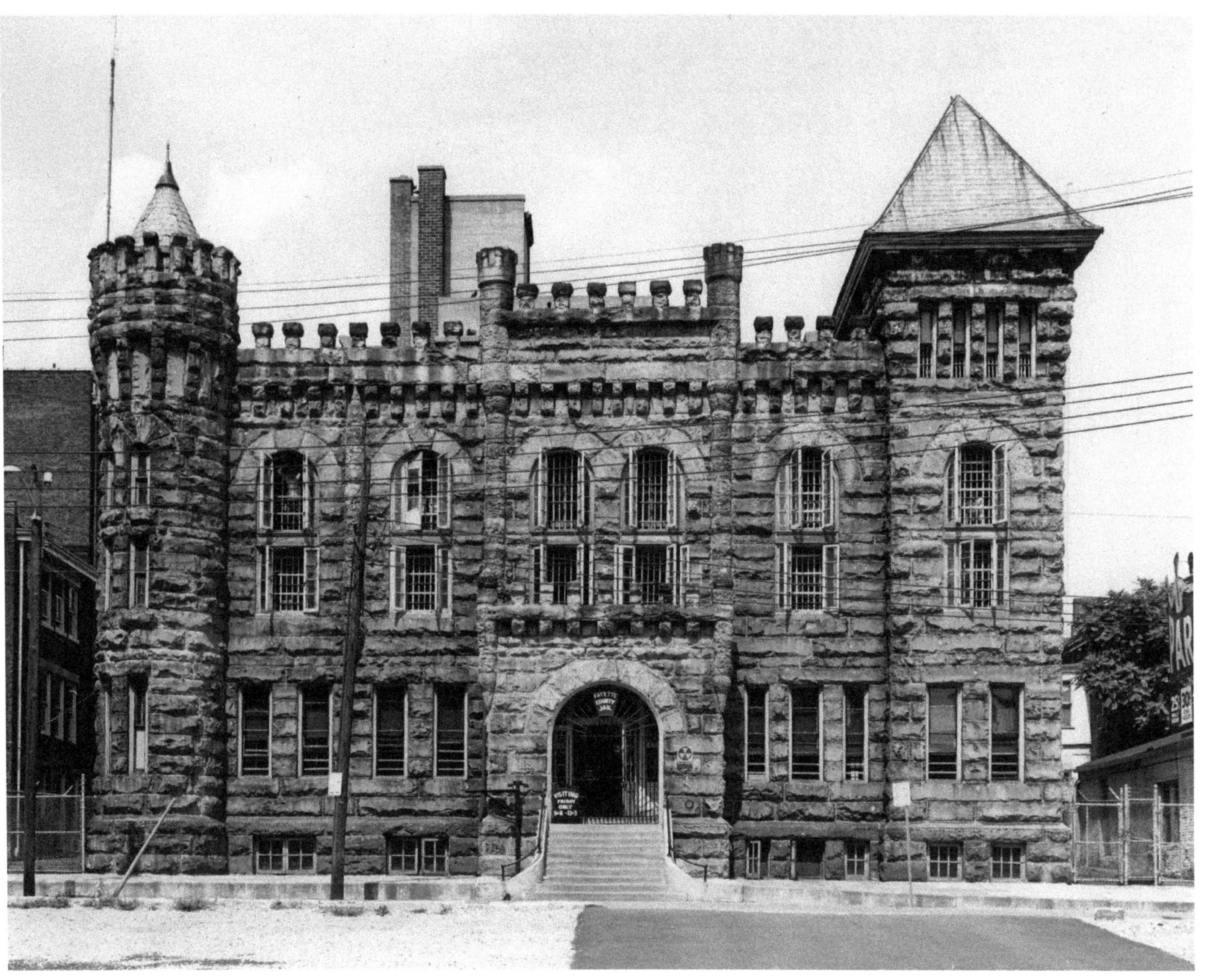

Security Trust Company Board of Directors, 1915.

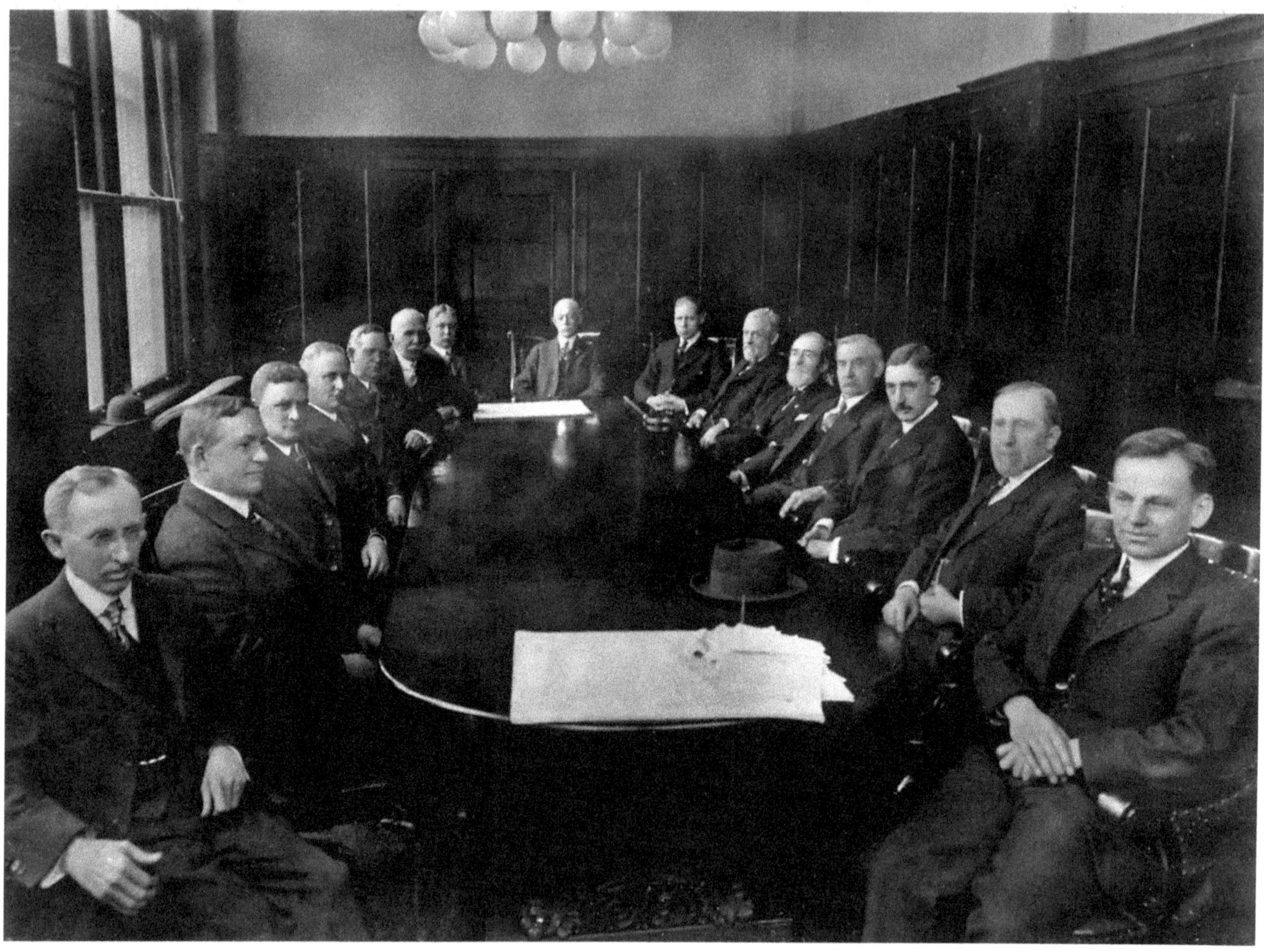

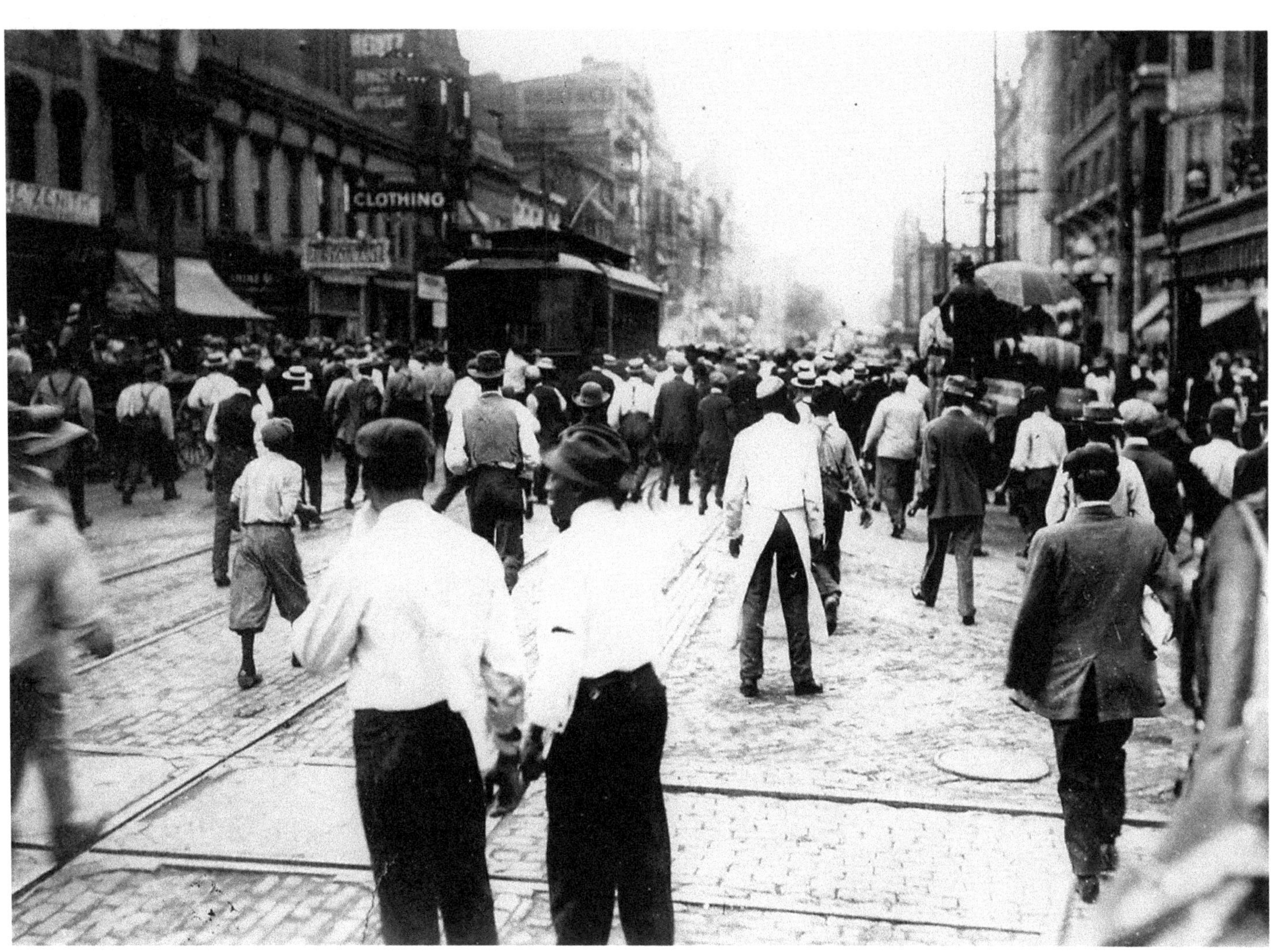


Streetcar strikers on Main Street, 1910.

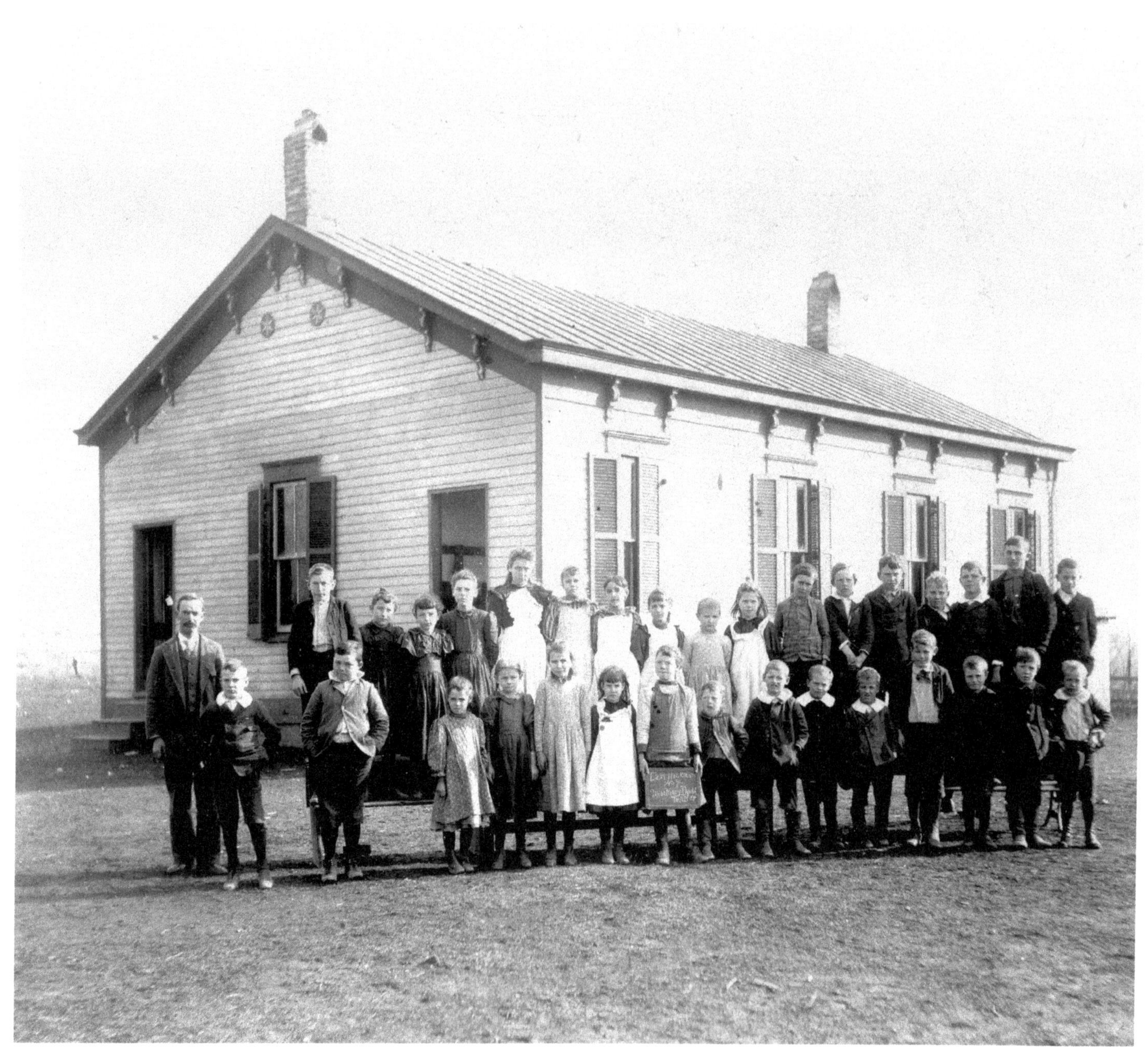

Mary Dodd's class at East Hickman School, 1901.

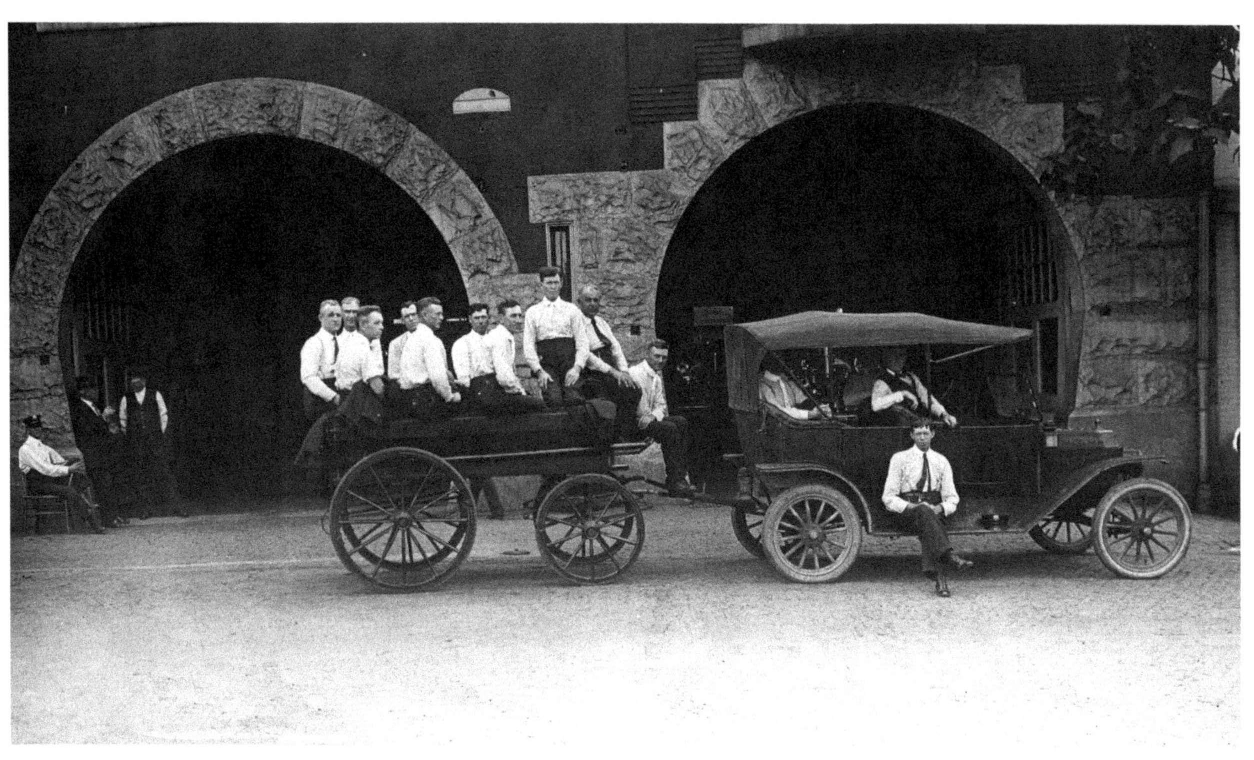

Fire Department volunteers who helped with hemp and wheat harvest during World War I, ca. 1918.

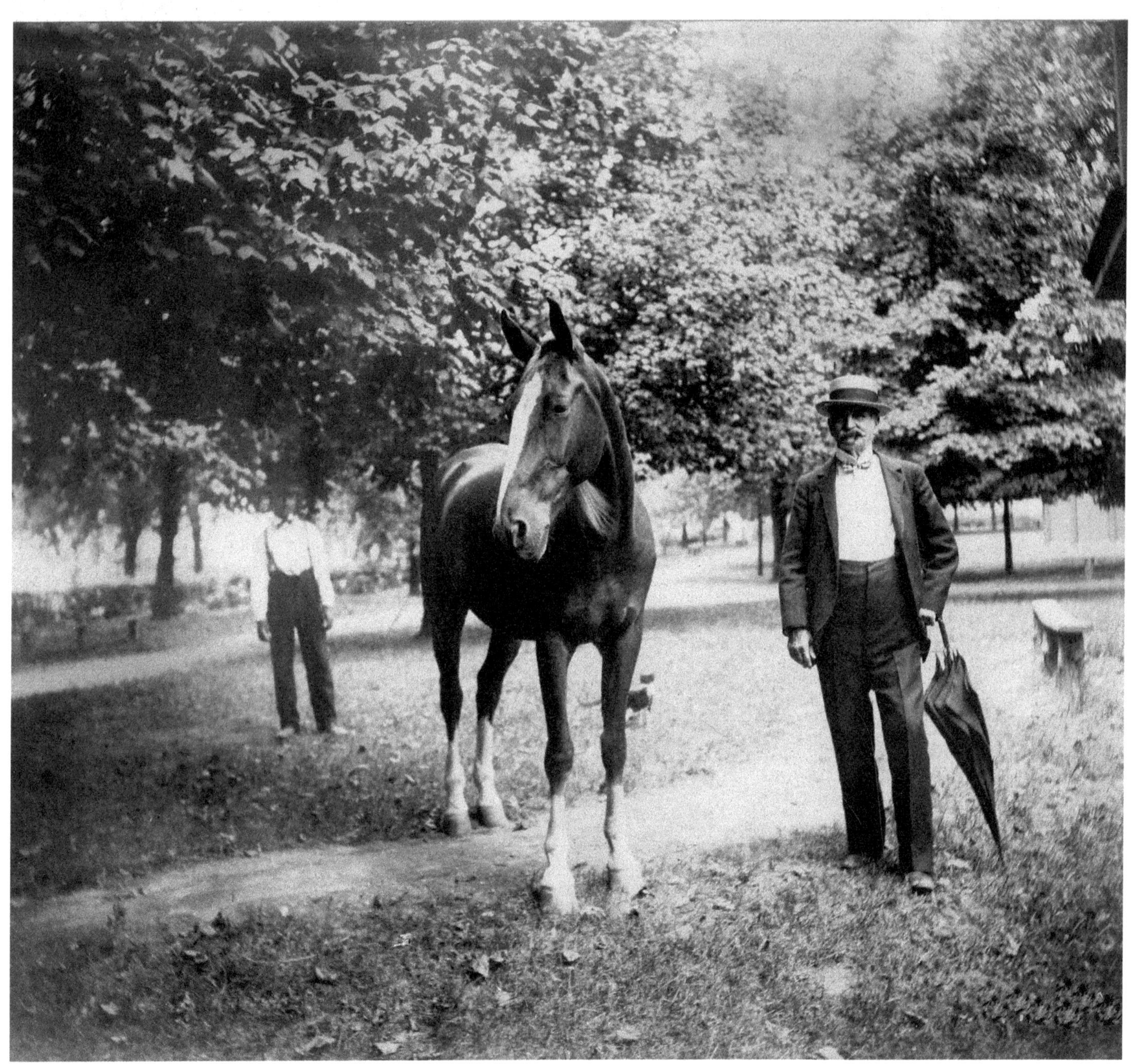

Henry Howard Gratz in Gratz Park, 1900.

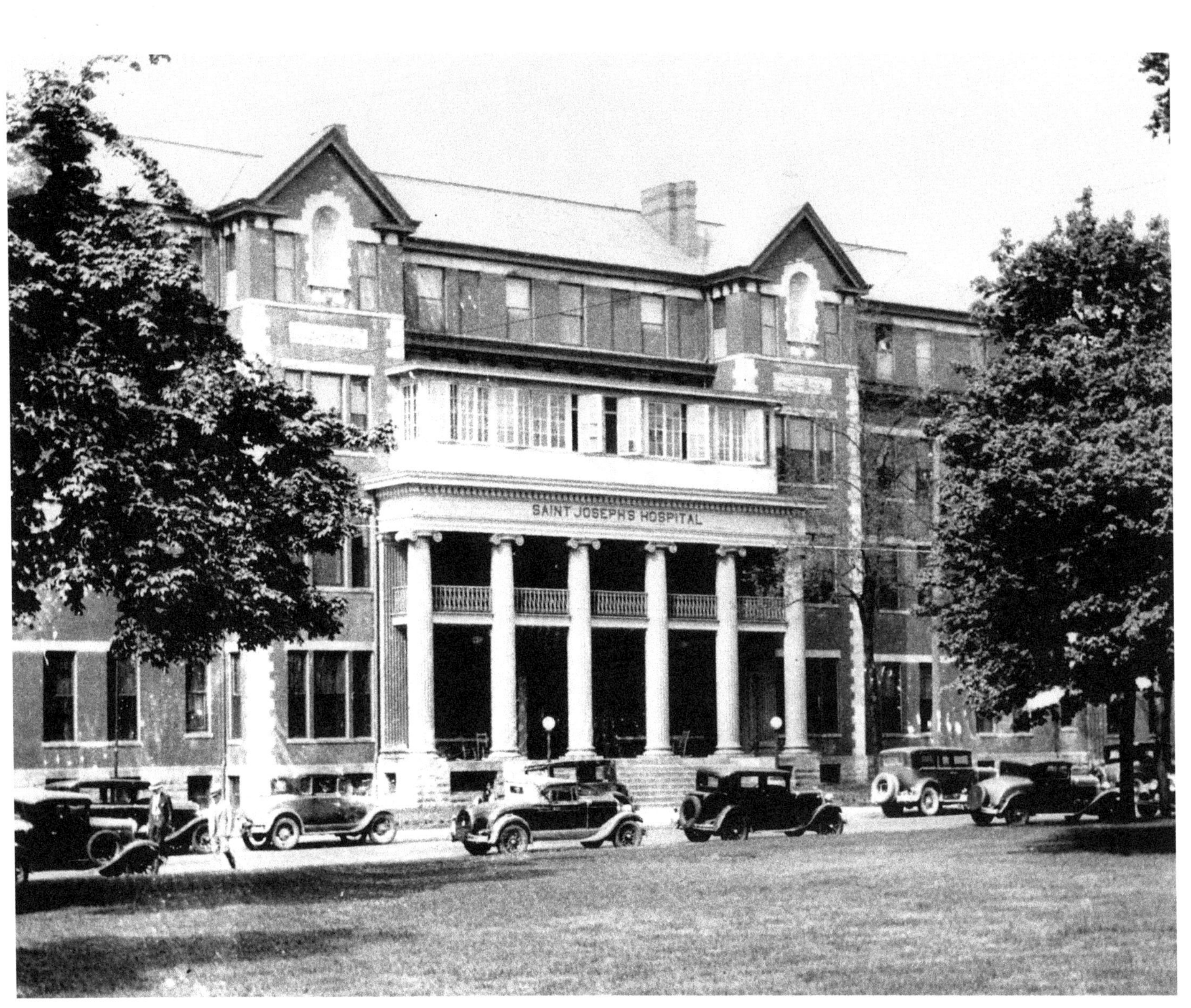


Saint Joseph's Hospital on Second Street (razed 1966), ca. 1910.

Carty Building (built 1871-72), cast iron façade, southwest corner of Main and Mill Streets, razed 1938.

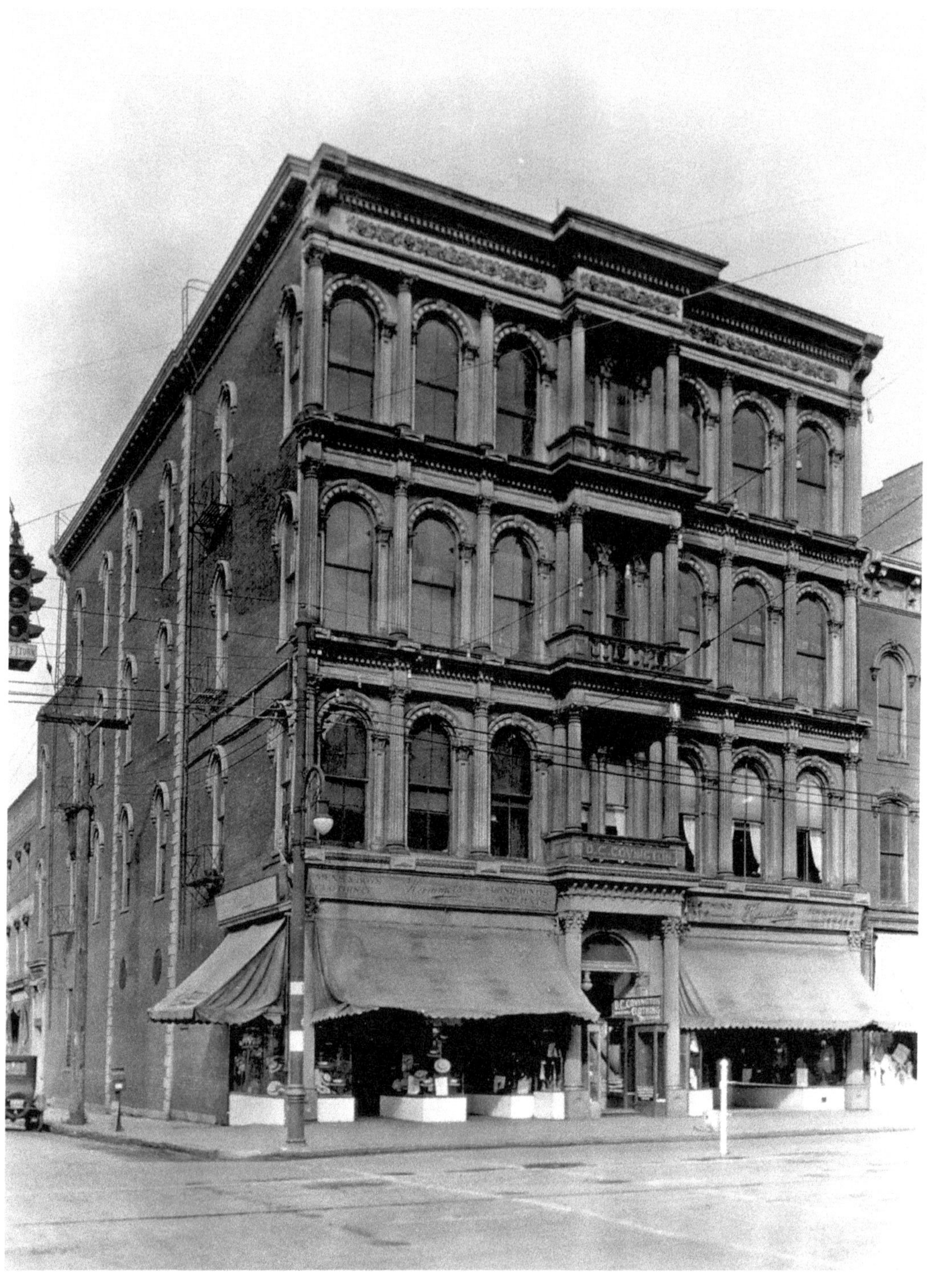

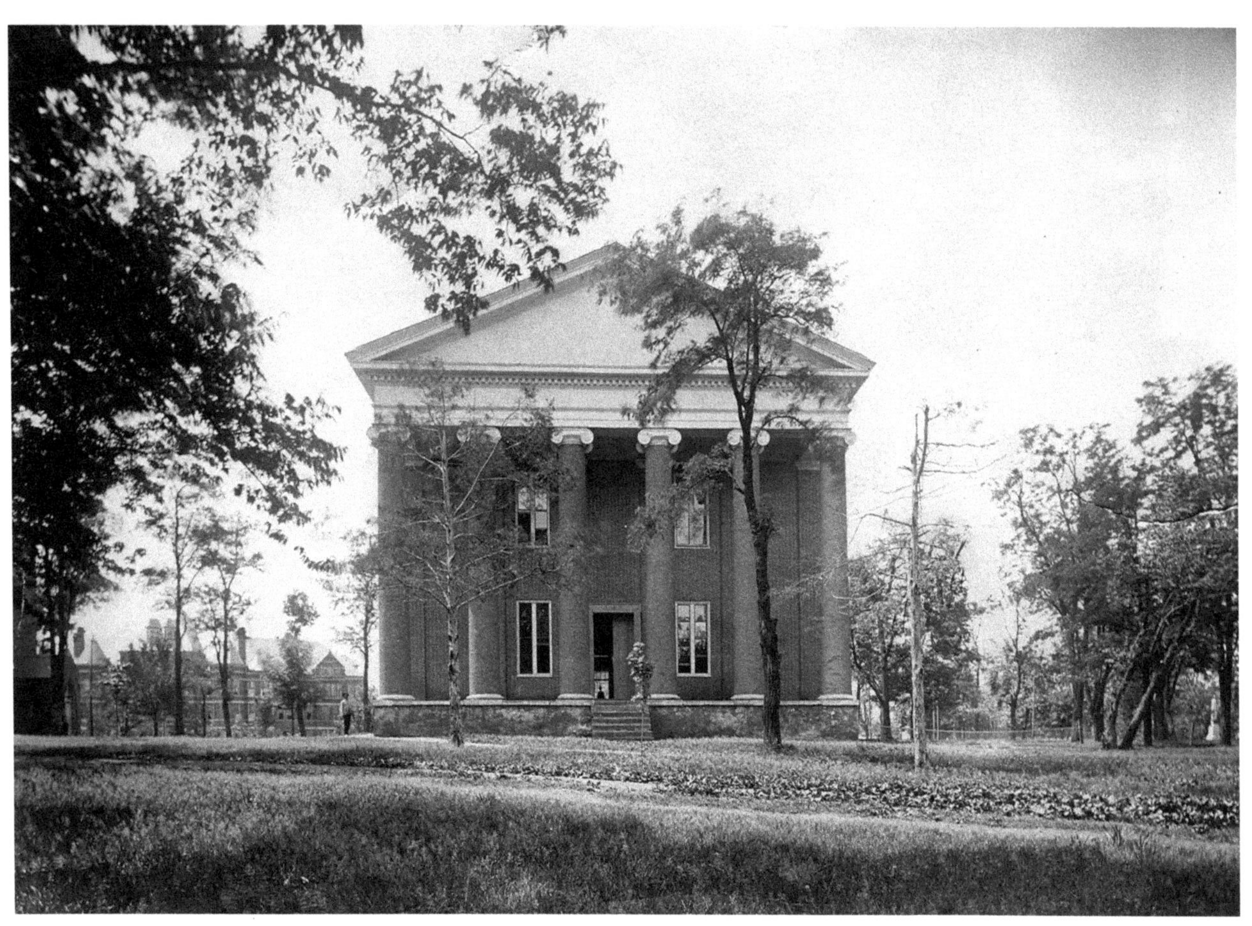

Giddings Hall at Georgetown College in 1901.

Banker's convention at Bellmont Woods, Oct. 1906.

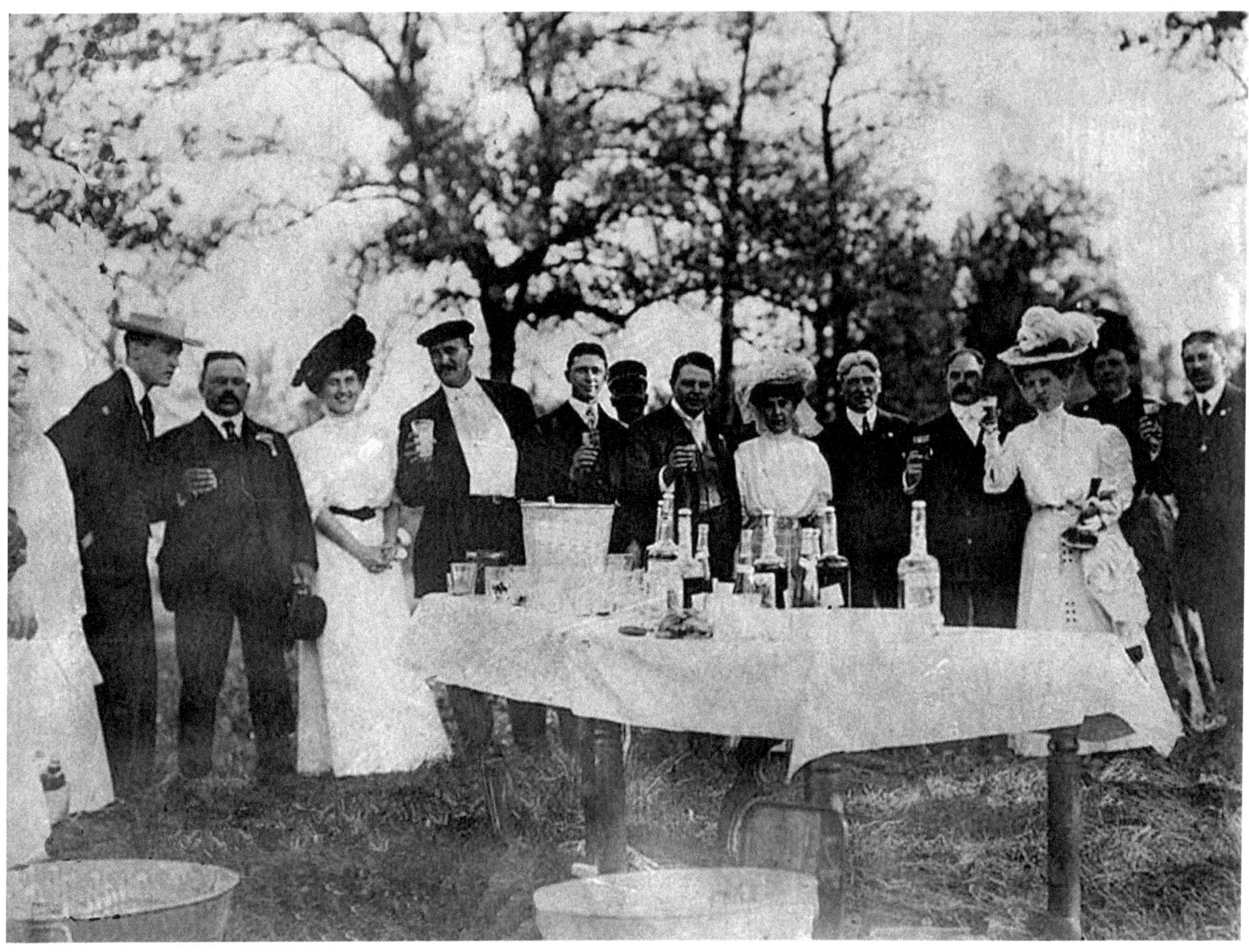

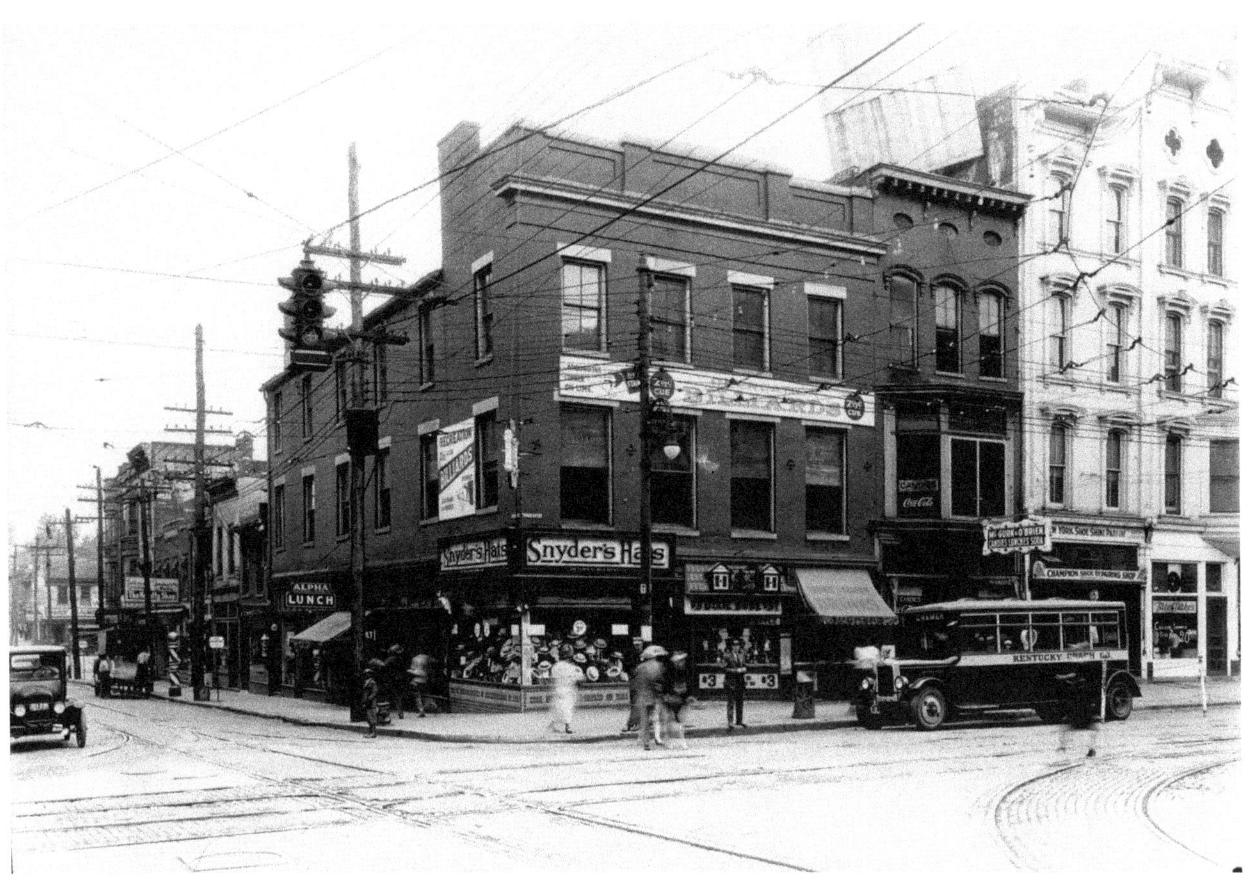


Urban vitality at the southwest corner of Main and Limestone Streets with early Crower bus, ca. 1930.

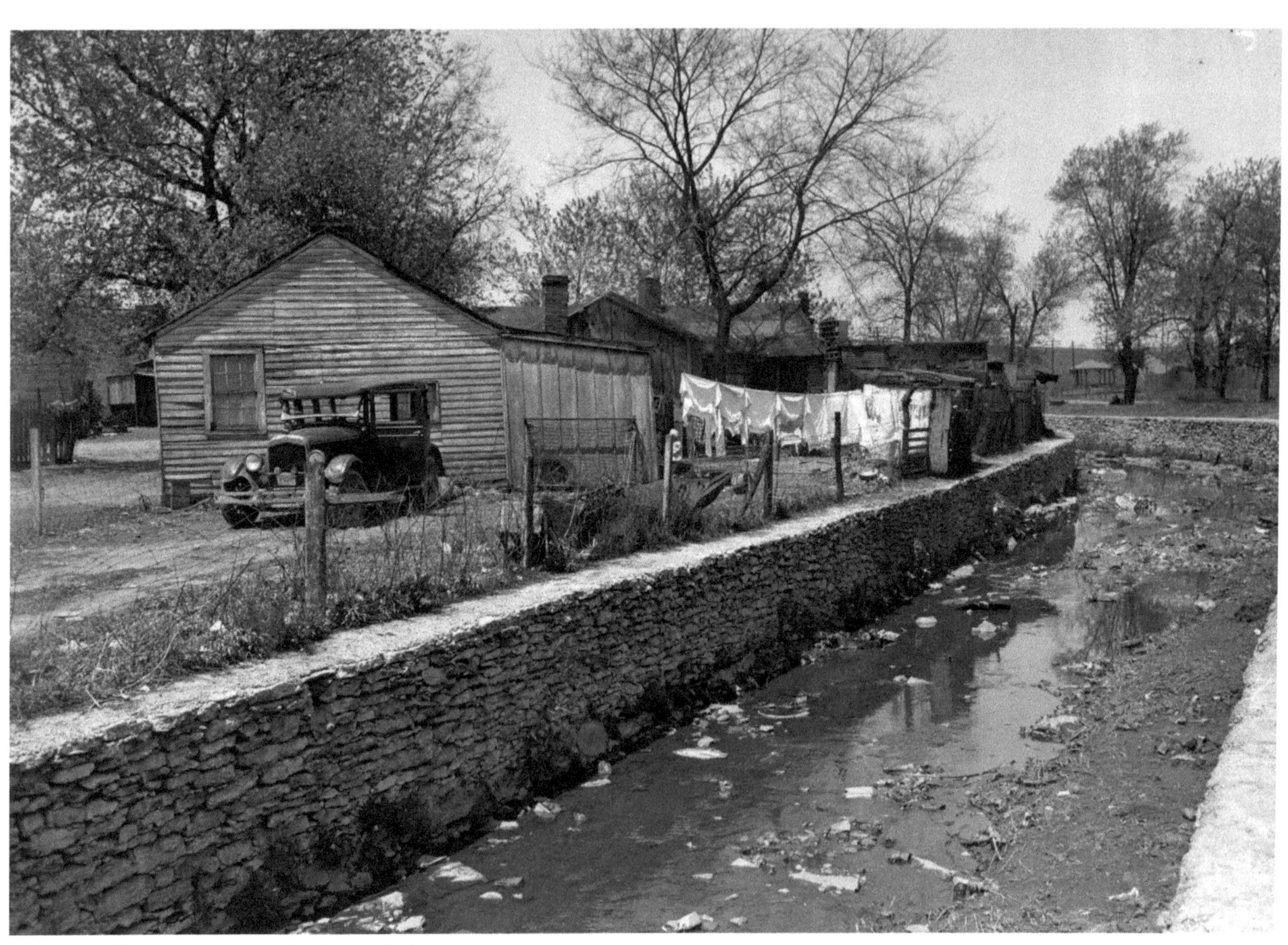

Town branch stream entering the city, early 20th century.

# Living Well in War and Depression

## 1920-1940

The First World War brought great changes in the country as a whole, but life in Lexington was being transformed slowly by other forces. Lexington contributed to the war effort in some outstanding ways and made great contributions far away from the city. At home, society was being changed by the automobile, by new forms of entertainment, by the availability of new devices that restructured the labor force and by grand social changes. Laura Clay, daughter of Lexington's great and colorful abolitionist Cassius Marcellus Clay, was a leader of the movement that would bring rights to women in 1920. Lexington was to produce many women who broke new ground for their sex. Black citizens were becoming professional leaders in their community. Lexington was spared most of the ethnic turmoil that swept the country in the young century—but not all. Anti-evolution forces were active in this town where John Scopes had graduated from the University of Kentucky.

Lexington has been a city of paradox. When new high schools were built in 1923, one was named for Jefferson Davis and one for Paul Lawrence Dunbar. There were many long established and prosperous businesses and banks but very little manufacturing. Somewhat isolated from eastern centers of culture, the city nonetheless supported a series of concerts and lectures which featured the greatest artists and minds of the day. Given the stereotype of Kentucky then current, Lexington was a seat of "high" culture. A new amusement park had popular appeal. Gambling at the tracks, the production of tobacco, houses of ill repute and the manufacture of Bourbon flourished along with the many churches that frowned on such activities.

In the hard times of the Depression, there was little money but most institutions held firm and most of the people, especially those with a connection to the land, could continue a pleasant existence. The repeal of prohibition in 1933 undoubtedly softened the blows for some. The Federal Narcotics Farm was built in the 1930's and brought new recognition to Lexington from remote and perhaps unsought sources. The "New Deal" was a good deal for the region especially considering improvements in the infrastructure through the Civilian Conservation Corps and the Public Works Administration. Throughout this period, Lexington grew in many positive ways. The development of Ashland Park on the lands of Henry Clay is emblematic of this growth. When war clouds covered Europe, Lexington was a fine place to live.

Old Saint Peter's Catholic Church on Limestone Street (built 1837), razed ca. 1928.

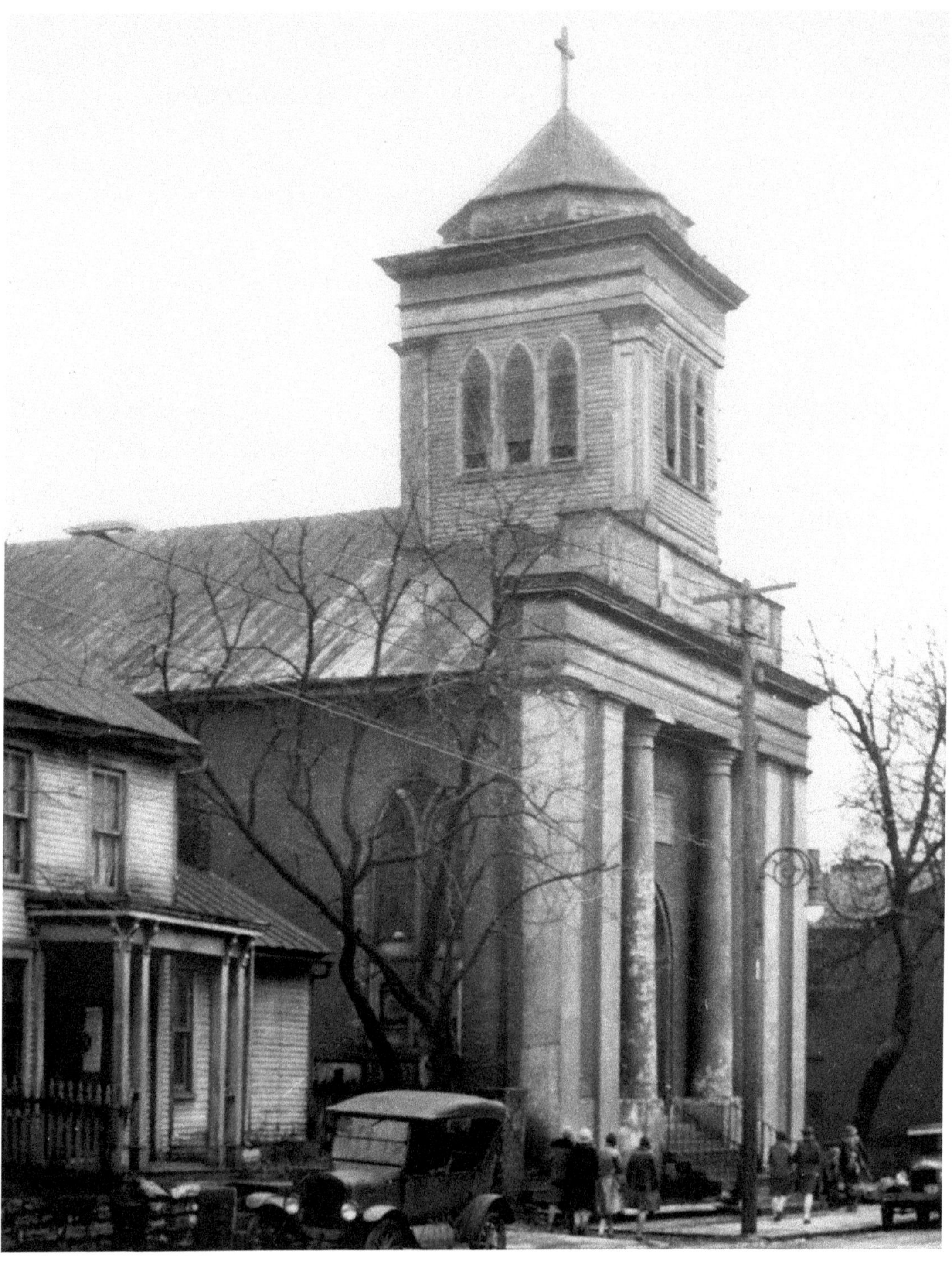

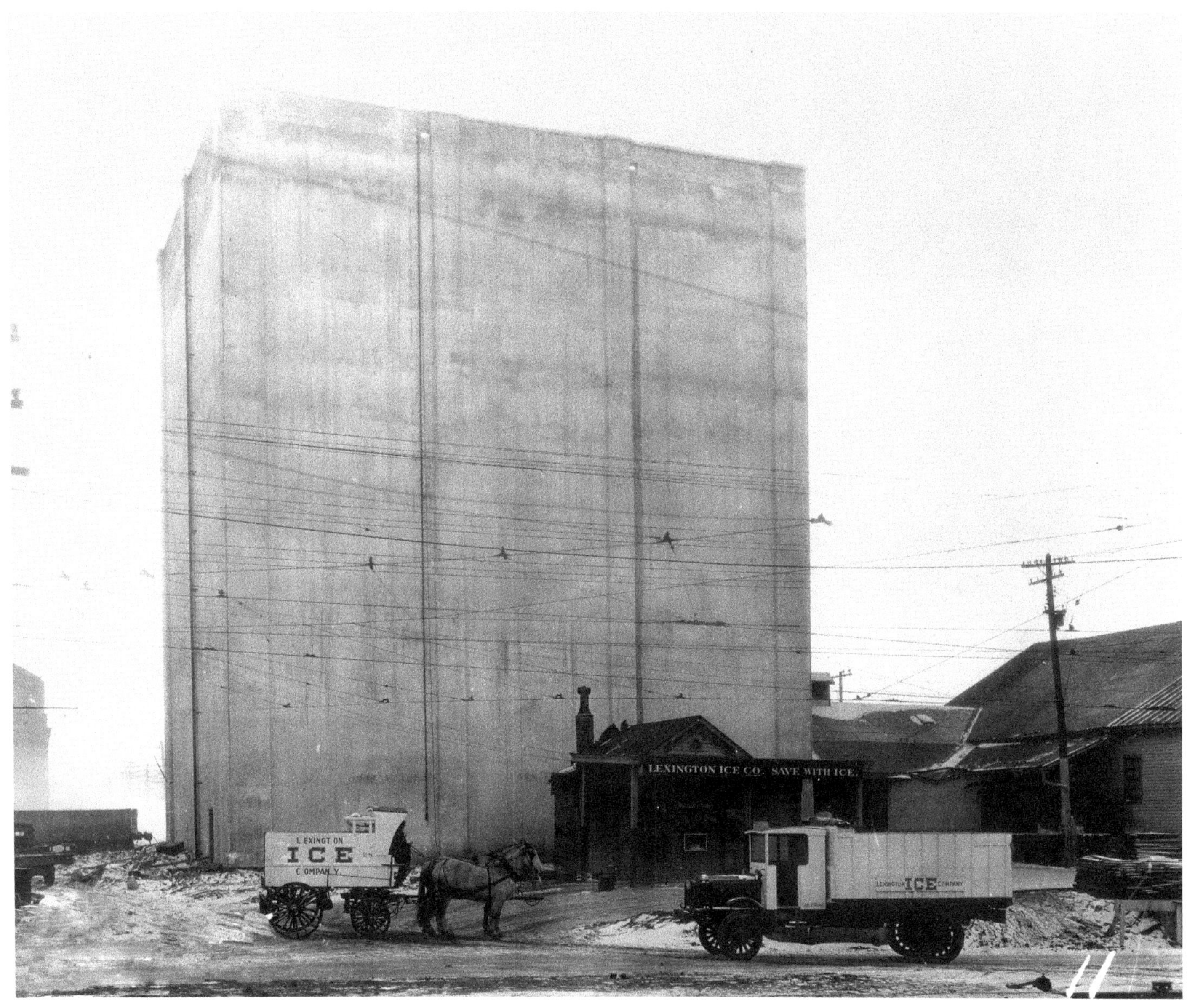


Ice Plant of Kentucky Utilities on Loudoun Avenue, 1929.

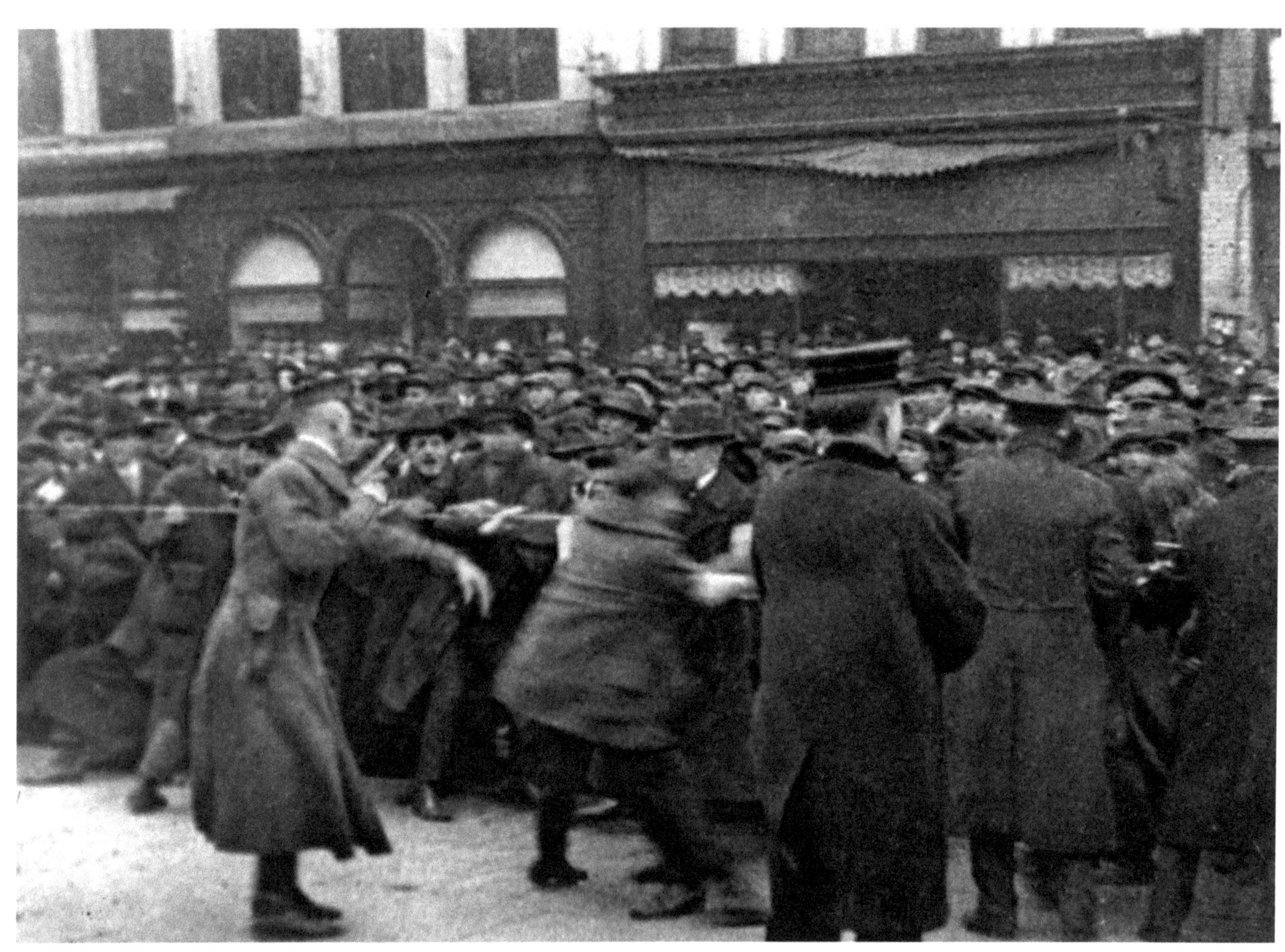

Lynch mob at the courthouse (the mob was repulsed with casualties and their intended victim later executed by law), 1920.

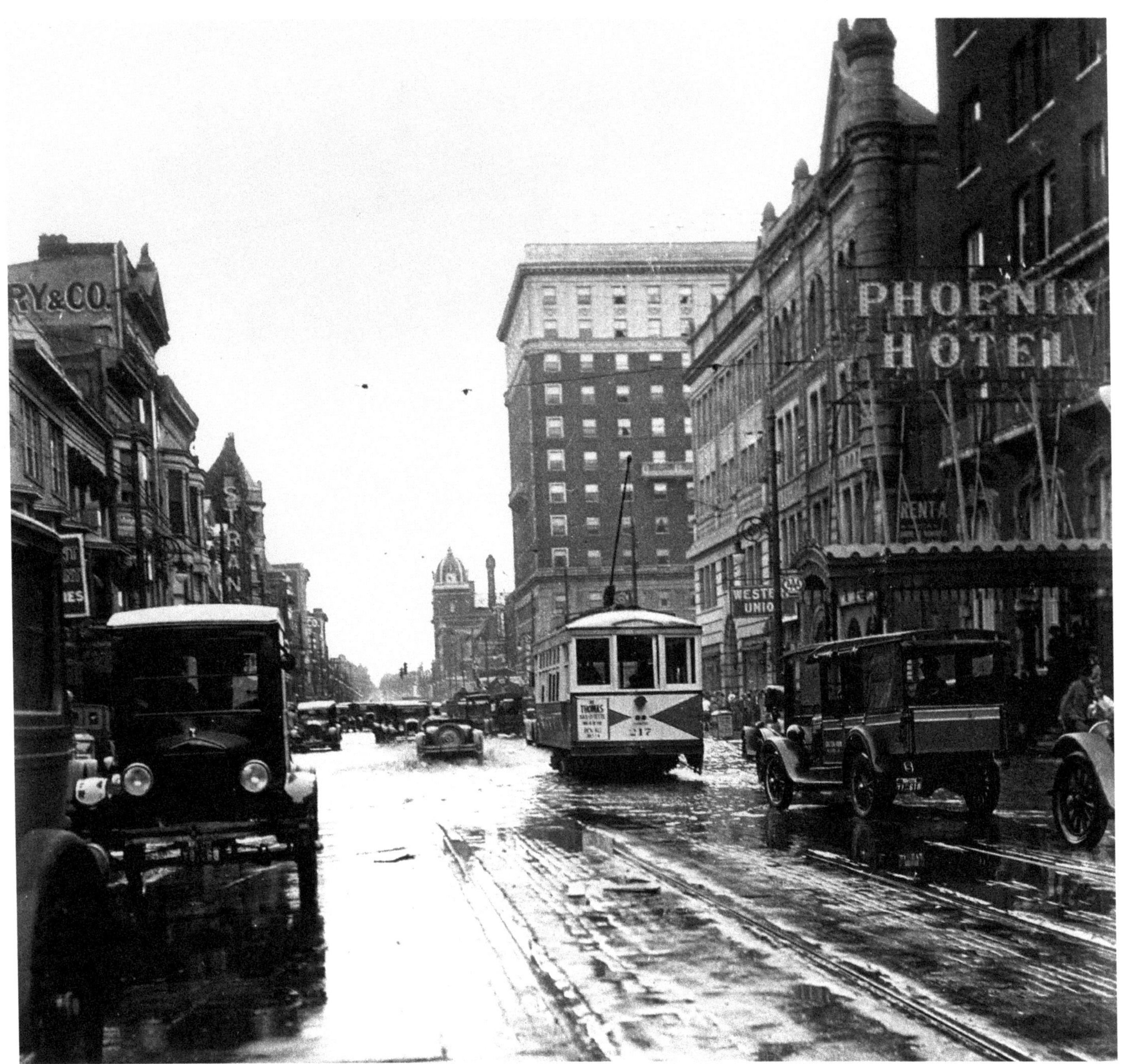


Main Street flooded, 1928.

Banquet at the Phoenix Hotel, 1938.

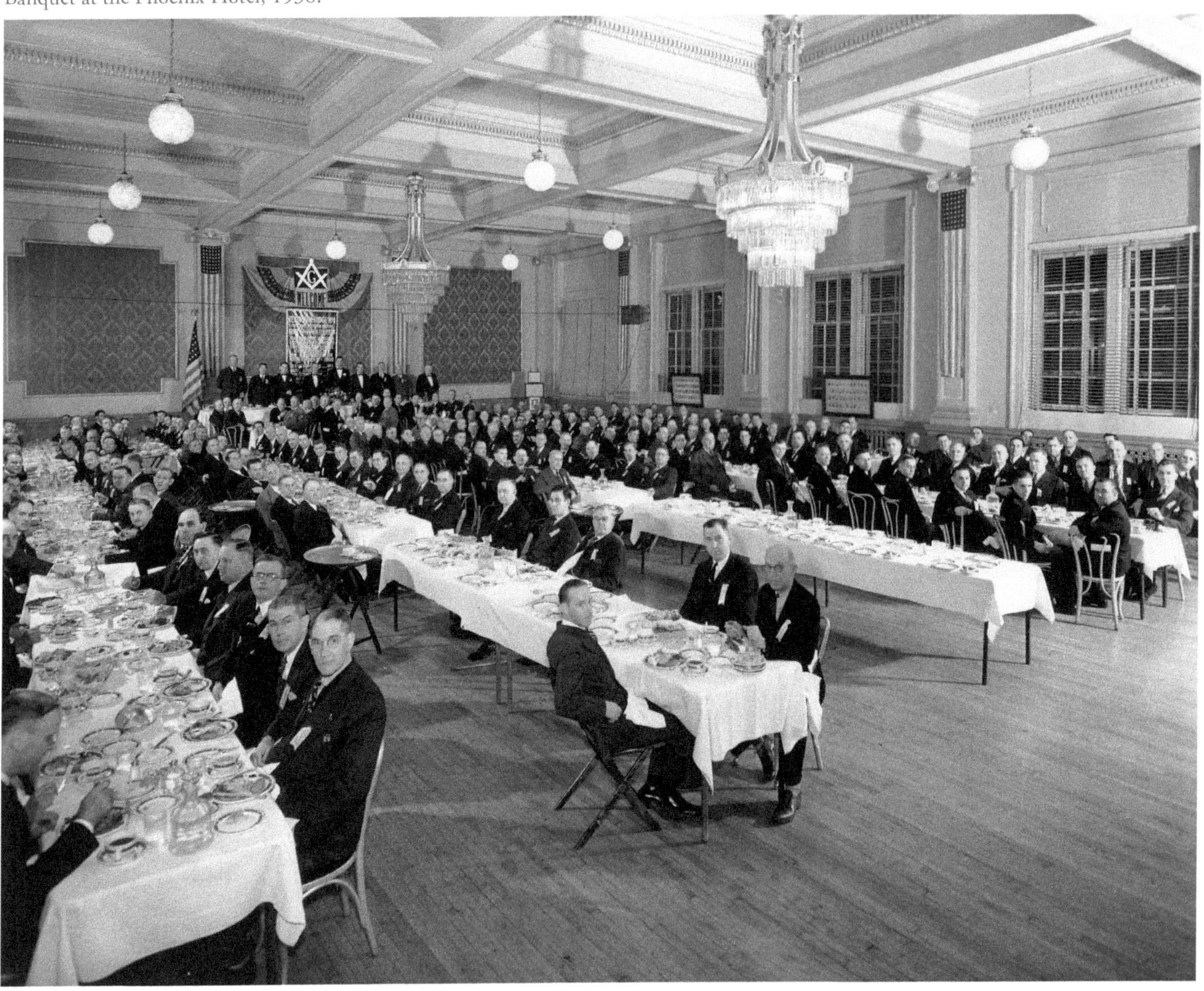

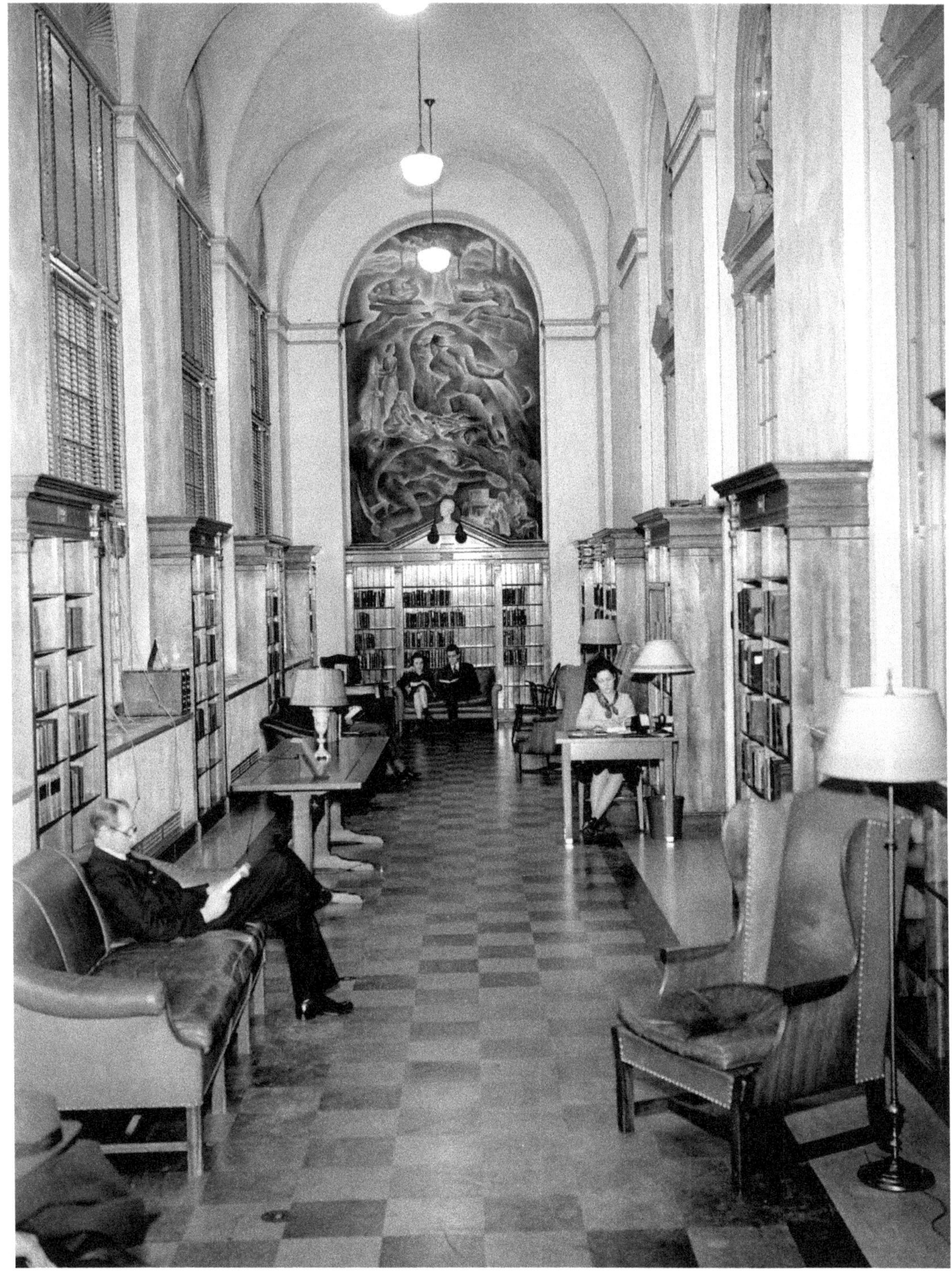

Margaret I. King Library browsing room at the University of Kentucky with Frank W. Long murals, 1939.

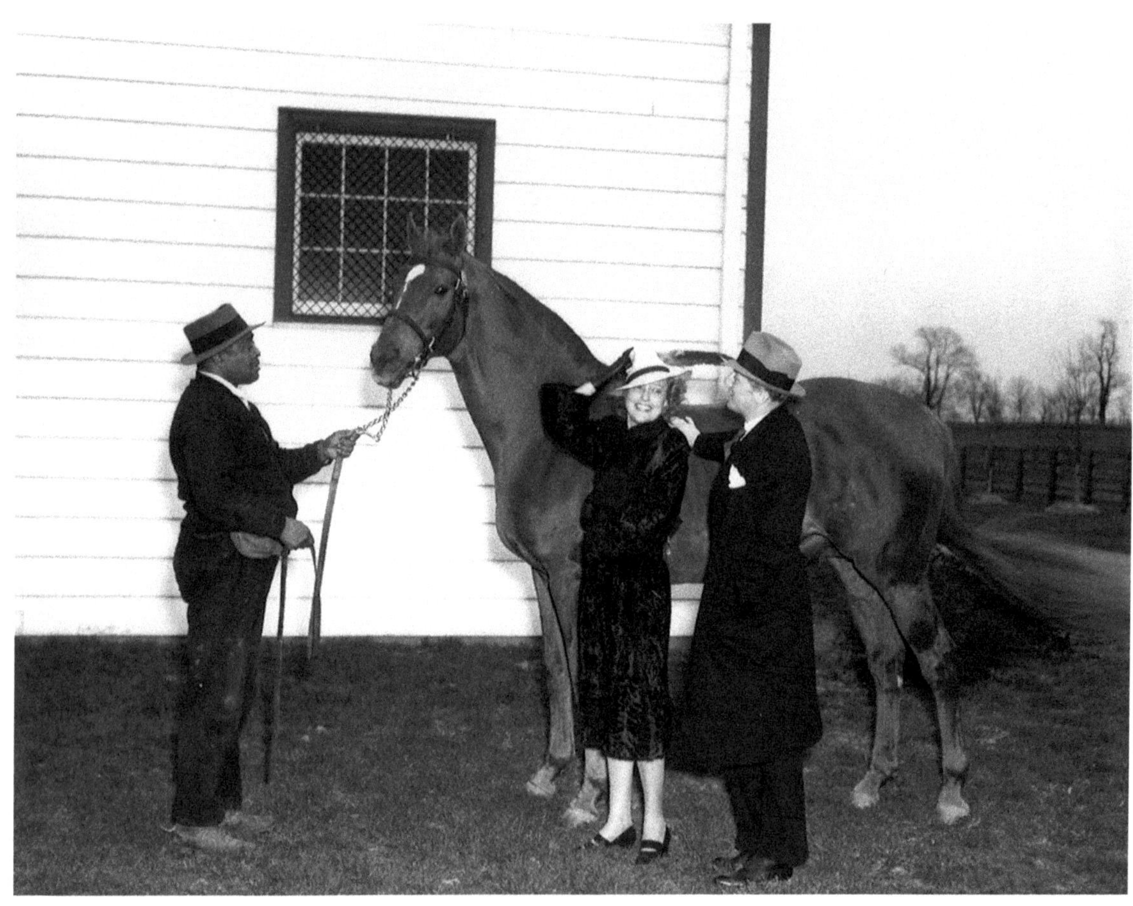

Man O'War and his groom Will Harbut visited by singer-actress Jeannette McDonald, 1939.

American Legion Parade on Main Street, 1931.

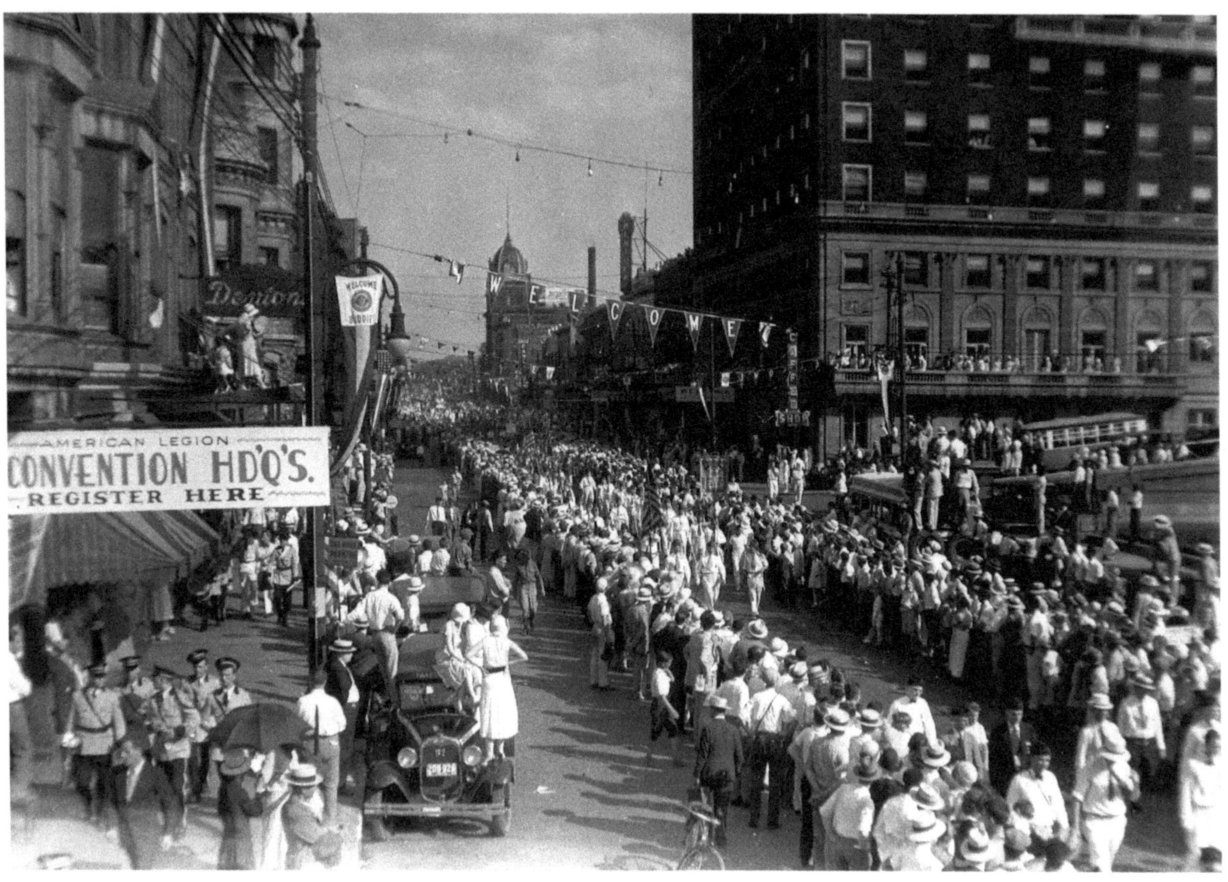

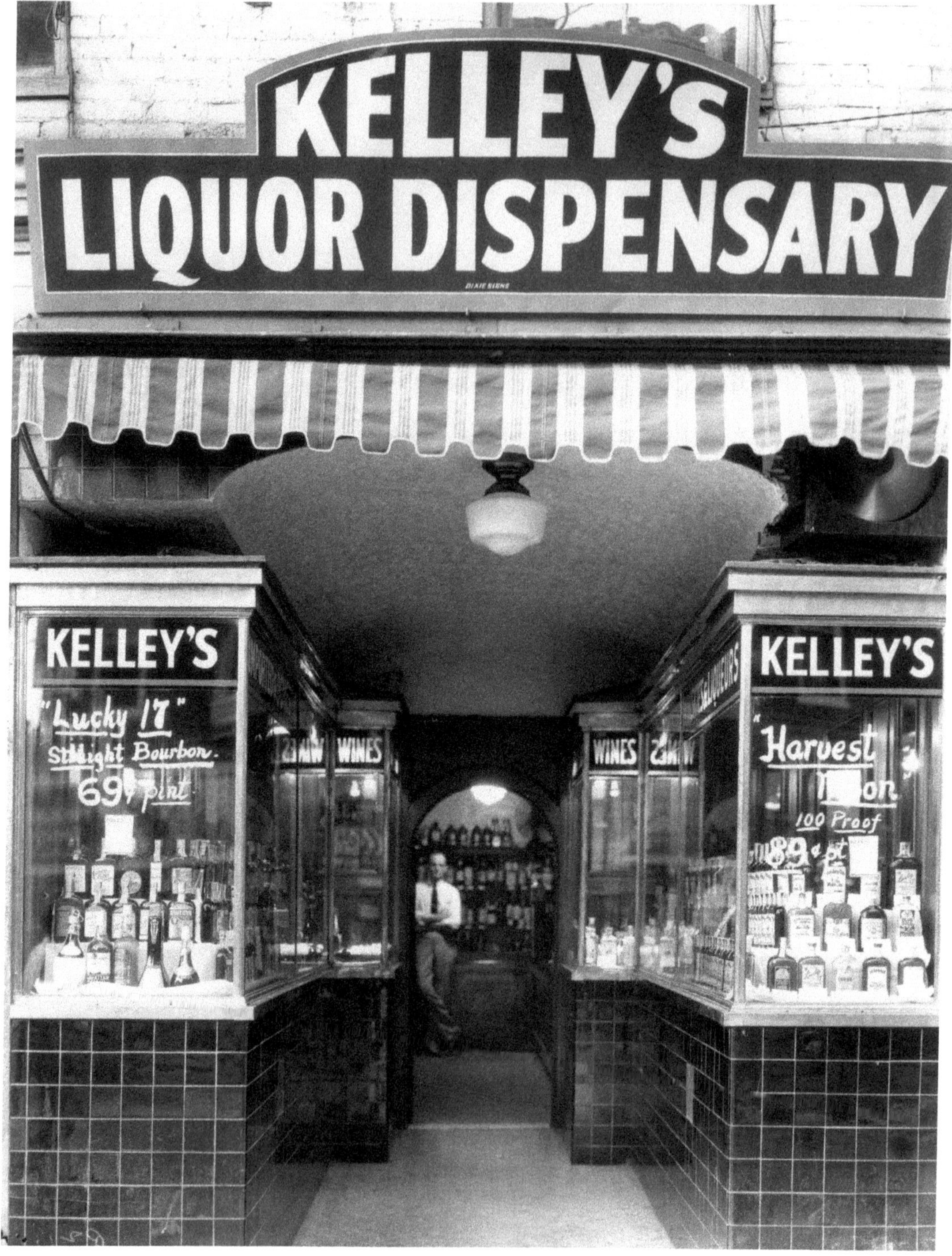


Kelley's Liquor store on Main Street, 1934.

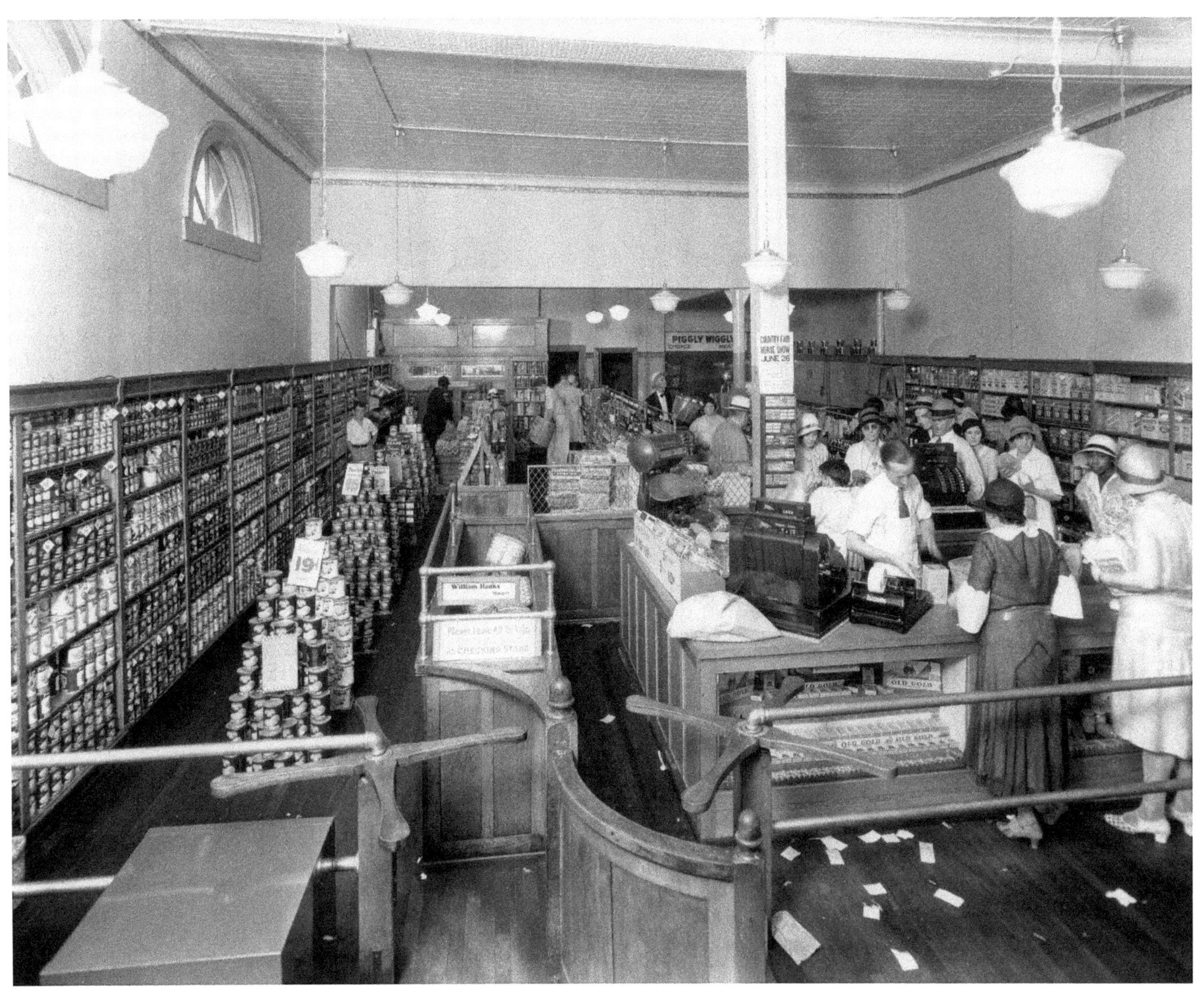


Piggly Wiggly new "self-service" grocery store at Broadway and Short Street, 1920.

Landover Lodge in Fayette Park, 1927.

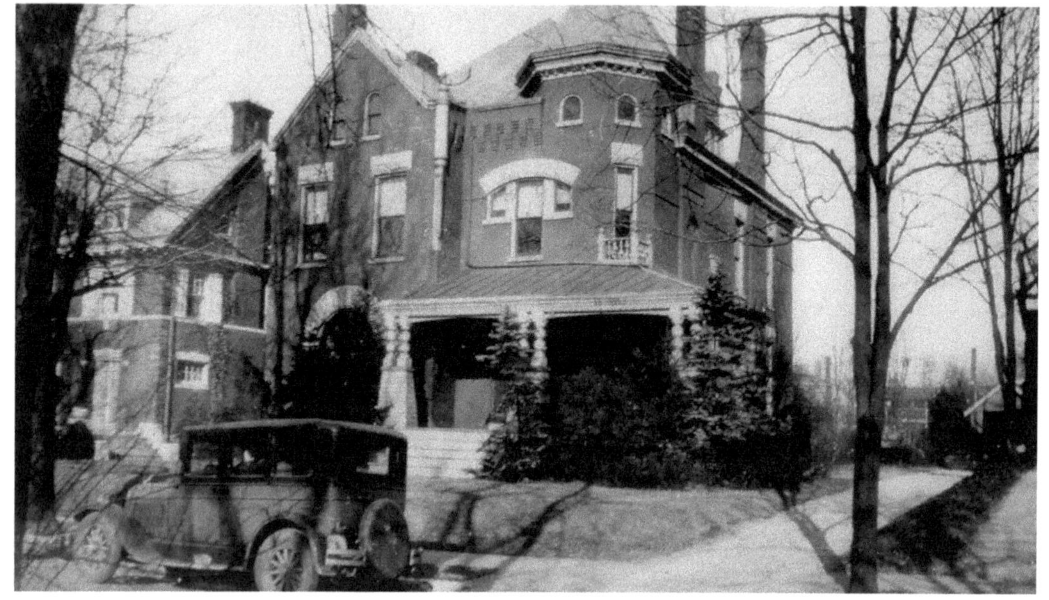

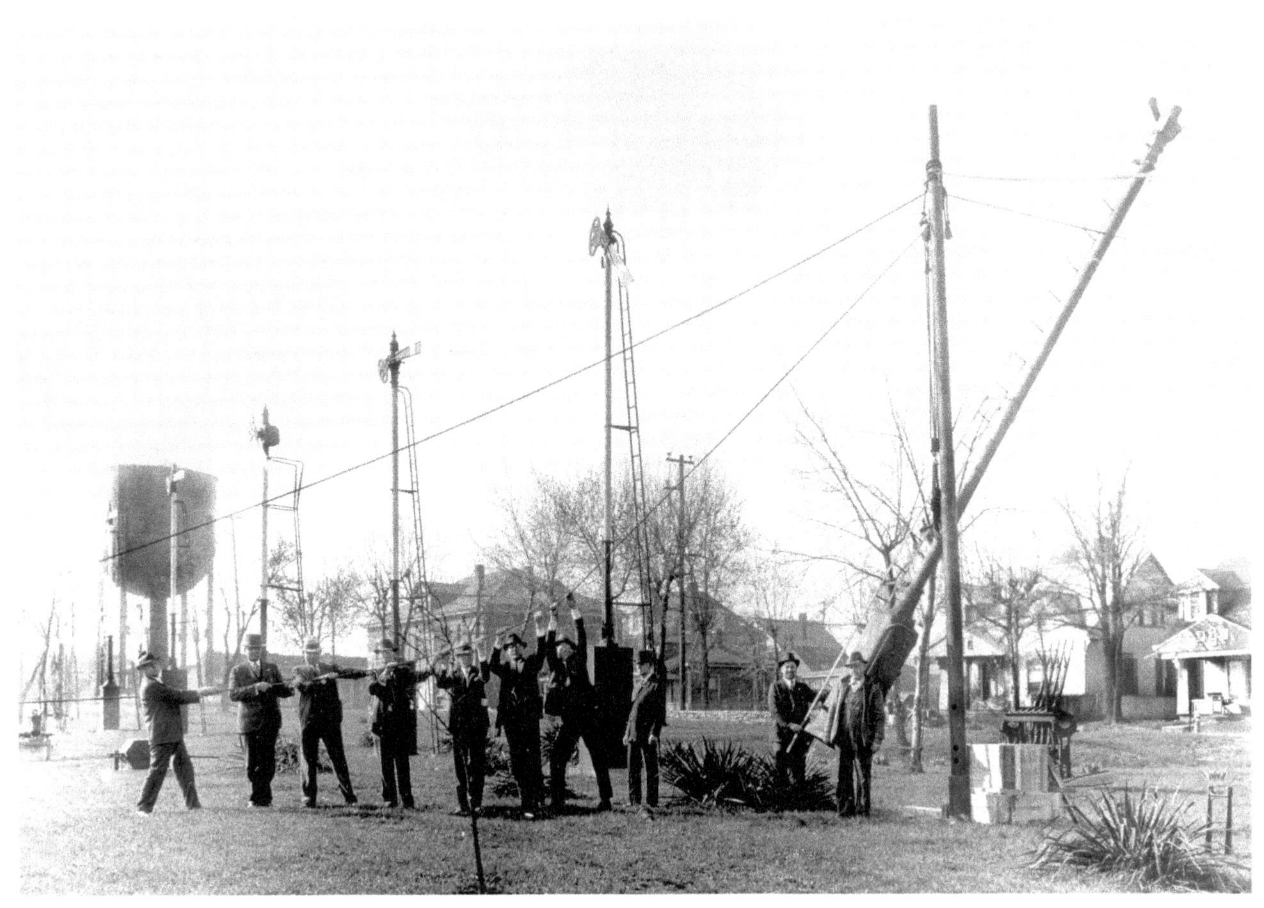

Hoisting a signal near Southern Station in Lexington in the 1930's.

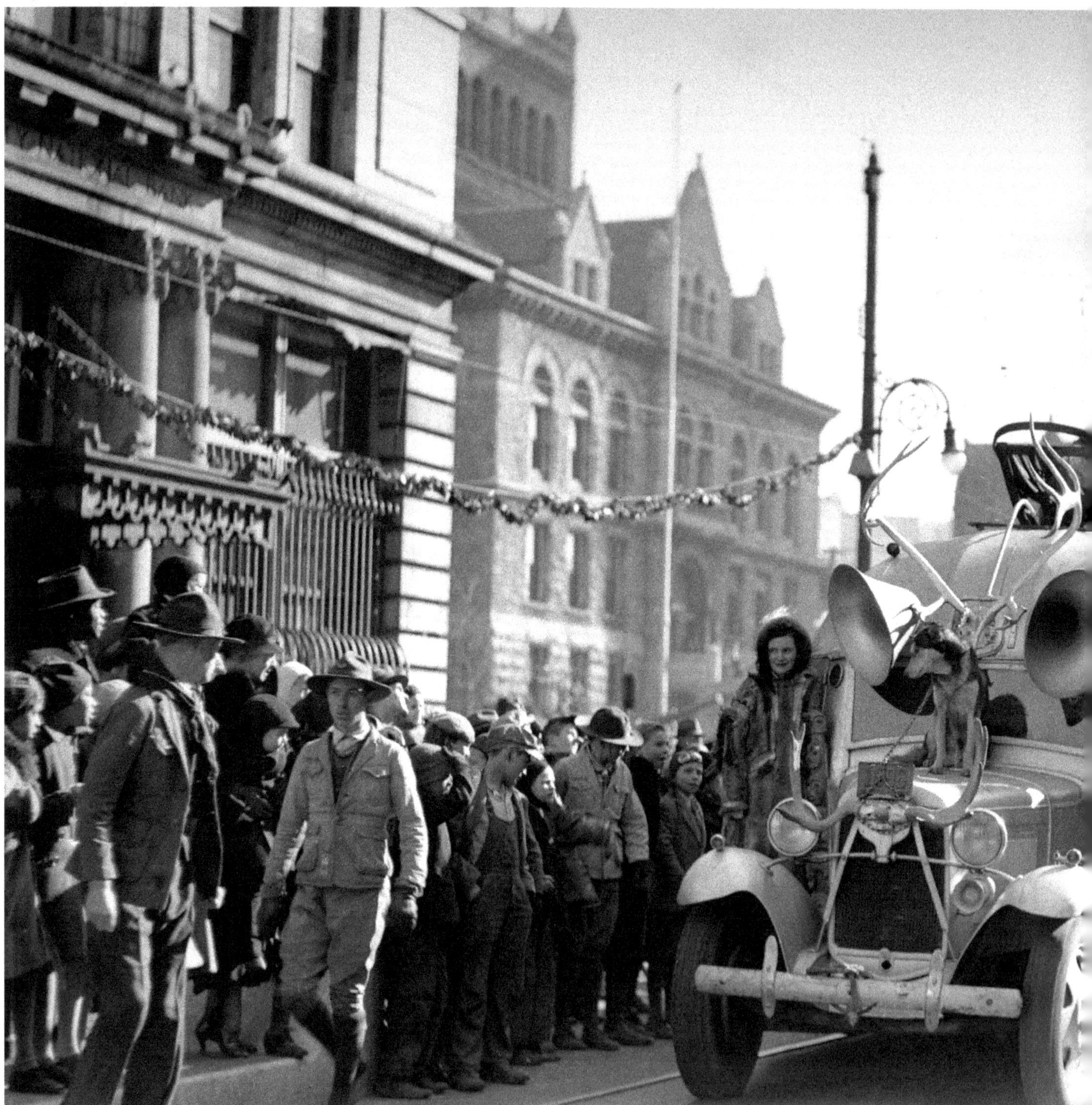

Christmas Parade on Main Street, 1935.

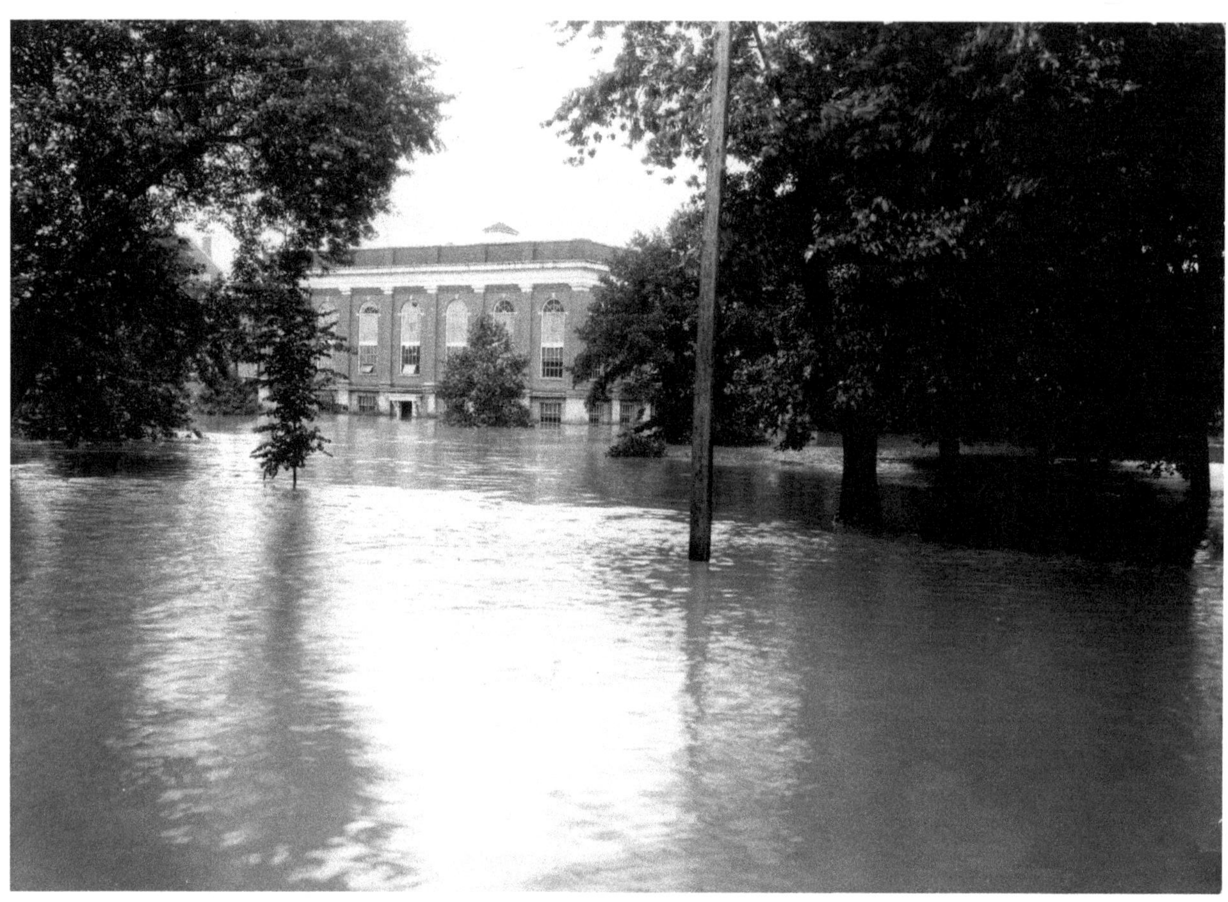

Flooded Alumni Gymnasium at the University of Kentucky, 1928.

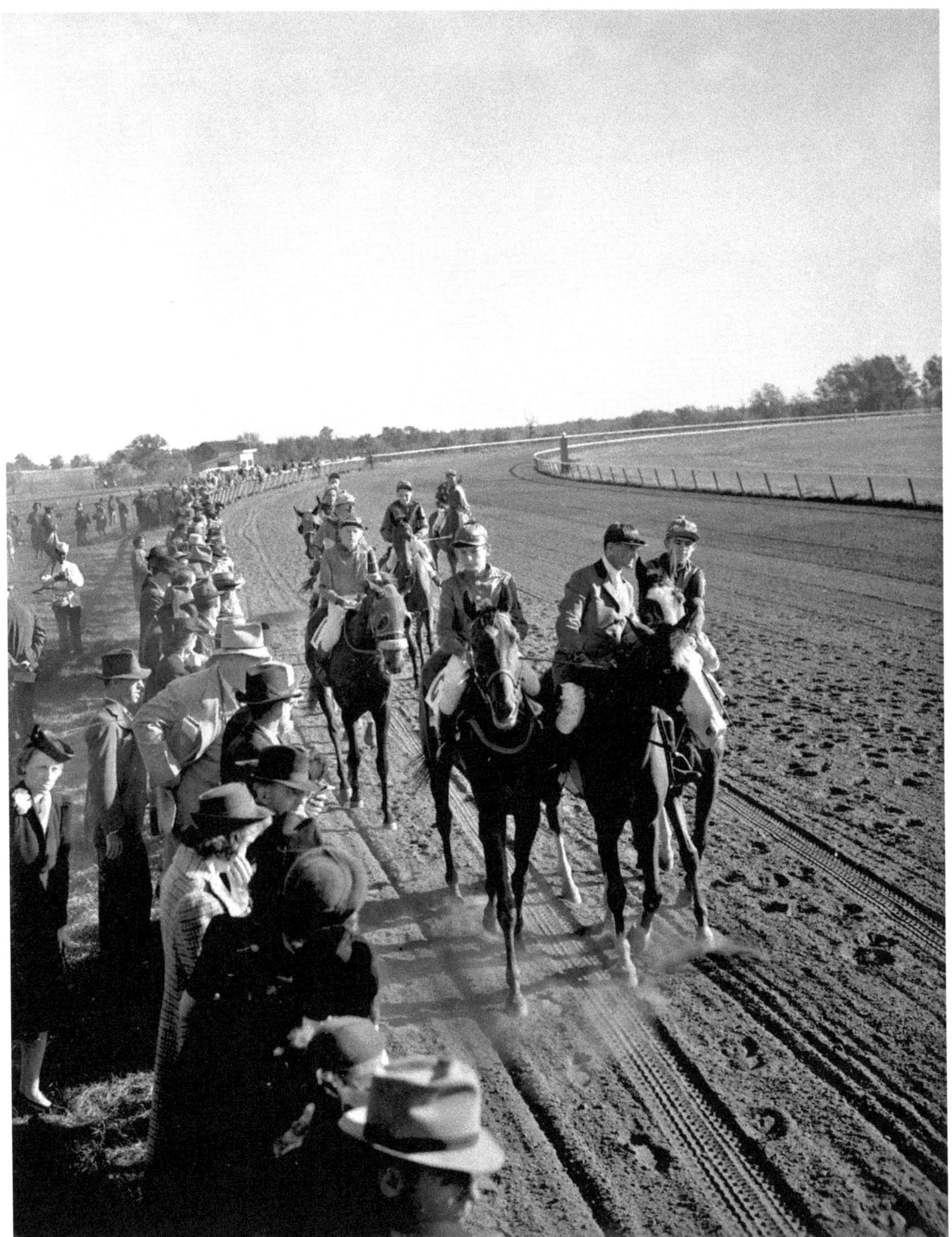

Prior to race at Keeneland,
1939.

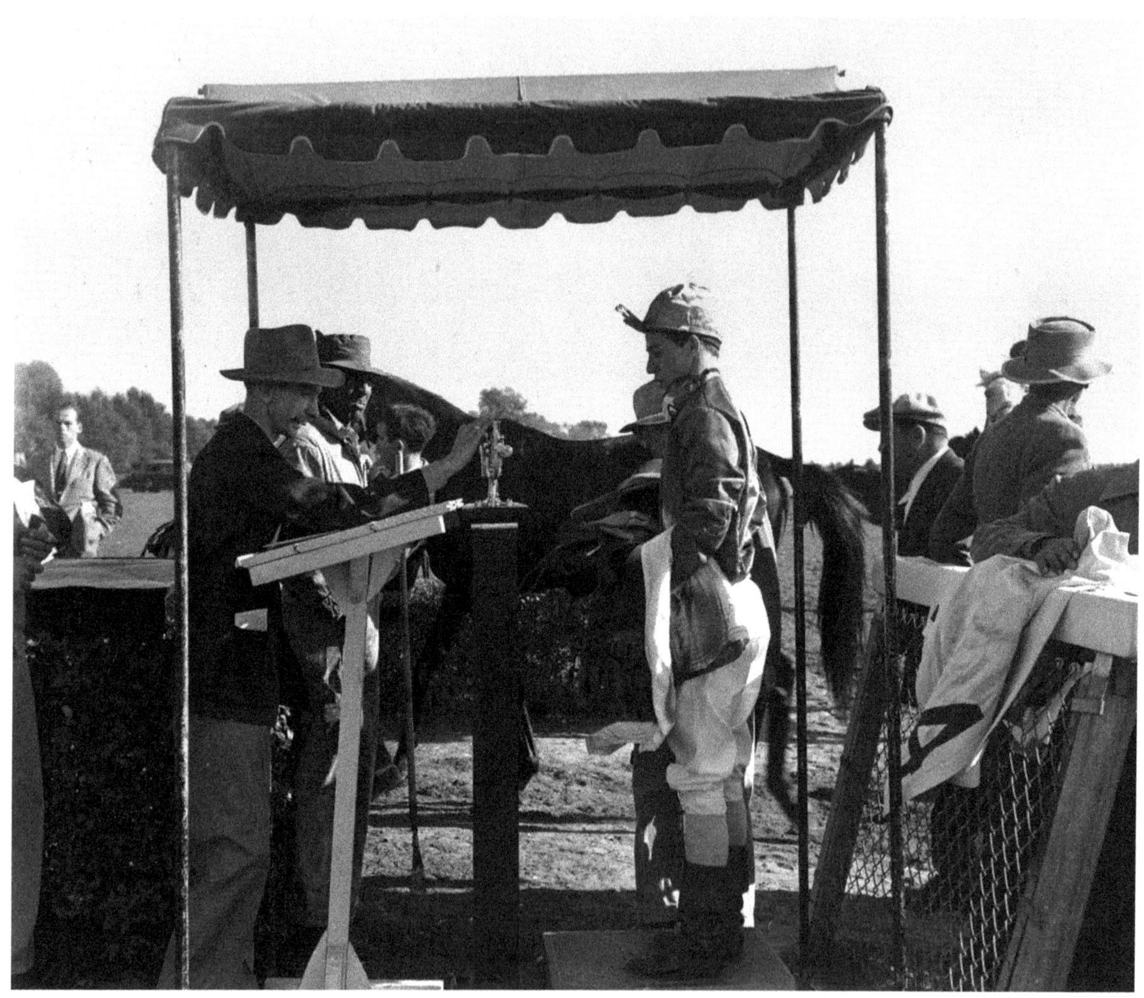

Jockey weighing out at Keeneland, 1939.

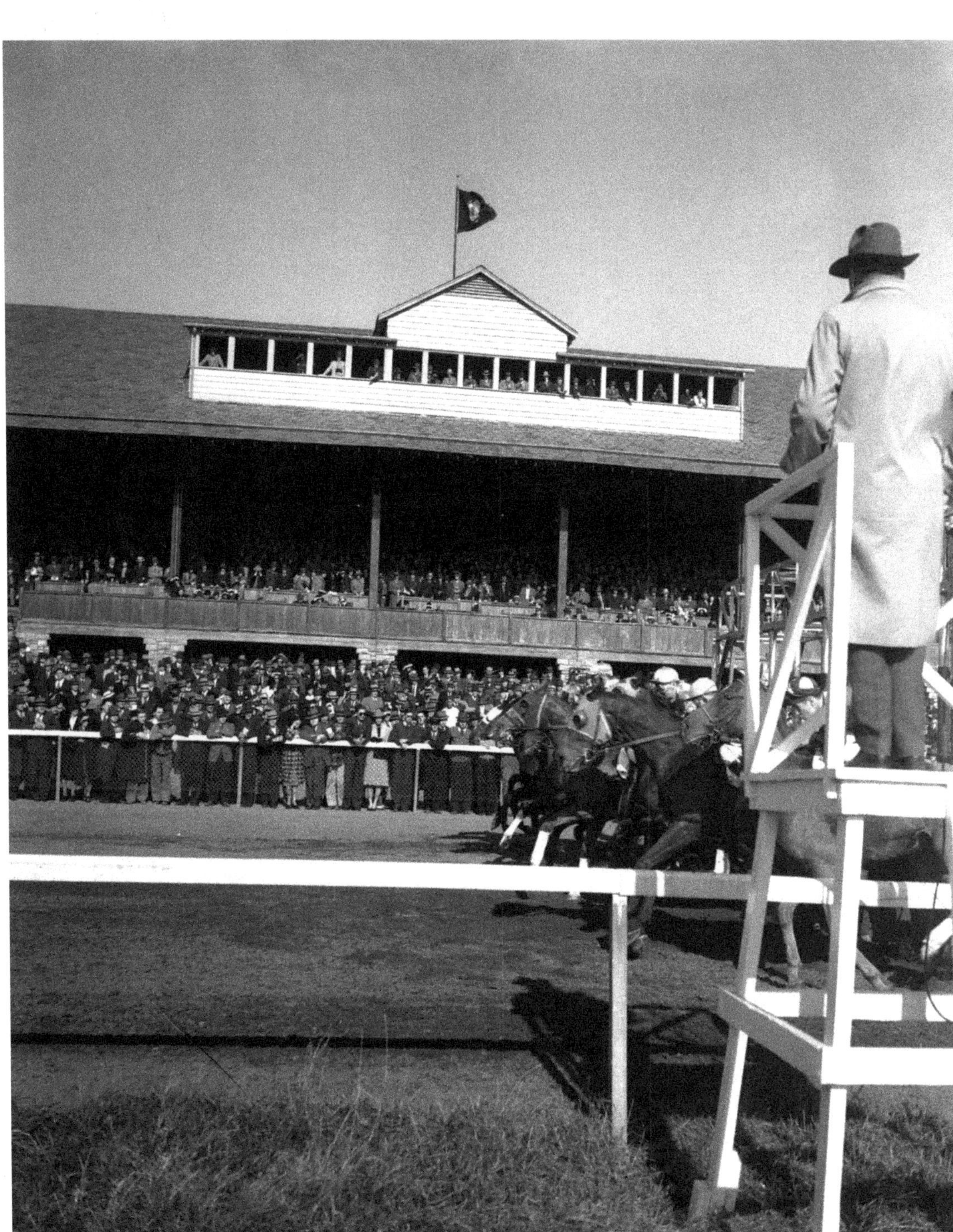

At the start of a race, Keeneland, 1939.

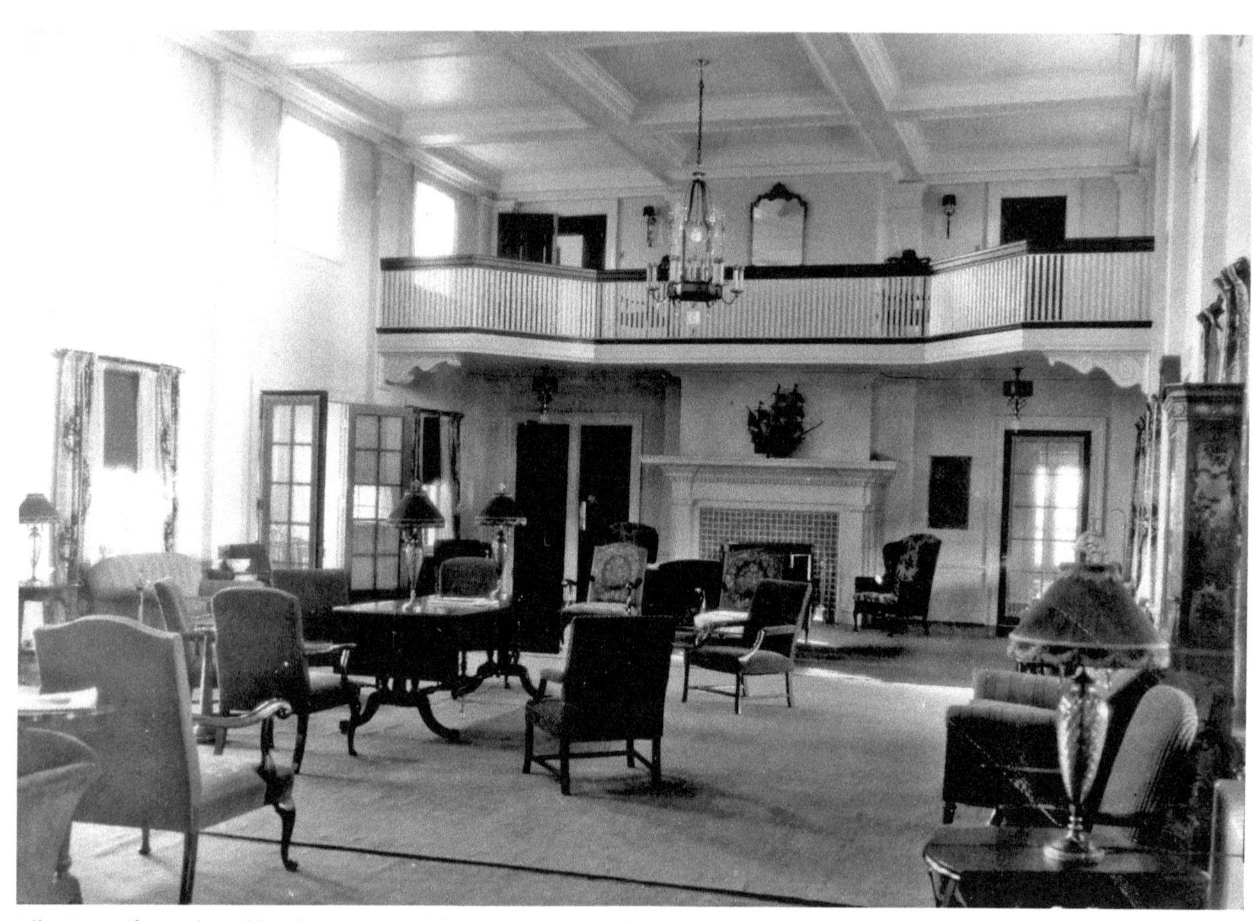

Idle Hour (formerly Ashland) Country Club interior, mid 20$^{th}$ century.

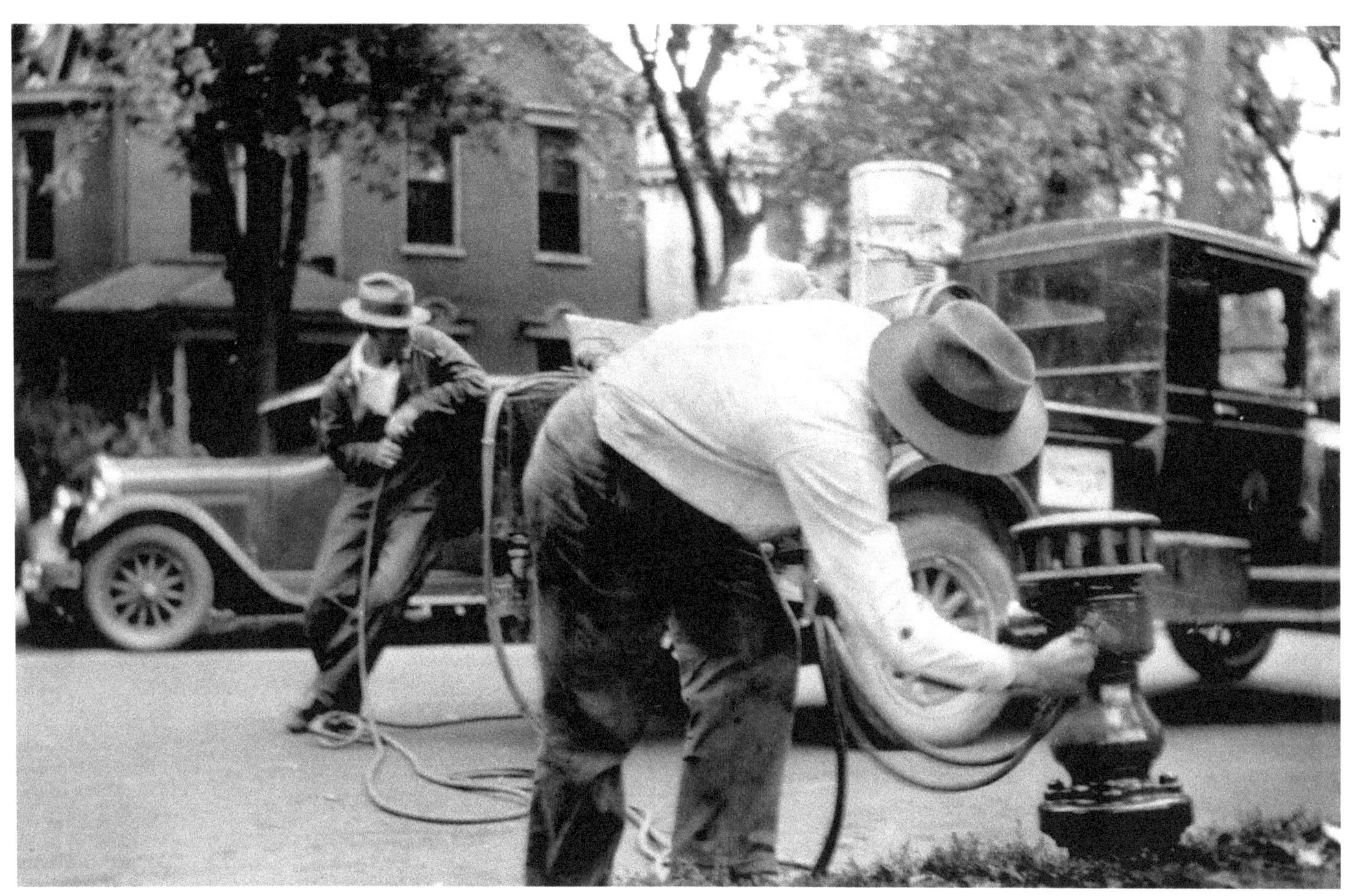

Checking a fire hydrant in the 1930's.

Professor Granville Terrel and his horse Katy arrive at the University of Kentucky after a 610 mile ride, 1927.

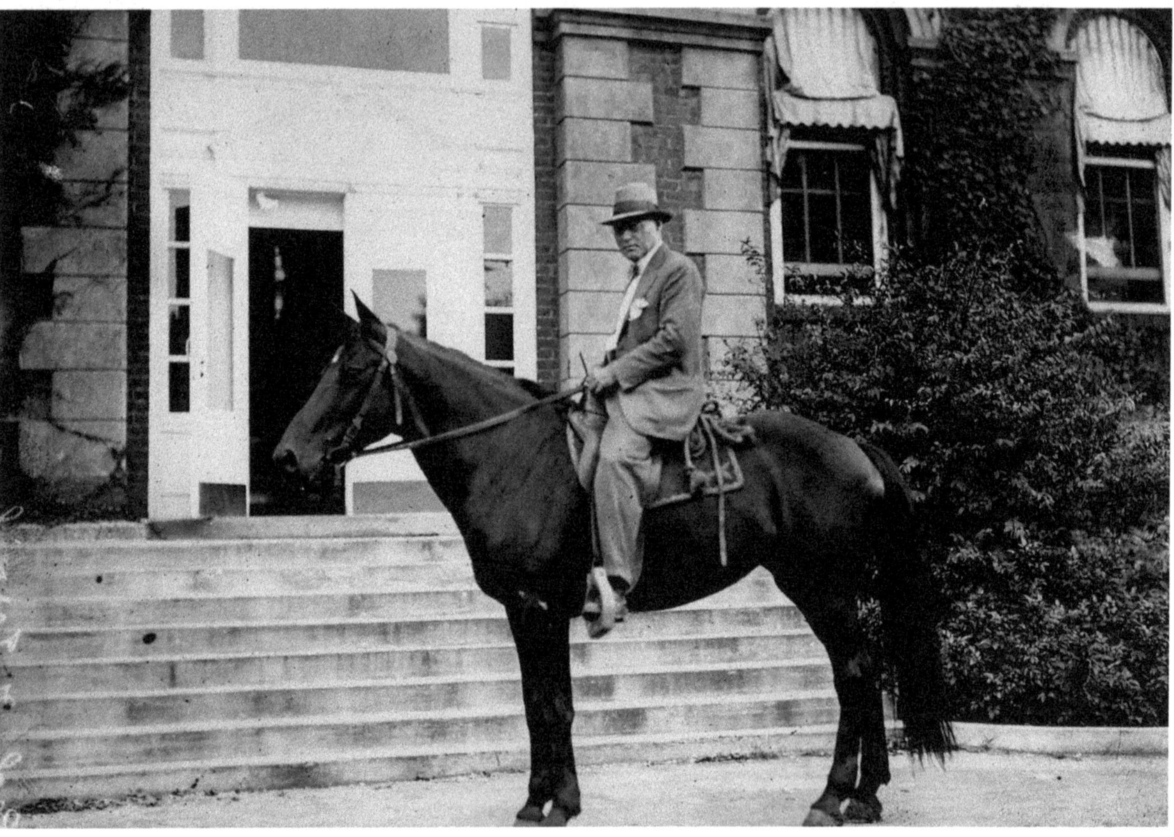

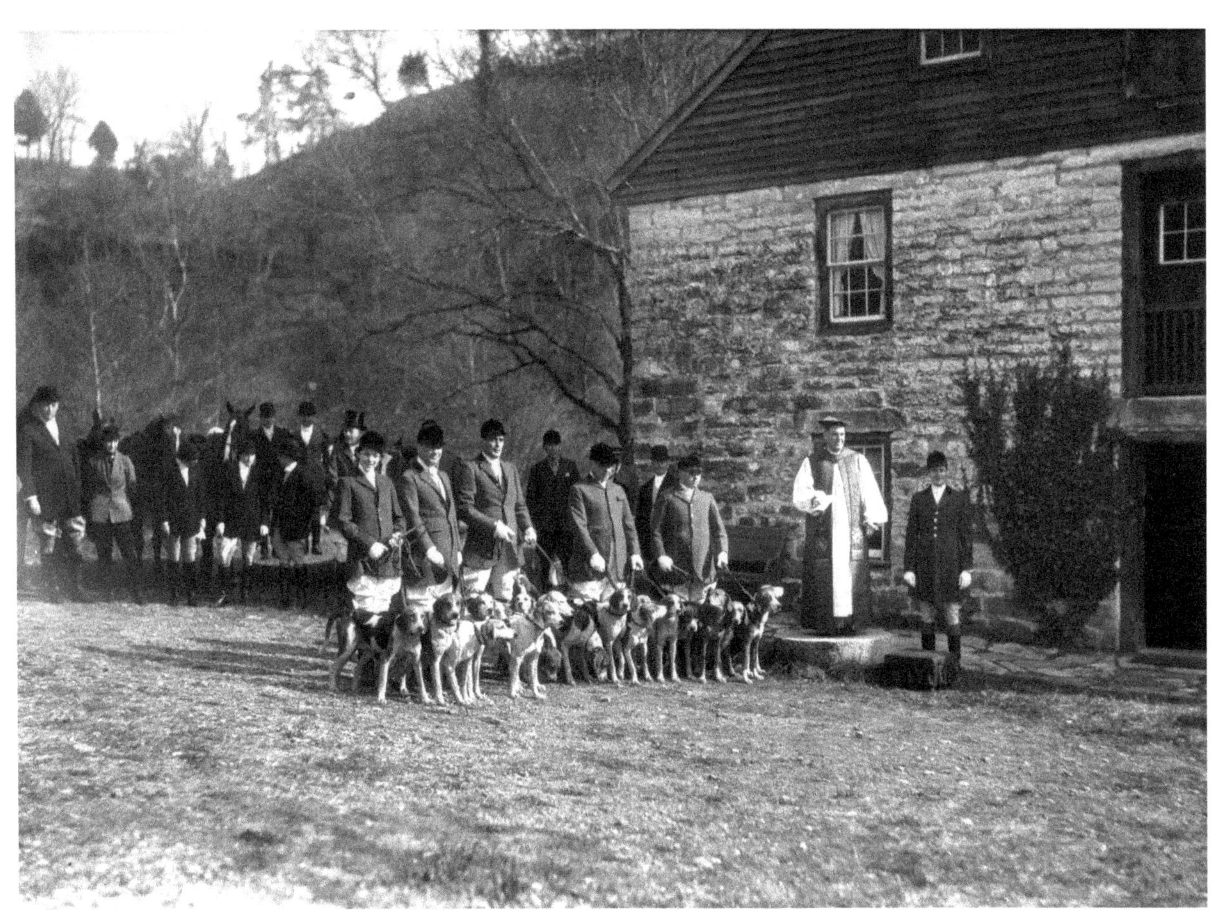

Bishop Abbott officiates at the Iroquois Hunt Club's
second Blessing of the Hounds, 1933.

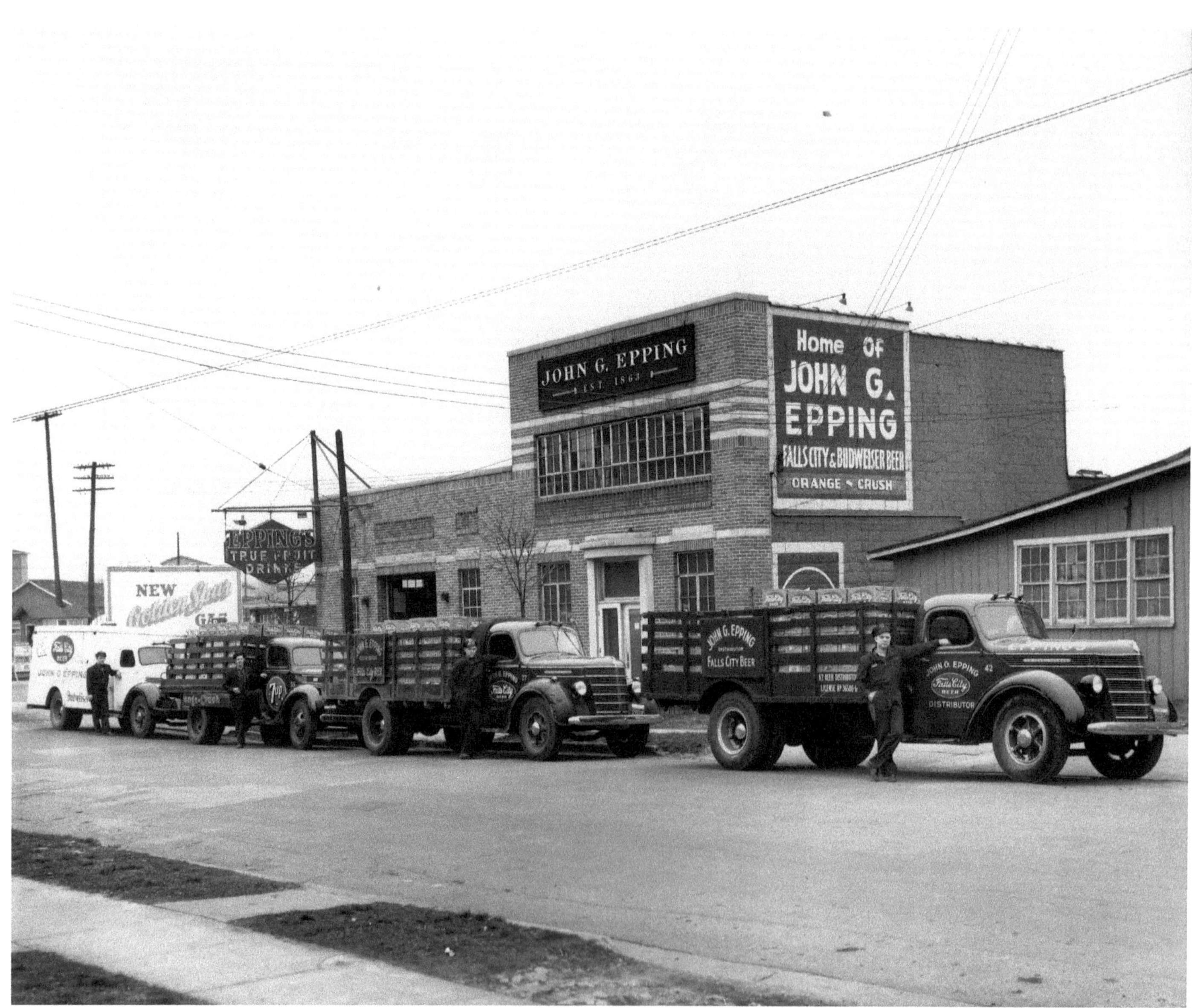

John G. Epping Bottling Works, March 1942.

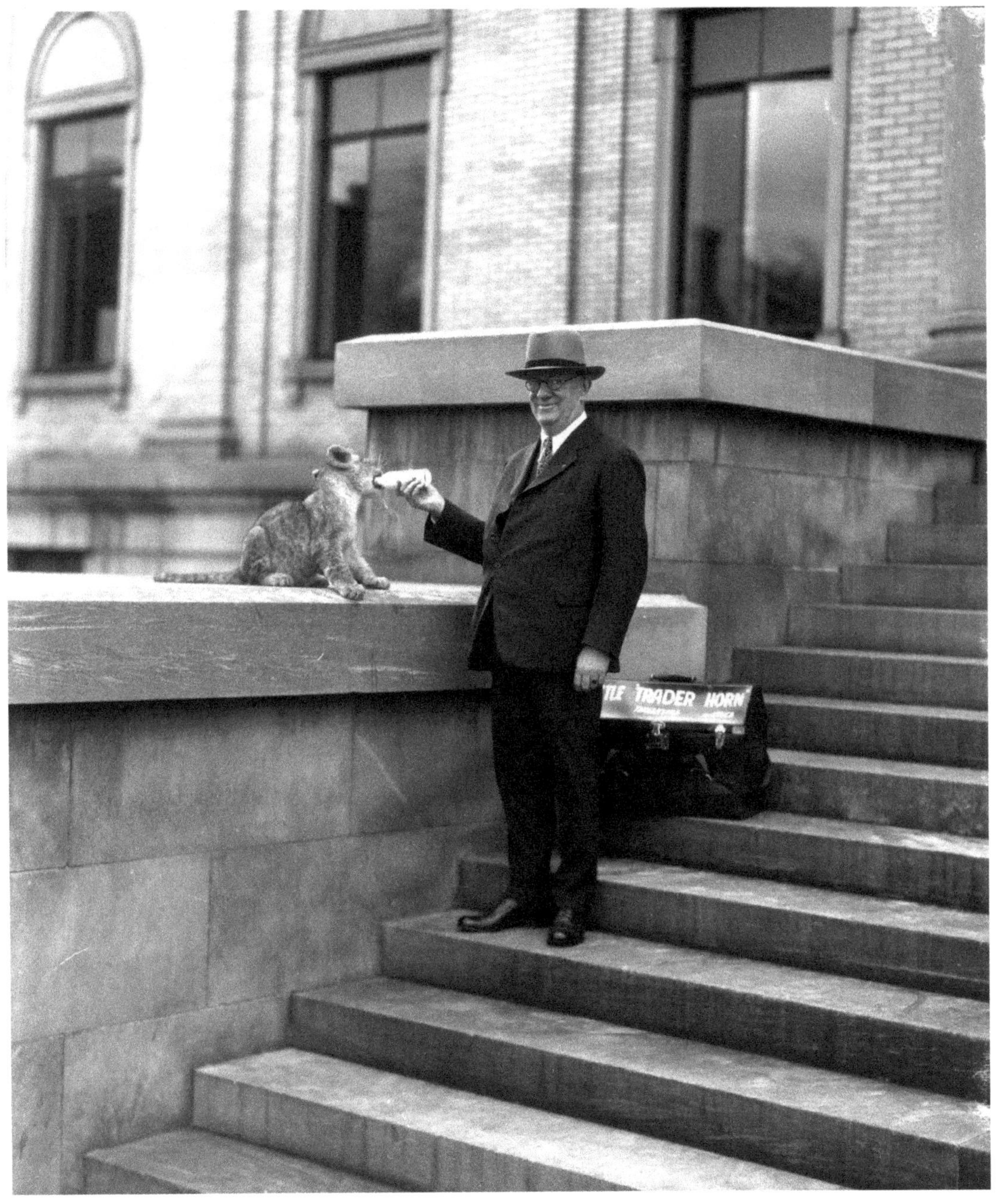


Mayor O'Brien and lion cub promote a film from the steps of City Hall, 1931.

Main Street in flood, 1928.

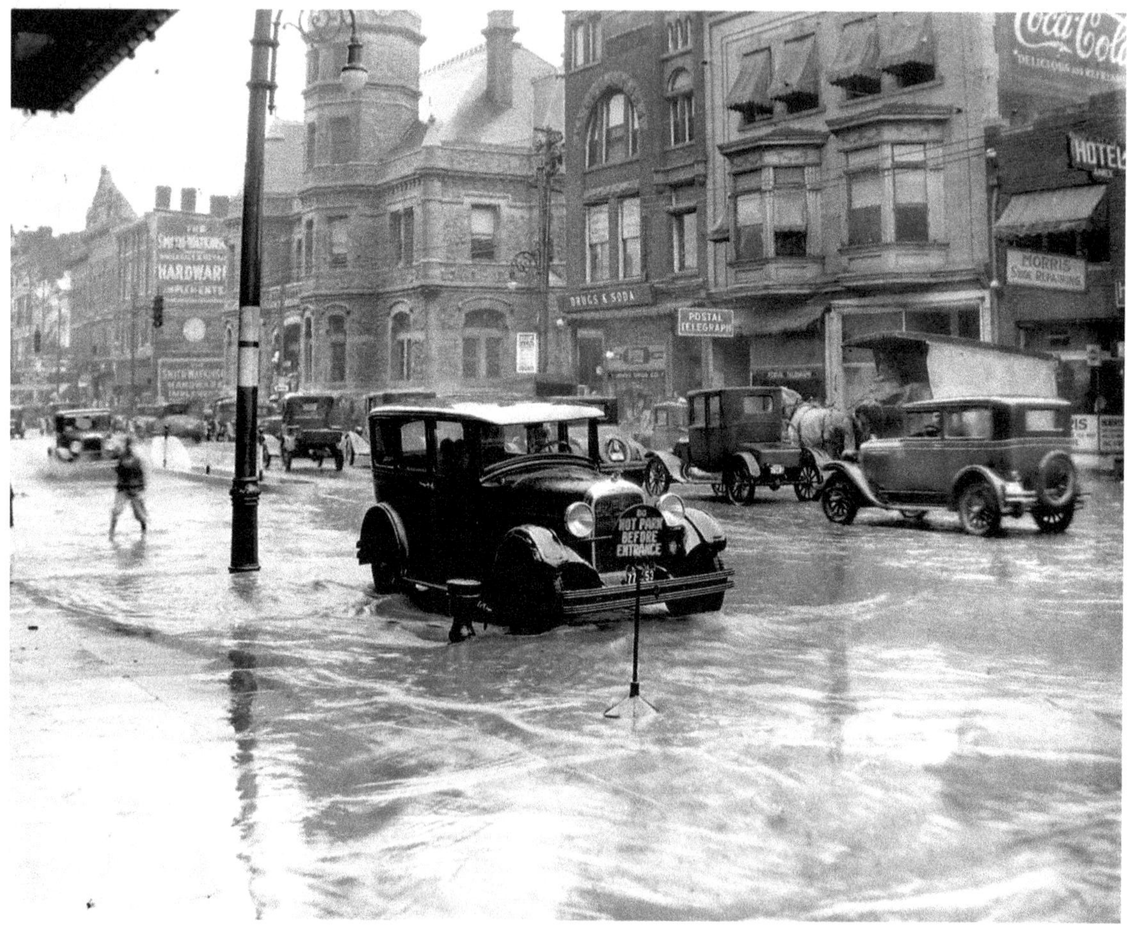

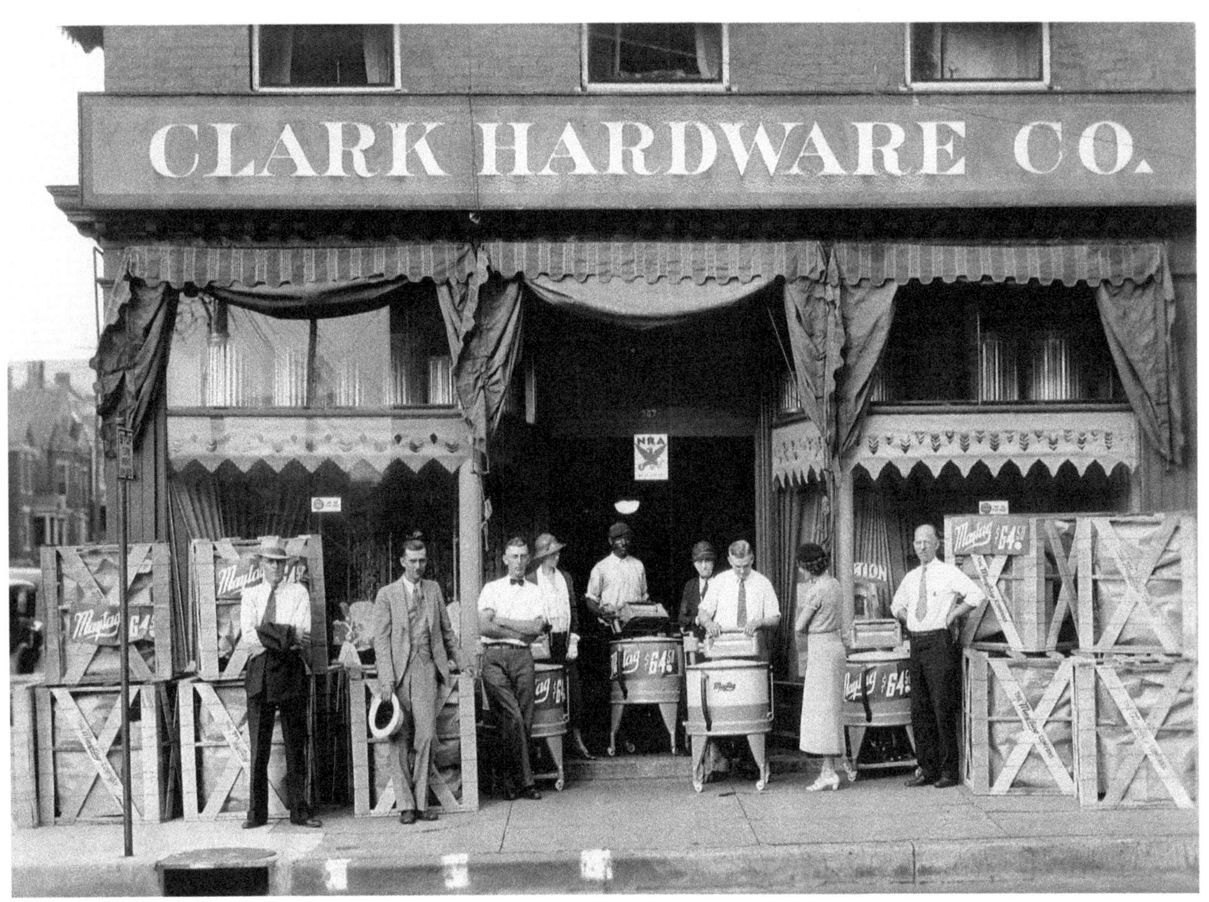


Clark's Hardware Store in 1933 after the arrival of a new shipment of Maytag washers.

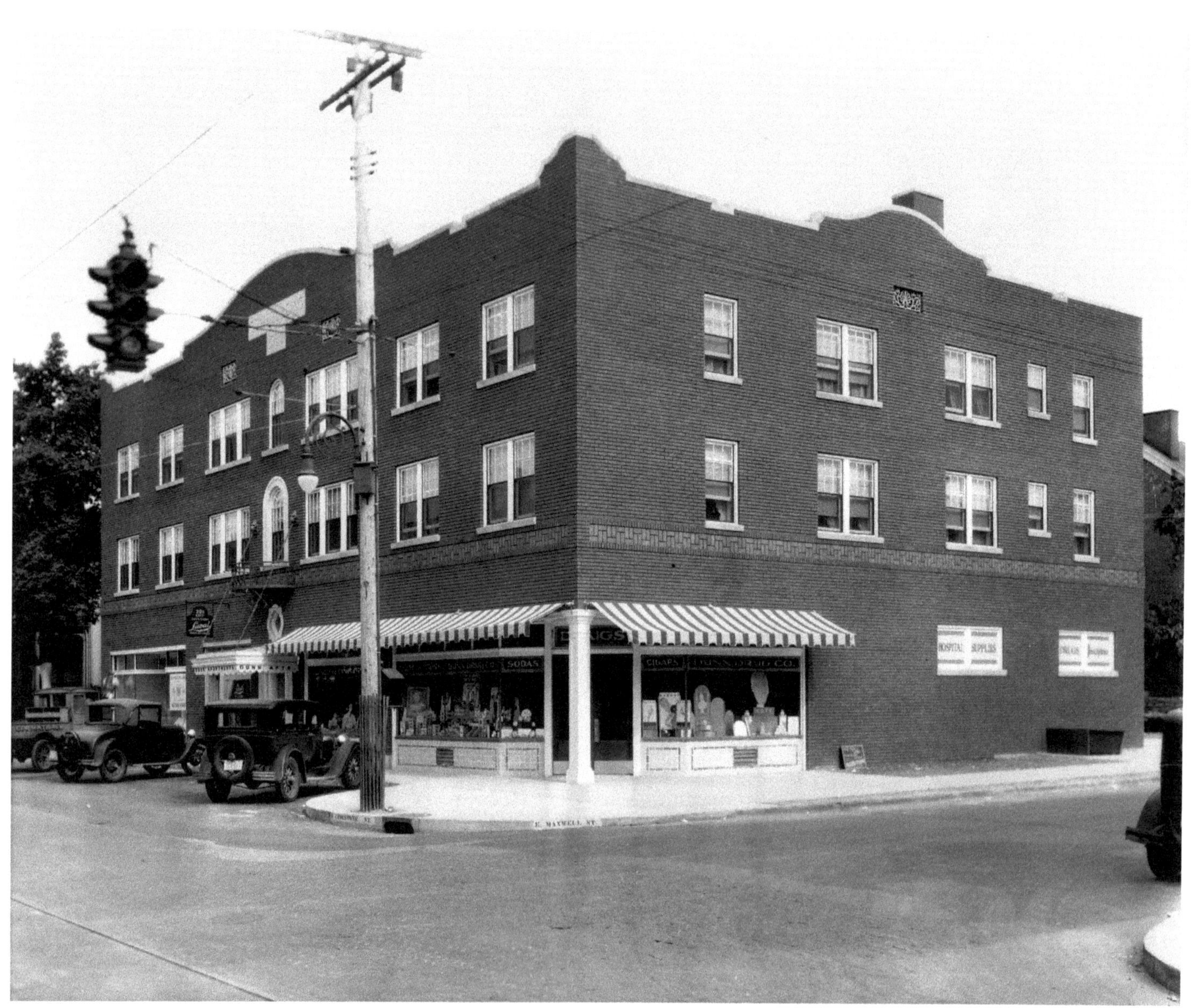

Dunn's Drug Store on South Limestone Street.

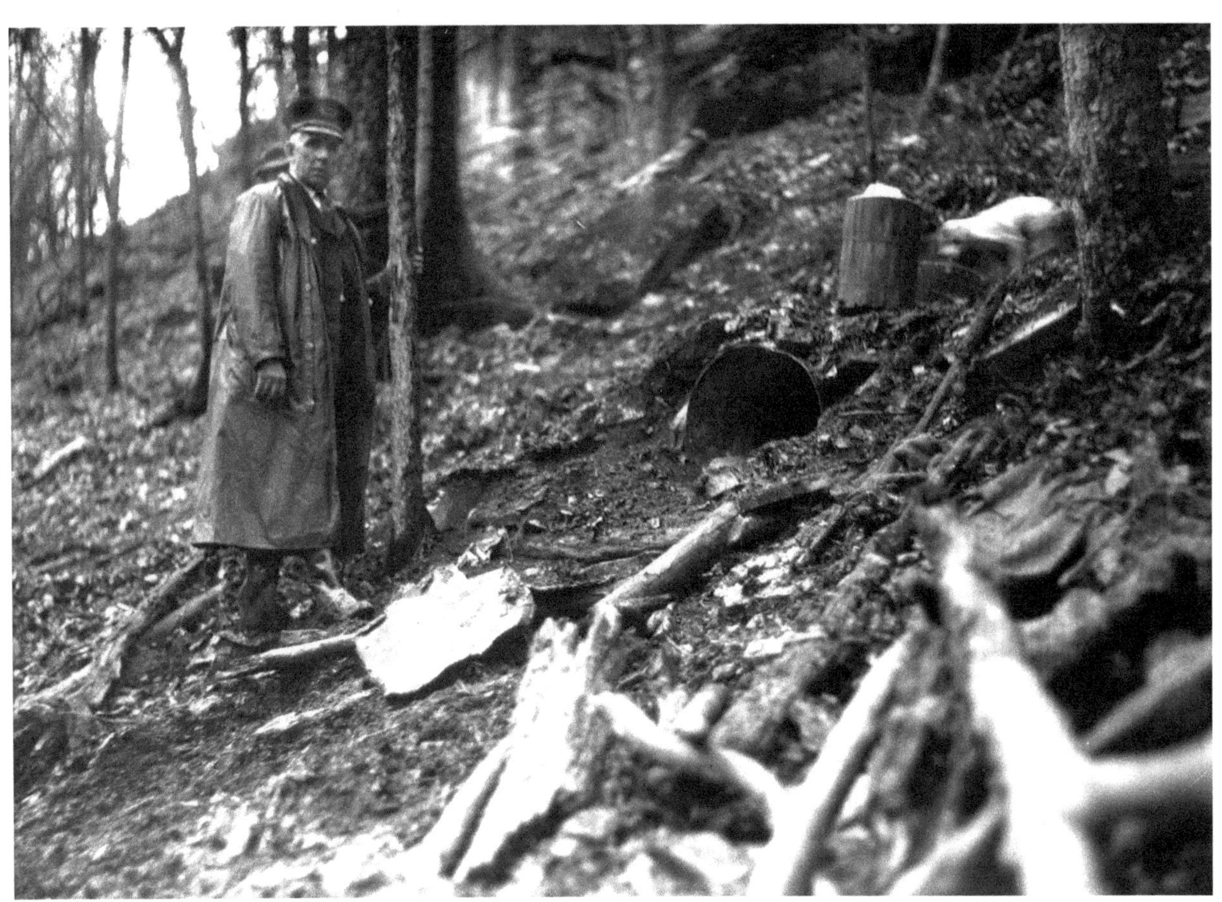

Raid on a moonshine still, 1931.

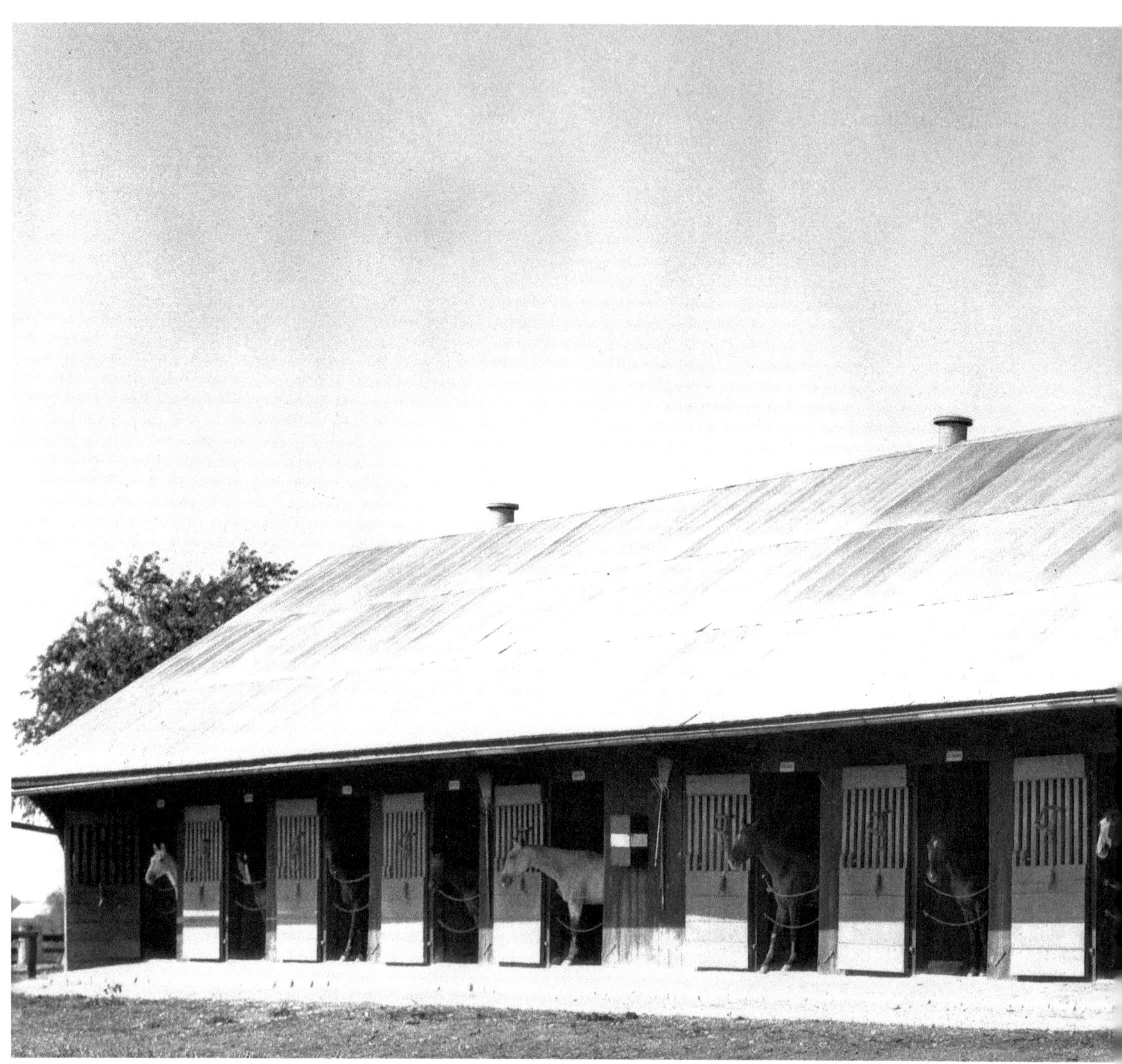

Barn at Hamburg Place, 1932.

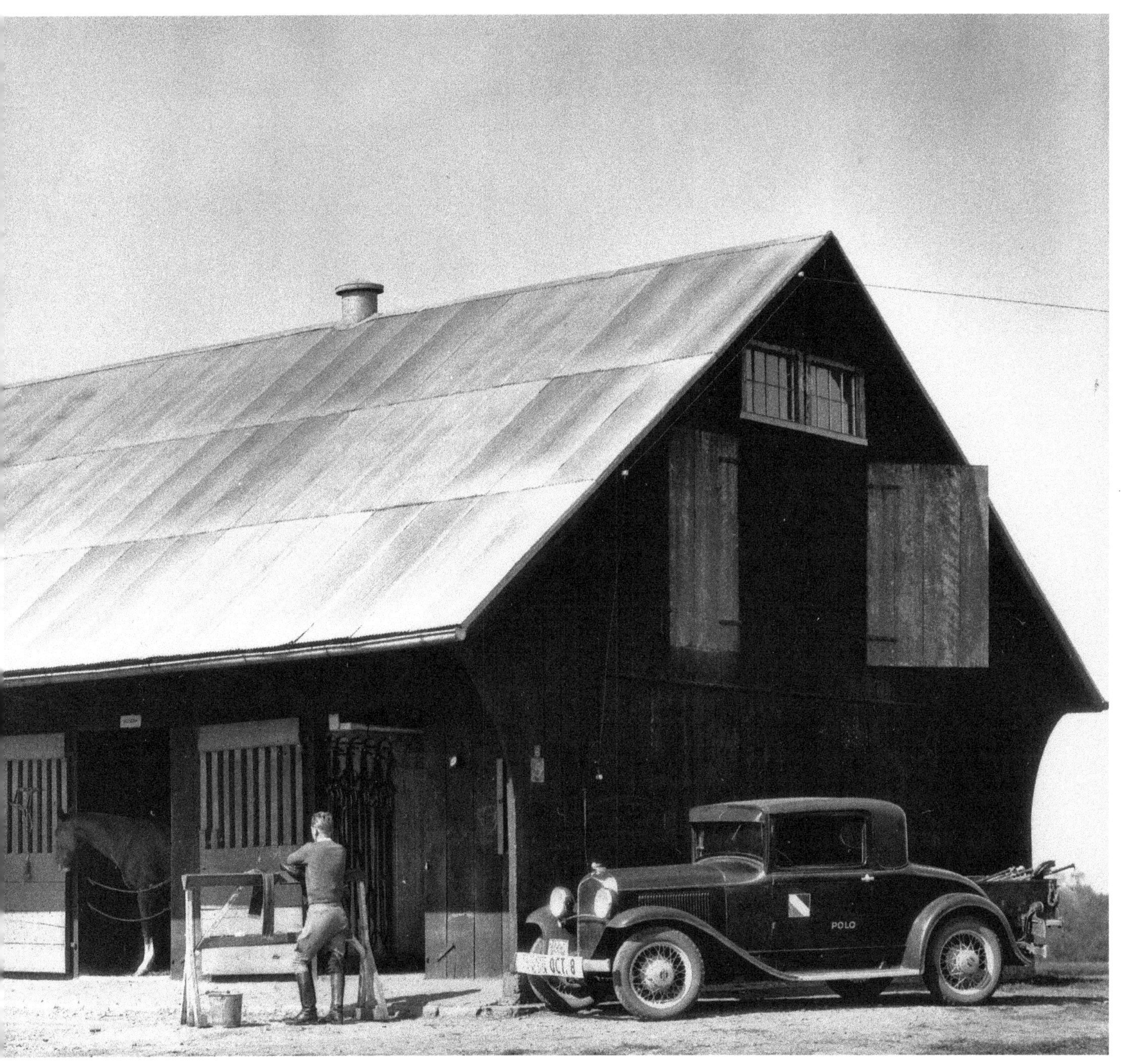
POLO
OCT. 8

Golfer Marion Miley and Mayor Thompson, 1935.

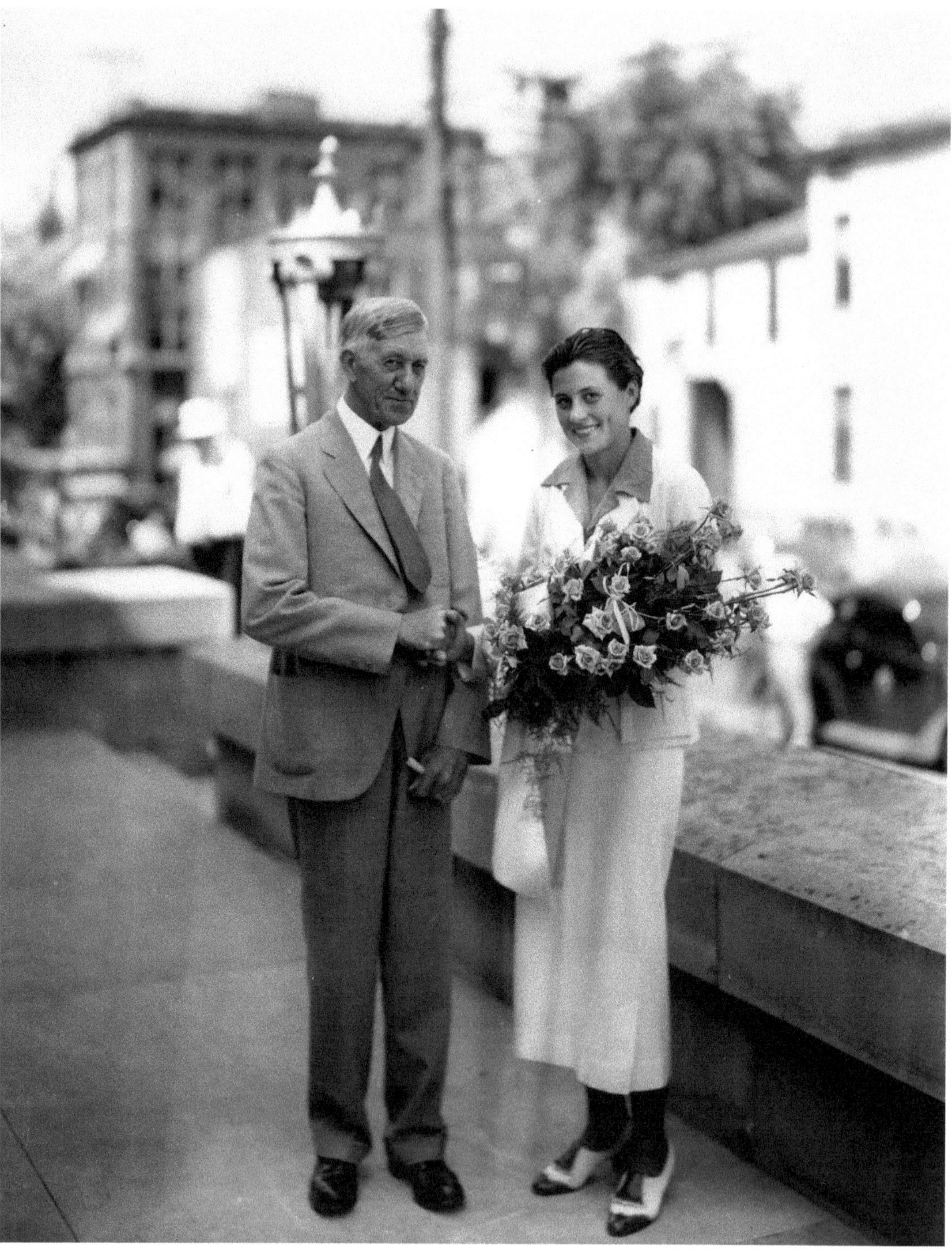

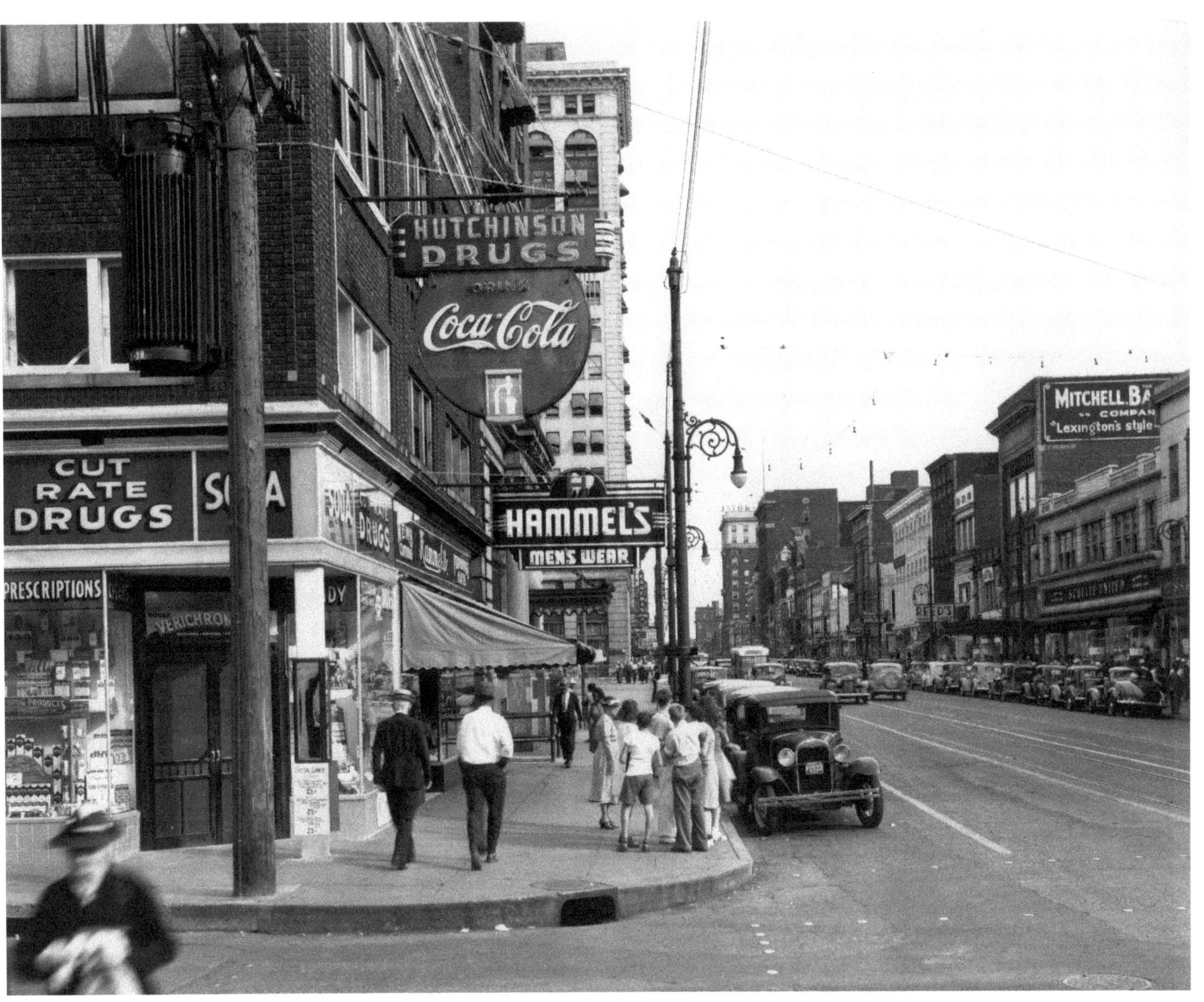


Hutchinson Drugs' West Main Street store (they had another store on East Main) with the Lafayette and new Phoenix Hotels in the distance, 1939.

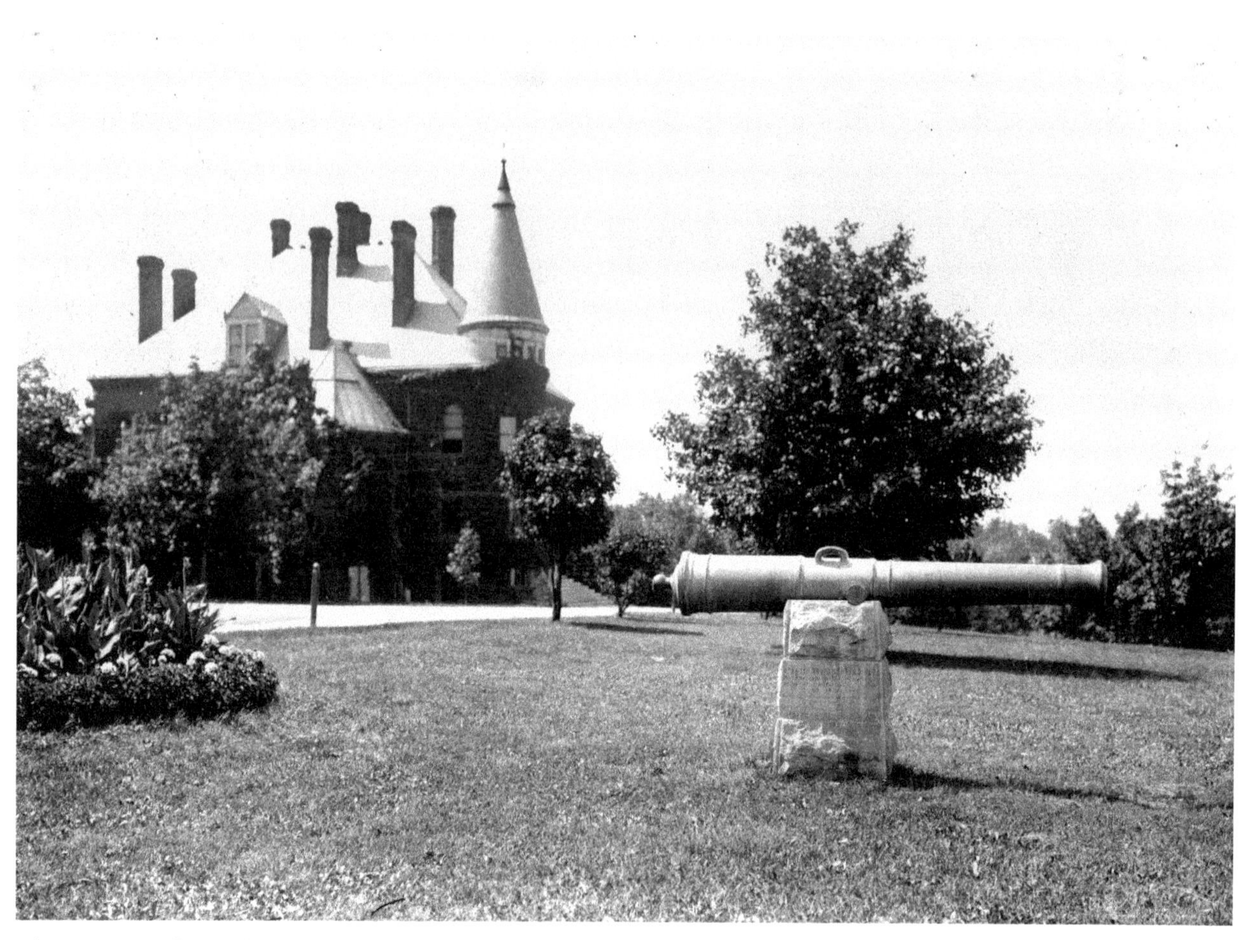

The cannon in front of the Main Building, used in the Spanish-American War.

Celebration at the Kentucky Theater, 1930.

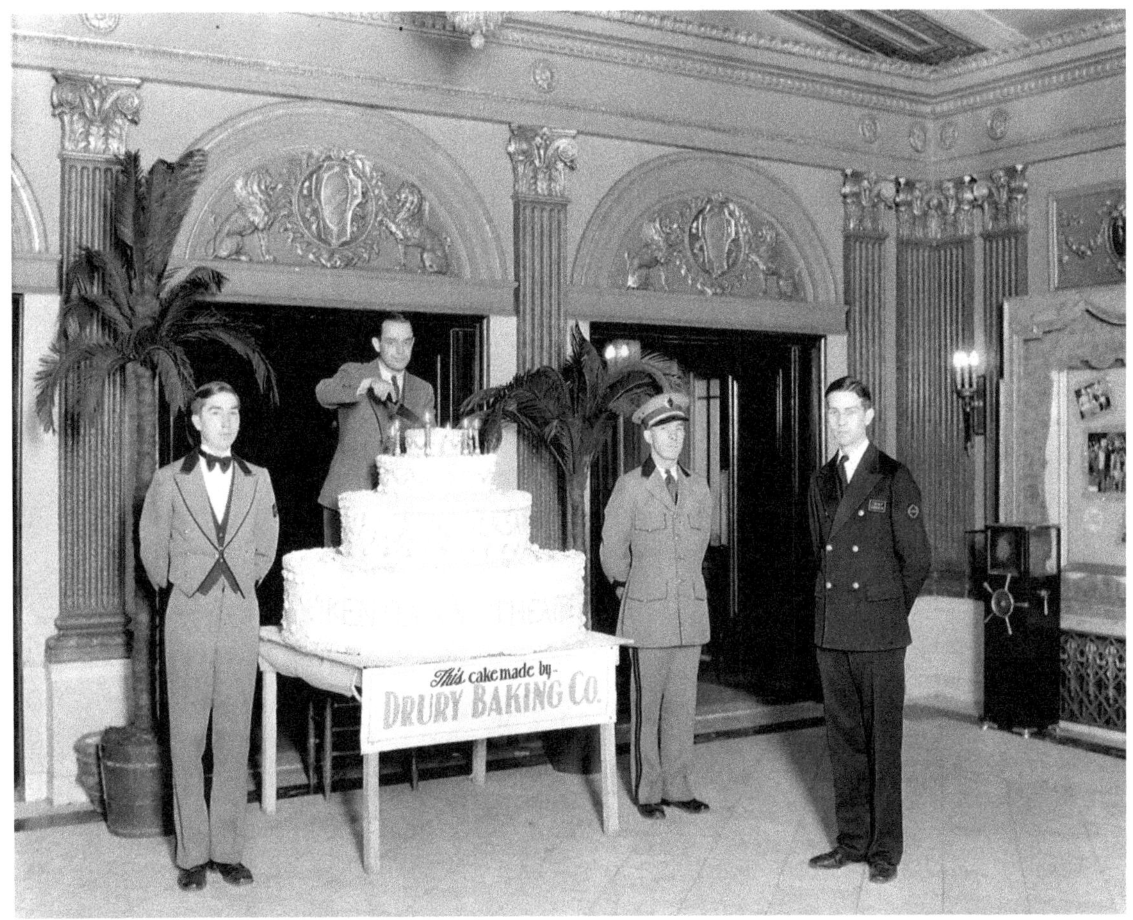

"Split" Democratic Convention on Cheapside, 1936.

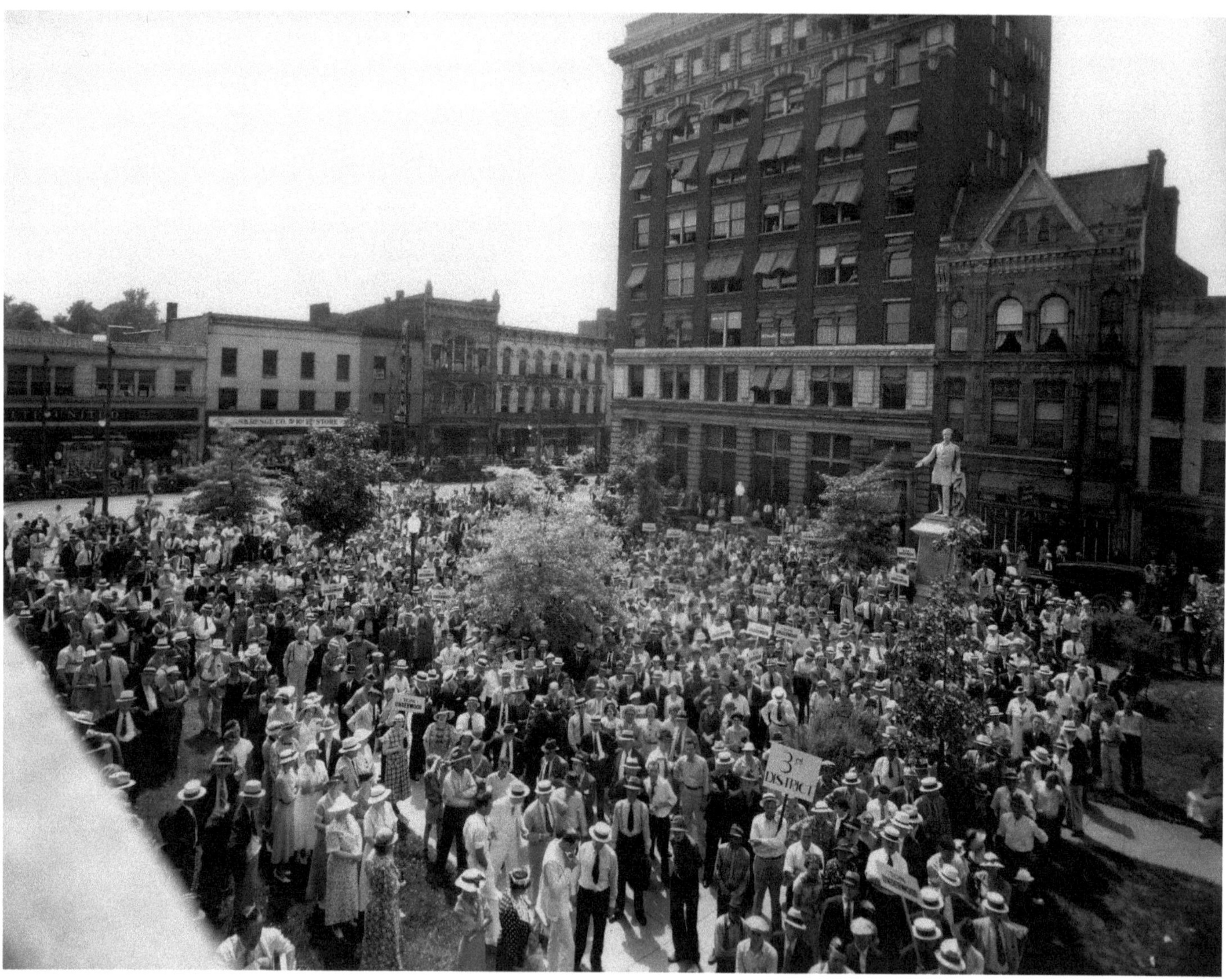

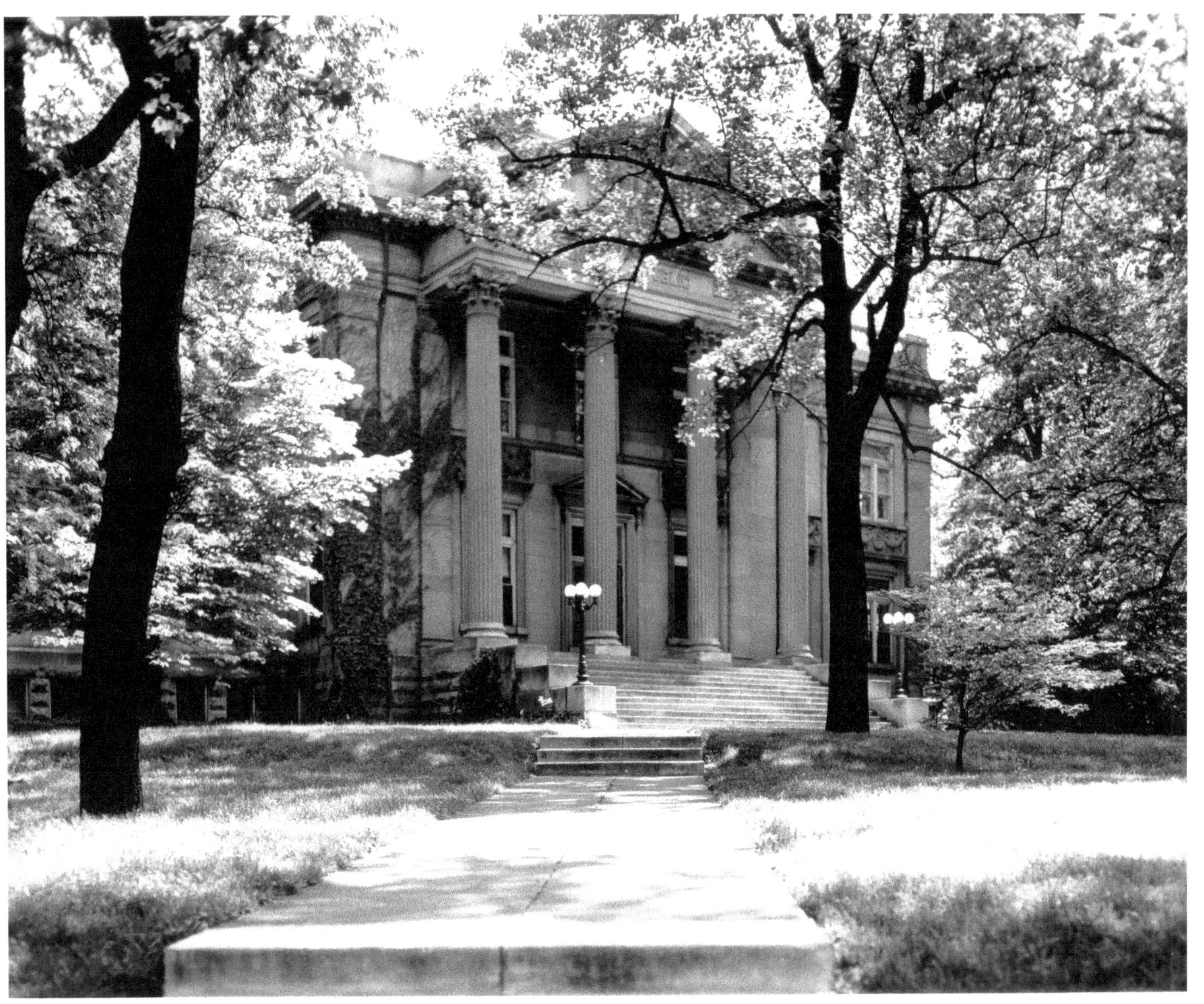

Lexington Public Library (built with a Carnegie grant of 1902) in Gratz Park, mid 20th century.

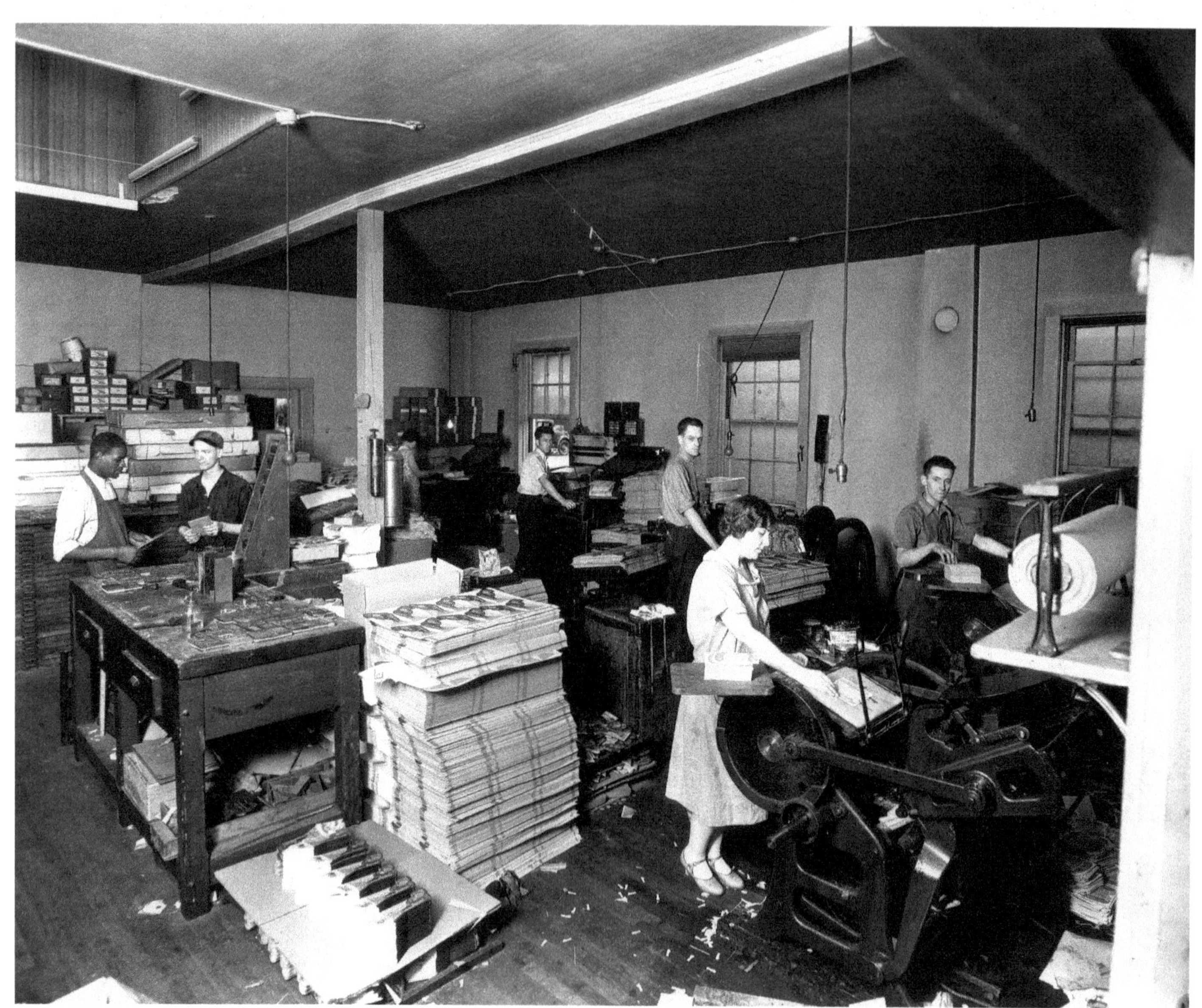
Printing at Spotswood Specialty Company, 1930.

The Gem House, was demolished in 1919 to make room for the Lafayette Hotel.

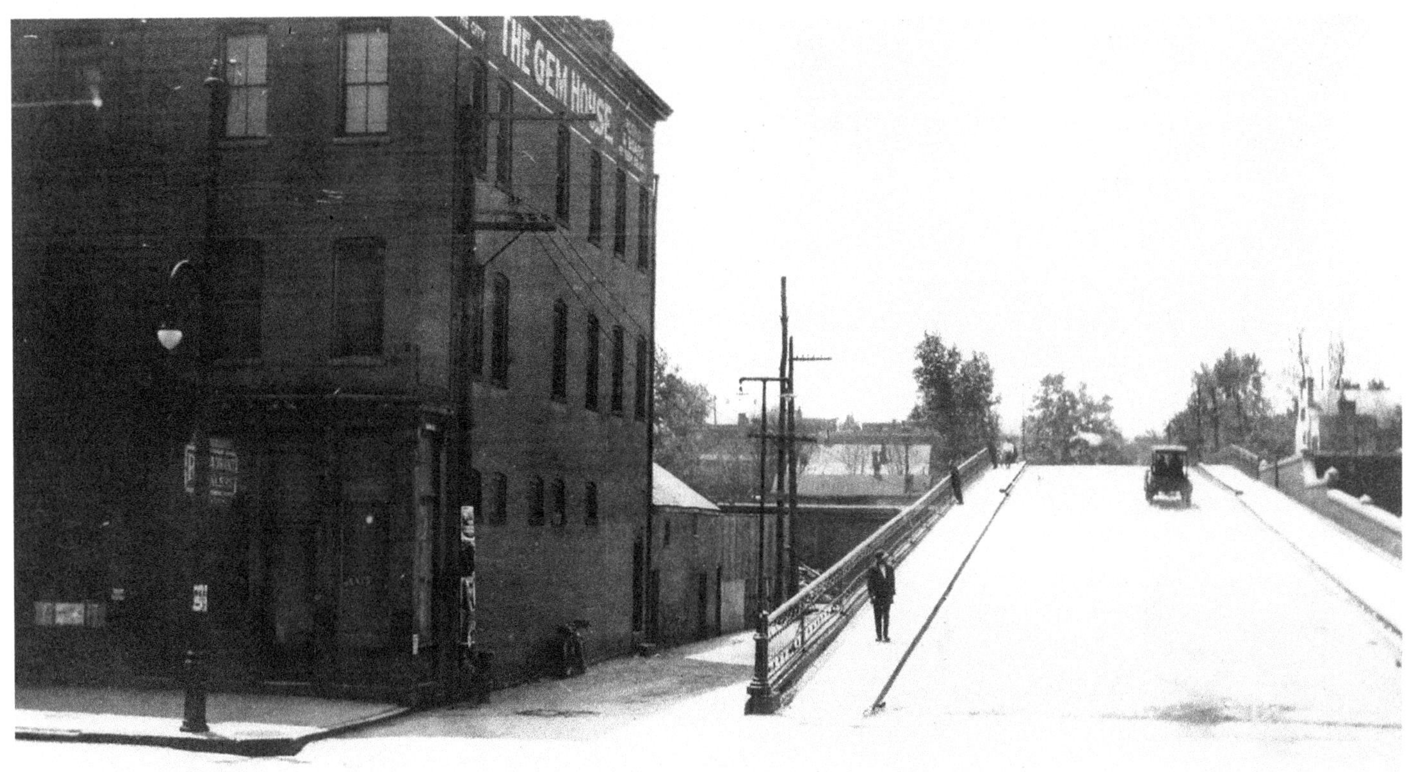

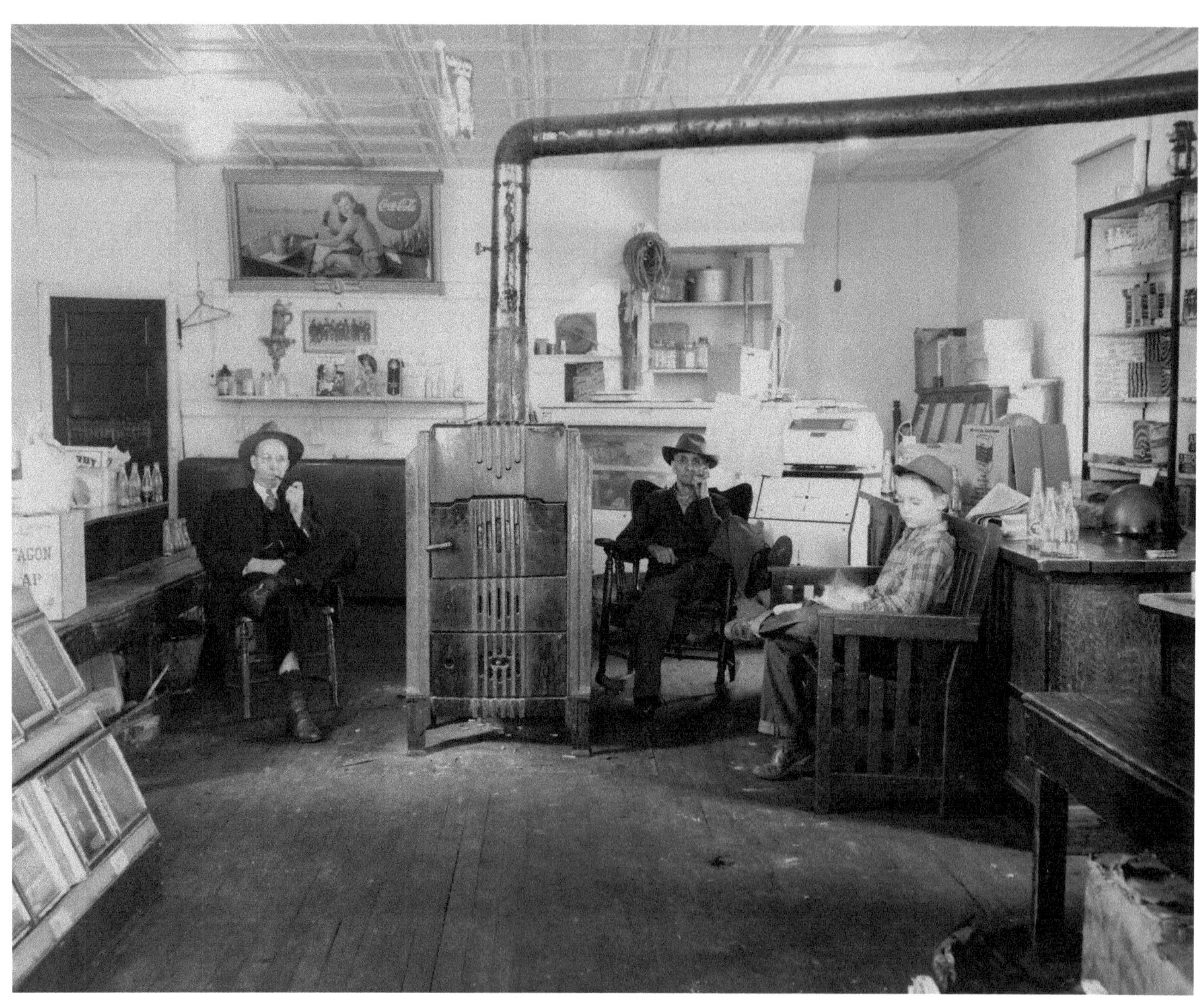


"Jot 'em Down" country store interior at Iron Work Pike and Russell Cave Road, 1944.

# Toward the Second Century

## 1941-1975

For one growing up and living in Lexington in the period from the Second World War until the city's bicentennial, life could be fine indeed. It was not far removed from the image fostered is several Hollywood movies set in the area at that time.

The citizens had early mobilized in preparation for possible conflict. Already the ladies had been assembling "Bundles for Britain". The Lexington Signal Depot at Avon, very near the city, was in operation by 1942. Support for the war was generous from many walks of life. As an agricultural center, Lexington had important contributions to make and made them. Irving Air Chute Company, one of the few local manufacturing industries, expanded.

After the war, life in Lexington returned to the rather quiet nature it had known for most of the century. Tobacco and the horse business flourished in the post war era. Returning soldiers brought expected expansion in education. Lexington entered the industrial age, with the blessings of clean industries. In the next decade Lexington was to be one of the fastest growing areas in the country and with that growth came problems of scale and planning. One very positive outcome due in part to the sound of new voices was felt in the civil rights movement. In 1963, Lexington had a Commission on Human Rights and saw the election of the first black city commissioner.

When Lexington embarked on urban renewal activities in the mid 1960's it was with mixed blessings. The preservation movement, then only in existence locally for about ten years, was not able to save significant neighborhoods and structures in the downtown. However, this urban renewal sparked some major achievements such as the removal of the railroad tracks crossing major thoroughfares and the formation of the Lexington Center Cooperation in 1972 that included among its components Rupp Arena. Adolph Rupp and "Bear" Bryant of UK basketball and football fame respectively must be considered among the most important Lexingtonians in the popular mind. Creation of the Kentucky Horse Park, where the cause of Lexington's international fame could be enshrined, was approved by the Commonwealth in 1972. As Lexington, Kentucky approached its bicentennial year another and most innovative and important change, initiated in 1972, was coming to fruition. Lexington and Fayette County were merged to form a city of "first-class" status.

Blacksmith shop of Stanley Bryant at Donerail north of Lexington, 1942.

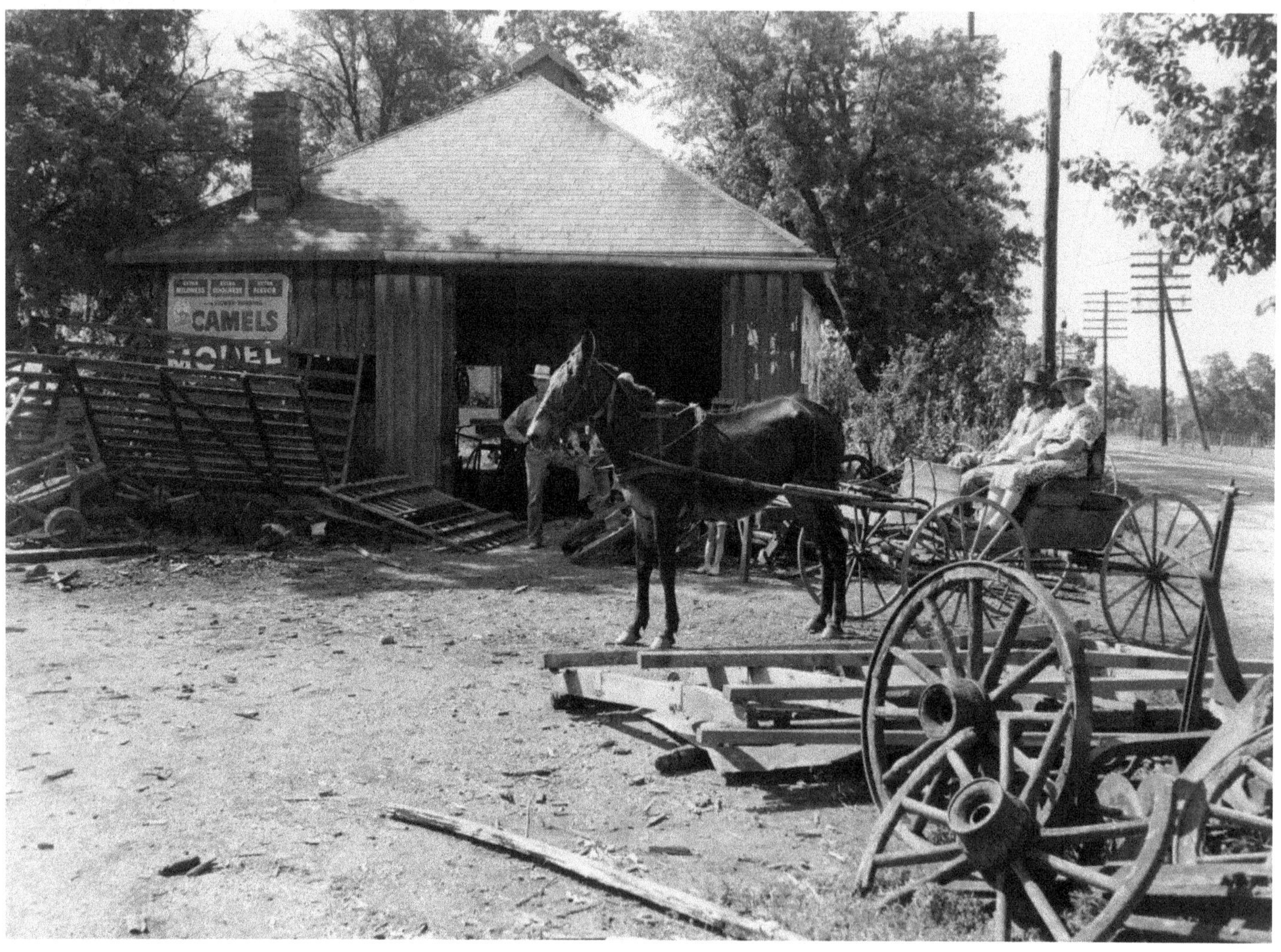

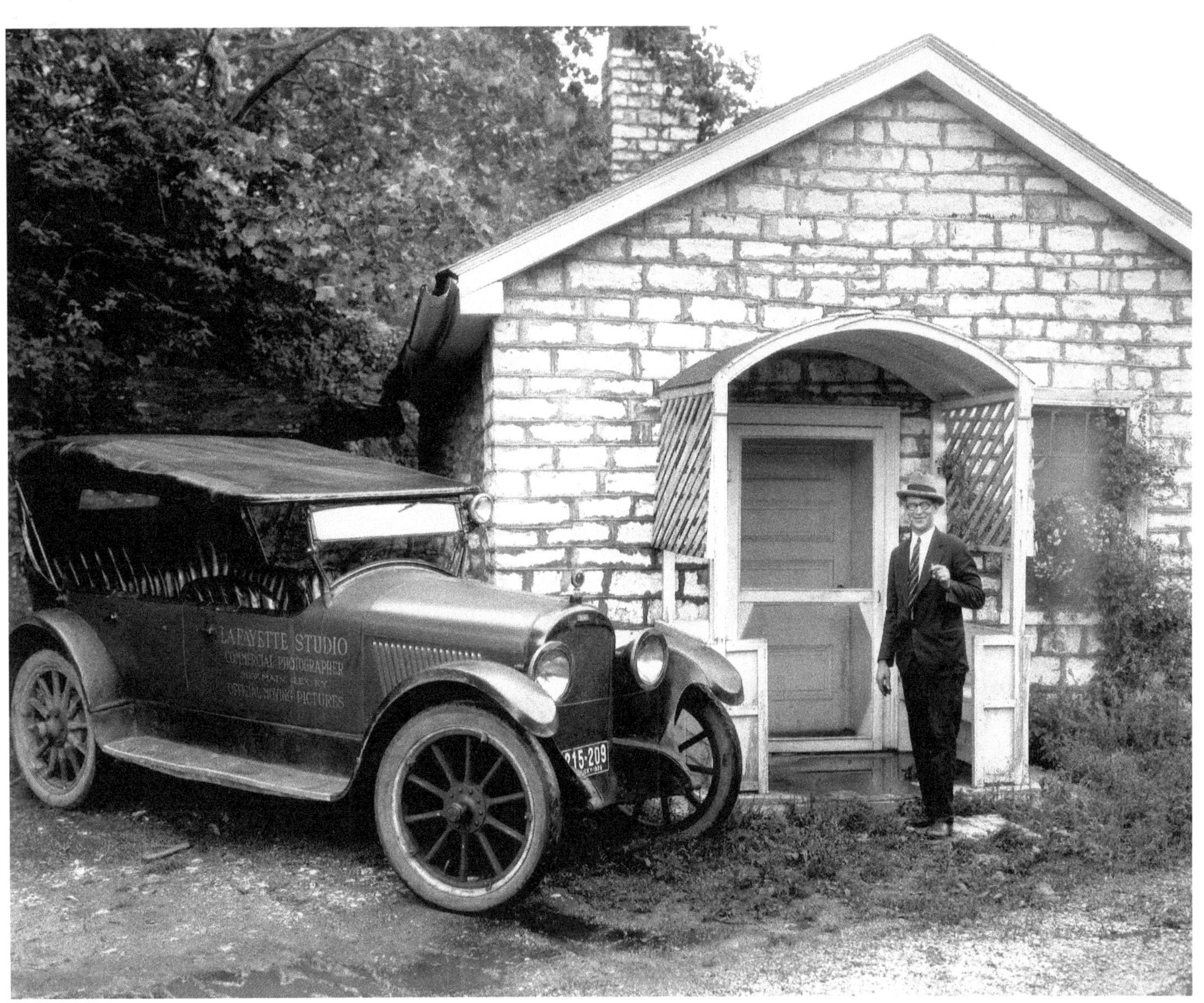


Photographer Robert J. Long standing next to a Lexington Minute Man Six automobile, manufactured in the early 1900's on West Main Street.

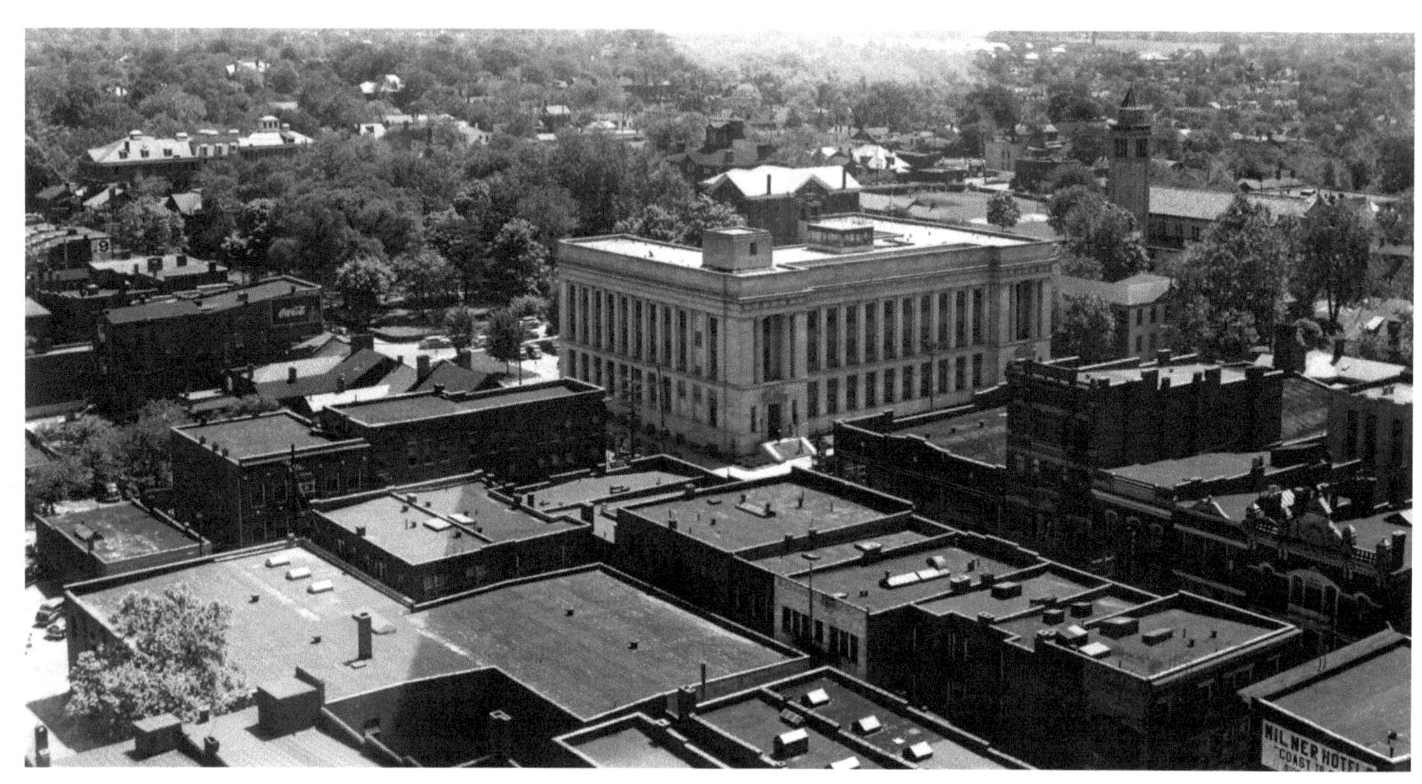


New Federal Post Office on Barr Street, 1941.

"Floral Hall" at the entrance to Red Mile after renovation and removal of cupola in mid 1900's.

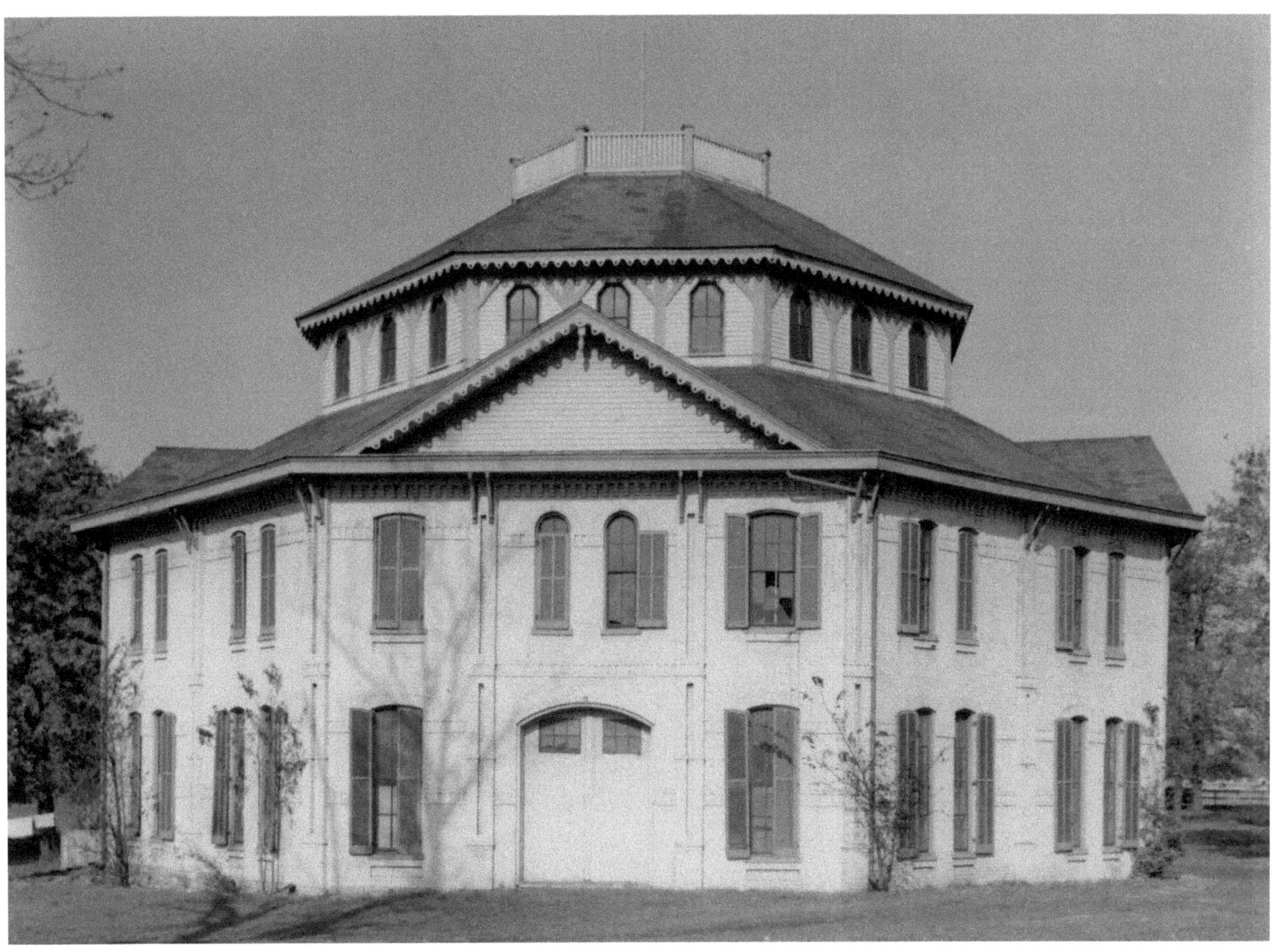

Greyhound Bus station, mid 20th century.

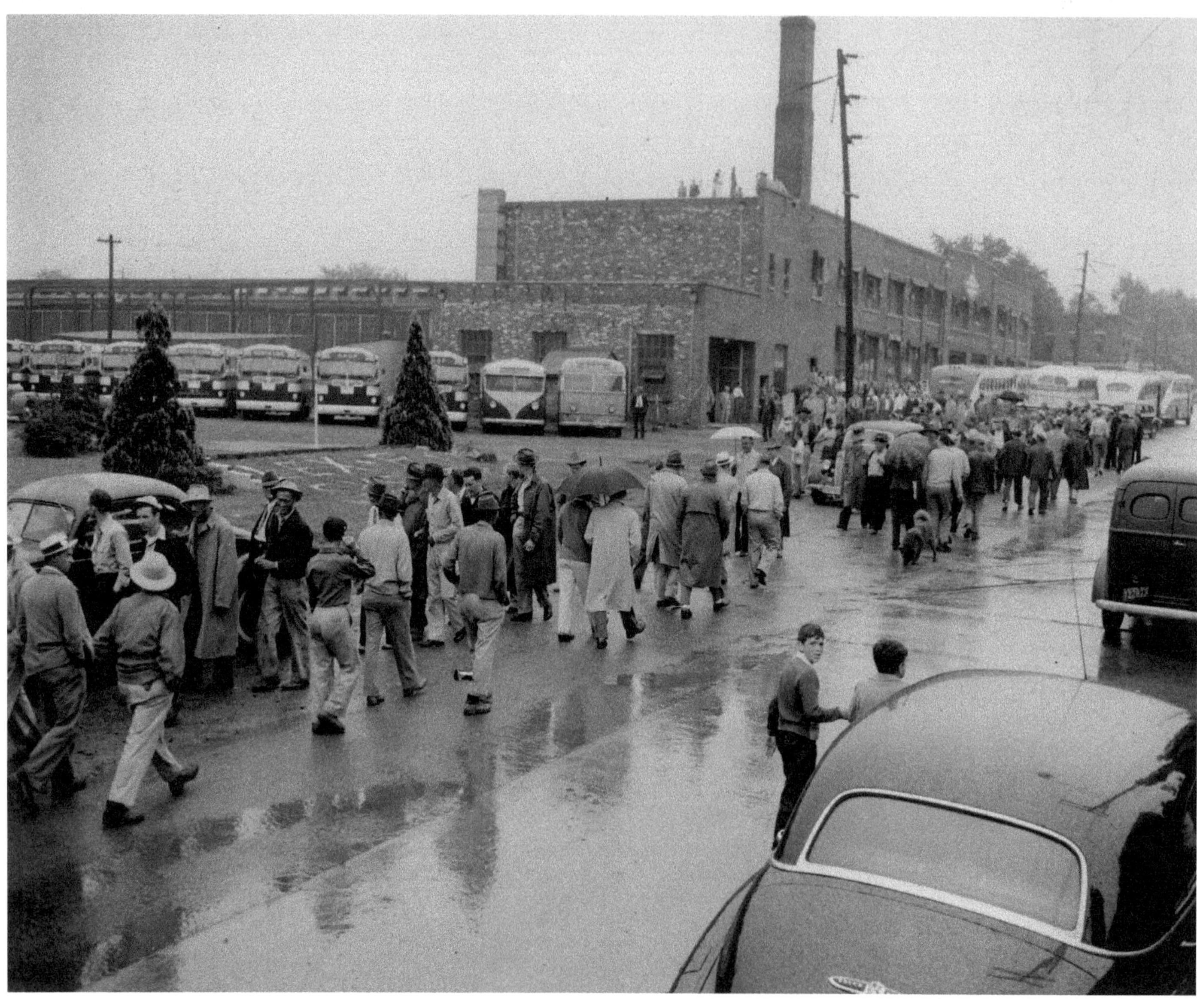

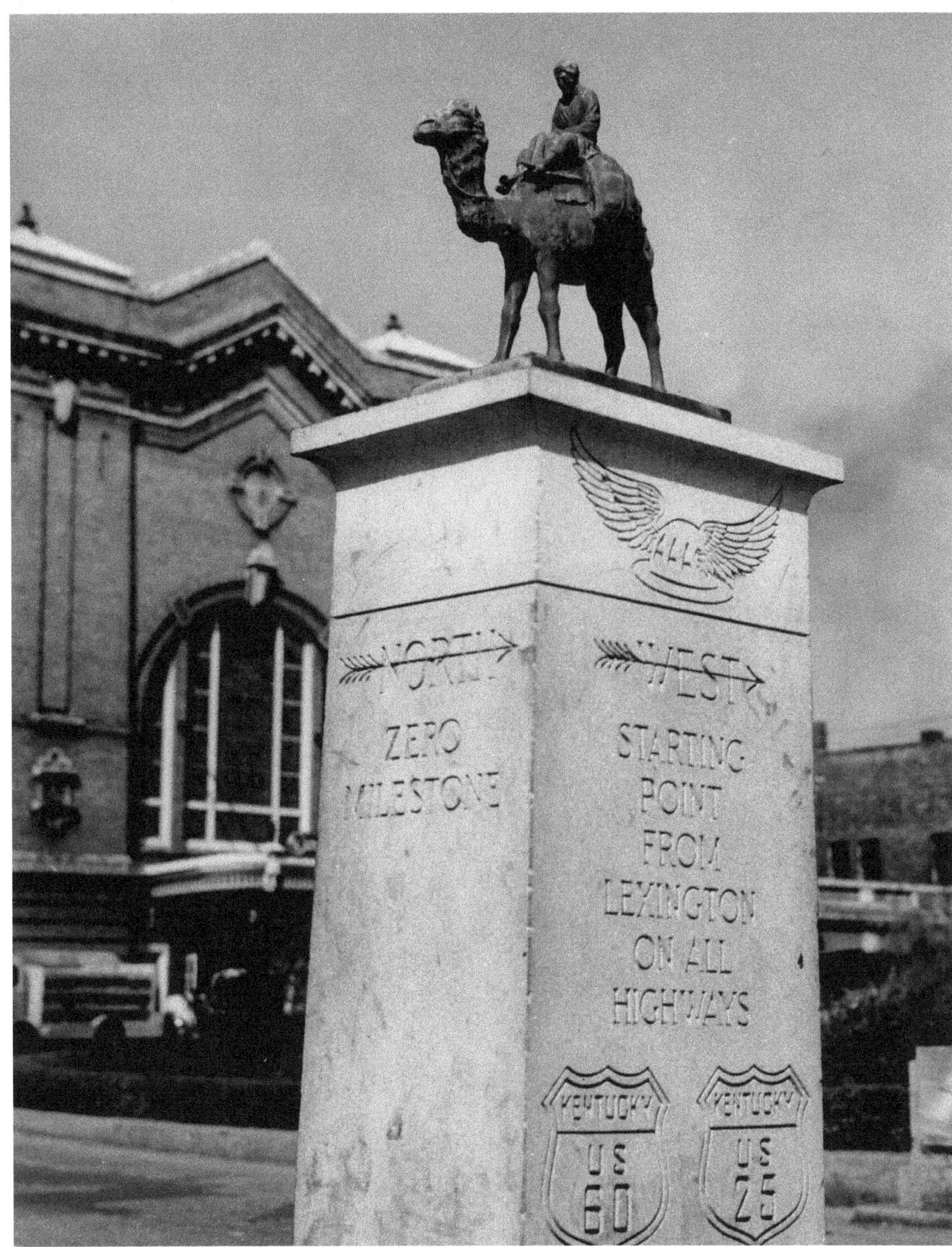


Lexington's movable zero mile marker (from which distances to the city are to be measured) positioned in front of Union Station, 1948.

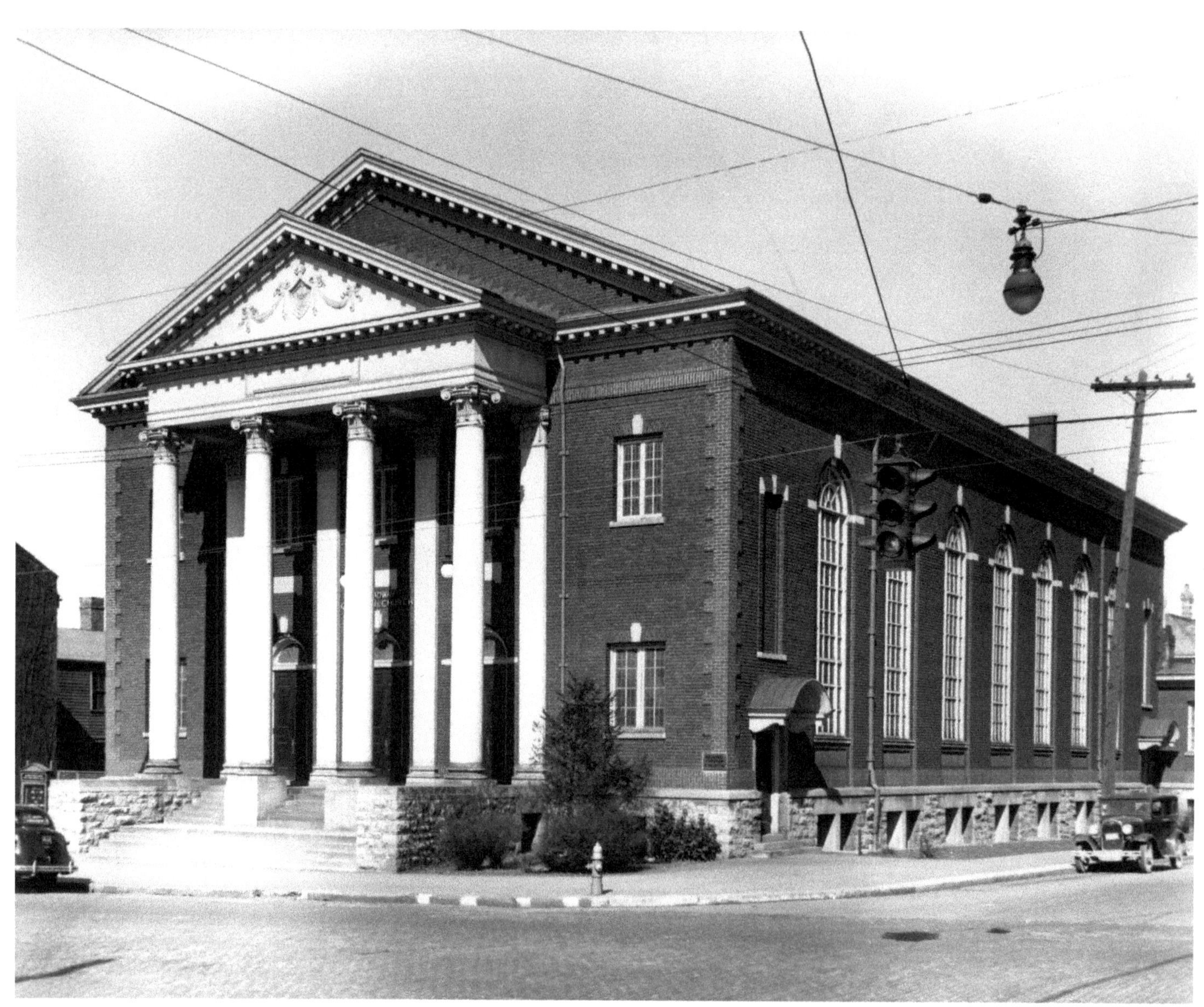

Broadway Christian Church (built 1917), 1943.

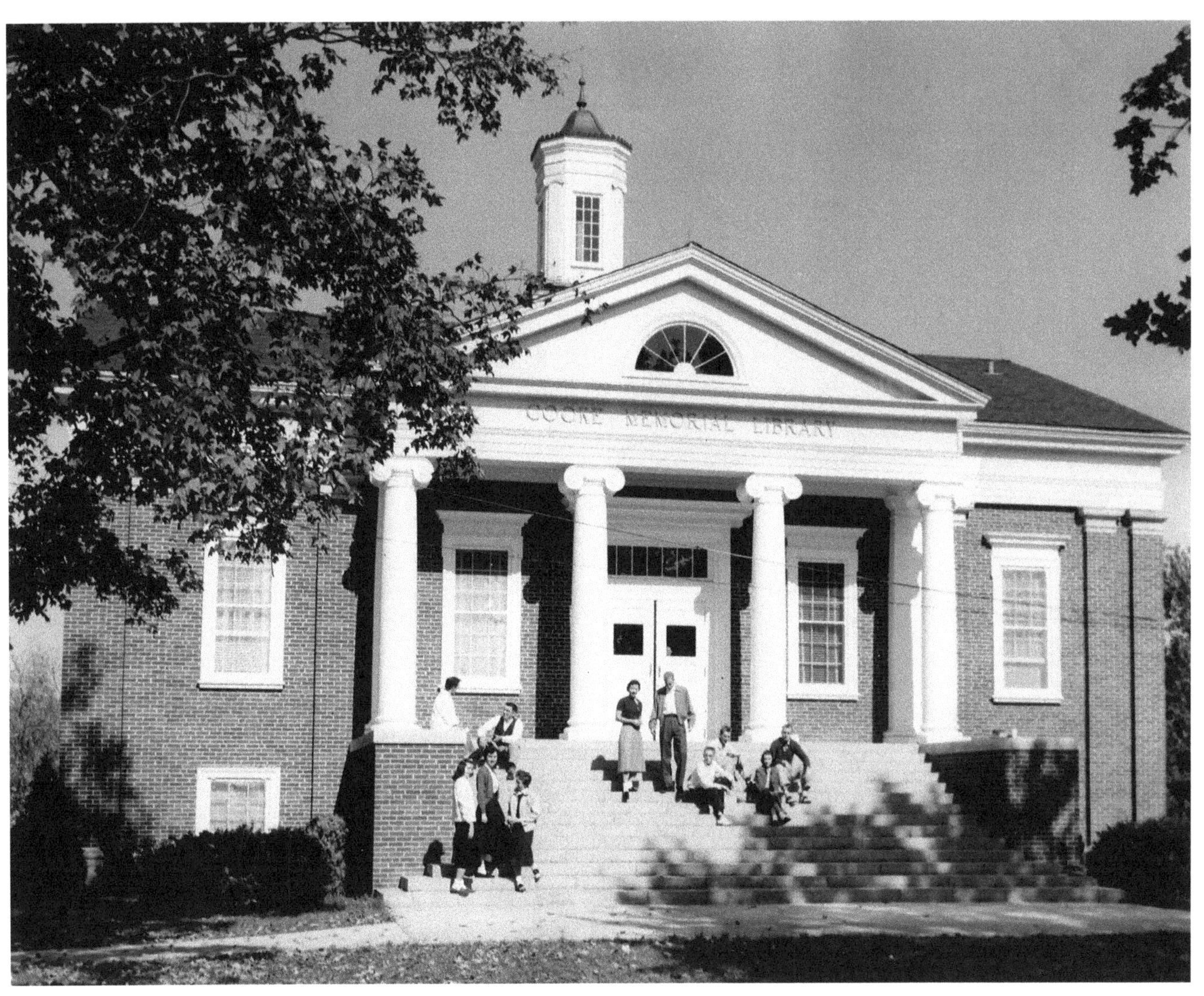


Cooke Memorial Library, Georgetown University.

Looking west down Main Street from Cheapside, 1947.

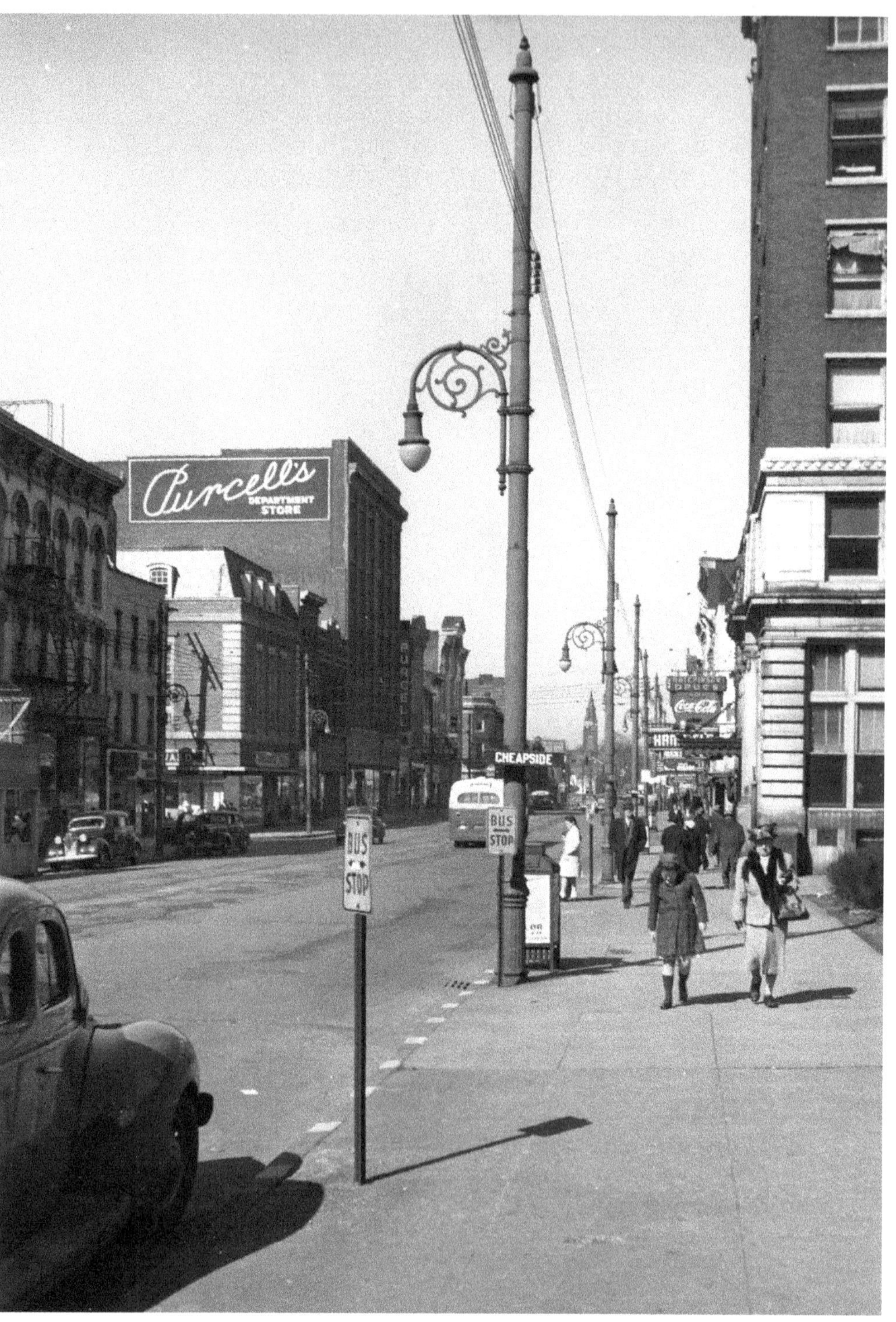

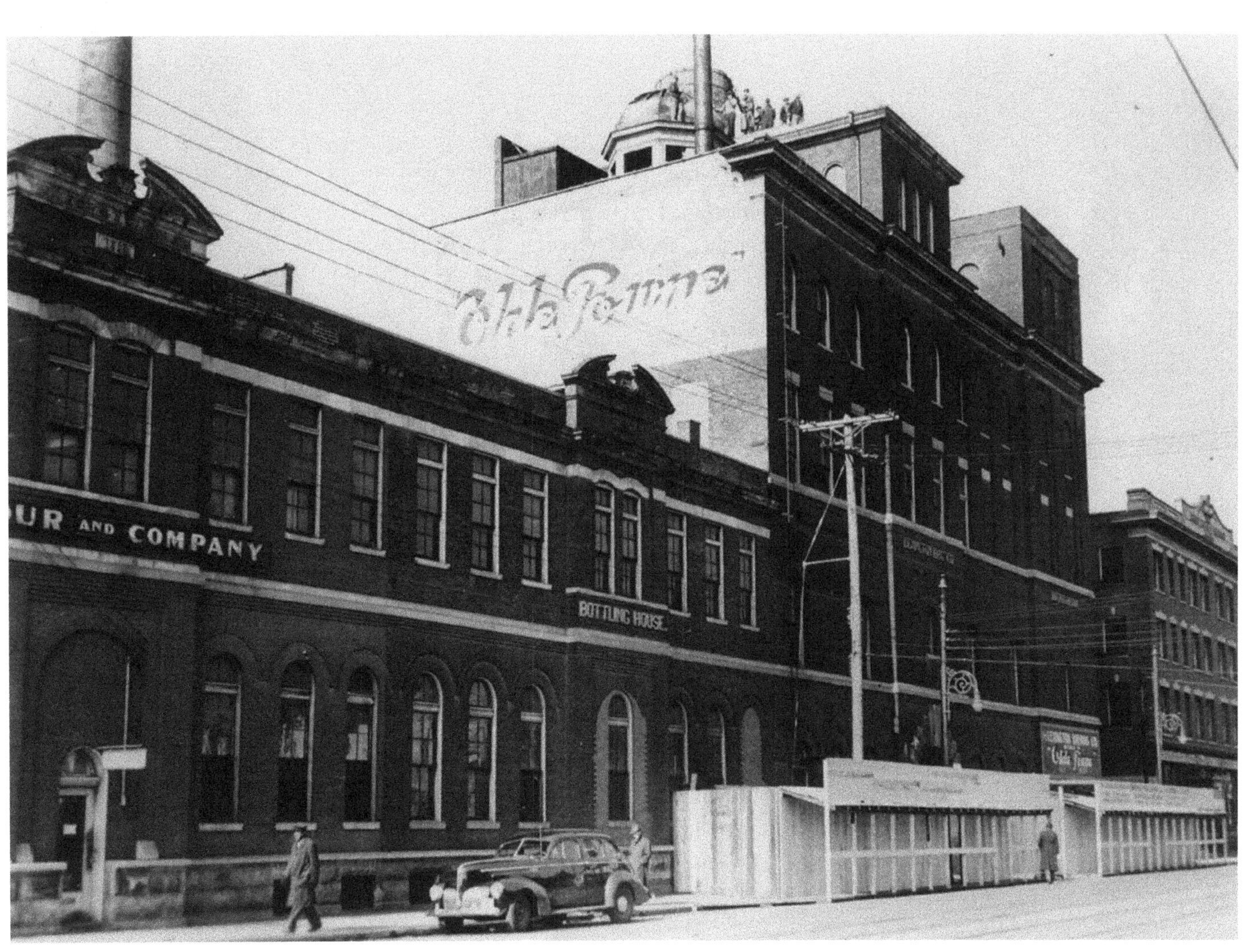


Lexington Brewery (built 1897) on East Main Street near Rose Street, early 20th century.

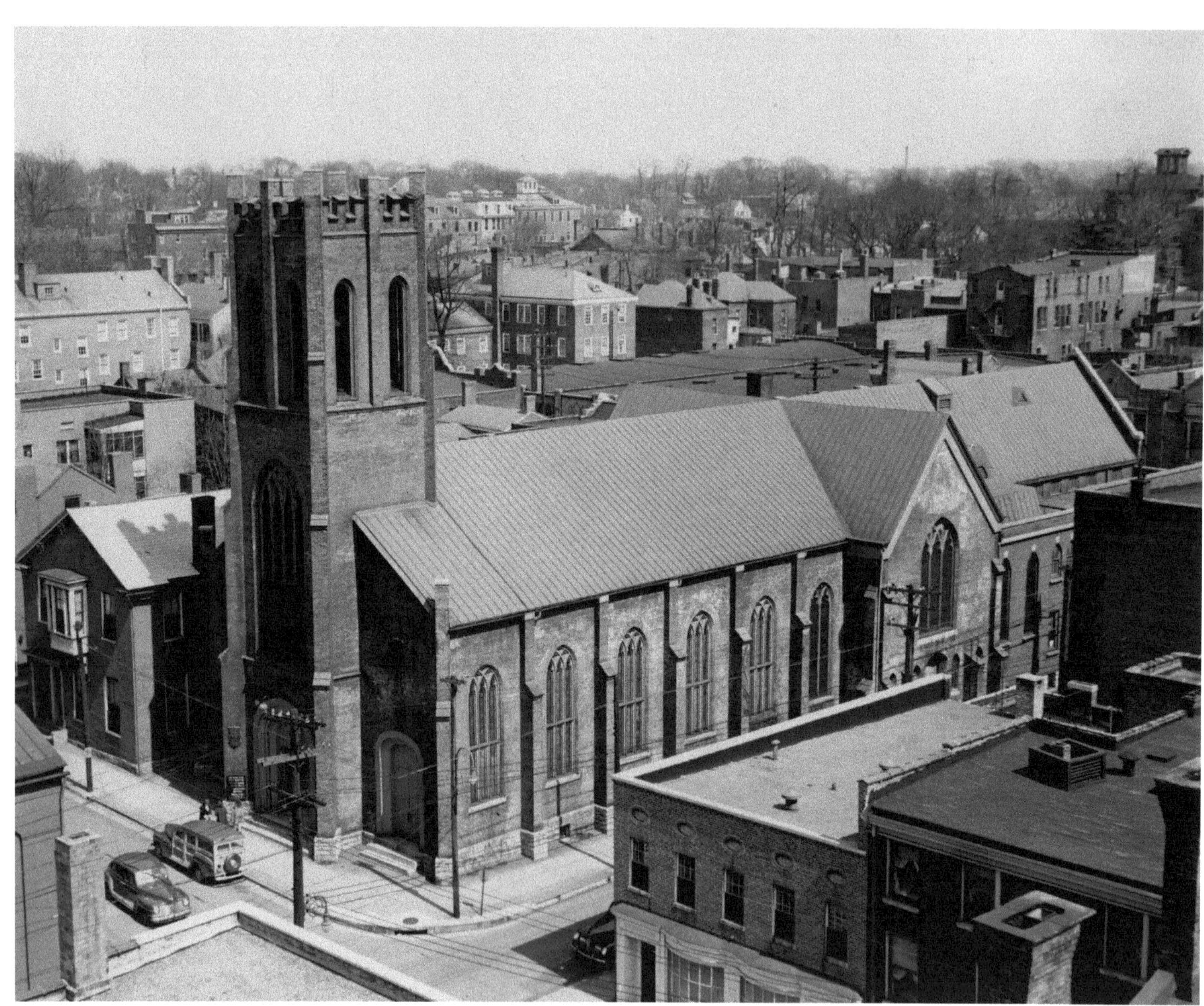

Christ Church Episcopal Cathedral on Market Street
(built 1847), 1943.

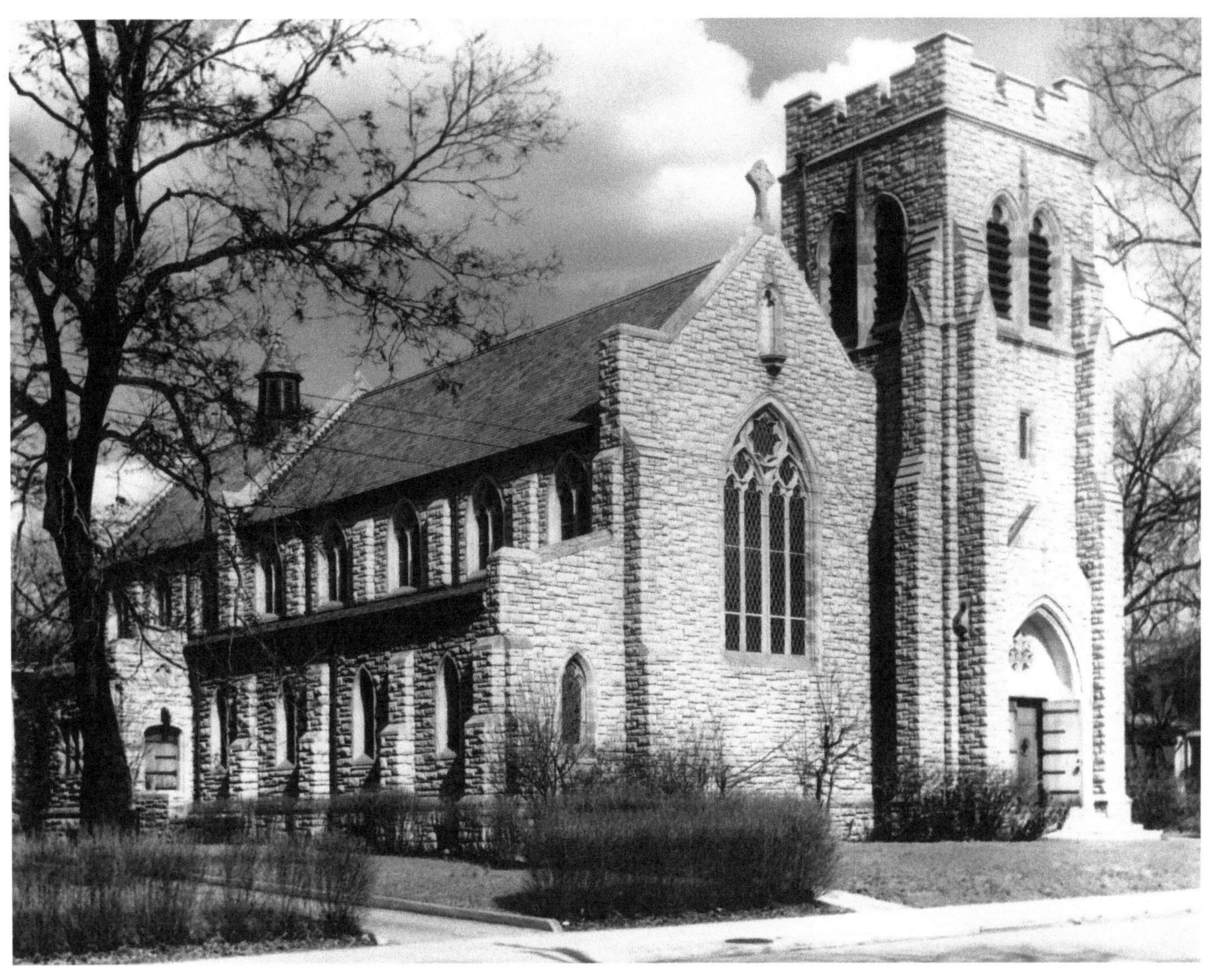

Good Shepherd Episcopal Church on East Main Street (built 1927), 1956.

Woodland Christian Church at Woodland Avenue and High Street, 1943.

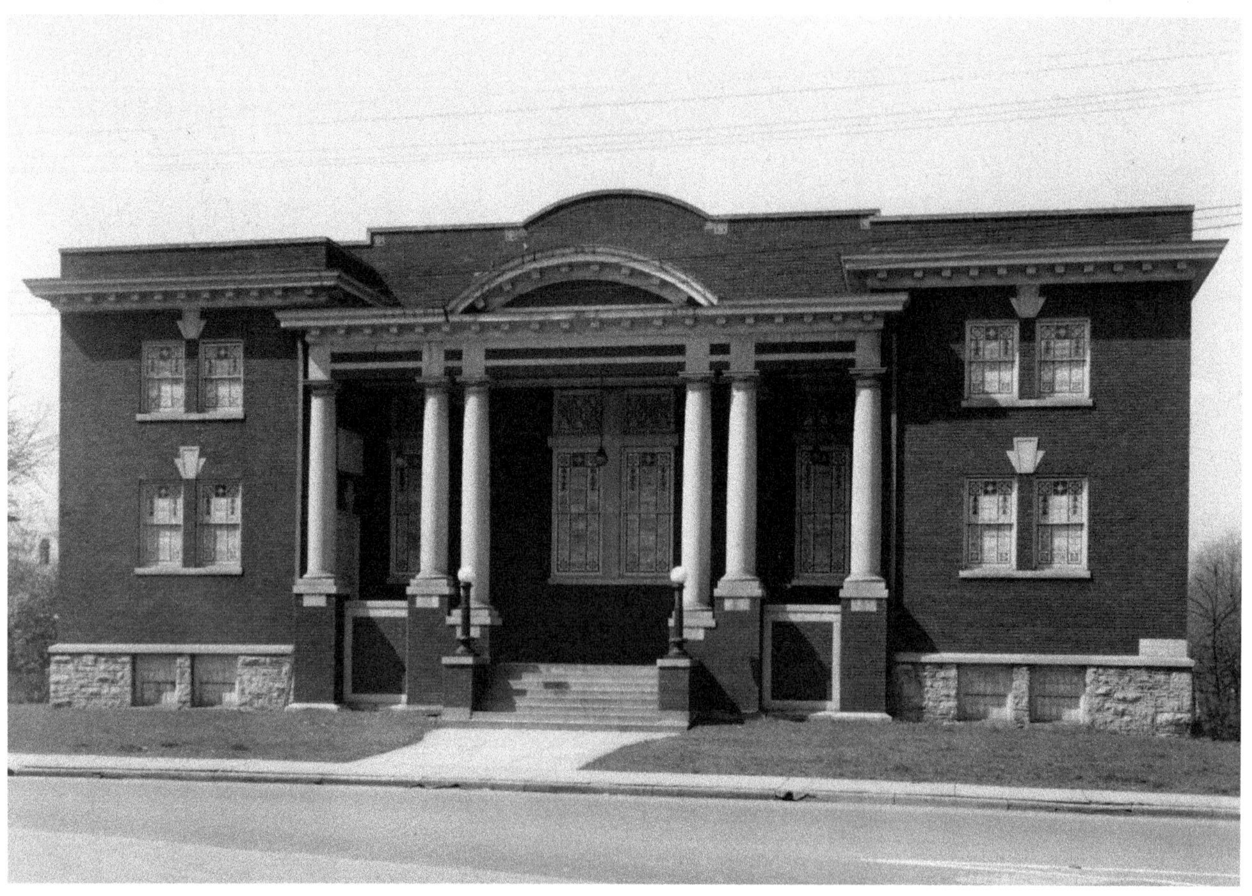

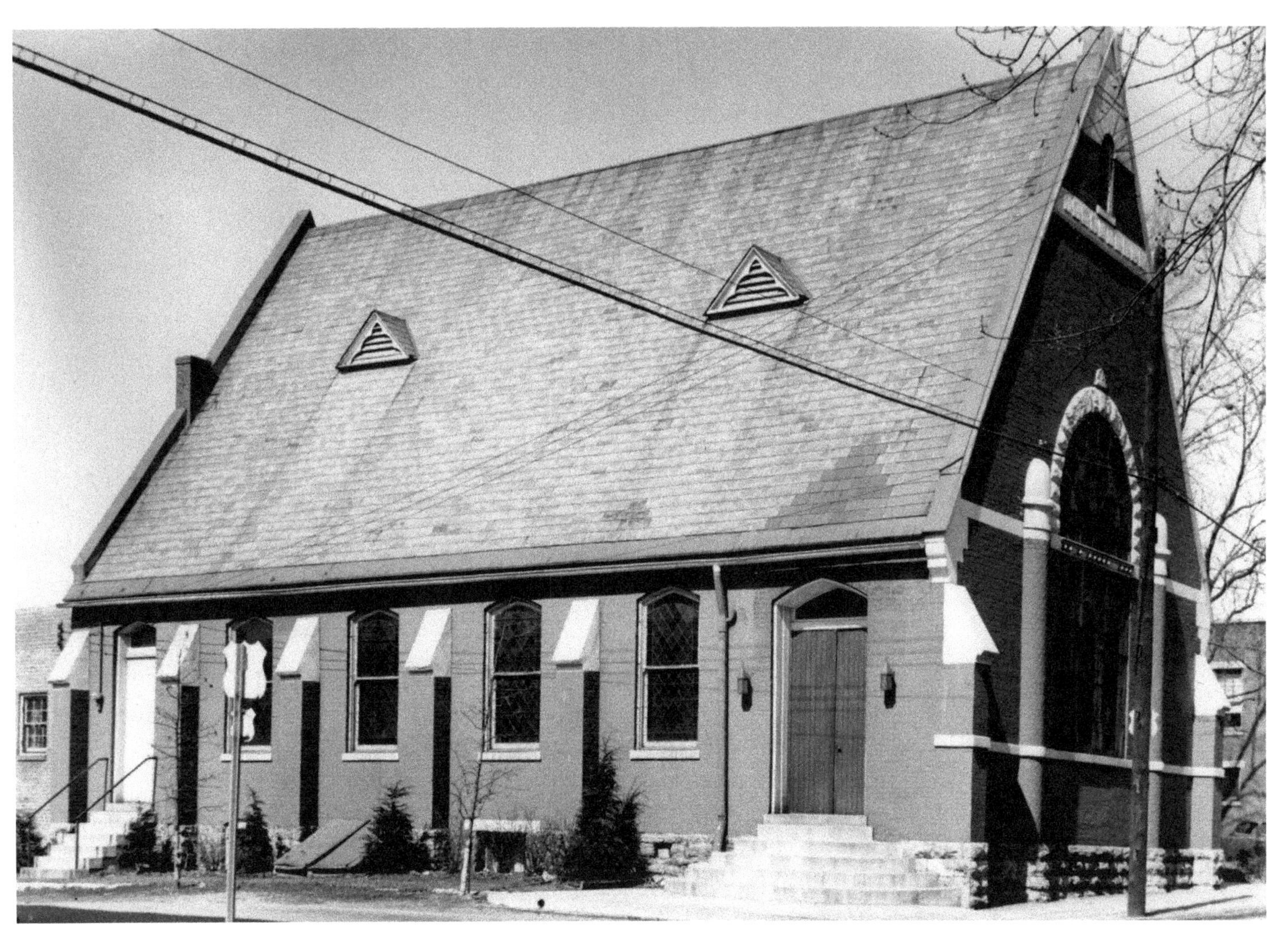

Ohavay Zion Synagogue (built as Maxwell Street Presbyterian Church in 1891, rededicated 1916), 1943.

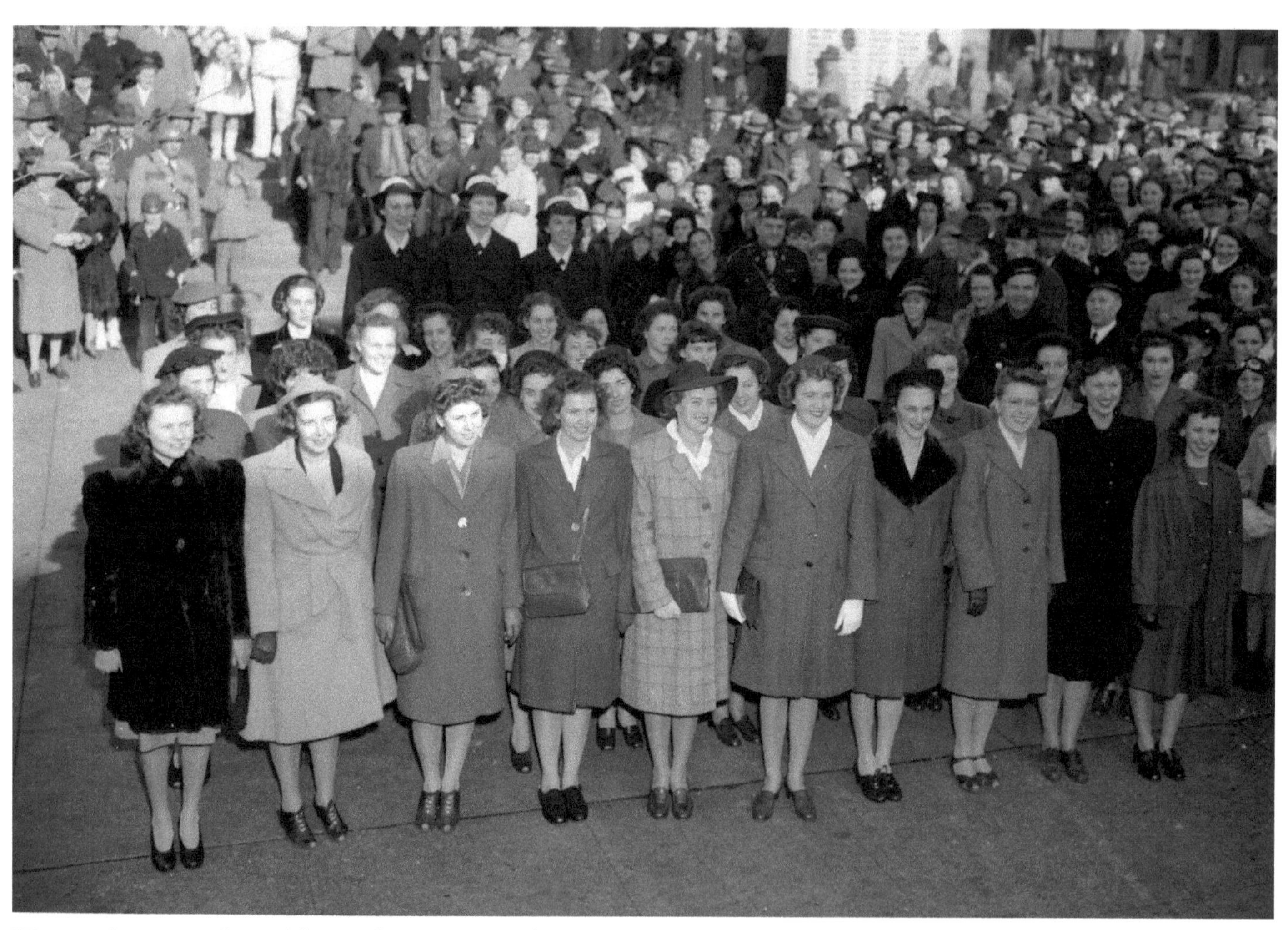

Waves newly sworn in front of the courthouse, 11 November 1943.

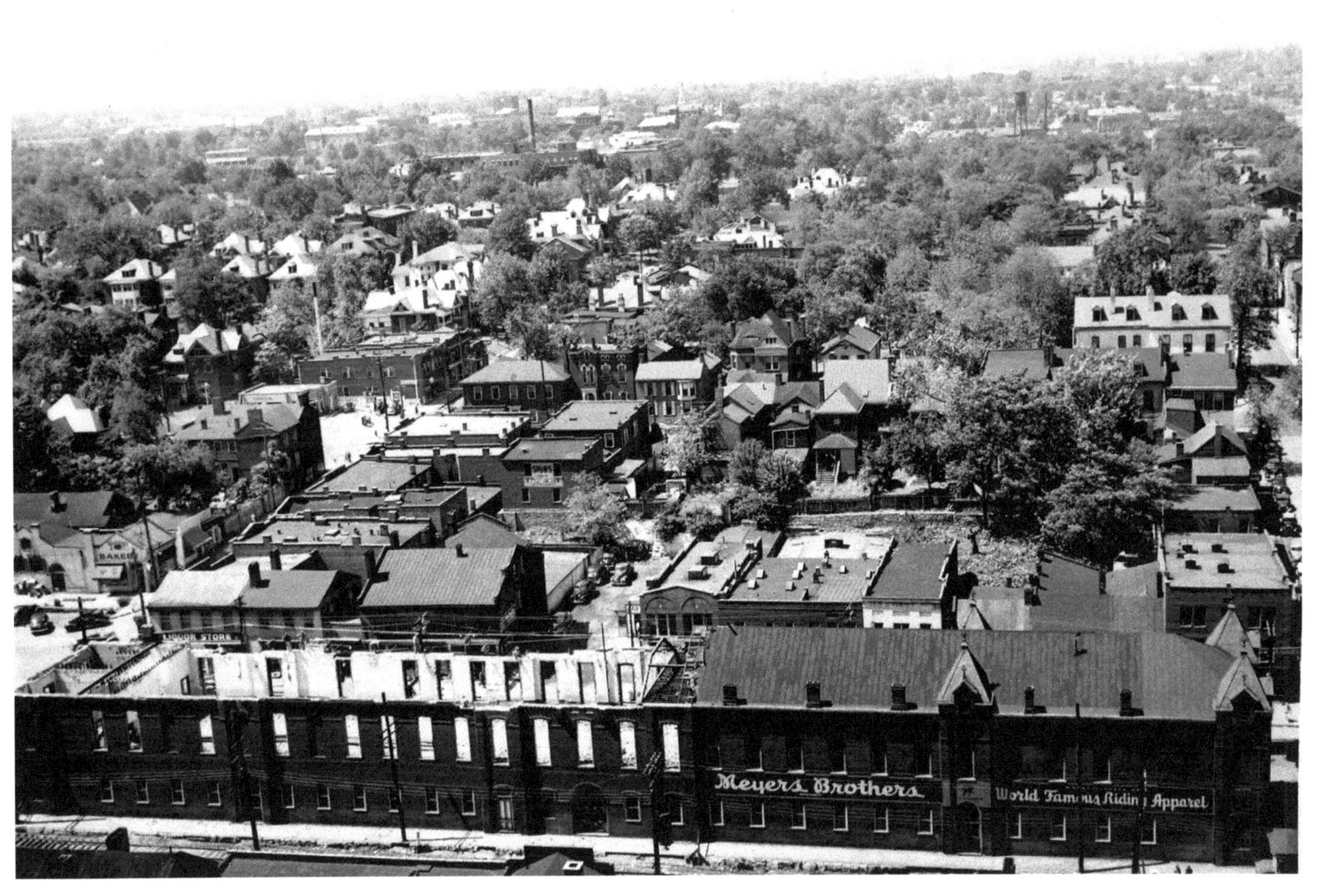


Jackson Hall, built in 1800's as the town marketplace, being razed in 1940's.

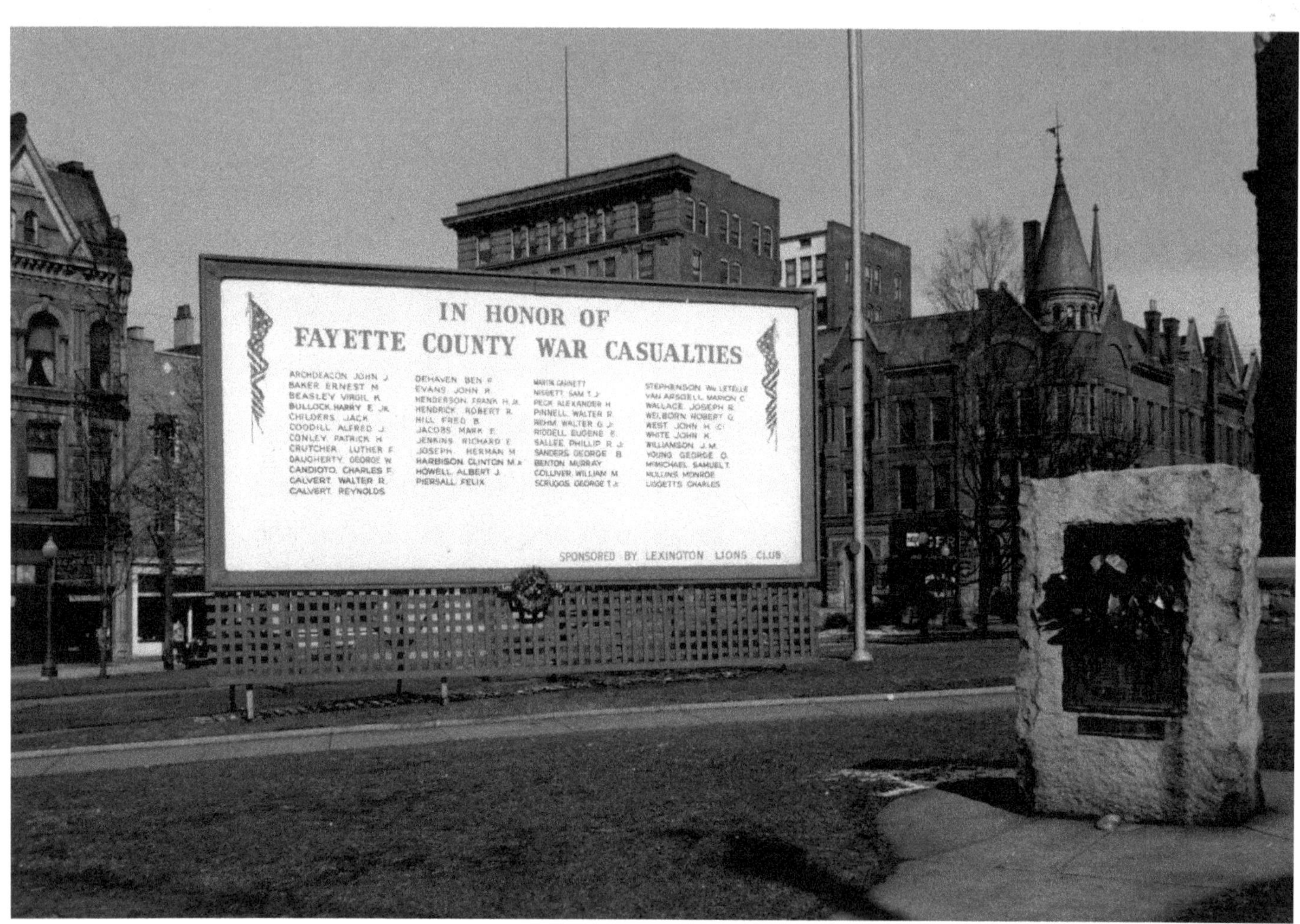

Fayette County War Casualties Sign, 1944.

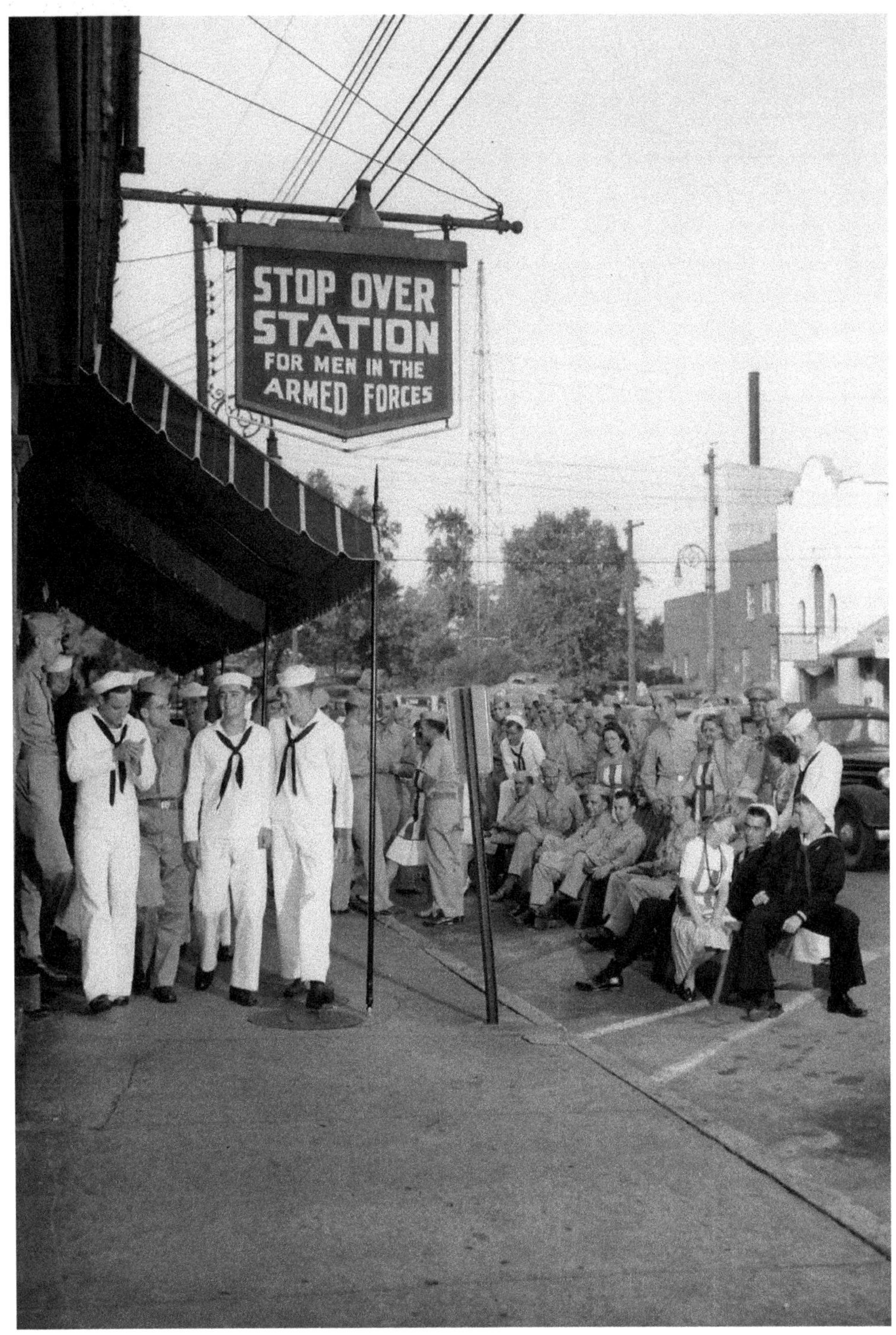


Locally sponsored "Stop over Station" for the troops on the Esplanade, 1942.

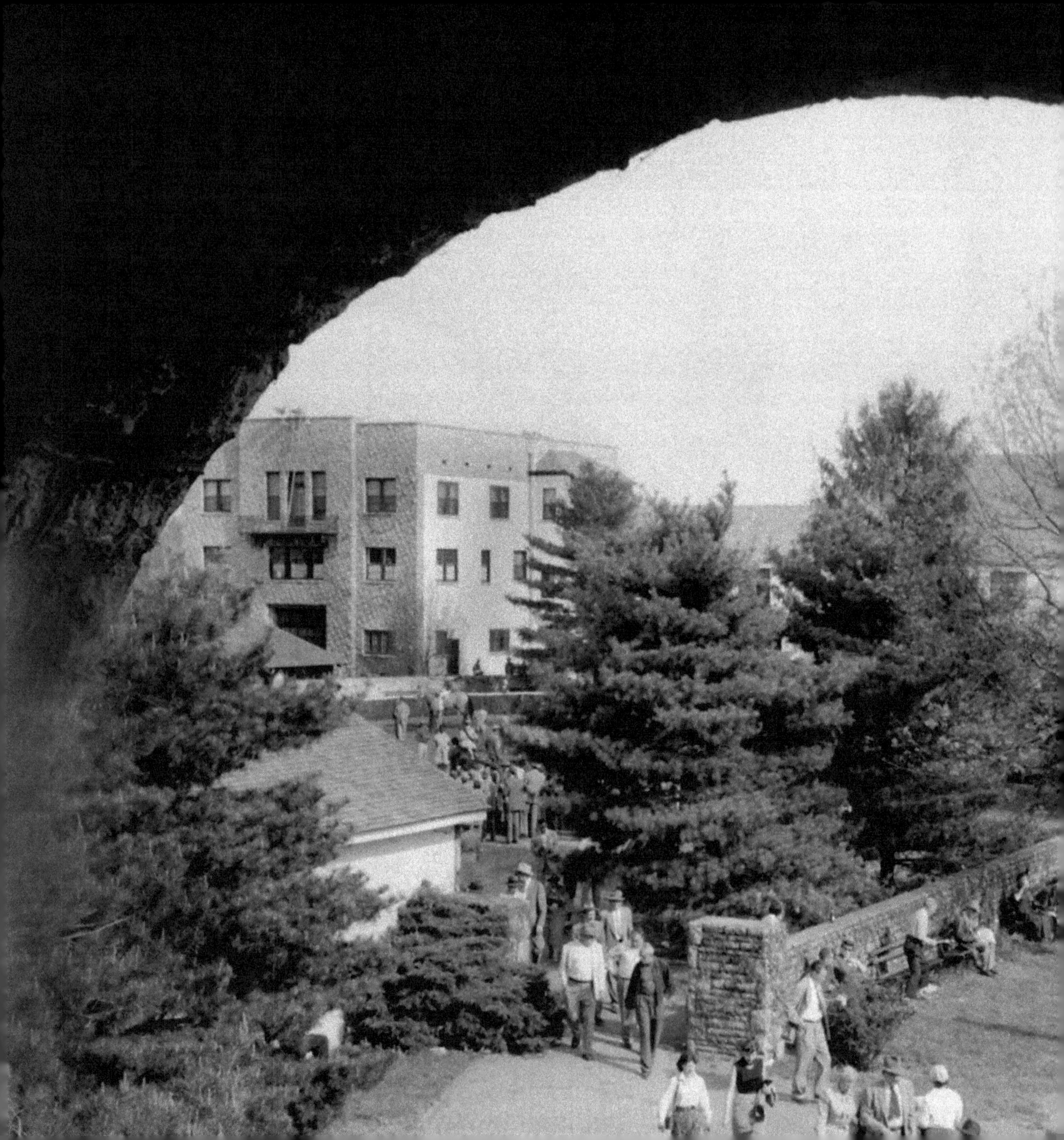

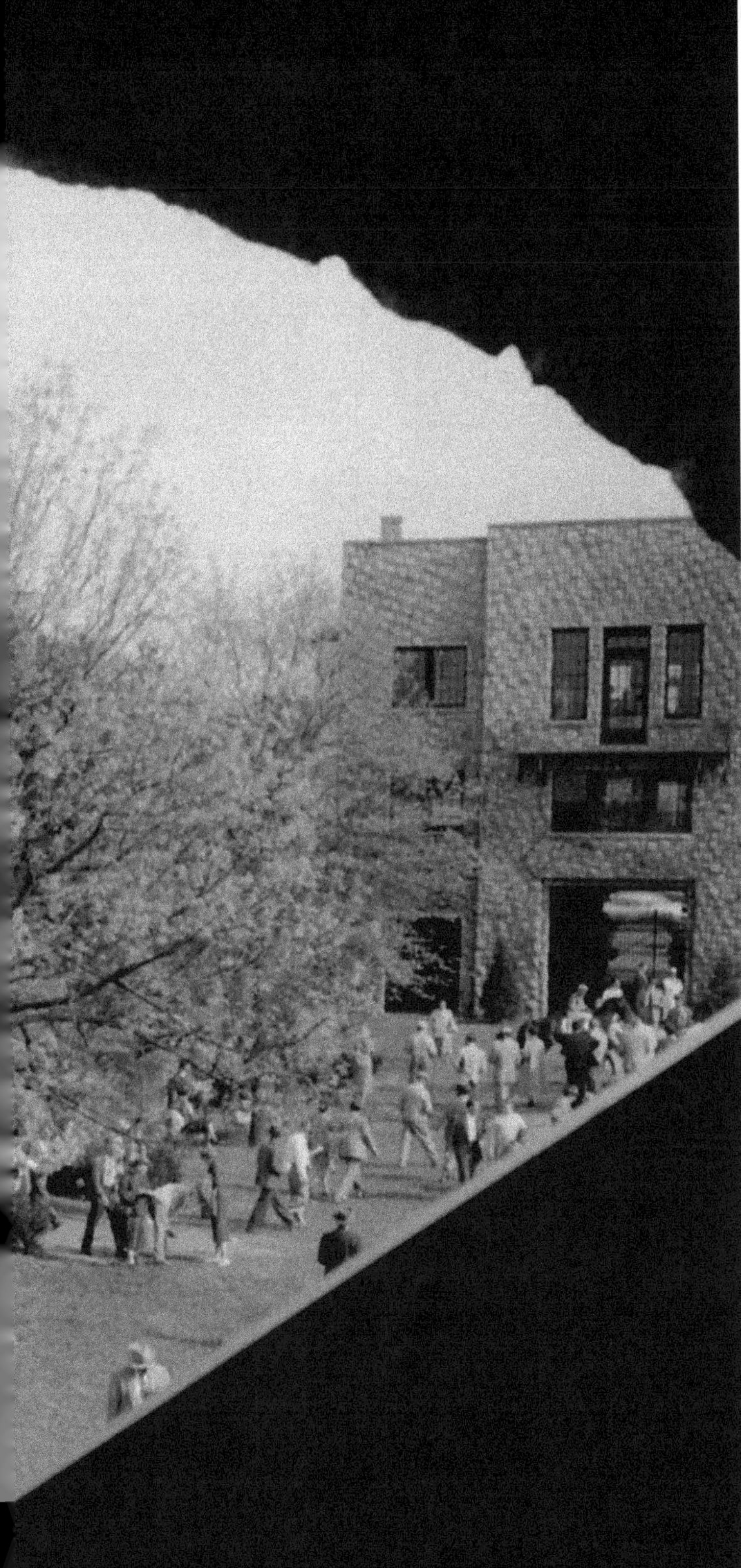

Archway at Keeneland.

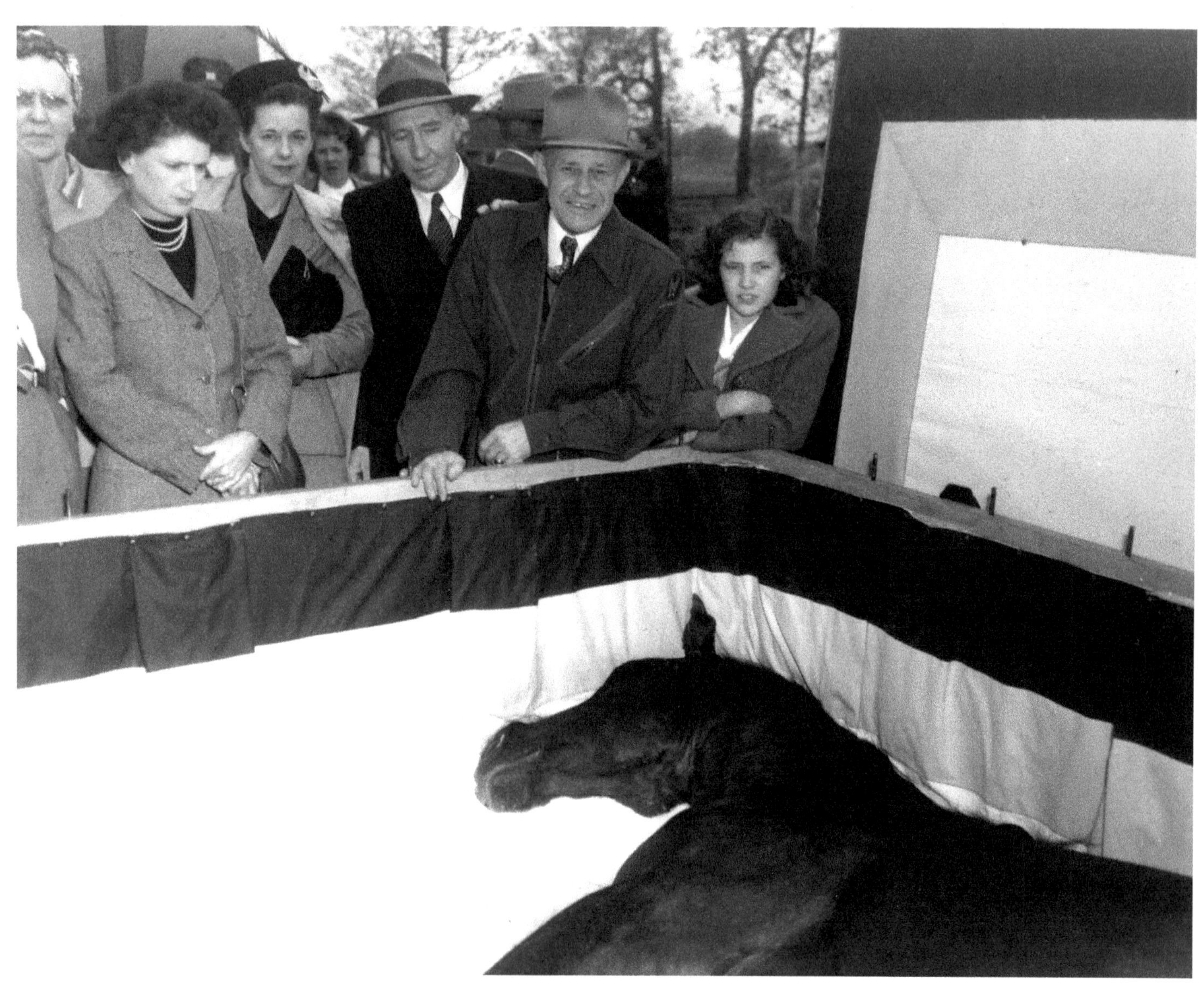

Funeral of Man O'War. November 1947.

Jockeys at Keeneland, c. 1950.

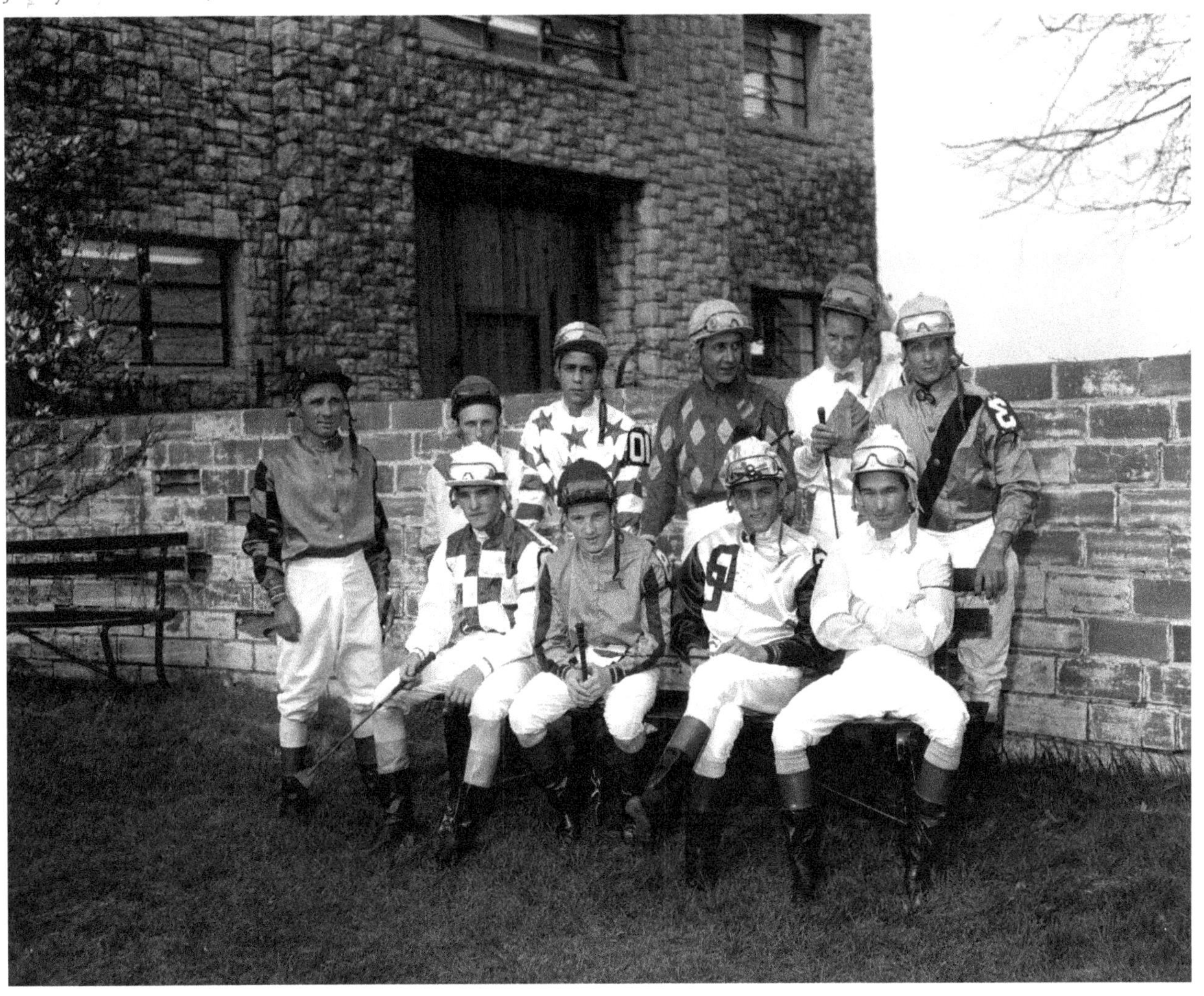

Photo, next page: Sale of Tige o' My Heart at Keeneland, 1957.

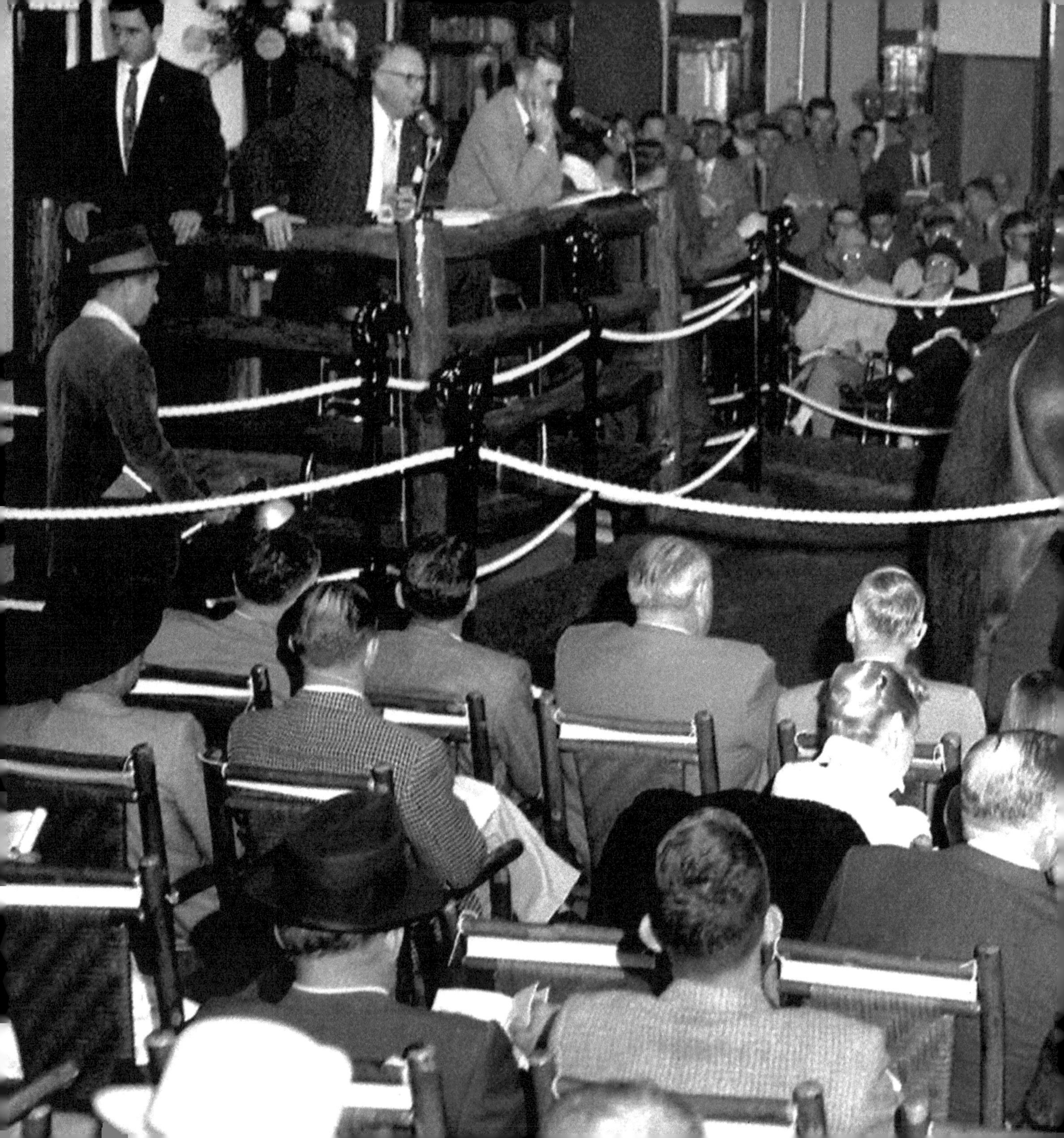

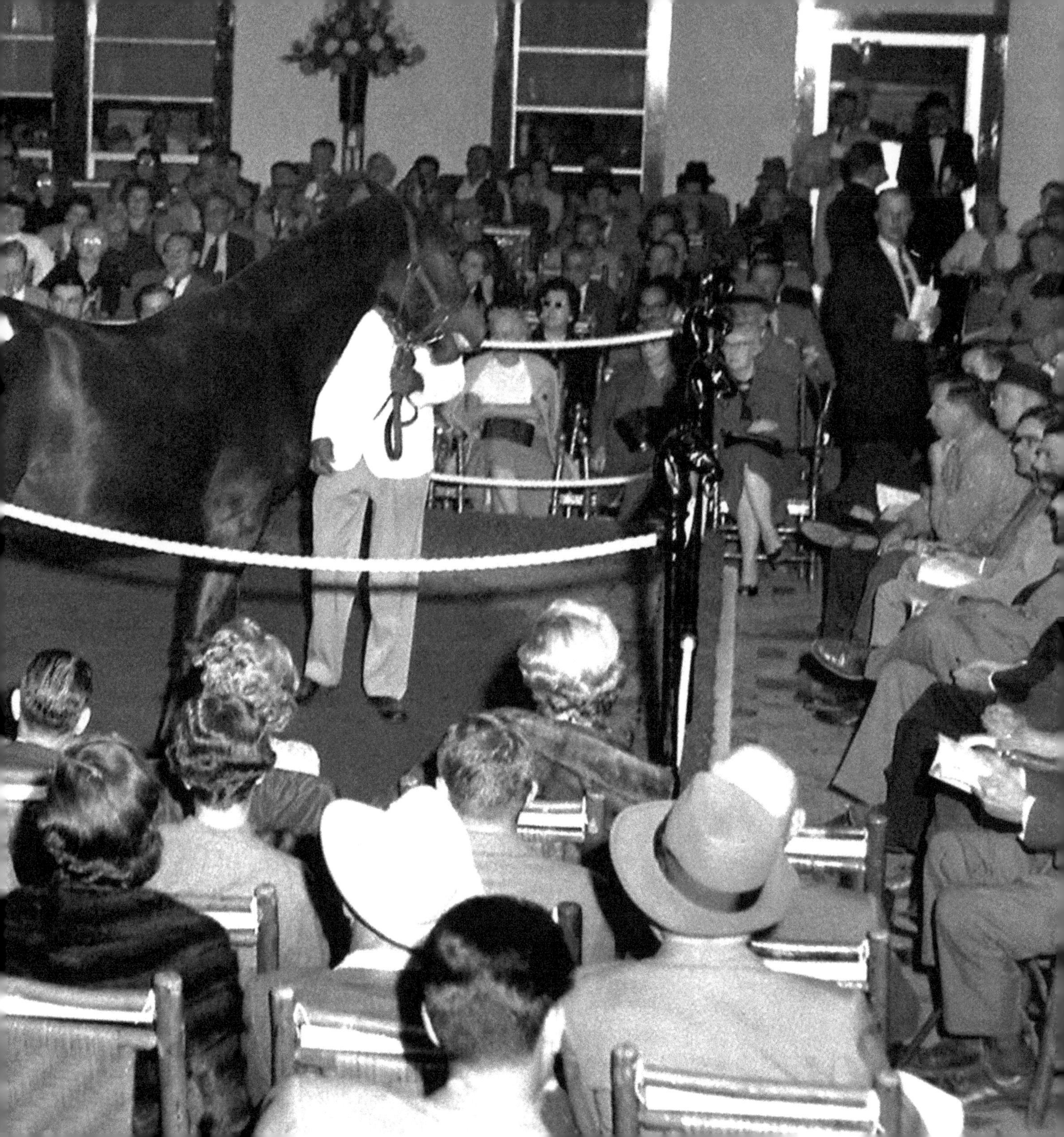

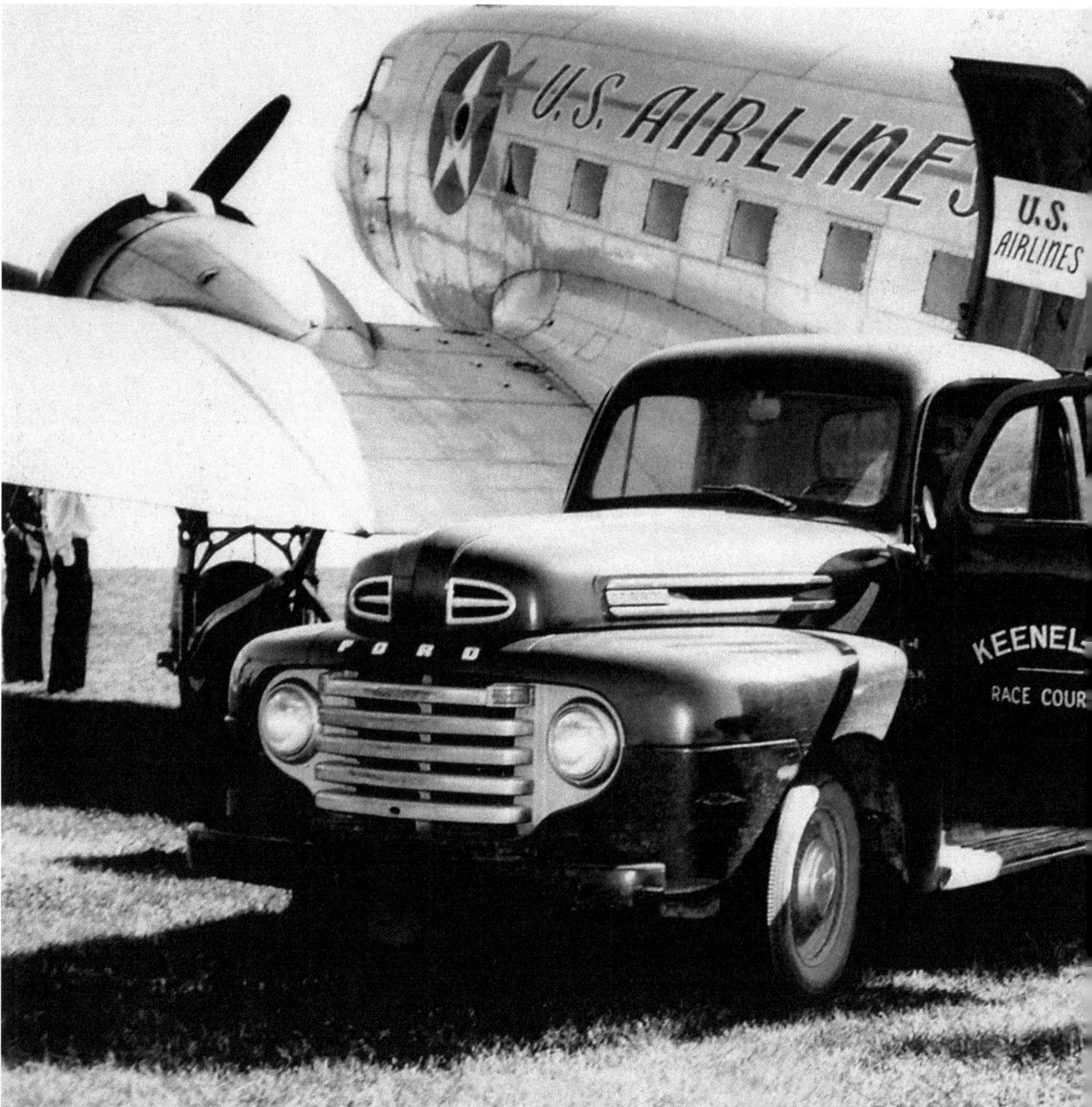
U.S. AIRLINES
U.S.
AIRLINES
FORD
KEENEL
RACE COUR

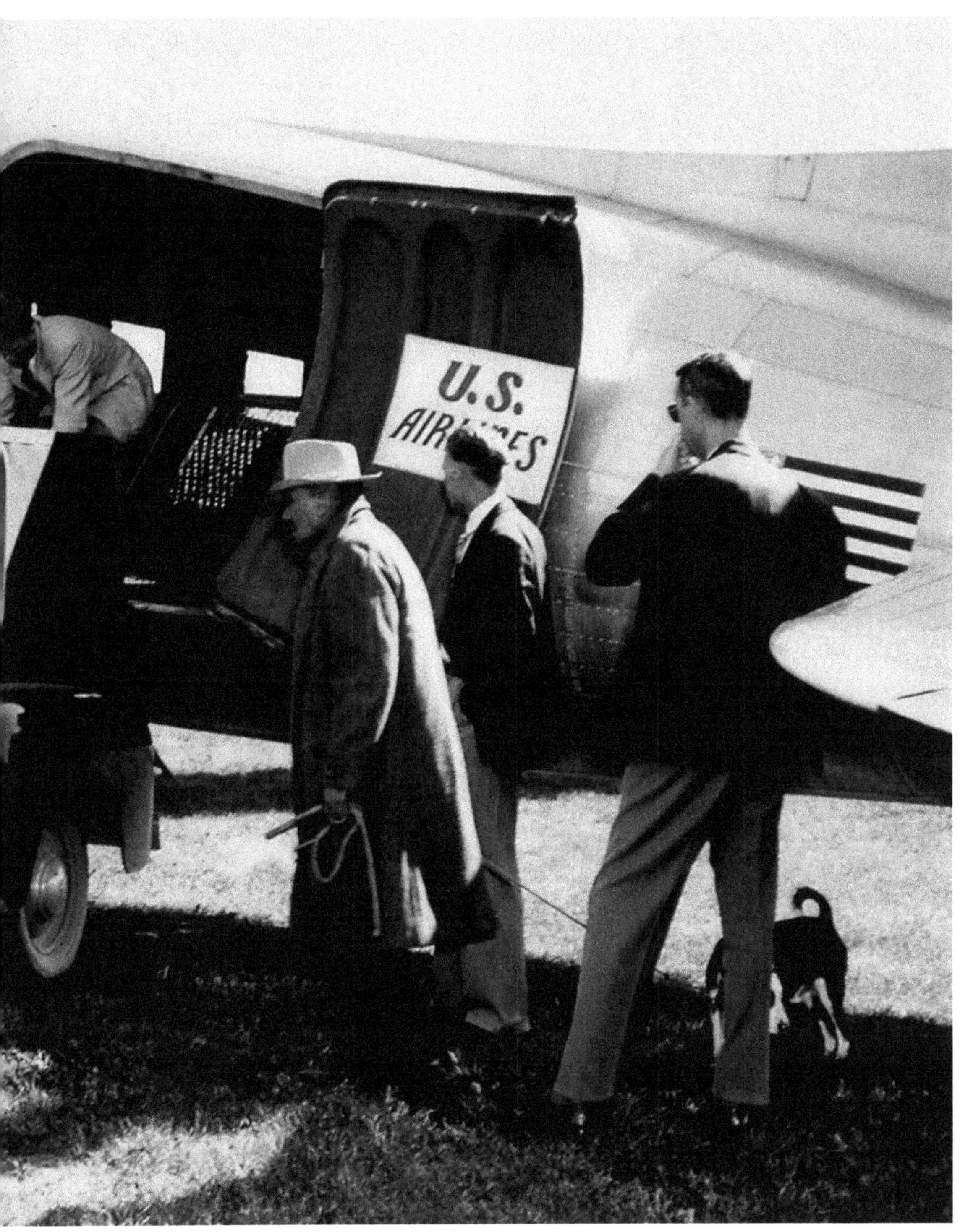


Tige o' My Heart being loaded onto transport plane at Blue Grass Airport, 1957.

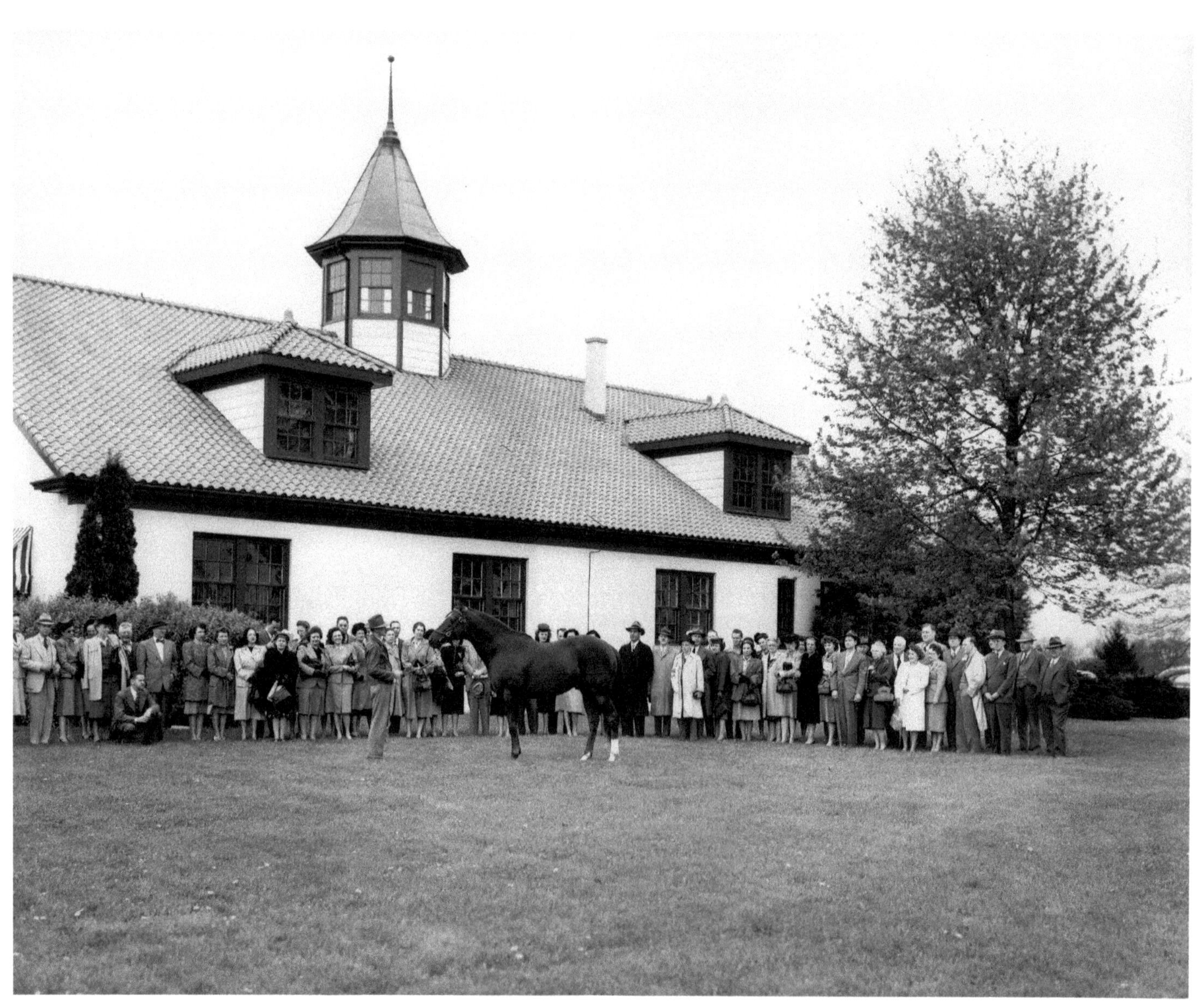

Whirlaway, 1941 Triple Crown winner, is admired by visitors to Calumet Farm on Versailles Road, 1947.

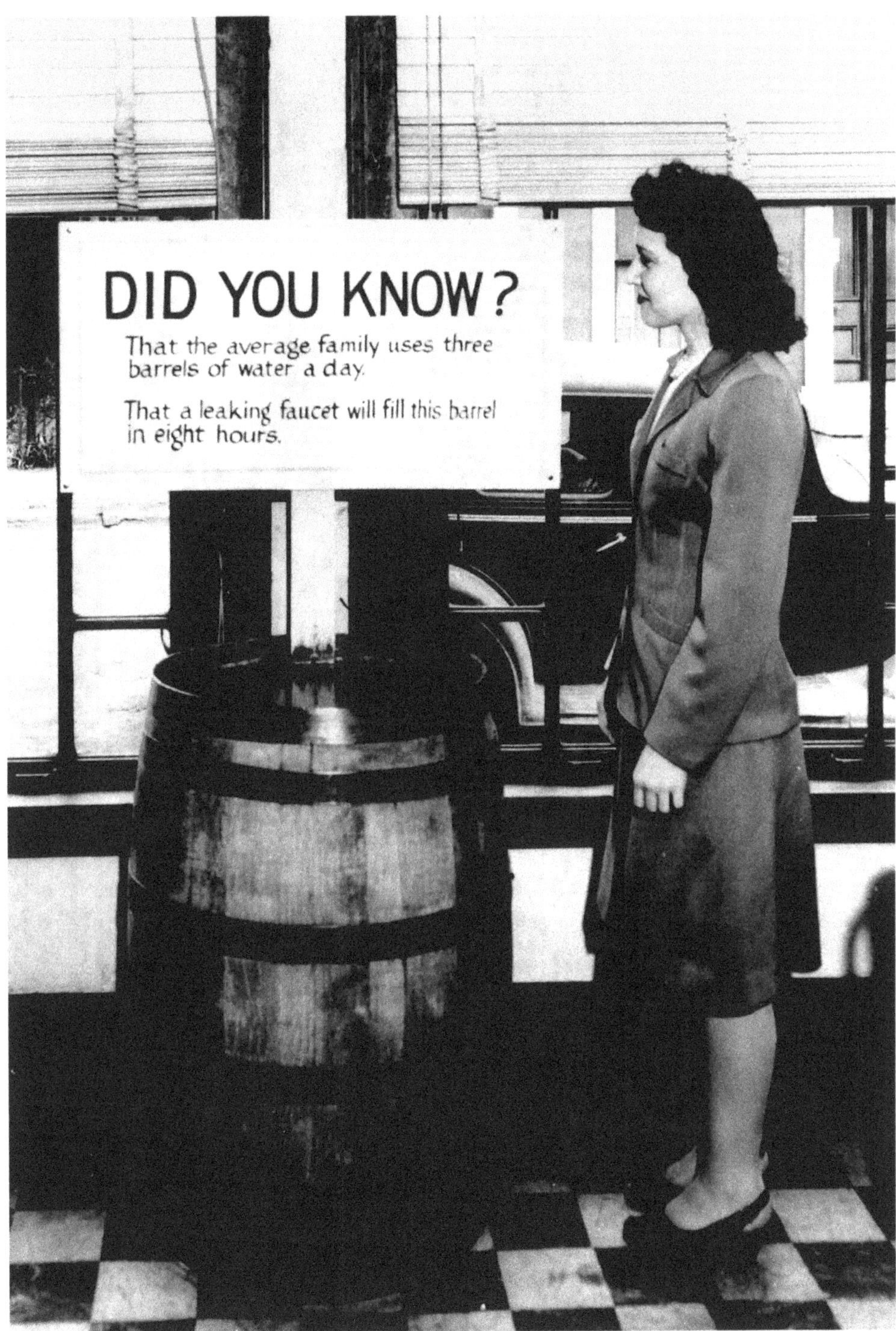


A public service ad by the Kentucky Water Service urged families to conserve water.

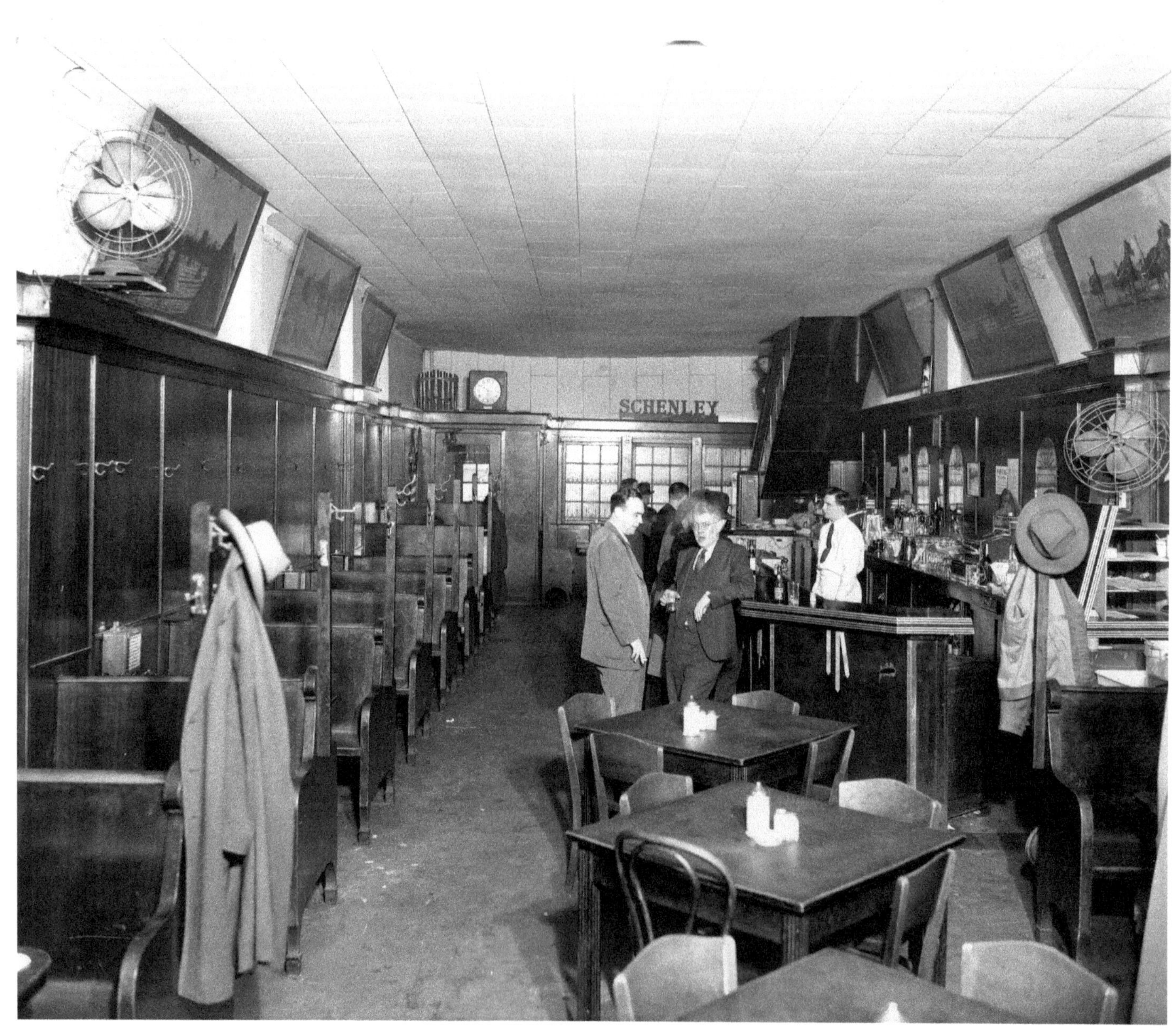


Interior of Keith's Restaurant (later The Golden Horseshoe) on Main Street, 1946.

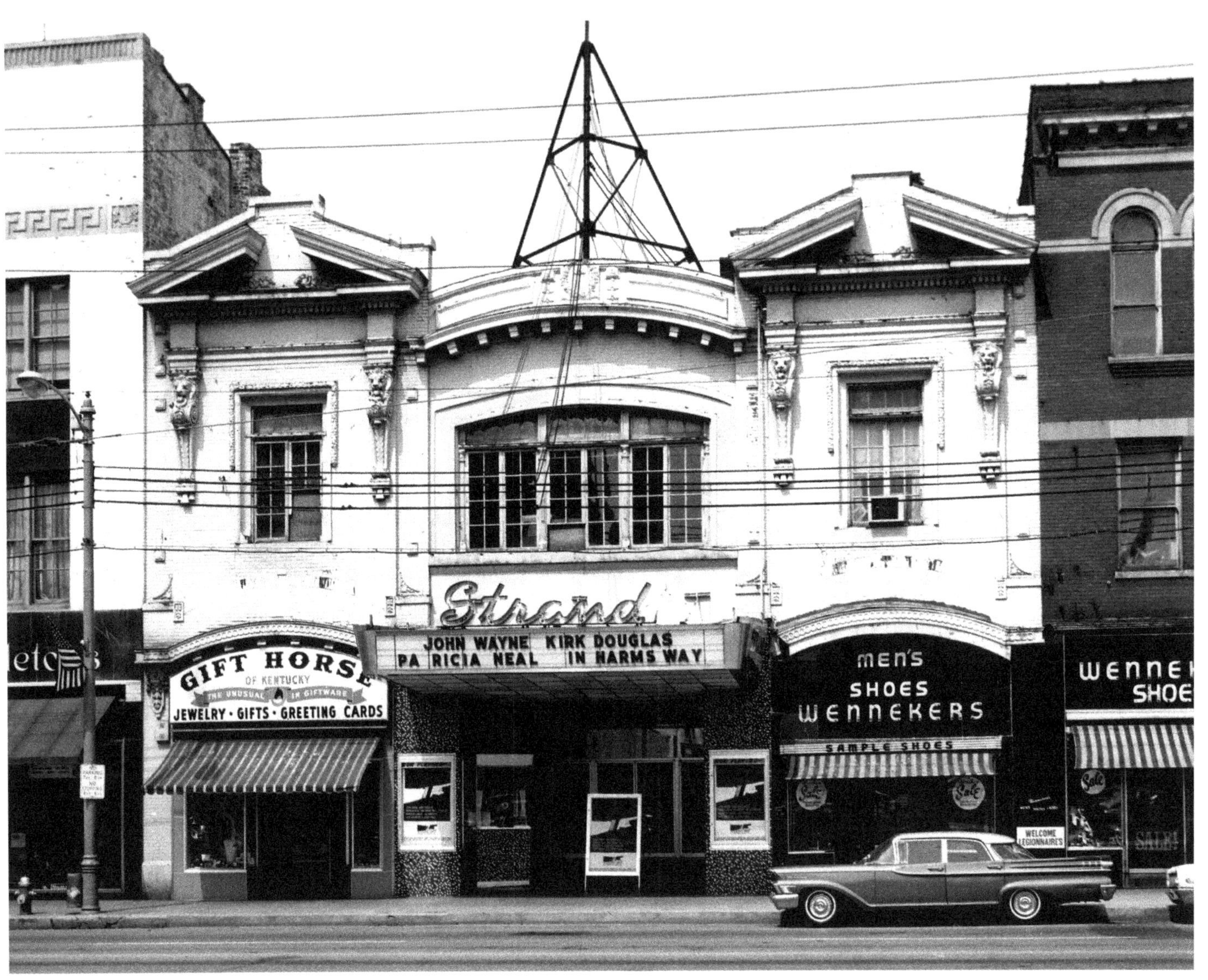


Strand Theater on Main Street (built as a livery stable about 1907, operated as theater from 1915 to 1973), mid 20th century.

Vogt Reel House (firehouse, built 1904) on Jefferson Street, 1965.

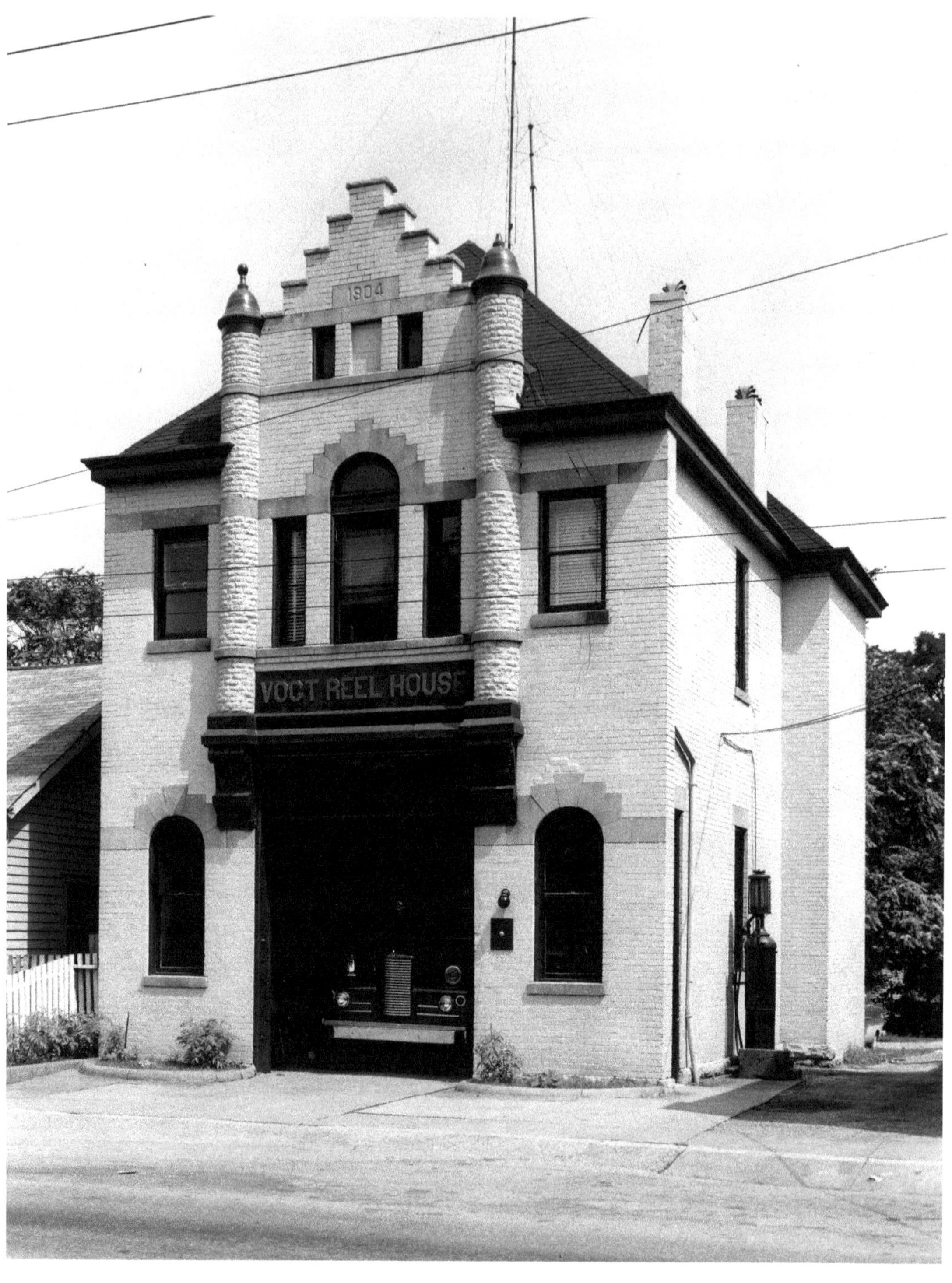

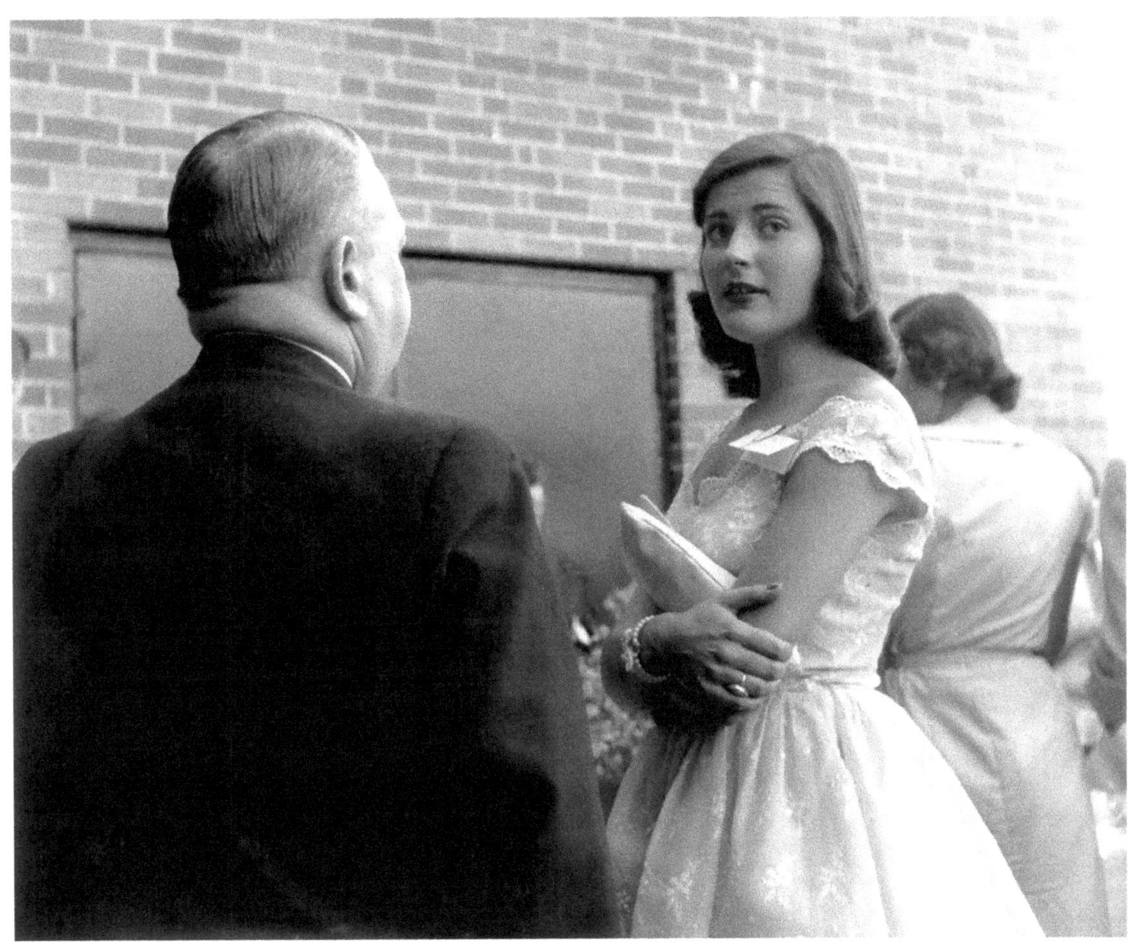

"Miss Kentucky" Ann Gillock at radio banquet in Lexington, 1957.

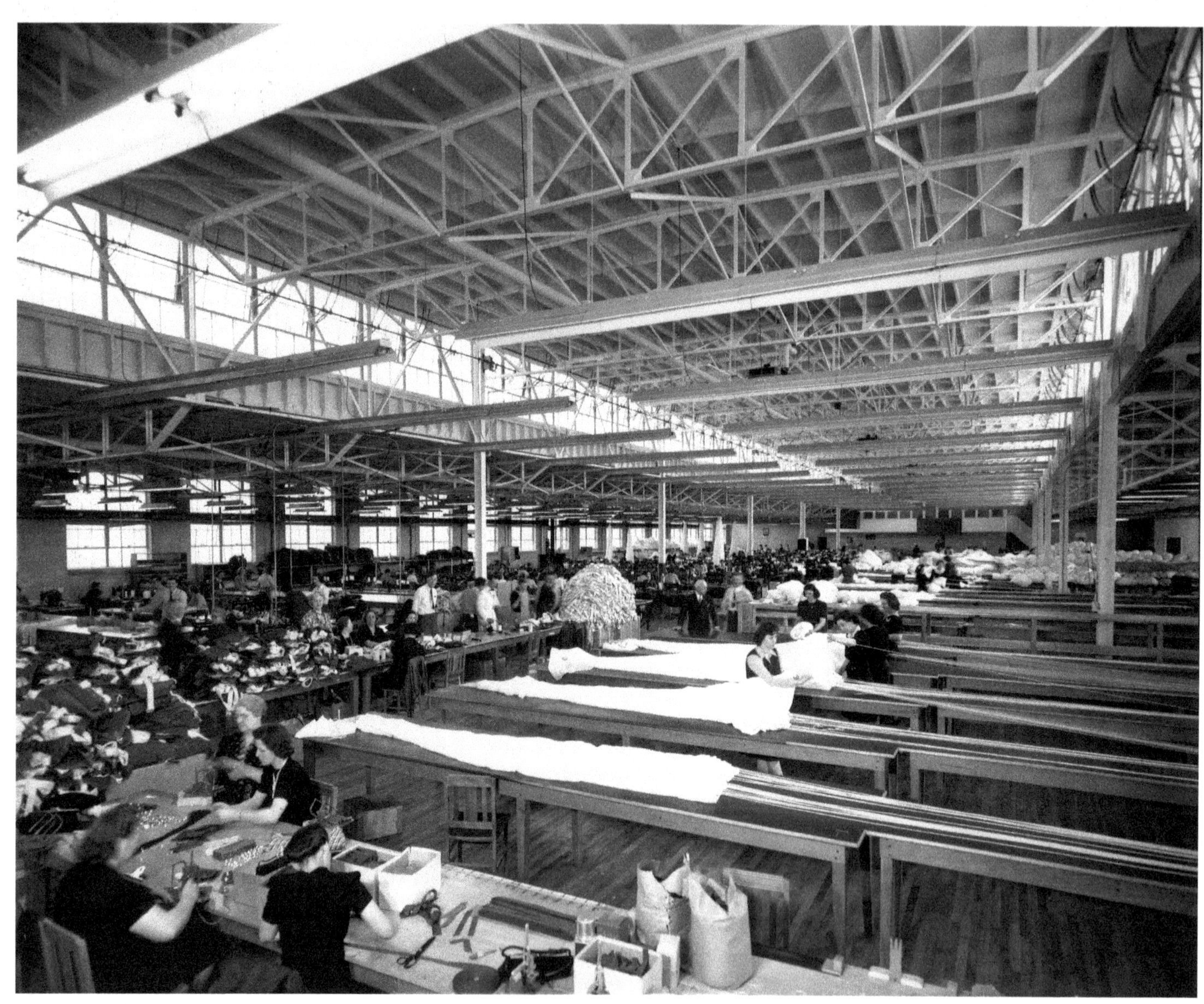

Women working at Irving Air Chute Company on Versailles Road (moved and expanded plant from Main Street in 1942), 1943.

Locals Betty Coed and the Debs perform at Joyland Park's dance casino on Paris Pike, 1940. National acts appeared there from time to time in the summer season.

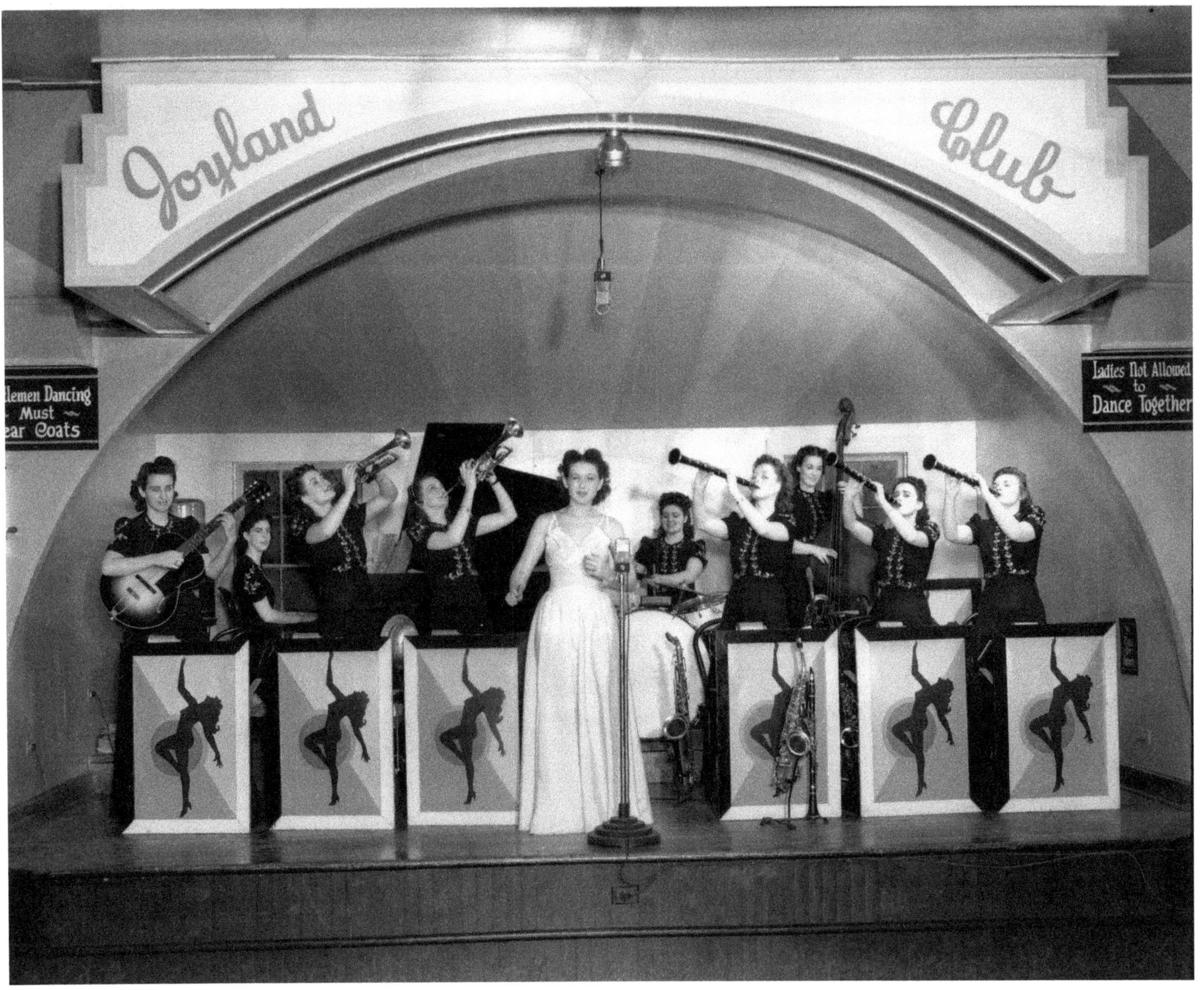

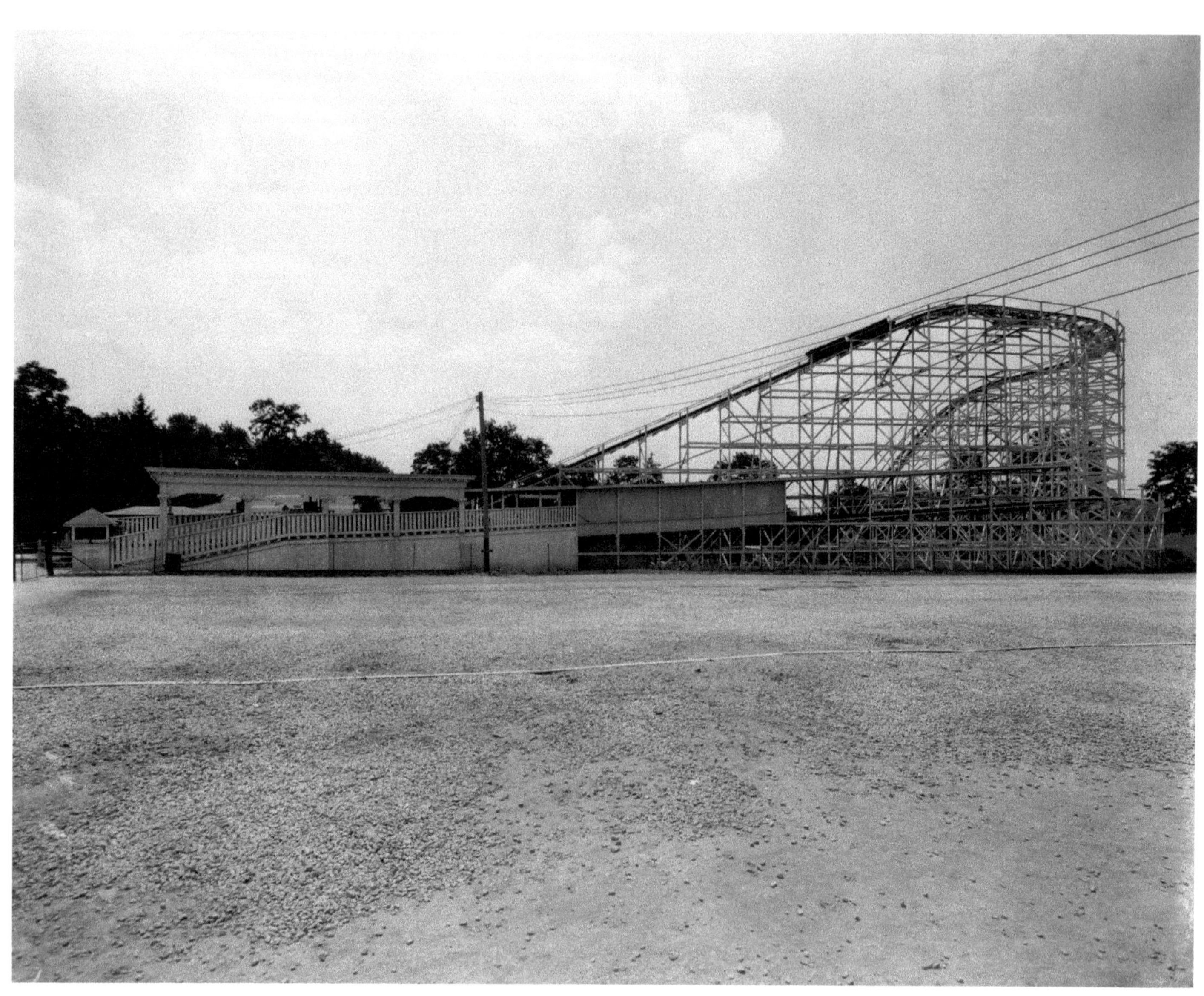

Roller coaster at Joyland Park, 1940.

Gathering at the Grand Army of the Republic plot
in the Lexington Cemetery, 1948.

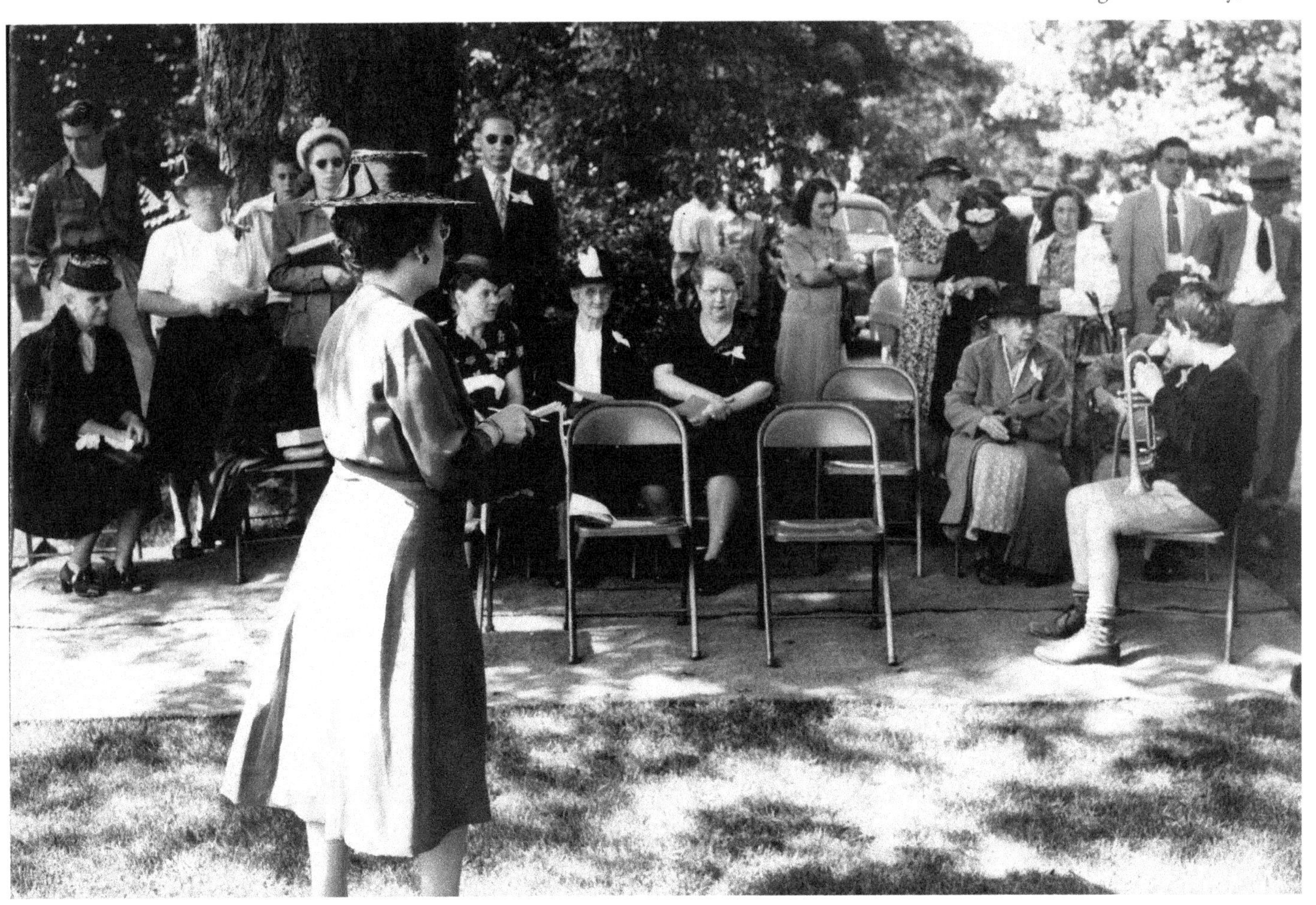

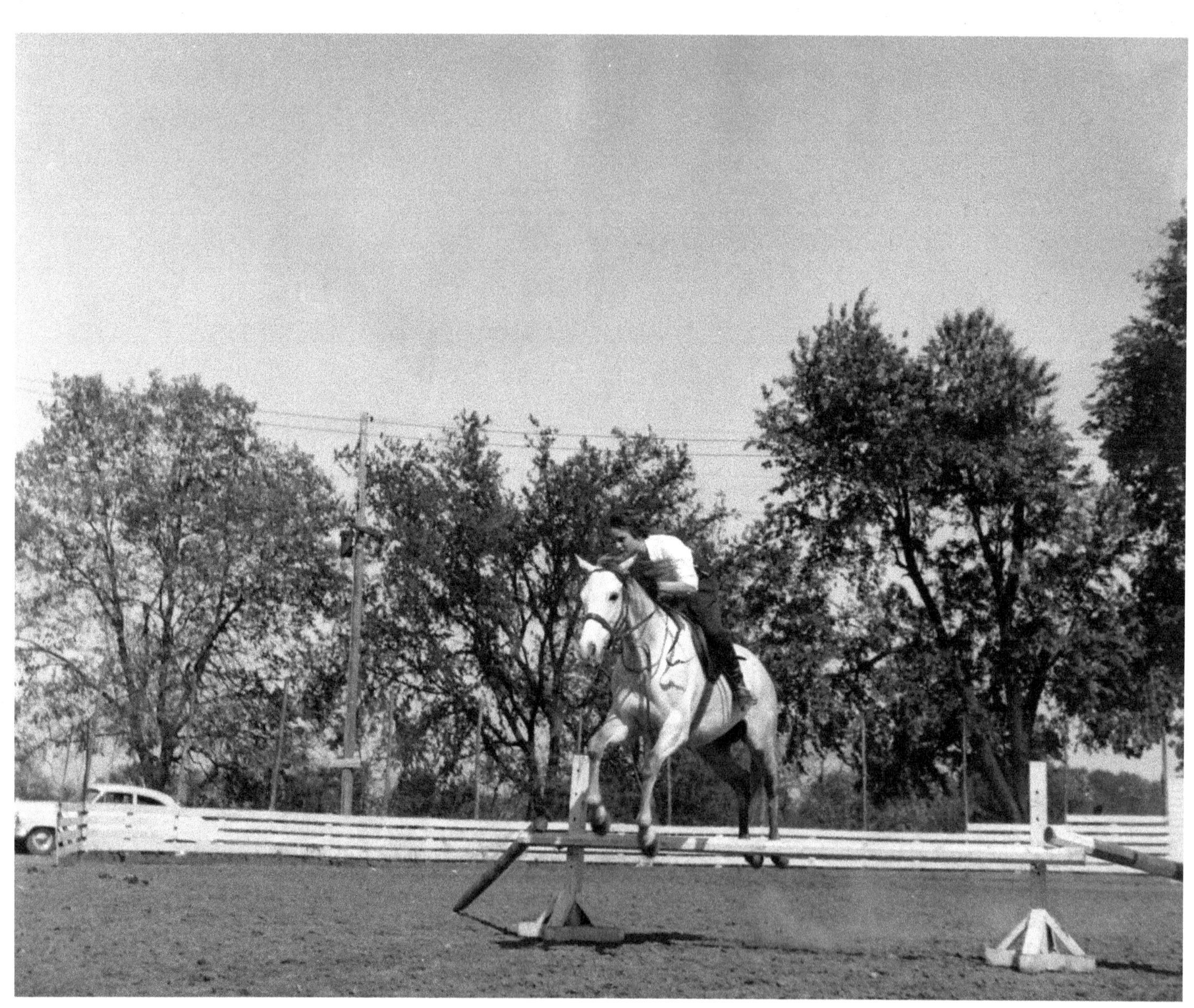

University of Kentucky equestrienne prepares for the Block and Bridle Horse Show at the trotting track, 1958.

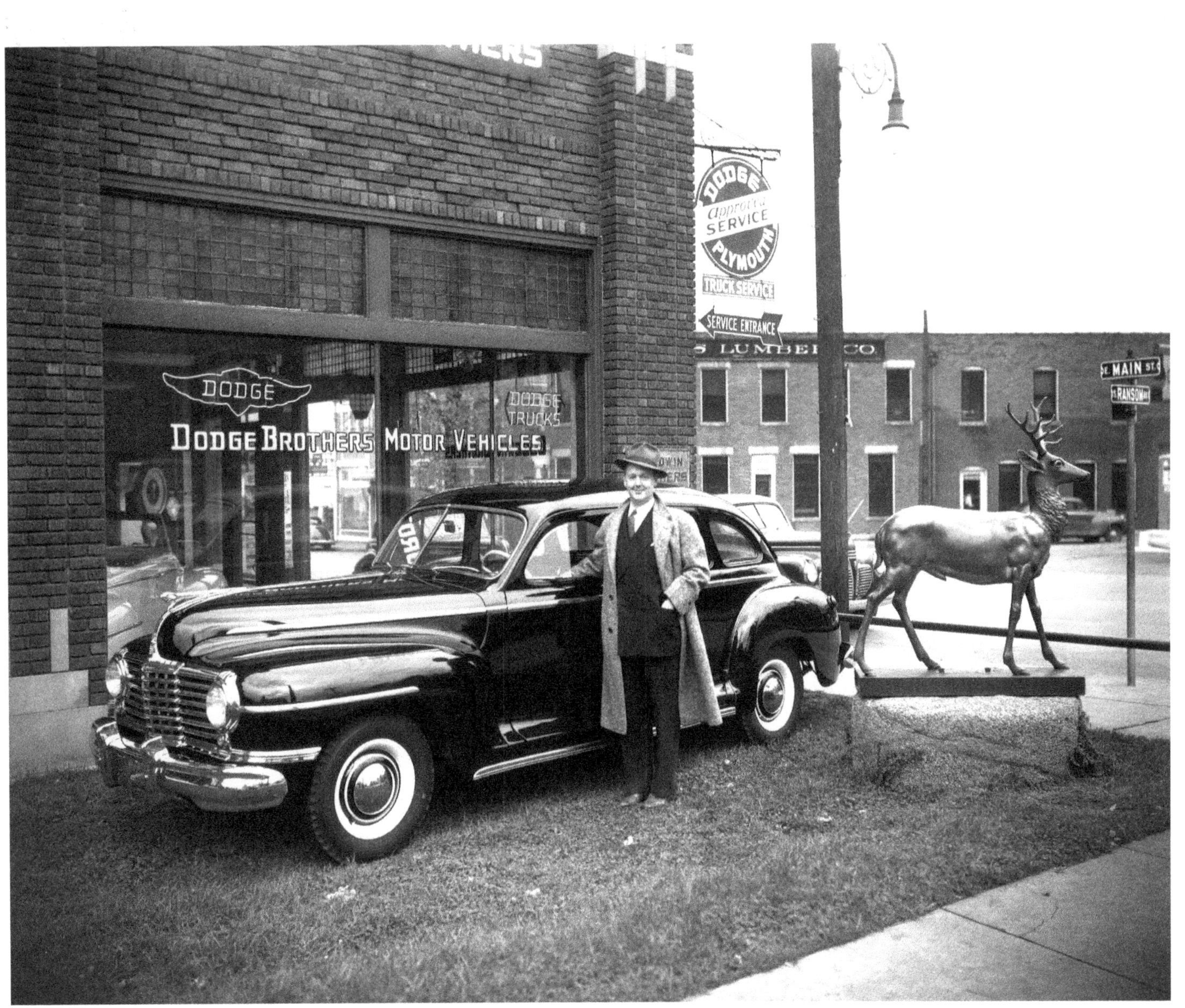


Goodwin Brothers automobile dealership on Main Street, 1941.

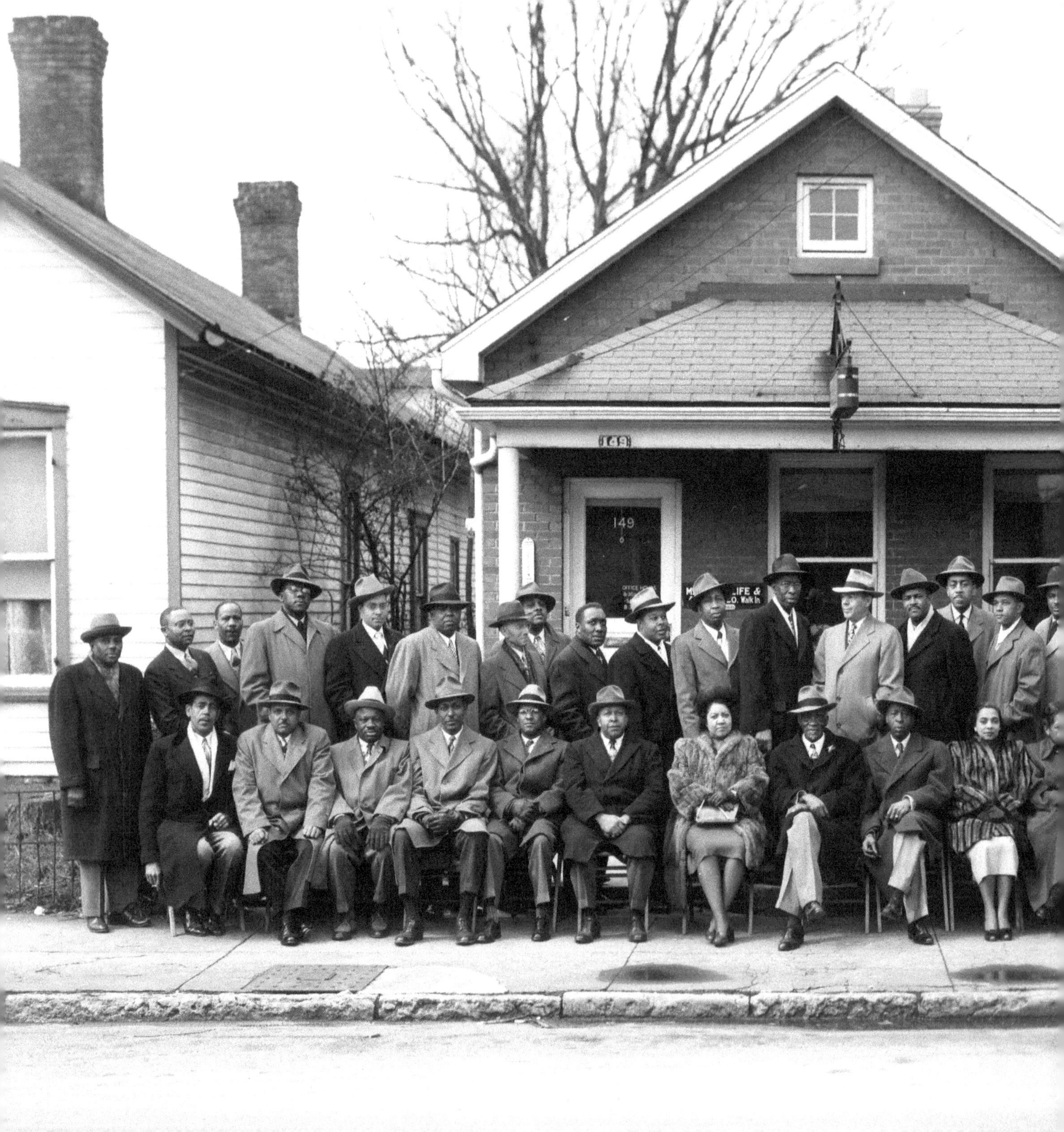
149
149
OFFICE HOURS
Walk In

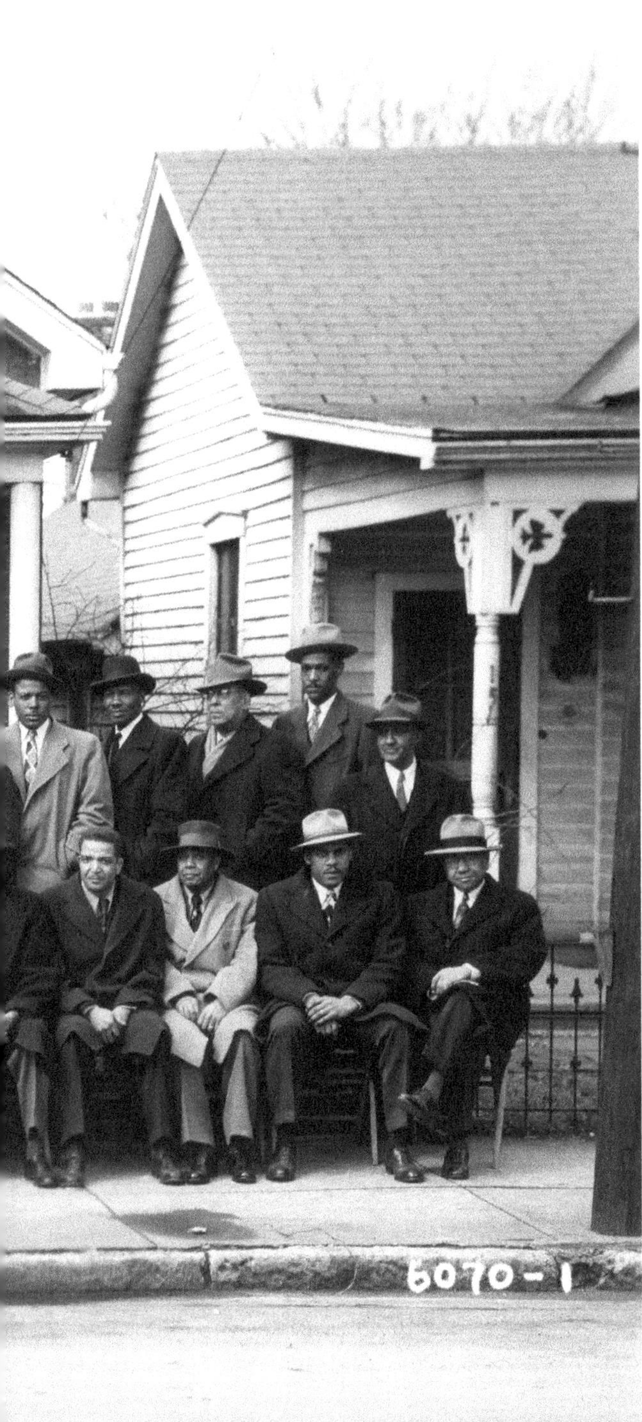


Mammoth Life Insurance Company (Kentucky's largest African-American owned business, founded in 1915) on Deweese Street, 1949.

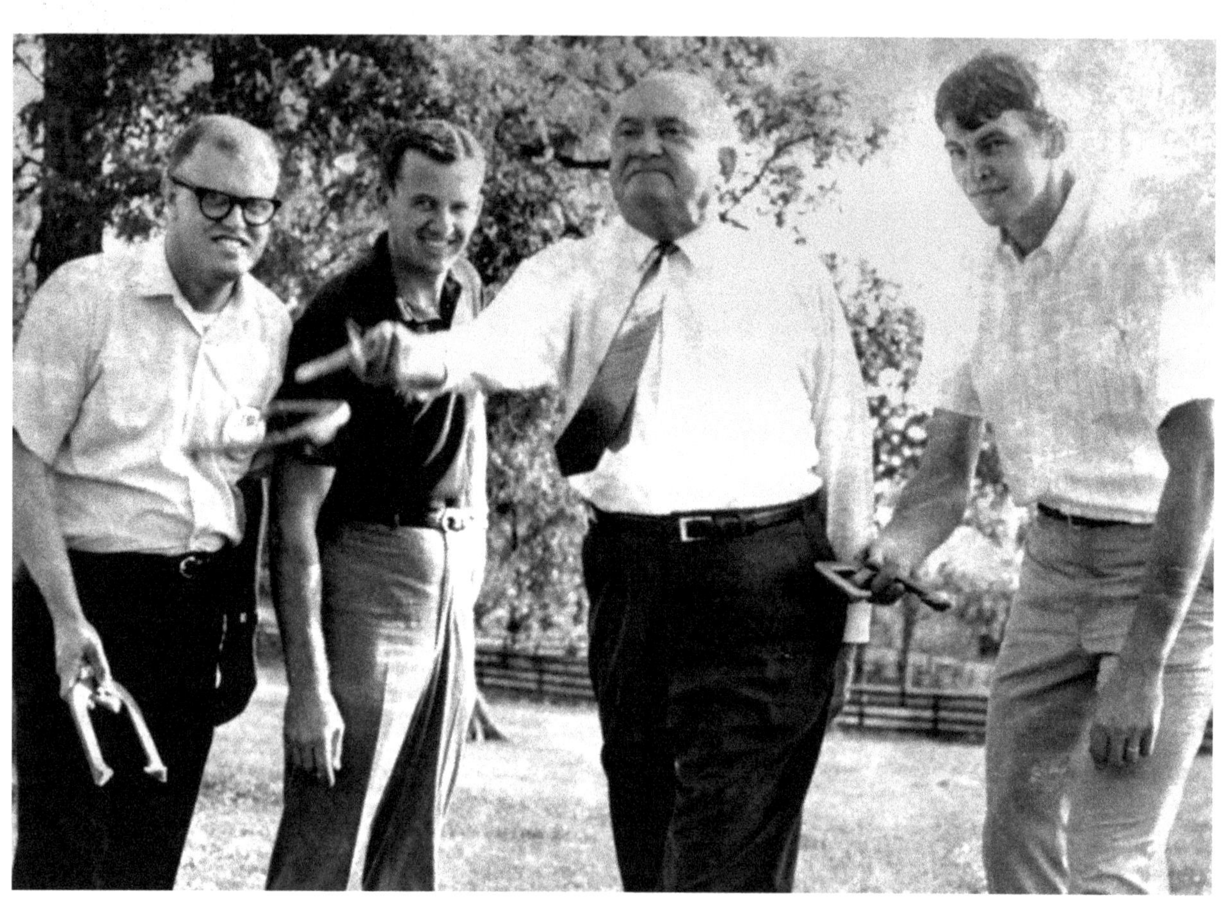

Basketball's Adolph Rupp (University of Kentucky coach 1930-71) playing horseshoes. Wildcat Dan Issel (far right), was later inducted into the NBA Hall of Fame.

Margaret I. King Library at the University of Kentucky (dedicated 1931), 1940.

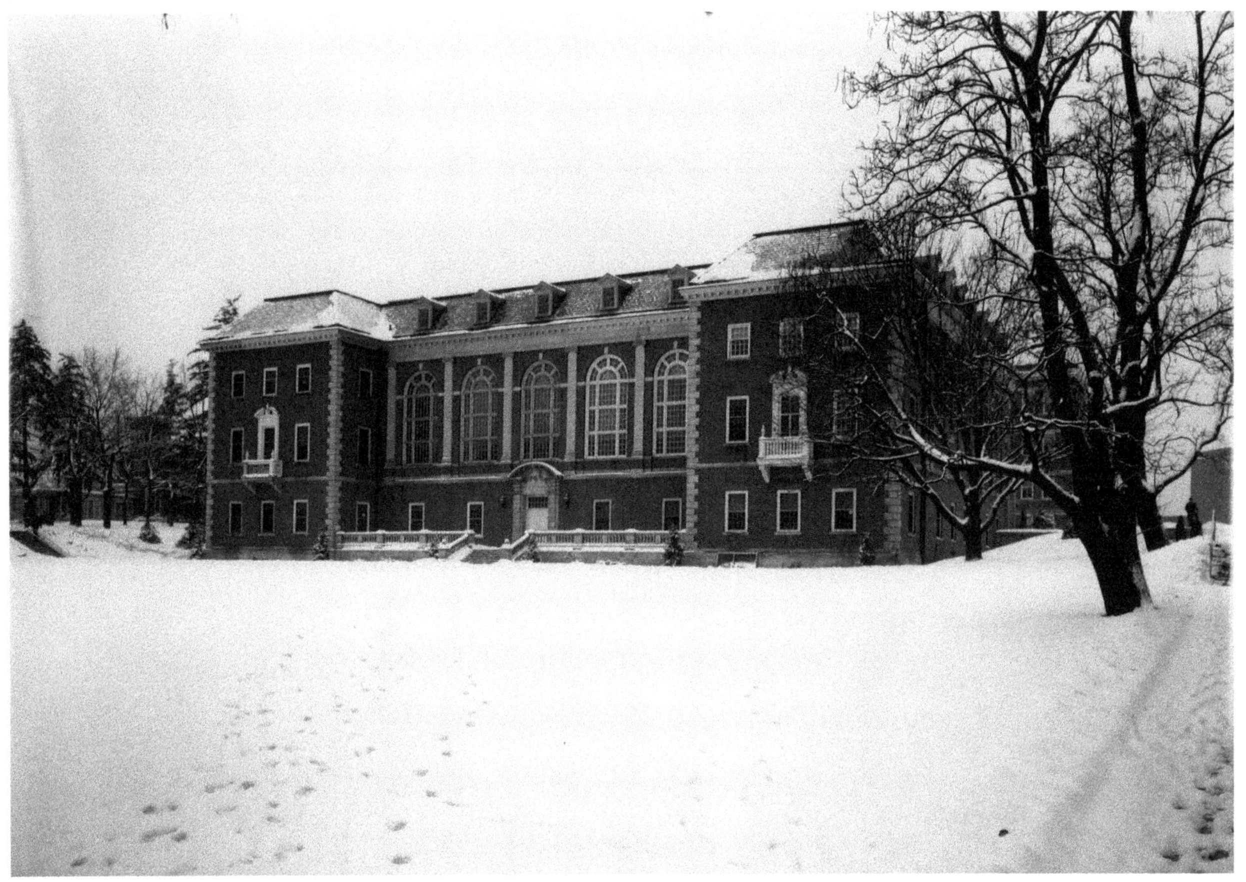

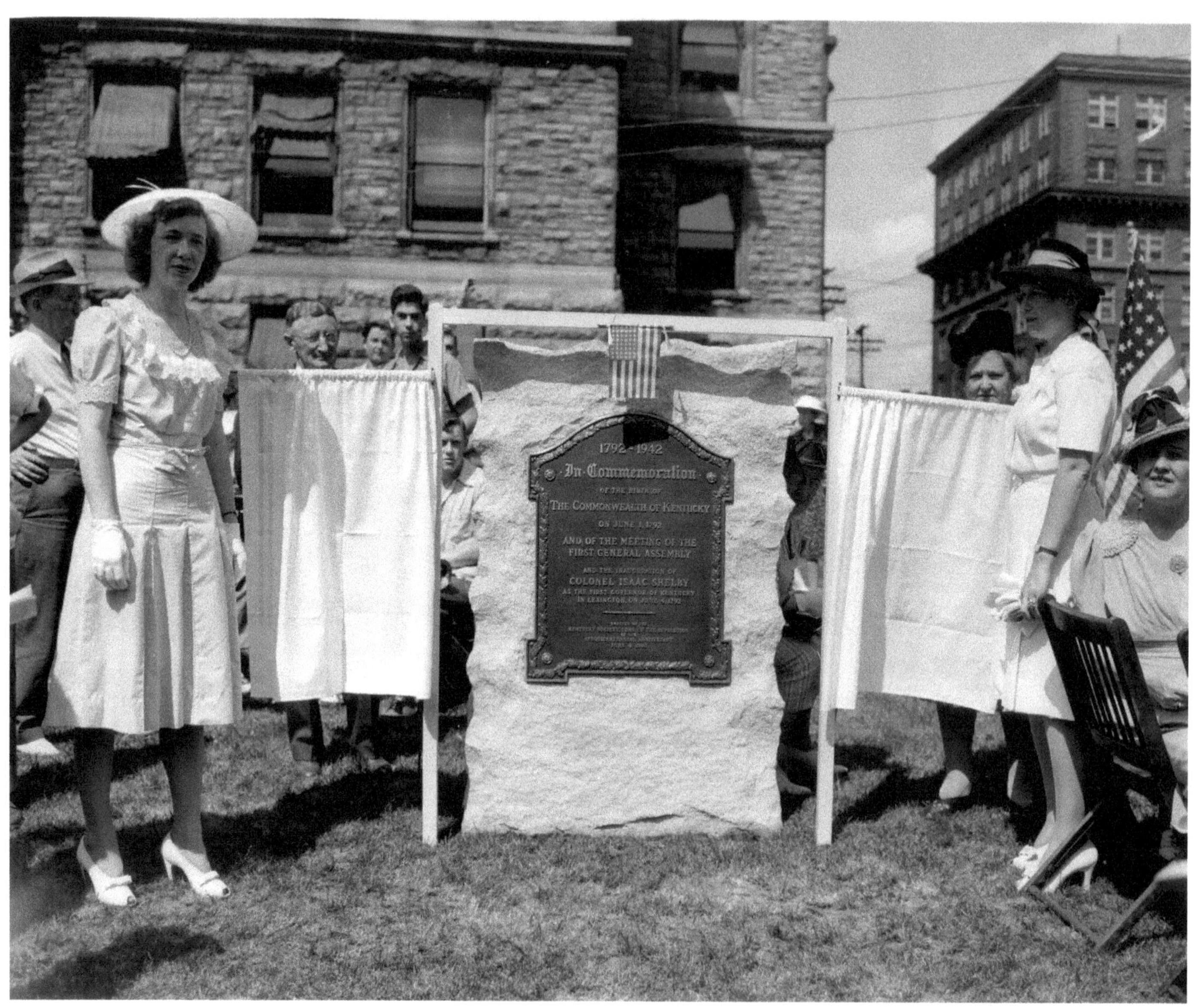


Monument celebrating Lexington's sesquicentennial reads: 1792-1942: In Commemoration of the Birth of the Commonwealth of Kentucky on June 1, 1792.

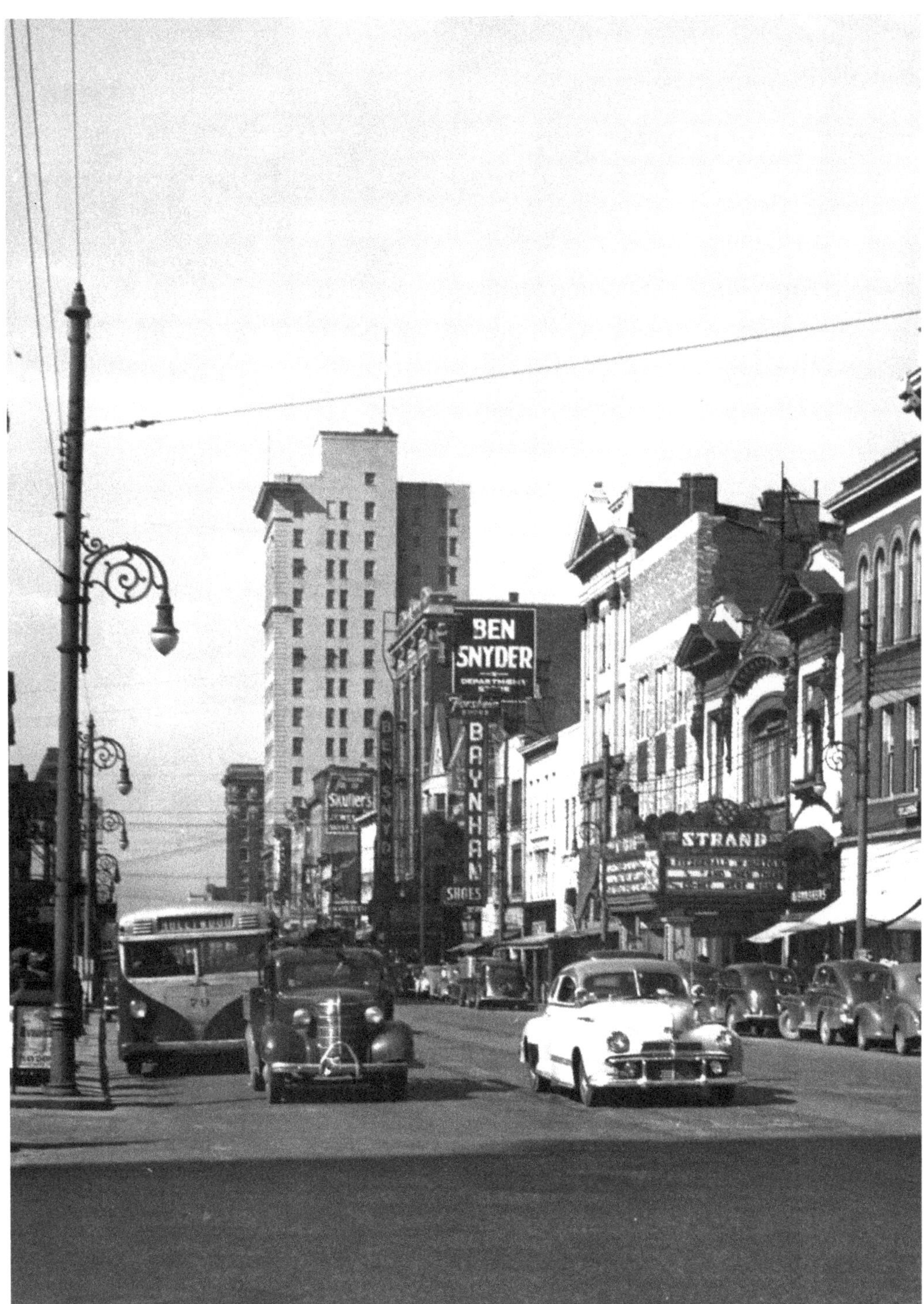


Looking west down Main Street from Union Station, 1944.

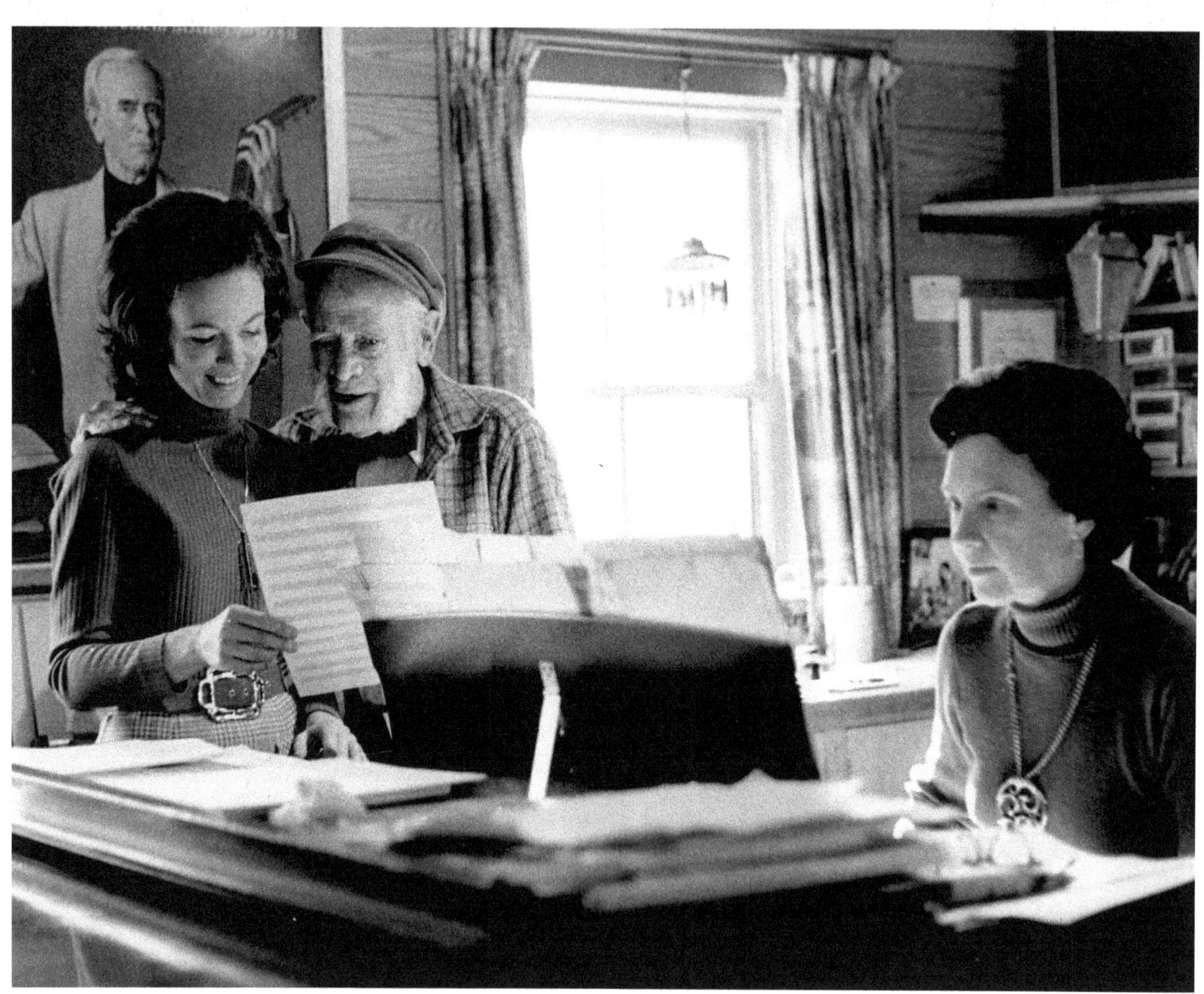

Kentucky native and renown balladeer John Jacob Niles (center) was the featured performer at the newly restored Lexington Opera House.

# Notes on the Photographs

These notes, listed by page number, attempt to include all aspects known of the photographs. The page number, photograph's title or description, photographer/collection, archive and call or box number when applicable identifies each of the photographs. While every attempt was made to collect all available data, in some cases complete data was unavailable due to the age and condition of some of the photographs and records.

**II College of the Bible**
kukav:2002:017
J. Soule Smith
Art Work of the Blue Grass Region of Kentucky
University of Kentucky Libraries

**VI View of Third Street**
kukav:2002av02:075
J. Soule Smith
Art Work of the Blue Grass Region of Kentucky
University of Kentucky Libraries

**X Street Car Center at Courthouse**
ktu:pa1:364
Bullock Photograph Collection
Transylvania University Library, Lexington, Ky.

**2. Funeral Procession of Senator Henry Clay**
kukuarp:1998ua002:3932
Louis Edward Nollau Collection
University of Kentucky Libraries

**3 Old Soldiers' Reunion**
ktu:pa1:36
Transylvania University Library, Lexington, Ky.
Bullock Photograph Collection

**4 Lexington's Third Courthouse**
kukav:pa62w8:0189
Wilson Family Photographic Collection
University of Kentucky Libraries

**5 Upper Market House**
Kukuarp:1998ua001:211_007
University of Kentucky Libraries
Louis Edward Nollau Collection

**6 Stage Coach**
ktu:pa1:52
Bullock Photograph Collection
Transylvania University Library, Lexington, Ky.

**7 Lexington Fire Department**
J. Winston Coleman, Jr. Photographic
Transylvania University Library, Lexington, Ky.

**8 Sheriff's Office**
ktu:pa1:31b
Bullock Photograph Collection
Transylvania University Library, Lexington, Ky.

**9 Hemp Field**
kukav:2002av02:042
J. Soule Smith
Art Work of the Blue Grass Region of Kentucky
University of Kentucky Libraries

**10 Madam Belle Brezing**
kukav:2003av1:007
Belle Brezing Photographic Collection
University of Kentucky Libraries

**11 Kentucky State Guard**
ktu:pa1:41
Transylvania University Library, Lexington, Ky.
Bullock Photograph Collection

**12 Morton High School Seniors**
kukarp:2001ua028:4754
Portrait Print Collection
University of Kentucky Libraries

**13 African American Baptism**
ktu:pa1:19
Bullock Photograph Collection
Transylvania University Library, Lexington, Ky.

**14 Lexington's Fifth Courthouse**
kukav:pa62m49:PA62M49_029
Lyle Family Photographic Collection
University of Kentucky Libraries

**15 Lexington's Post Office**
kukav:2002av02:002
J. Soule Smith
Art Work of the Blue Grass Region of Kentucky
University of Kentucky Libraries

**16. Courthouse at Main and Cheapside**
kukav:80pa121:0071
Louis Edward Nollau High Bridge Collection
University of Kentucky Libraries

**17 Cheapside**
kukav:pa62w8:0191
Wilson Family Photographic Collection
University of Kentucky Libraries

**18 The Straus Building**
ktu:pa1:25a
Bullock Photograph Collection
Transylvania University Library, Lexington, Ky.

**19 Broadway**
kukav:2002av02:090
J. Soule Smith
Art Work of the Blue Grass Region of Kentucky
University of Kentucky Libraries

**20 Central Christian Church**
kukav:2002av02:027
J. Soule Smith
Art Work of the Blue Grass Region of Kentucky
University of Kentucky Libraries

**21 Lexington Cemetary Entrance**
kukav:2002av02:007
J. Soule Smith
Art Work of the Blue Grass Region of Kentucky
University of Kentucky Libraries

**22 Hanover**
Kukav:2002av02:033
J. Soule Smith
Art Work of the Blue Grass Region of Kentucky
University of Kentucky Libraries

**23 Chenosa Lake**
ktu:pa1:340
Bullock Photograph Collection
Transylvania University Library, Lexington, Ky.

**24 Asylum gatehouse**
J. Winston Coleman, Jr. Photographic
Transylvania University Library, Lexington, Ky.

**25 Eastern Kentucky Asylum for the Insane**
kukav:2002av02:030
J. Soule Smith
Art Work of the Blue Grass Region of Kentucky
University of Kentucky Libraries

**26 Hopemont**
ktu:pa1:30a
Bullock Photograph Collection
Transylvania University Library, Lexington, Ky.

**27 Mule drawn trolleys**
ktu:pa1:46b
Bullock Photograph Collection
Transylvania University Library, Lexington, Ky.

**28 Orphan Asylum**
ktu:pa1:230
Bullock Photograph Collection
Transylvania University Library, Lexington, Ky.

**29 Phoenix Hotel**
kukav:2002av02:091
J. Soule Smith
Art Work of the Blue Grass Region of Kentucky
University of Kentucky Libraries

**30 Lexington Opera House**
kukav:2002av02:031
J. Soule Smith
Art Work of the Blue Grass Region of Kentucky
University of Kentucky Libraries

**32 Red Mile Grandstand**
J. Winston Coleman, Jr. Photographic
Transylvania University Library, Lexington, Ky.

**33 Morgan's Men**
pa79w1:166
Samuel M. Wilson Photographic Collection
University of Kentucky Libraries

**34 View on Broadway, ca. 1898**
kukav:2002av02:088
J. Soule Smith
Art Work of the Blue Grass Region of Kentucky
University of Kentucky Libraries

**36 Bryan Station Memorial**
Kukav:2002av02:001
J. Soule Smith
Art Work of the Blue Grass Region of Kentucky
University of Kentucky Libraries

**38 Kentucky Association Racetrack**
ktu:pa1:44b
Bullock Photograph Collection
Transylvania University Library, Lexington, Ky.

**39 Old Morrison**
ktu:pa1:451a
Bullock Photograph Collection
Transylvania University Library, Lexington, Ky.

**40 Monument to John. C. Breckinridge**
kukav:2002av02:032
J. Soule Smith
Art Work of the Blue Grass Region of Kentucky
University of Kentucky Libraries

**42 Masterson's Station**
kukav:2002av02:023
J. Soule Smith
Art Work of the Blue Grass Region of Kentucky
University of Kentucky Libraries

**43 Lyon Firehouse**
ktu:pa1:452
Bullock Photograph Collection
Transylvania University Library, Lexington, Ky.

**44 Revival In Woodlawn Park**
ktu:pa1:45b
Bullock Photograph Collection
Transylvania University Library, Lexington, Ky.

**46 Main Street, 1898**
kukav:2002av02:051
J. Soule Smith
Art Work of the Blue Grass Region of Kentucky
University of Kentucky Libraries

**48 Fayette County Jail**
J. Winston Coleman, Jr. Photographic
Transylvania University Library, Lexington, Ky.

**49 Gratz Kitchen**
Ktu:pa1:211
Bullock Photograph Collection
Transylvania University Library, Lexington, Ky.

**50 Hamilton College**
Kukav:2002av02:038
J. Soule Smith
Art Work of the Blue Grass Region of Kentucky
University of Kentucky Libraries

**52 Short Street**
kukav:2002av02:108
J. Soule Smith
Art Work of the Blue Grass Region of Kentucky
University of Kentucky Libraries

**54 Women and Christian Temperance Union**
kukav:2002av02:060
J. Soule Smith
Art Work of the Blue Grass Region of Kentucky
University of Kentucky Libraries

**55 Agricultural and Mechanical College of Kentucky**
kukav:2002av02:070
J. Soule Smith
Art Work of the Blue Grass Region of Kentucky
University of Kentucky Libraries

**56 Johnson School**
kukav:2002av02:060
J. Soule Smith
Art Work of the Blue Grass Region of Kentucky
University of Kentucky Libraries

**57 Aerial View of Short Street**
ktu:pa1:370
Bullock Photograph Collection
Transylvania University Library,
Lexington, Ky.

**58 Stable on Limestone**
J. Winston Coleman, Jr. Photographic
Transylvania University Library,
Lexington, Ky.

**59 Sayre Female Institute**
ktu:pa1:600
Transylvania University Library,
Lexington, Ky.
Bullock Photograph Collection

**60 Students on the lawn of Sayre Female Institute**
ktu:pa1:601
Bullock Photograph Collection
Transylvania University Library,
Lexington, Ky.

**61 Floral Hall**
J. Winston Coleman, Jr. Photographic
Transylvania University Library,
Lexington, Ky.

**62 Police Station on Water Street**
ktu:pa1:48b
Bullock Photograph Collection
Transylvania University Library,
Lexington, Ky.

**64 County Officials on Courthouse Steps**
ktu:pa1:38
Bullock Photograph Collection
Transylvania University Library,
Lexington, Ky.

**65 Northern Bank Building**
ktu:pa1:278
Bullock Photograph Collection
Transylvania University Library,
Lexington, Ky.

**66 Ringling Brothers Parade**
Ktu:pa1:378
Bullock Photograph Collection
Transylvania University Library,
Lexington, Ky.

**67 St. Paul's Catholic Church**
ktu:pa1:502
Bullock Photograph Collection
Transylvania University Library,
Lexington, Ky.

**68 Soliders at Union Station**
Kukarp:1998au001:53_002
Louis Edward Nollau Collection
University of Kentucky Libraries

**69 Golden Jubilee**
kukarp:1998au001:175_0001
Louis Edward Nollau Collection
University of Kentucky Libraries

**70 Choir of Second Presbyterian Church**
kukarp:1998ua01:360_0001
Louis Edward Nollau Collection
University of Kentucky Libraries

**71 Training Recruits Arrive**
kukarp:1998ua002:53_0003
Louis Edward Nollau Collection
University of Kentucky Libraries

**72 Mule carts excavating for spillway**
Photo courtesy of Kentucky American Water Company

**73 Lexington State College Band**
kukarp:1998ua001:042_0036
Louis Edward Nollau Collection
University of Kentucky Libraries

**74 Davidson School**
ktu:pa1:210
Bullock Photograph Collection
Transylvania University Library,
Lexington, Ky.

**75 Police station**
Ktu:pa1:218
Bullock Photograph Collection
Transylvania University Library,
Lexington, Ky.

**76 Streetcar accident**
Ktu:pa1:366
Bullock Photograph Collection
Transylvania University Library,
Lexington, Ky.

**77 Elegant High Street**
Ktu:pa1:307
Bullock Photograph Collection
Transylvania University Library,
Lexington, Ky.

**78 Old Mount Horeb Church**
Ktu:pa1:273
Bullock Photograph Collection
Transylvania University Library,
Lexington, Ky.

**79 Electric streetcar passing Phoenix Hotel**
Ktu:pa1:368
Bullock Photograph Collection
Transylvania University Library,
Lexington, Ky.

**80 Main and Broadway**
ktu:pa1:367
Bullock Photograph Collection
Transylvania University Library,
Lexington, Ky.

**81 Woodland Park Auditorium**
J. Winston Coleman, Jr. Photographic
Transylvania University Library,
Lexington, Ky.

**82 Interior of Main Street Christian**
J. Winston Coleman, Jr. Photographic
Transylvania University Library,
Lexington, Ky.

**83 Short Street during construction of National Bank**
J. Winston Coleman, Jr. Photographic
Transylvania University Library,
Lexington, Ky.

**84 Main and Upper Street**
J. Winston Coleman, Jr. Photographic
Transylvania University Library,
Lexington, Ky.

**85 Old Central Fire Department**
J. Winston Coleman, Jr. Photographic
Transylvania University Library,
Lexington, Ky.

**86 Prominent Horsemen**
J. Winston Coleman, Jr. Photographic
Transylvania University Library,
Lexington, Ky.

**87 Coal Company on Broadway**
J. Winston Coleman, Jr. Photographic
Transylvania University Library,
Lexington, Ky.

**88 Fire companies race at trotting track**
J. Winston Coleman, Jr. Photographic
Transylvania University Library,
Lexington, Ky.

**90 Mary Todd Lincoln's girlhood home**
pa62w8:0188
Wilson Family Photographic Collection
University of Kentucky Libraries

**91 Jail on Short Street**
J. Winston Coleman, Jr. Photographic
Transylvania University Library,
Lexington, Ky.

**92 Security Trust Company Board of Directors**
J. Winston Coleman, Jr. Photographic
Transylvania University Library,
Lexington, Ky.

**93 Streetcar strikers**
J. Winston Coleman, Jr. Photographic
Transylvania University Library,
Lexington, Ky.

**94 Mary Dodd's class at East Hickan School**
kukav:80pa132:0023
Massillon Alexander Cassidy
Fayette County Schools Photographic Collection
University of Kentucky Libraries

**95 Fire department volunteers**
kukarp:1998ua001:392_0003
Louis Edward Nollau Collection
University of Kentucky Libraries

**96 Henry Howard Gratz**
ktu:pa1:520
Bullock Photograph Collection
Transylvania University Library,
Lexington, Ky.

**97 St. Joseph Hospital**
J. Winston Coleman, Jr. Photographic
Transylvania University Library,
Lexington, Ky.

**98 Carty Building**
J. Winston Coleman, Jr. Photographic
Transylvania University Library,
Lexington, Ky.

**99 Giddings Hall at Georgetown College**
Georgetown College Library
Special Collections

**100 Bankers Convention in Bellmont Woods**
ktu:pa1:522
Transylvania University Library,
Lexington, Ky.
Bullock Photograph Collection

**101 Main and Limestone with Crowler Bus**
kukuarp:1998ua002:3960
Louis Edward Nollau Collection
University of Kentucky Libraries

**102 Town Branch**
J. Winston Coleman, Jr. Photographic
Transylvania University Library,
Lexington, Ky.

**104 Old Saint Peter's Catholic Church**
J. Winston Coleman, Jr. Photographic
Transylvania University Library,
Lexington, Ky.

**105 Ice Plant**
J. Winston Coleman, Jr. Photographic
Transylvania University Library,
Lexington, Ky.

**106 Lynch mob at the courthouse**
J. Winston Coleman, Jr. Photographic
Transylvania University Library,
Lexington, Ky.

**107 Main Street during 1928 flood**
J. Winston Coleman, Jr. Photographic
Transylvania University Library,
Lexington, Ky.

**108 Banquet at Phoenix Hotel**
J. Winston Coleman, Jr. Photographic
Transylvania University Library,
Lexington, Ky.

**109 Library browsing room**
kukav:lstudio:0890041
Lafayette Studio Collection
University of Kentucky Libraries

**110 Man O' War with Jeannette McDonald**
kukav:lstudio:0890011
Lafayette Studio Collection
University of Kentucky Libraries

**111 American Legion Parade**
kukav:lstudio:0890024
Lafayette Studio Collection
University of Kentucky Libraries

**112 Kelley's Liquor Dispensary**
kukav:lstudio:0890206
Lafayette Studio Collection
University of Kentucky Libraries

**113 Piggly Wiggly**
kukav:lstudio:0890202
Lafayette Studio Collection
University of Kentucky Libraries

**114 Lodge in Fayette Park**
kukav:pa62w8:0490
Wilson Family Photographic
Collection
University of Kentucky Libraries

**115 Hoisting a Signal**
kukuarp:1998ua002:4226
Louis Edward Nollau Collection
University of Kentucky Libraries

**116 Christmas Parade on Main Street**
kukav:lstudio:0890034
Lafayette Studio Collection
University of Kentucky Libraries

**117 Flooded Alumni Gymnasium**
kukarp:1998ua001:186_0005
Louis Edward Nollau Collection
University of Kentucky Libraries

**118 Prior to race at Keeneland**
Keeneland Library

**119 Jockey weighing in**
Keeneland Library

**120 At the start of the race**
Keeneland Library

**122 Idle Hour**
kukarp:1998ua002:3950
Louis Edward Nollau Collection
University of Kentucky Libraries

**123 Checking a fire hydrant**
Photo courtesy of Kentucky American
Water

**124 Professor Granville Terrel**
kukarp:2001ua028:4613
Louis Edward Nollau Collection
University of Kentucky Libraries

**125 Blessing of the Hounds**
J. Winston Coleman, Jr. Photographic
Transylvania University Library,
Lexington, Ky.

**126 Epping Bottling Works**
kukav:lstudio:0890201
Lafayette Studio Collection
University of Kentucky Libraries

**127 Mayor O'Brien with Nubian lion cub**
kukav:lstudio:0890241
Lafayette Studio Collection
University of Kentucky Libraries

**128 Main Street in flood**
kukav:lstudio:0890122
Lafayette Studio Collection
University of Kentucky Libraries

**129 Clark's Hardware**
Kukav:lstudio:0890030
Lafayette Studio Collection
University of Kentucky Libraries

**130 Dunn's Drug Store on South Limestone Street**
Kukav:lstudio:0890101
Lafayette Studio Collection
University of Kentucky Libraries

**131 Raid on moonshine still**
Kukav:lstdio:0890023
Lafayette Studio Collection
University of Kentucky Libraries

**132 Hamburg Place**
Kukav:lstudio:0890081
Lafayette Studio Collection
University of Kentucky Libraries

**134 Marion Miley**
Kukav:lstudio:0890138
Lafayette Studio Collection
University of Kentucky Libraries

**135 Hutchinson Drugs on West Main Street**
kukav:lstudio:0890152
Lafayette Studio Collection
University of Kentucky Libraries

**136 Cannon in front of the Main Building at UK**
kukuarp:1998ua001:182_0002
Louis Edward Nollau
University of Kentucky Libraries

**137 Kentucky Theater**
Kukav:lstudio:0890238
Lafayette Studio Collection
University of Kentucky Libraries

**138 Democratic Convention**
Kukav:lstudio:0890128
Lafayette Studio Collection
University of Kentucky Libraries

**139 Lexington Public Library**
kukav:1997av27:2535
James Edwin Ed Weddle Photographic Collection
University of Kentucky Libraries

**140 Spotswood Specialty Company**
Kukav:lstudio:0890053
Lafayette Studio Collection
University of Kentucky Libraries

**141 The Gem House**
J. Winston Coleman, Jr. Photographic
Transylvania University Library,
Lexington, Ky.

**142 Jot 'em Down**
J. Winston Coleman, Jr. Photographic
Transylvania University Library,
Lexington, Ky.

**144 Blacksmith shop**
J. Winston Coleman, Jr. Photographic
Transylvania University Library,
Lexington, Ky.

**145 Robert J. Long**
kukav:lstudio:0890193
Lafayette Studio Collection
University of Kentucky Libraries

**146 Federal Post Office**
J. Winston Coleman, Jr. Photographic
Transylvania University Library,
Lexington, Ky.

**147 Renovated Floral Hall**
J. Winston Coleman, Jr. Photographic
Transylvania University Library,
Lexington, Ky.

**148 Greyhound Bus Station**
J. Winston Coleman, Jr. Photographic
Transylvania University Library,
Lexington, Ky.

**149 Mile marker**
J. Winston Coleman, Jr. Photographic
Transylvania University Library,
Lexington, Ky.

**150 Broadway Christian**
J. Winston Coleman, Jr. Photographic
Transylvania University Library,
Lexington, Ky.

**151 Cooke Memorial Library**
Georgetown University
Special Collections

**152 West on Main Street**
J. Winston Coleman, Jr. Photographic
Transylvania University Library,
Lexington, Ky.

**153 Lexington Brewery**
J. Winston Coleman, Jr. Photographic
Transylvania University Library,
Lexington, Ky.

**154 Christ Church Episcopal Cathedral**
J. Winston Coleman, Jr. Photographic
Transylvania University Library,
Lexington, Ky.

**155 Good Shepherd**
J. Winston Coleman, Jr. Photographic
Transylvania University Library,
Lexington, Ky.

**156 Woodland Christian Church**
J. Winston Coleman, Jr. Photographic
Transylvania University Library,
Lexington, Ky.

**157 Ohavay Zion Synagogue**
J. Winston Coleman, Jr. Photographic
Transylvania University Library,
Lexington, Ky.

**158 Newly sworn WAVES in front of Courthouse**
J. Winston Coleman, Jr. Photographic
Transylvania University Library,
Lexington, Ky.

**159 Jackson Hall**
J. Winston Coleman, Jr. Photographic
Transylvania University Library,
Lexington, Ky.

**160 War Casualties Monument**
J. Winston Coleman, Jr. Photographic
Transylvania University Library,
Lexington, Ky.

**161 Stop Over Station**
J. Winston Coleman, Jr. Photographic
Transylvania University Library,
Lexington, Ky.

**162 Archway at Keeneland**
Keeneland Library

**164 Funeral for Man O' War**
J. Winston Coleman, Jr. Photographic
Transylvania University Library,
Lexington, Ky.

**165 Jockeys at Keeneland**
Keeneland Library

**166 Sale of Tige O' My Heart**
Keeneland Library

**168 Tige O' My Heart loaded onto airplane**
Keeneland Library

**170 Whirlaway**
Kukav:lstudio:0890189
Lafayette Studio Collection
University of Kentucky Libraries

**171 Public service ad**
027-psa
Photo courtesy of Kentucky American Water

**172 Keith's Restaurant**
Kukav:lstudio:0890187
Lafayette Studio Collection
University of Kentucky Libraries

**173 Strand Theater**
J. Winston Coleman, Jr. Photographic
Transylvania University Library,
Lexington, Ky.

**174 Vogt Reel House**
J. Winston Coleman, Jr. Photographic
Transylvania University Library,
Lexington, Ky.

**175 "Miss Kentucky" Ann Gillock**
kukav:79pa104:0588
Radio Photographic Collection
University of Kentucky Libraries

**176 Irving Air Chute Company**
lstudio:0890179
Lafayette Studio Collection
University of Kentucky Libraries

**177 Betty Coed and the Debs**
lstudio:0890156
Lafayette Studio Collection
University of Kentucky Libraries

**178 Roller coaster at Joyland**
lstudio:0890123
Lafayette Studio Collection
University of Kentucky Libraries

**179 GAR at Lexington Cemetery**
kukav:61m158:020
Neville Family Papers
University of Kentucky Libraries

**180 University of Kentucky equestrienne**
kukarp:2001ua028:1962
Portrait Print Collection
University of Kentucky Libraries

**181 Goodwin Brothers**
lstudio:0890171
Lafayette Studio Collection
University of Kentucky Libraries

**182 Mammoth Life Insurance**
lstudio:0890195
Lafayette Studio Collection
University of Kentucky Libraries

**184 Adolph Rupp**
kukarp:2001ua028:3946
Portrait Print Collection
University of Kentucky Libraries

**185 Margaret I. King Library**
kukav:lstudio:0890042
Lafayette Studio Collection
University of Kentucky Libraries

**186 Sesquicentennial monument**
kukav:pa51w13:3
Samuel M. Wilson: Kentucky Sesquicentennial Collection
University of Kentucky Libraries

**187 West on Main Street from Union Station**
J. Winston Coleman, Jr. Photographic
Transylvania University Library,
Lexington, Ky.

**188 John Jacob Niles**
Archives of The Lexington Opera
House/Lexington Center Corp

**198 View across courthouse lawn**
J. Winston Coleman, Jr. Photographic
Transylvania University Library,
Lexington, Ky.

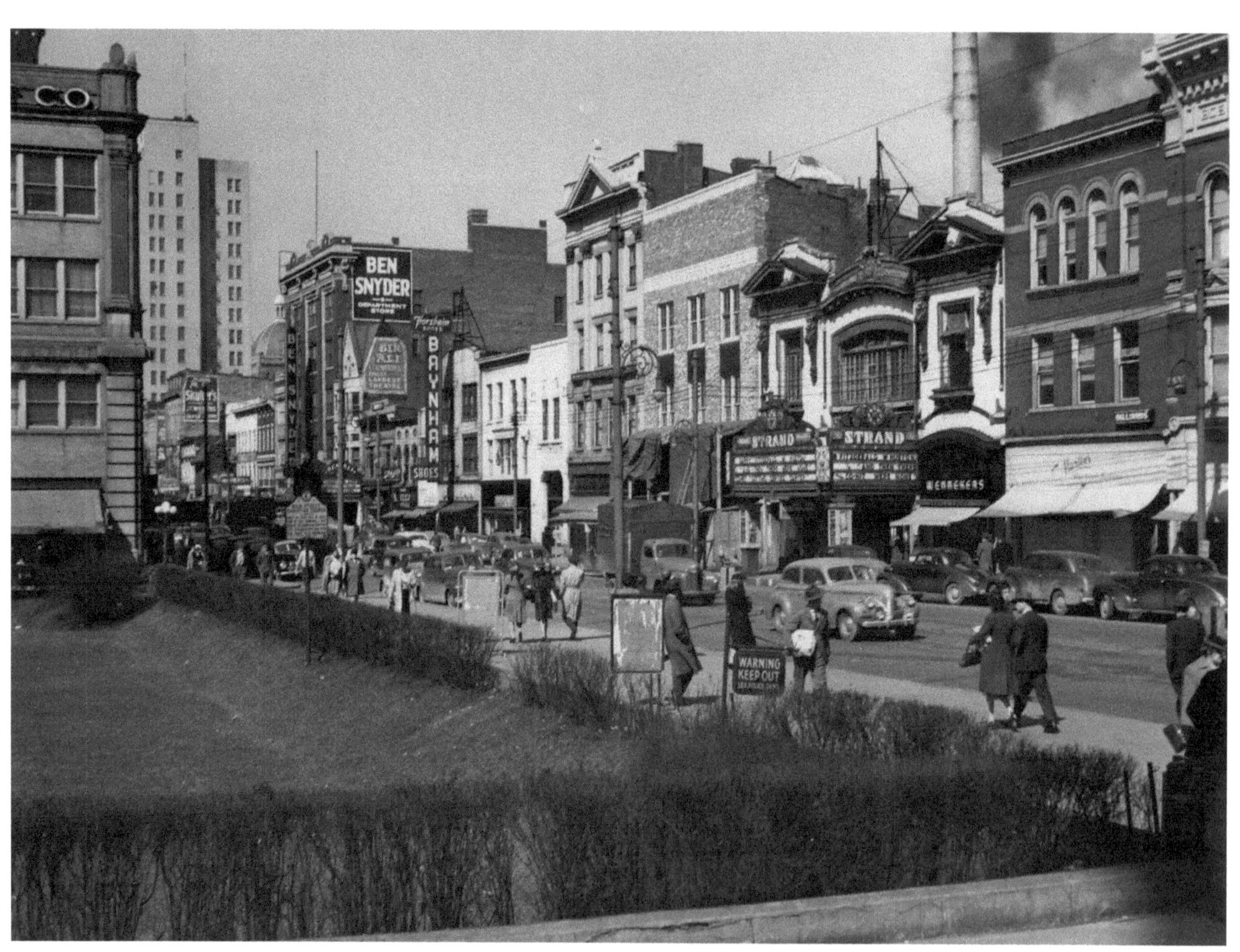


Looking across courthouse lawn onto Main Street, mid 1940's.

# HISTORIC PHOTOS OF LEXINGTON

From early on, Lexington earned a reputation for innovation in arts, commerce and education. The frontier city's accomplishments in education, architecture, and economics far exceeded the expectations of its Eastern counterparts. Four wars and urban redevelopment have repeatedly altered the city's landscape and culture. Through its changes, Lexington has endured and prospered through the persistence and innovation of its civic leaders.

This volume, Historic Photos of Lexington, captures the journey in still photography collected from the finest archives in private and public collections. The book follows life, government, education and events spanning two centuries of Lexington's history. It captures unique and rare scenes through the lenses of hundreds of historic photographers. The images portray the events and people important to Lexington's history.

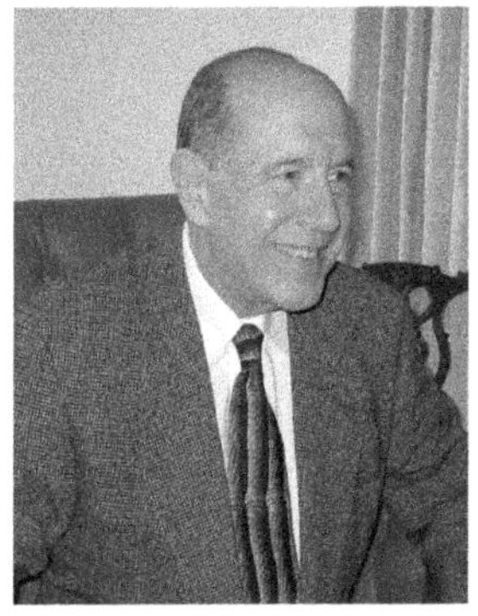

W. Gay Reading is a native Lexingtonian with roots in early central Kentucky. He graduated from Washington & Lee University with a BA in History and Fine Arts and holds an MFA in Theatre Design from Case-Western Reserve University.

He has worked in several capacities for the University of Kentucky, the Blue Grass Trust for Historic Preservation, and as proprietor of a private press. He is currently a partner in Greentree Antiques and Tearoom in downtown Lexington, where he lives, and serves as a board officer of the Headley-Whitney Museum for decorative arts and the Warwick Foundation that promotes the legacy of architectural historian and cultural scholar Clay Lancaster.

He returned to Lexington, Kentucky, after serving in the infantry in Viet Nam and has never left for long.

WWW.TURNERPUBLISHING.COM

www.ingramcontent.com/pod-product-compliance
Lightning Source LLC
LaVergne TN
LVHW070458120826
845154LV00019BA/28

* 9 7 8 1 6 8 3 3 6 9 1 4 1 *